It feels like I was all "Wow, volume 20 already" just a few weeks ago, and now here we are at volume 30. Thank you so much for reading! This series may seem long, but there are tons and tons of scenes that I've cut to make sure it wasn't even longer. Sometimes I think I might be too scared my readers will get bored with me. I want to try my hand at a chapter or three where the characters just kind of lounge around someone's room chatting the whole time. Not that I have the courage to actually do it!

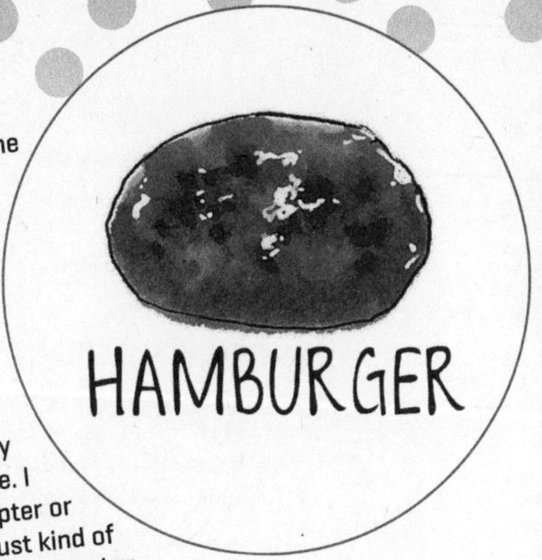

HAMBURGER

HARUICHI FURUDATE began his manga career when he was 25 years old with the one-shot *Ousama Kid* (King Kid), which won an honorable mention for the 14th Jump Treasure Newcomer Manga Prize. His first series, *Kiben Gakuha, Yotsuya Sensei no Kaidan* (Philosophy School, Yotsuya Sensei's Ghost Stories), was serialized in Weekly Shonen Jump in 2010. In 2012, he began serializing *Haikyu!!* in Weekly Shonen Jump, where it became his most popular work to date.

D0925390

HAIKYU!!

VOLUME 30
SHONEN JUMP Manga Edition

Story and Art by
HARUICHI FURUDATE

Translation **1** **ADRIENNE BECK**
Touch-Up Art & Lettering **2** **ERIKA TERRIQUEZ**
Design **3** **JULIAN [JR] ROBINSON**
Editor **4** **MARLENE FIRST**

HAIKYU!! © 2012 by Haruichi Furudate
All rights reserved.
First published in Japan in 2012 by SHUEISHA Inc., Tokyo.
English translation rights arranged by SHUEISHA Inc.

Printed in the U.S.A.

Published by VIZ Media, LLC
P.O. Box 77010
San Francisco, CA 94107

10 9 8 7 6 5 4 3 2 1
First printing, January 2019

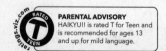

SHONEN JUMP MANGA

JACKET: Karasuno

HAIKYU!!

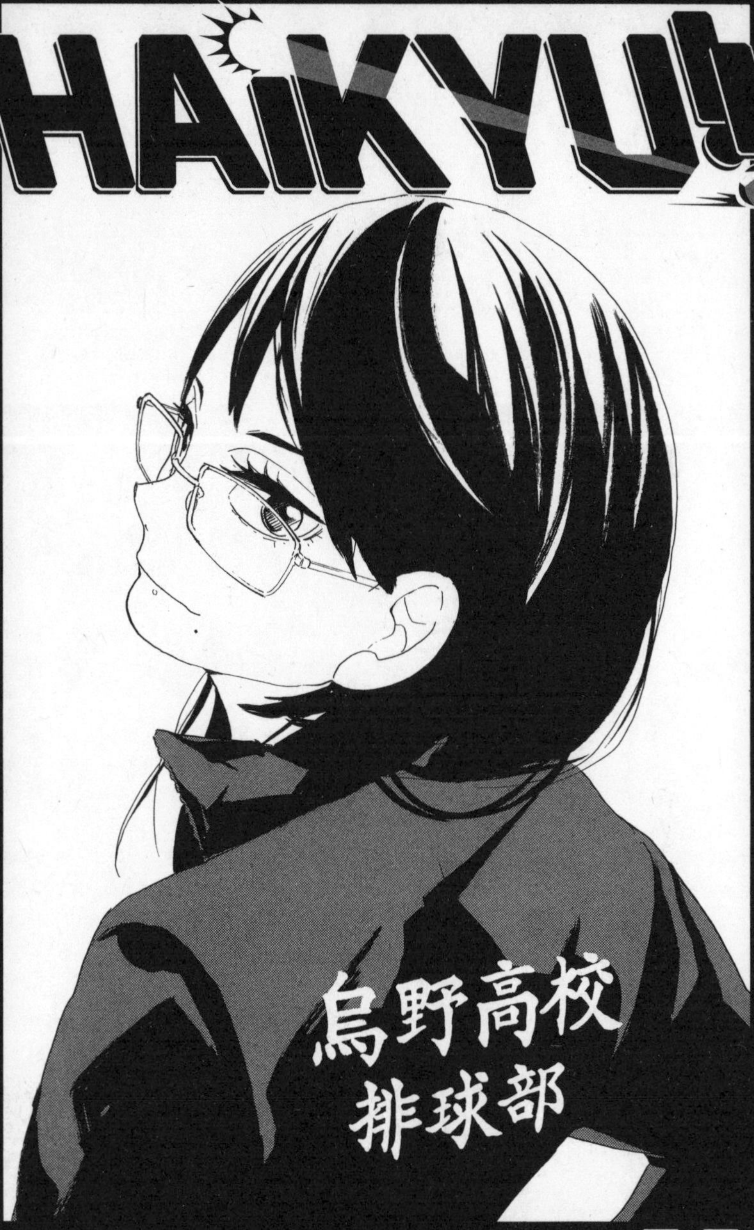
烏野高校
排球部

HARUICHI
FURUDATE

30

BROKEN HEART

Karasuno High School Volleyball Club

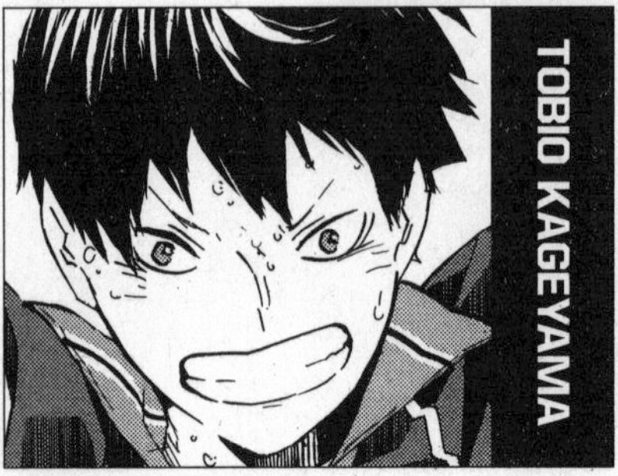

TOBIO KAGEYAMA

1ST YEAR / SETTER

His instincts and athletic talent are so good that he's like a "king" who rules the court. Demanding and egocentric.

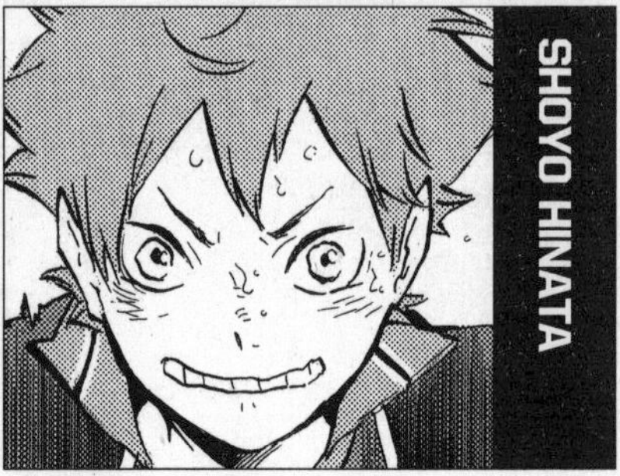

SHOYO HINATA

1ST YEAR / MIDDLE BLOCKER

Even though he doesn't have the best body type for volleyball, he is super athletic. Gets nervous easily.

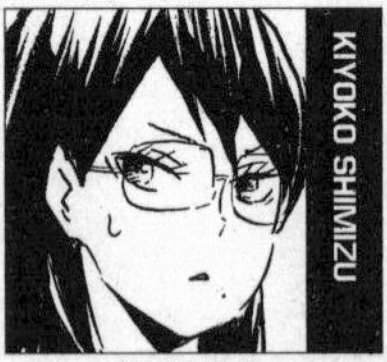

KIYOKO SHIMIZU

3RD YEAR
MANAGER

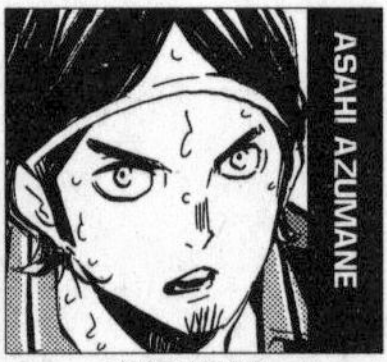

ASAHI AZUMANE

3RD YEAR
WING SPIKER

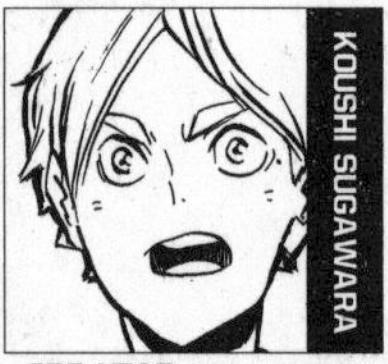

KOUSHI SUGAWARA

3RD YEAR (VICE CAPTAIN)
SETTER

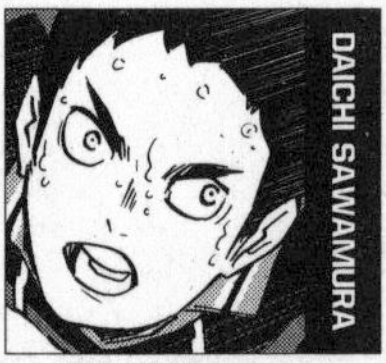

DAICHI SAWAMURA

3RD YEAR (CAPTAIN)
WING SPIKER

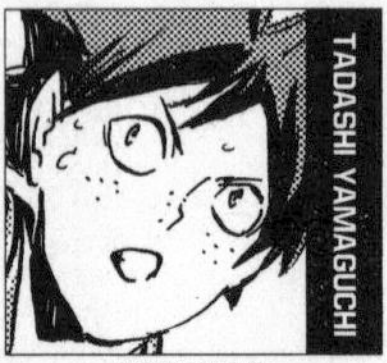

TADASHI YAMAGUCHI

1ST YEAR
MIDDLE BLOCKER

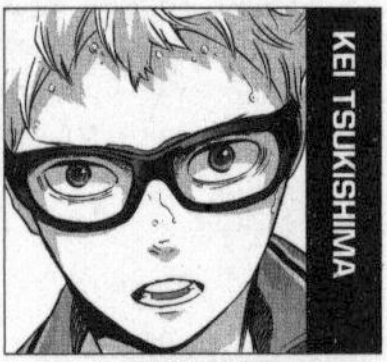

KEI TSUKISHIMA

1ST YEAR
MIDDLE BLOCKER

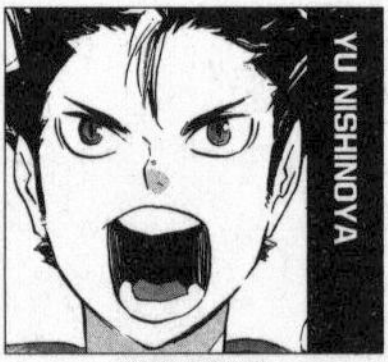

YU NISHINOYA

2ND YEAR
LIBERO

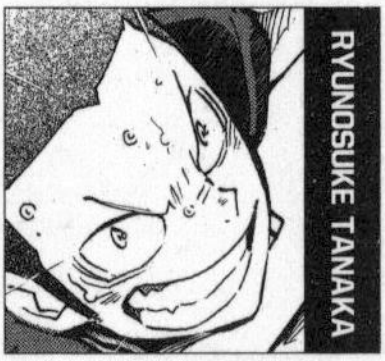

RYUNOSUKE TANAKA

2ND YEAR
WING SPIKER

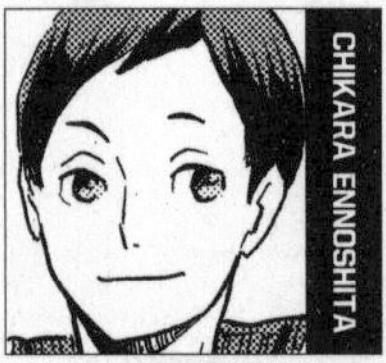

CHIKARA ENNOSHITA

2ND YEAR
WING SPIKER

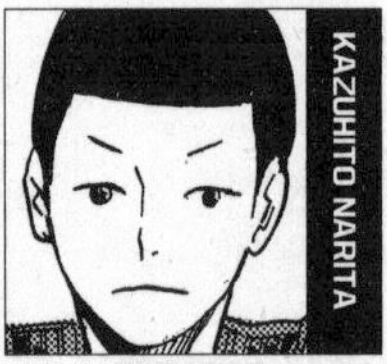

KAZUHITO NARITA

2ND YEAR
MIDDLE BLOCKER

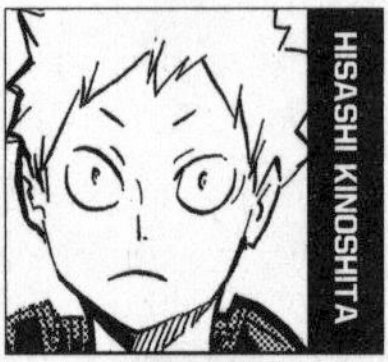

HISASHI KINOSHITA

2ND YEAR
WING SPIKER

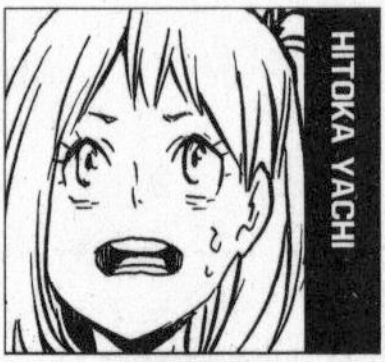

HITOKA YACHI

1ST YEAR
MANAGER

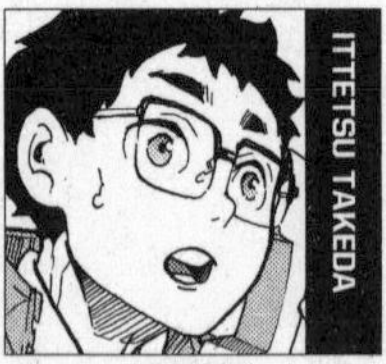

ITTETSU TAKEDA

ADVISER

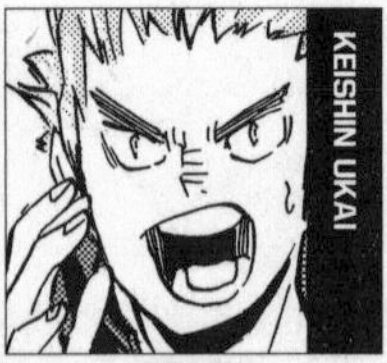

KEISHIN UKAI

COACH

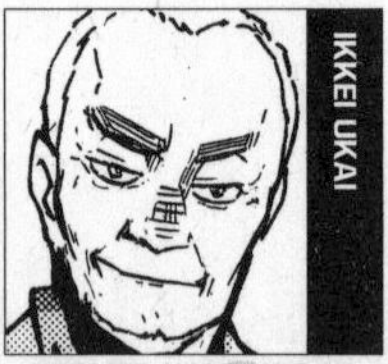

IKKEI UKAI

FORMER HEAD COACH

CHARACTERS

NATIONAL SPRING TOURNAMENT ARC

Inarizaki Volleyball Club

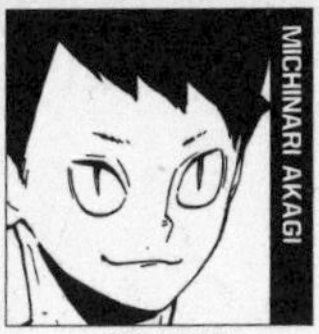
MICHINARI AKAGI
3RD YEAR
LIBERO

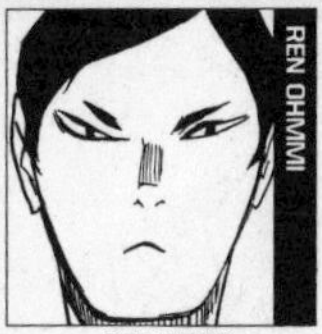
REN OHMIMI
3RD YEAR
MIDDLE BLOCKER

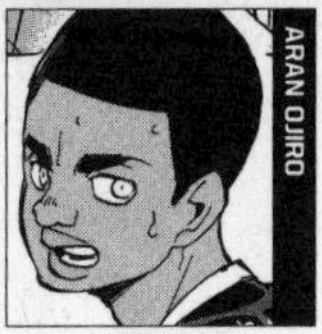
ARAN OJIRO
3RD YEAR
WING SPIKER

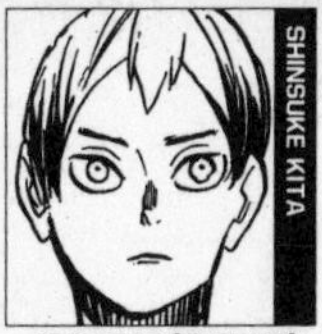
SHINSUKE KITA
3RD YEAR (CAPTAIN)
WING SPIKER

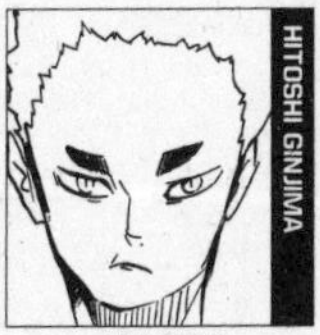
HITOSHI GINJIMA
2ND YEAR
WING SPIKER

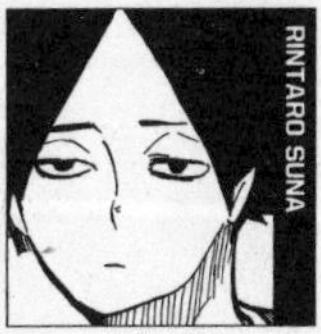
RINTARO SUNA
2ND YEAR
MIDDLE BLOCKER

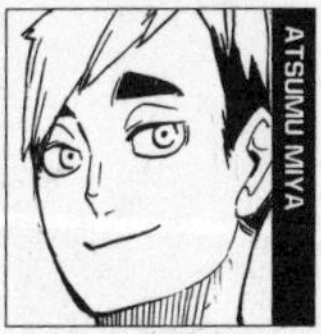
ATSUMU MIYA
2ND YEAR
SETTER

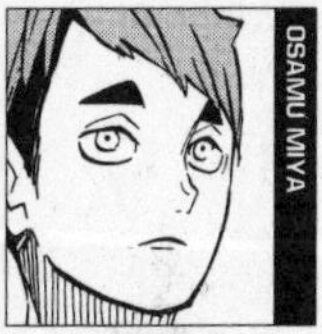
OSAMU MIYA
2ND YEAR
WING SPIKER

Nekoma Volleyball Club

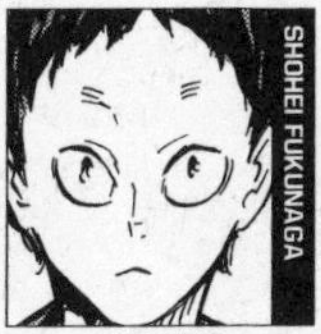
SHOHEI FUKUNAGA
2ND YEAR
WING SPIKER

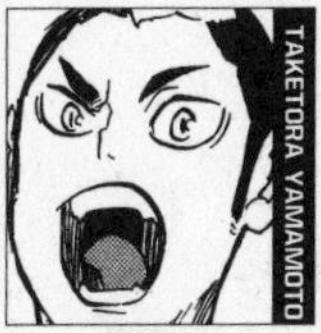
TAKETORA YAMAMOTO
2ND YEAR
WING SPIKER

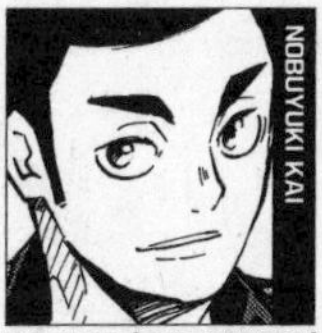
NOBUYUKI KAI
3RD YEAR (VICE CAPTAIN)
WING SPIKER

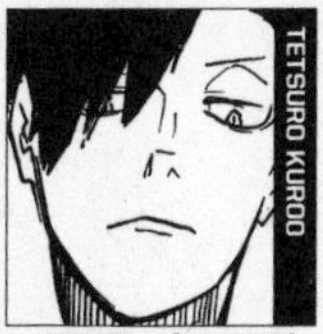
TETSURO KUROO
3RD YEAR (CAPTAIN)
MIDDLE BLOCKER

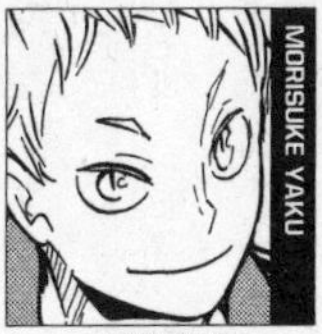
MORISUKE YAKU
3RD YEAR
LIBERO

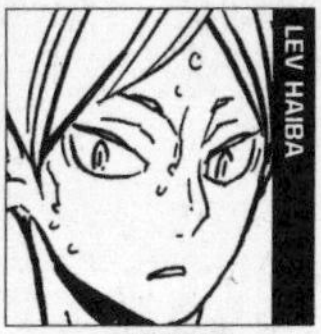
LEV HAIBA
1ST YEAR
MIDDLE BLOCKER

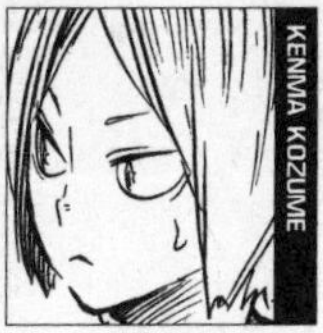
KENMA KOZUME
2ND YEAR
SETTER

Ever since he saw the legendary player known as "the Little Giant" compete at the national volleyball finals, Shoyo Hinata has been aiming to be the best volleyball player ever! He decides to join the volleyball club at his middle school and gets to play in an official tournament during his third year. His team is crushed by a team led by volleyball prodigy Tobio Kageyama, also known as "the King of the Court." Swearing revenge on Kageyama, Hinata graduates middle school and enters Karasuno High School, the school where the Little Giant played. However, upon joining the club, he finds out that Kageyama is there too! The two of them bicker constantly, but they bring out the best in each other's talents and become a powerful combo. It's day 2 of the Spring Tournament. Saeko's taiko drumming group arrives and breaks the influence of Inarizaki's marching band over Karasuno's rhythm. However, without warning, Inarizaki's star players, the Miya twins, use their own version of the Freak Quick! Karasuno flounders under the unexpected assault, but Tsukishima's quick thinking and Hinata's switch to commit blocking Osamu Miya gets things back under control. Yamaguchi's service ace gives Karasuno its first lead, and Kageyama, hoping to grab another point in a row, dashes past the net to chase down a botched dig...

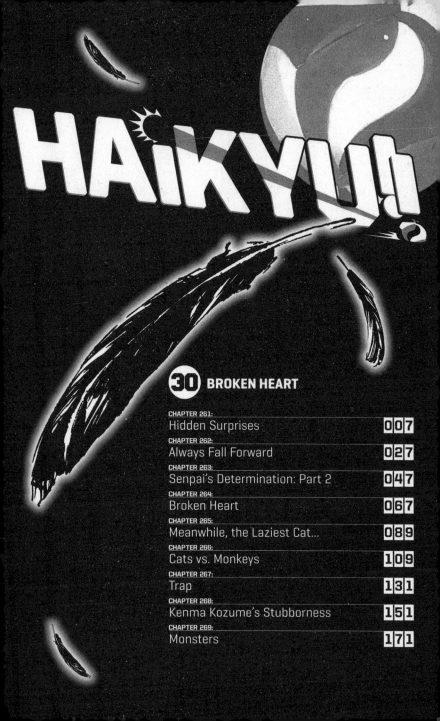

HAIKYU!!

30 BROKEN HEART

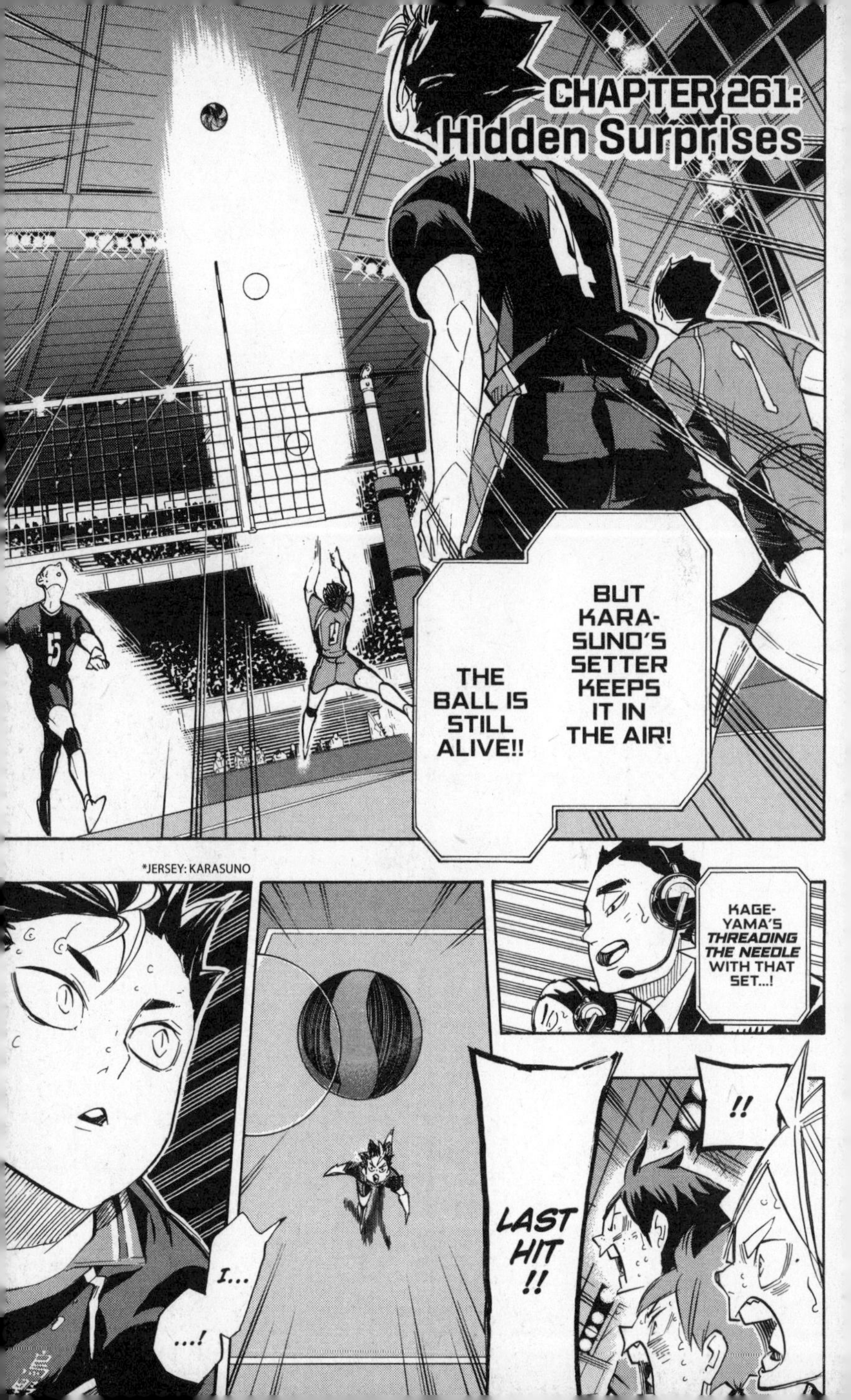
CHAPTER 261:
Hidden Surprises
BUT KARASUNO'S SETTER KEEPS IT IN THE AIR!
THE BALL IS STILL ALIVE!!
*JERSEY: KARASUNO
KAGEYAMA'S *THREADING THE NEEDLE* WITH THAT SET...!
!!
LAST HIT !!
I...
...!

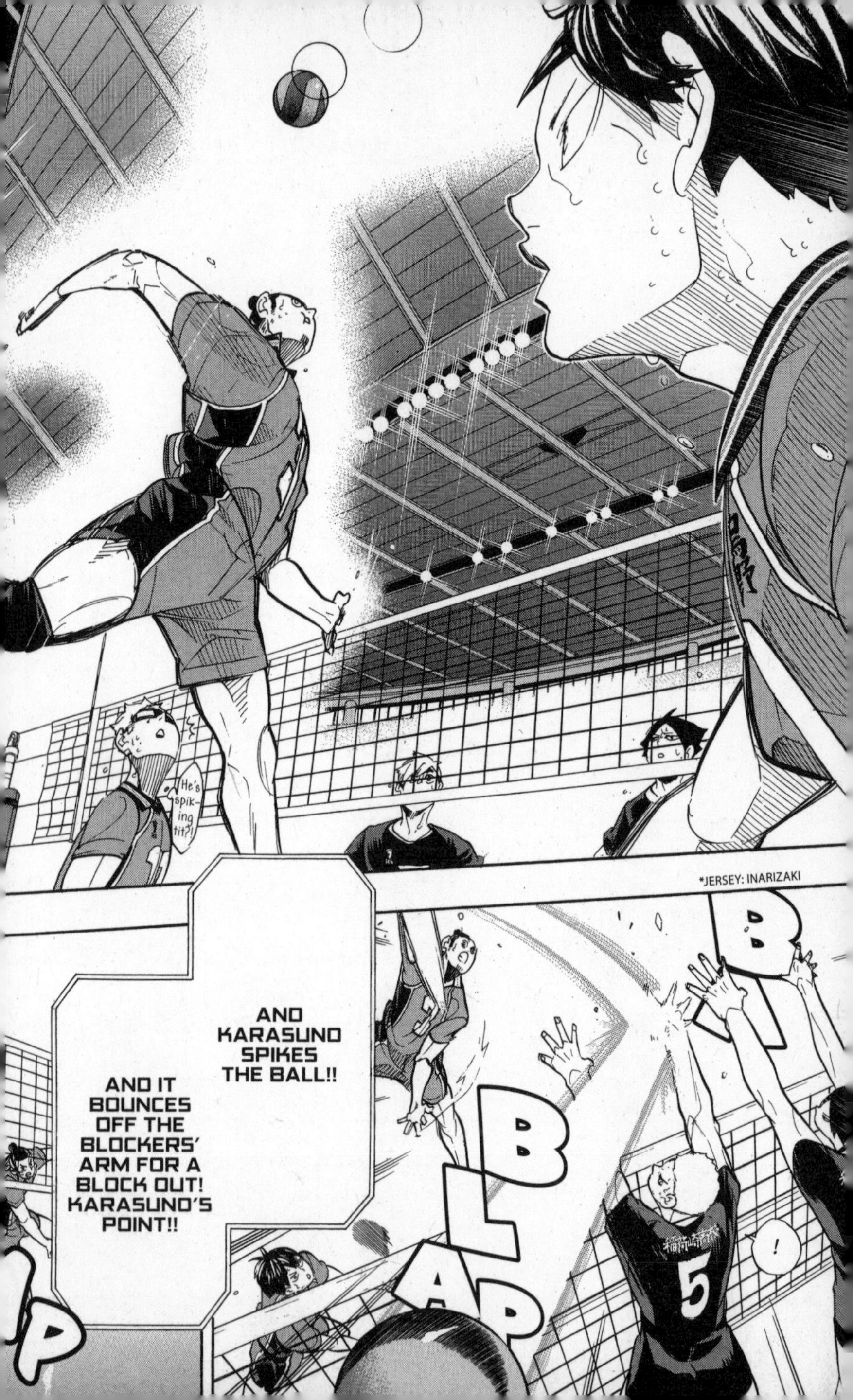
He's spik-ing tit?!
*JERSEY: INARIZAKI
AND KARASUNO SPIKES THE BALL!!
AND IT BOUNCES OFF THE BLOCKERS' ARM FOR A BLOCK OUT! KARASUNO'S POINT!!
BLAP
!

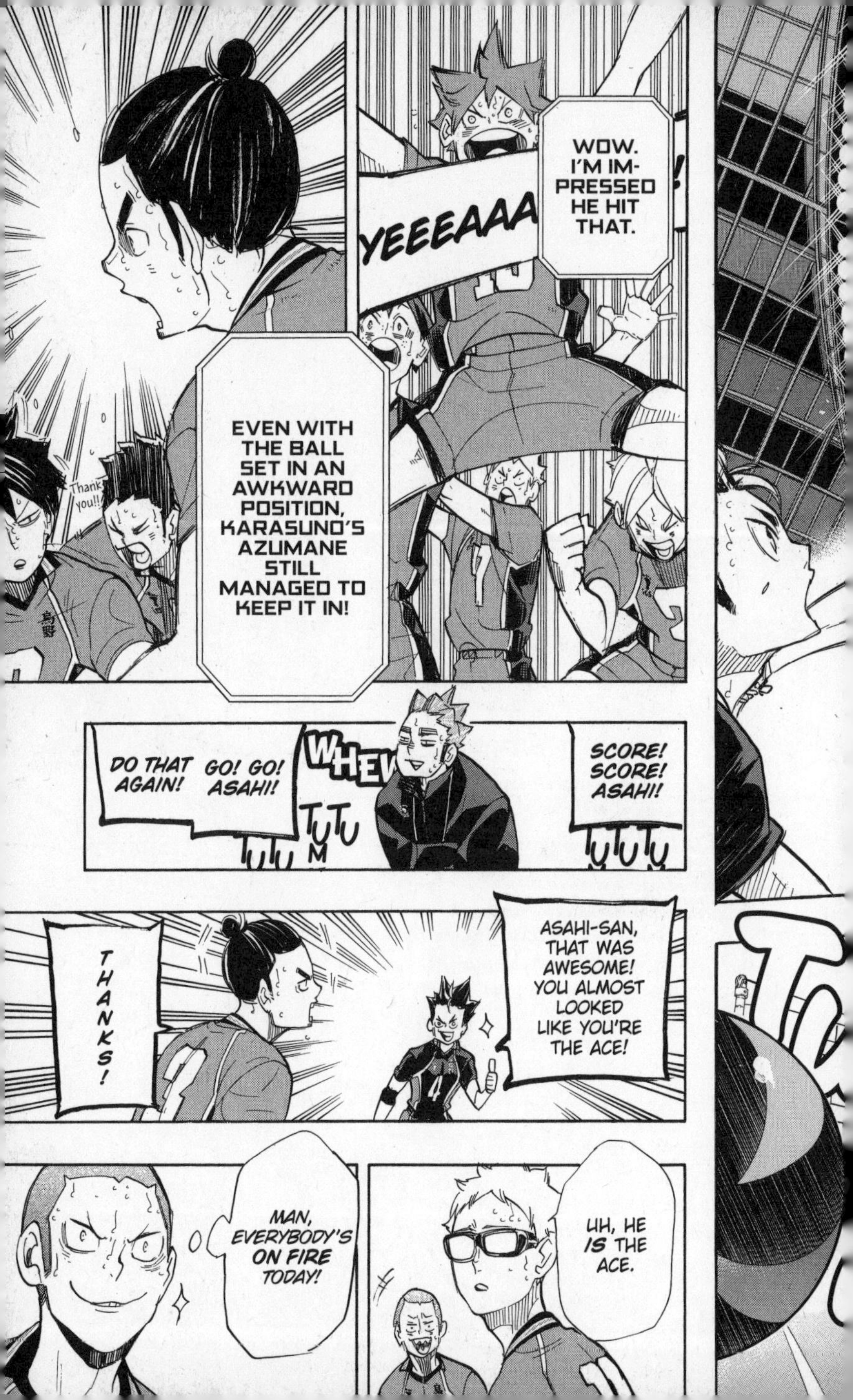
WOW. I'M IMPRESSED HE HIT THAT.
YEEEAAA
EVEN WITH THE BALL SET IN AN AWKWARD POSITION, KARASUNO'S AZUMANE STILL MANAGED TO KEEP IT IN!
Thank you!!
SCORE! SCORE! ASAHI!
GO! GO! ASAHI!
DO THAT AGAIN!
ASAHI-SAN, THAT WAS AWESOME! YOU ALMOST LOOKED LIKE YOU'RE THE ACE!
THANKS!
UH, HE IS THE ACE.
MAN, EVERYBODY'S ON FIRE TODAY!

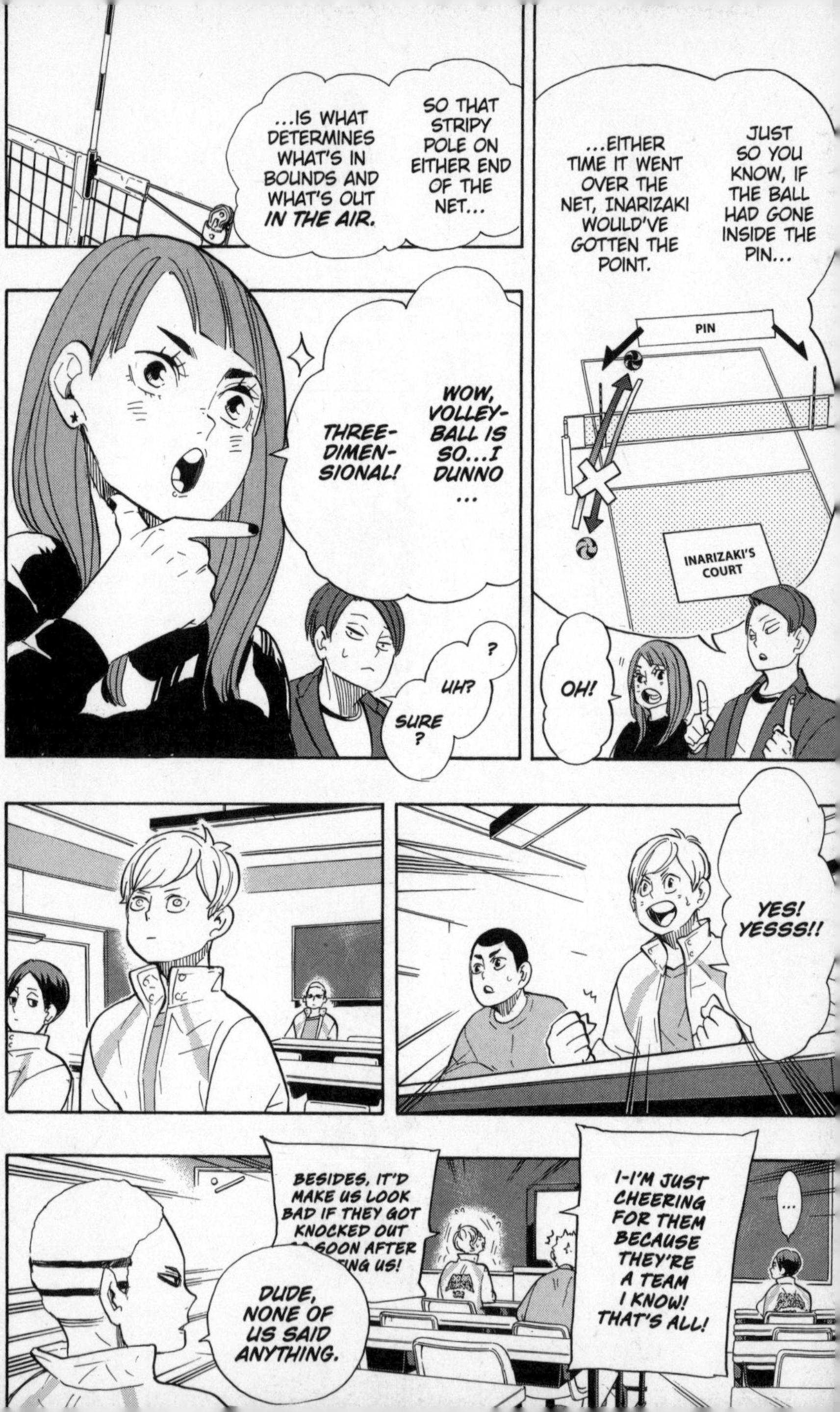
JUST SO YOU KNOW, IF THE BALL HAD GONE INSIDE THE PIN...
...EITHER TIME IT WENT OVER THE NET, INARIZAKI WOULD'VE GOTTEN THE POINT.
PIN
INARIZAKI'S COURT
OH!
SO THAT STRIPY POLE ON EITHER END OF THE NET...
...IS WHAT DETERMINES WHAT'S IN BOUNDS AND WHAT'S OUT IN THE AIR.
WOW, VOLLEYBALL IS SO...I DUNNO...
THREE-DIMENSIONAL!
?
UH?
SURE?
YES! YESSS!!
...
I-I'M JUST CHEERING FOR THEM BECAUSE THEY'RE A TEAM I KNOW! THAT'S ALL!
BESIDES, IT'D MAKE US LOOK BAD IF THEY GOT KNOCKED OUT SOON AFTER ING US!
DUDE, NONE OF US SAID ANYTHING.

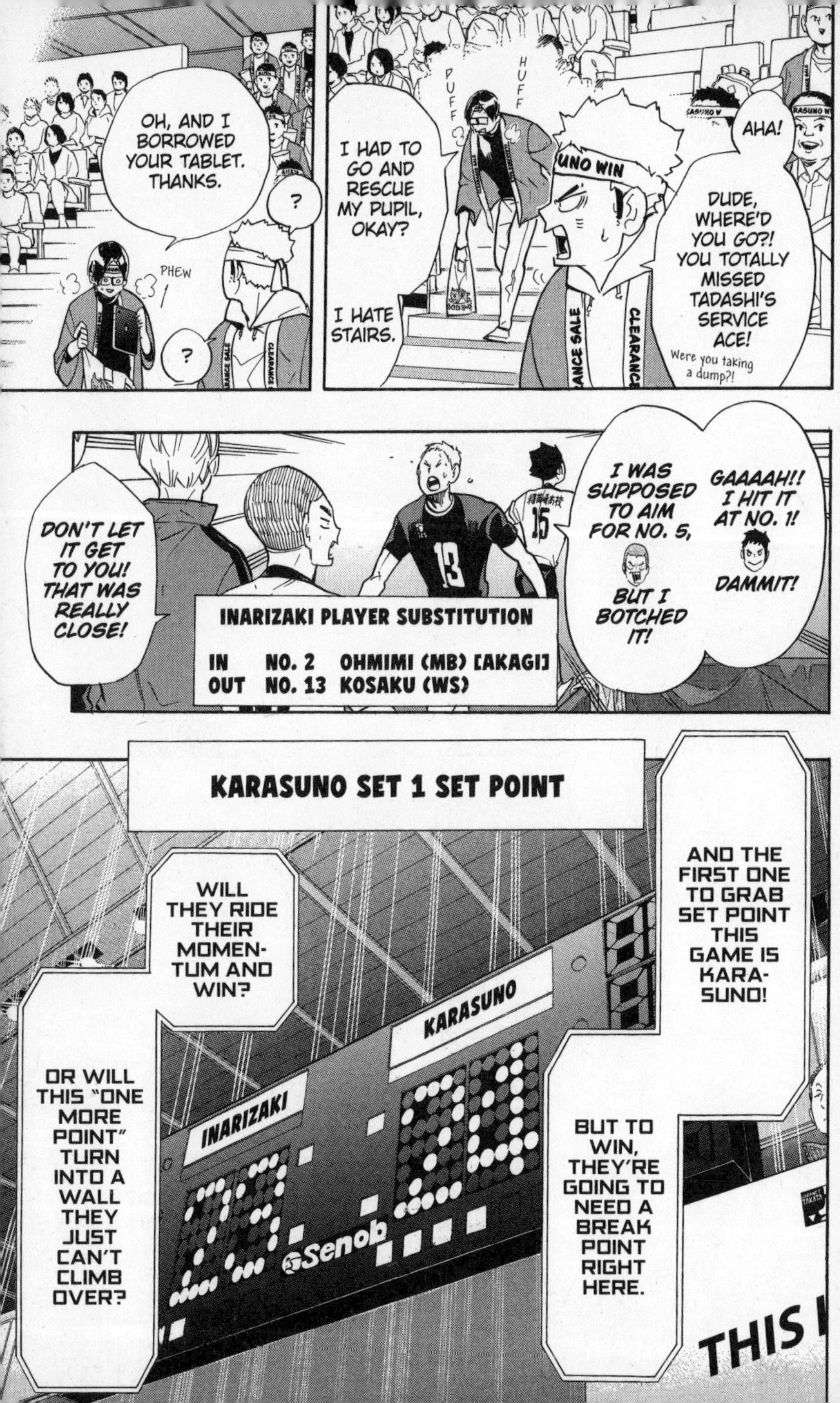
AHA!
DUDE, WHERE'D YOU GO?! YOU TOTALLY MISSED TADASHI'S SERVICE ACE!
Were you taking a dump?!
HUFF
PUFF
I HAD TO GO AND RESCUE MY PUPIL, OKAY?
I HATE STAIRS.
OH, AND I BORROWED YOUR TABLET. THANKS.
?
PHEW
?
GAAAAH!! I HIT IT AT NO. 1! DAMMIT!
I WAS SUPPOSED TO AIM FOR NO. 5, BUT I BOTCHED IT!
DON'T LET IT GET TO YOU! THAT WAS REALLY CLOSE!
INARIZAKI PLAYER SUBSTITUTION
IN NO. 2 OHMIMI (MB) [AKAGI]
OUT NO. 13 KOSAKU (WS)
KARASUNO SET 1 SET POINT
AND THE FIRST ONE TO GRAB SET POINT THIS GAME IS KARASUNO!
WILL THEY RIDE THEIR MOMENTUM AND WIN?
KARASUNO
INARIZAKI
Senob
BUT TO WIN, THEY'RE GOING TO NEED A BREAK POINT RIGHT HERE.
OR WILL THIS "ONE MORE POINT" TURN INTO A WALL THEY JUST CAN'T CLIMB OVER?
THIS I

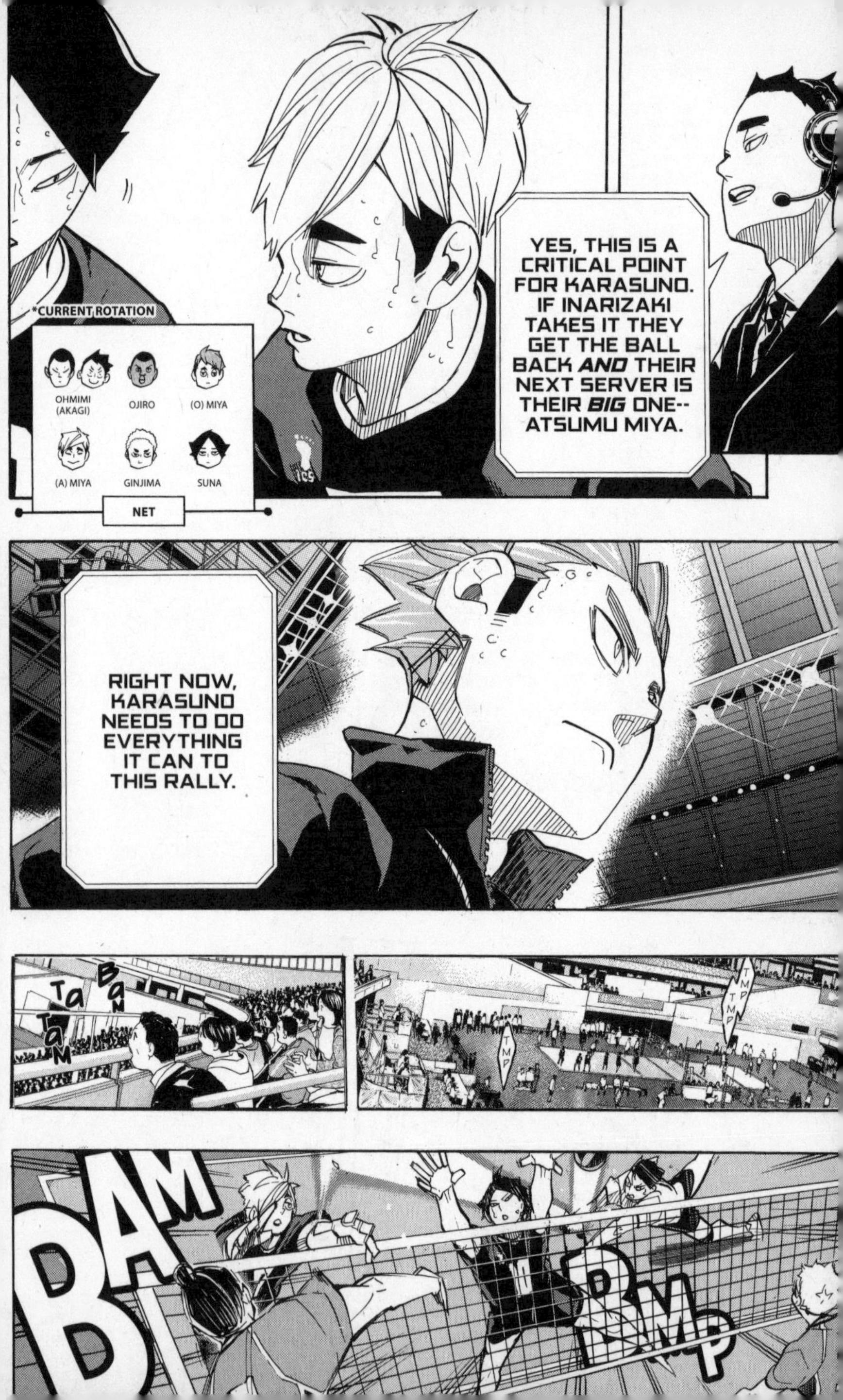
YES, THIS IS A CRITICAL POINT FOR KARASUNO. IF INARIZAKI TAKES IT THEY GET THE BALL BACK *AND* THEIR NEXT SERVER IS THEIR *BIG* ONE--ATSUMU MIYA.
*CURRENT ROTATION
OHMIMI (AKAGI)
OJIRO
(O) MIYA
(A) MIYA
GINJIMA
SUNA
NET
RIGHT NOW, KARASUNO NEEDS TO DO EVERYTHING IT CAN TO THIS RALLY.
TMP
TMP
TMP
TMP
Ta
Ba
Tam
BAM
BOMP

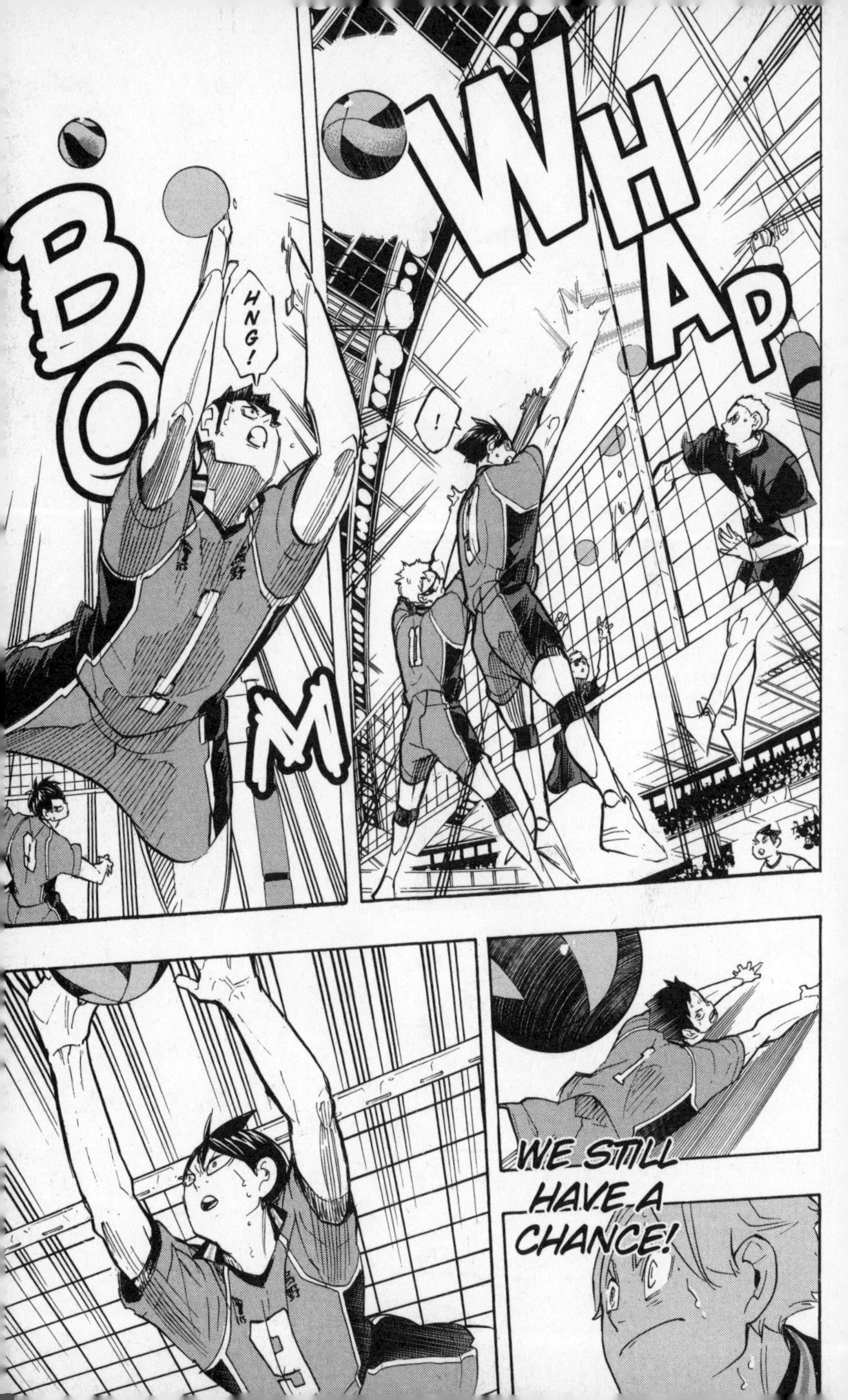
WHAP
!
BOOM
HNG!
WE STILL HAVE A CHANCE!

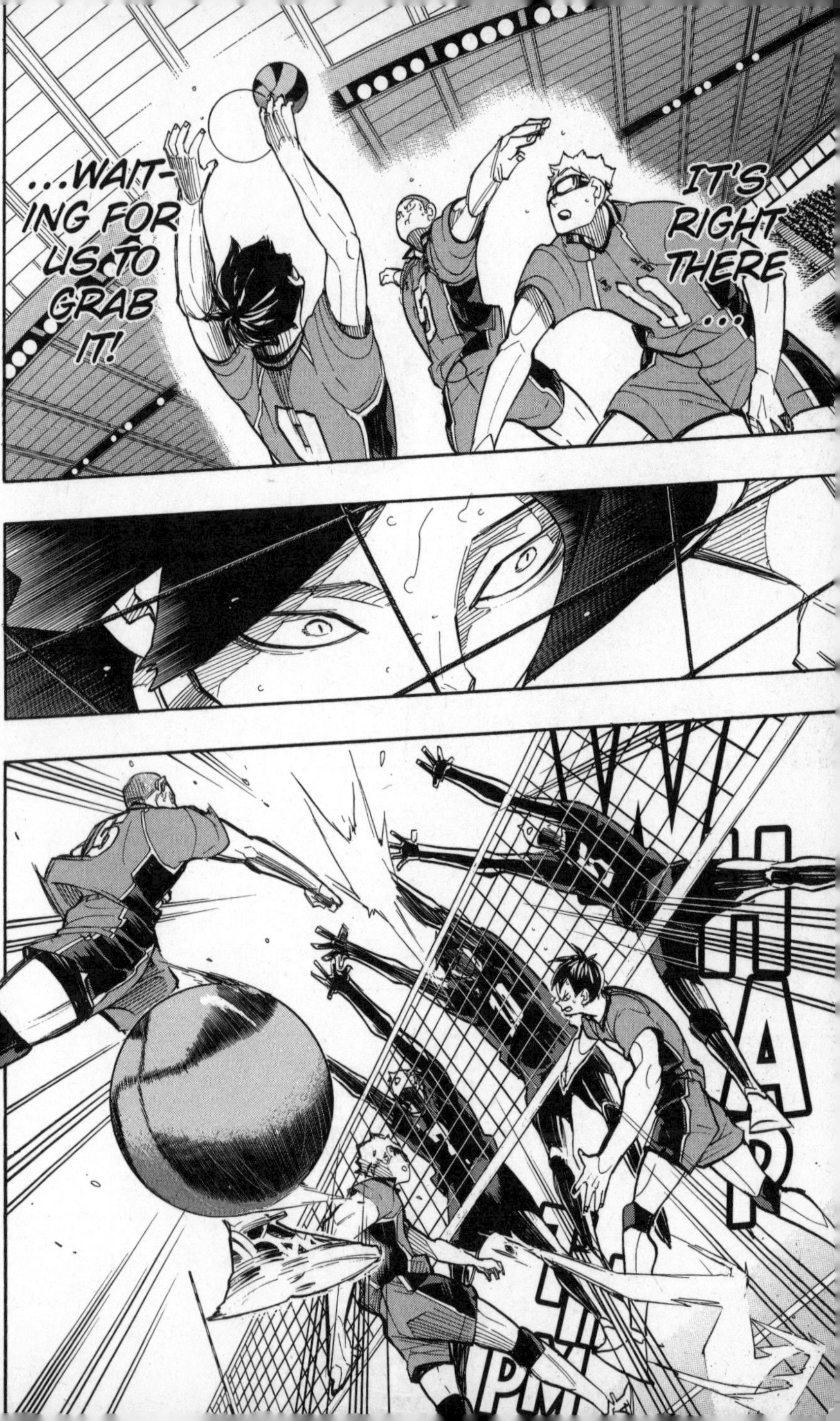
IT'S RIGHT THERE...
...WAIT-ING FOR US TO GRAB IT!

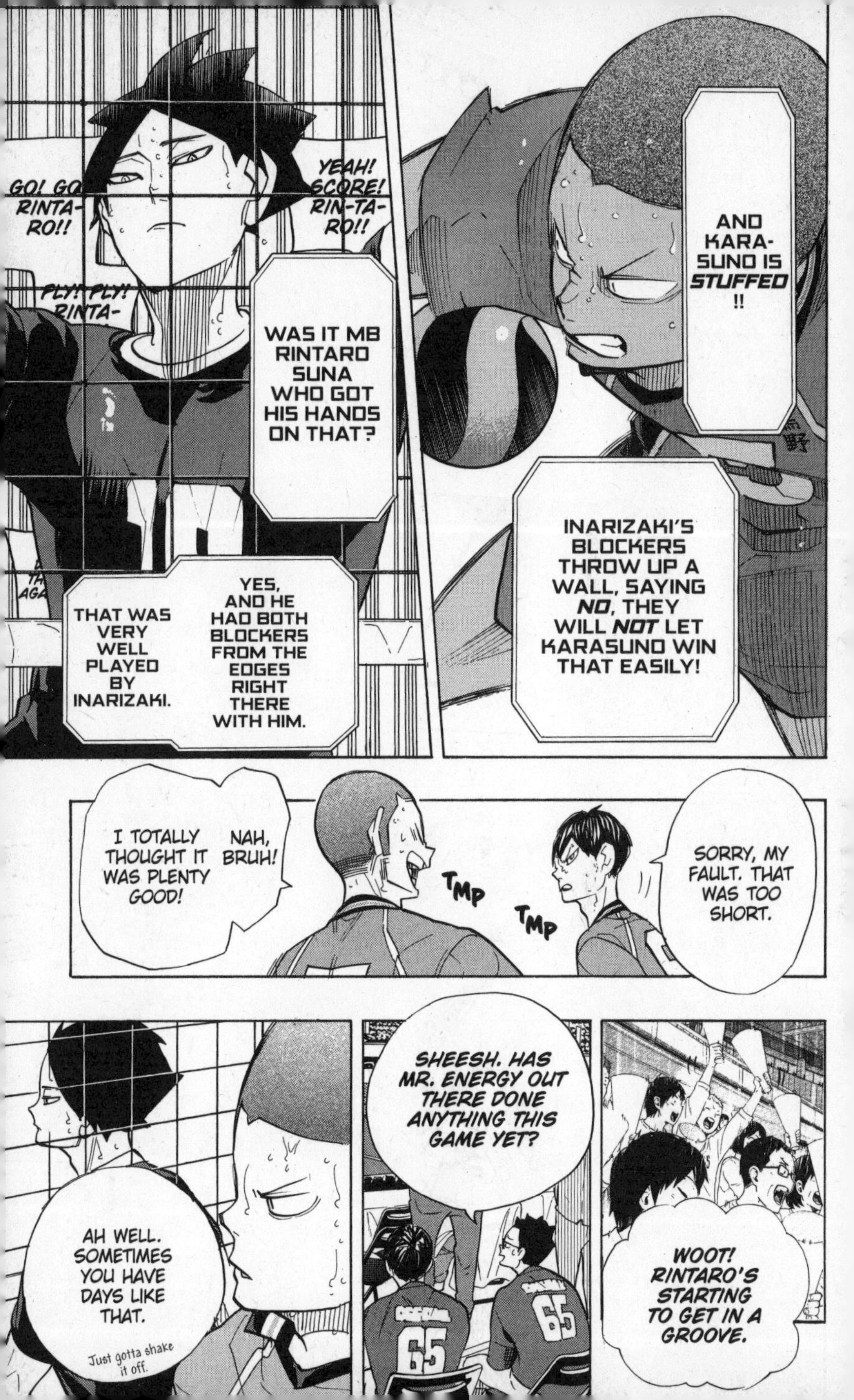
AND KARA-SUNO IS STUFFED!!
INARIZAKI'S BLOCKERS THROW UP A WALL, SAYING NO, THEY WILL NOT LET KARASUNO WIN THAT EASILY!
YEAH! SCORE! RIN-TA-RO!!
GO! GO! RINTA-RO!!
FLY! FLY! RINTA-
WAS IT MB RINTARO SUNA WHO GOT HIS HANDS ON THAT?
YES, AND HE HAD BOTH BLOCKERS FROM THE EDGES RIGHT THERE WITH HIM.
THAT WAS VERY WELL PLAYED BY INARIZAKI.
SORRY, MY FAULT. THAT WAS TOO SHORT.
TMP
TMP
NAH, BRUH!
I TOTALLY THOUGHT IT WAS PLENTY GOOD!
WOOT! RINTARO'S STARTING TO GET IN A GROOVE.
SHEESH. HAS MR. ENERGY OUT THERE DONE ANYTHING THIS GAME YET?
AH WELL. SOMETIMES YOU HAVE DAYS LIKE THAT.
Just gotta shake it off.

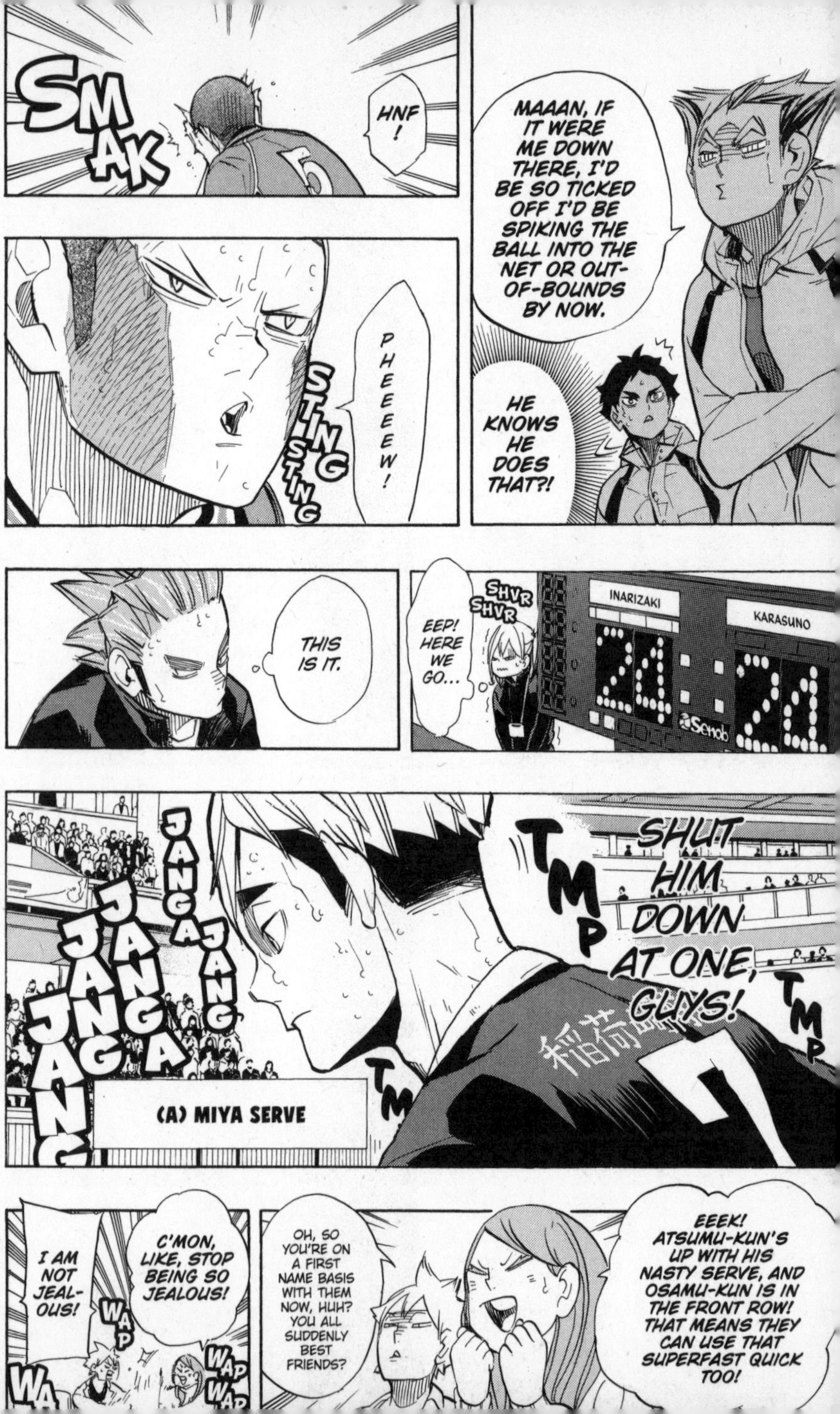
MAAAN, IF IT WERE ME DOWN THERE, I'D BE SO TICKED OFF I'D BE SPIKING THE BALL INTO THE NET OR OUT-OF-BOUNDS BY NOW.
HE KNOWS HE DOES THAT?!
HNF!
SMAK
PHEEEEW!
STING STING STING
SHVR SHVR
EEP! HERE WE GO...
INARIZAKI
KARASUNO
24 : 20
Senob
THIS IS IT.
SHUT HIM DOWN AT ONE, GUYS!
TMP TMP TMP
JANGA JANG JANGA JANGA JANGA JANG
(A) MIYA SERVE
EEEK! ATSUMU-KUN'S UP WITH HIS NASTY SERVE, AND OSAMU-KUN IS IN THE FRONT ROW! THAT MEANS THEY CAN USE THAT SUPERFAST QUICK TOO!
OH, SO YOU'RE ON A FIRST NAME BASIS WITH THEM NOW, HUH? YOU ALL SUDDENLY BEST FRIENDS?
C'MON, LIKE, STOP BEING SO JEALOUS!
I AM NOT JEAL-OUS!
WAP WAP WAP WA

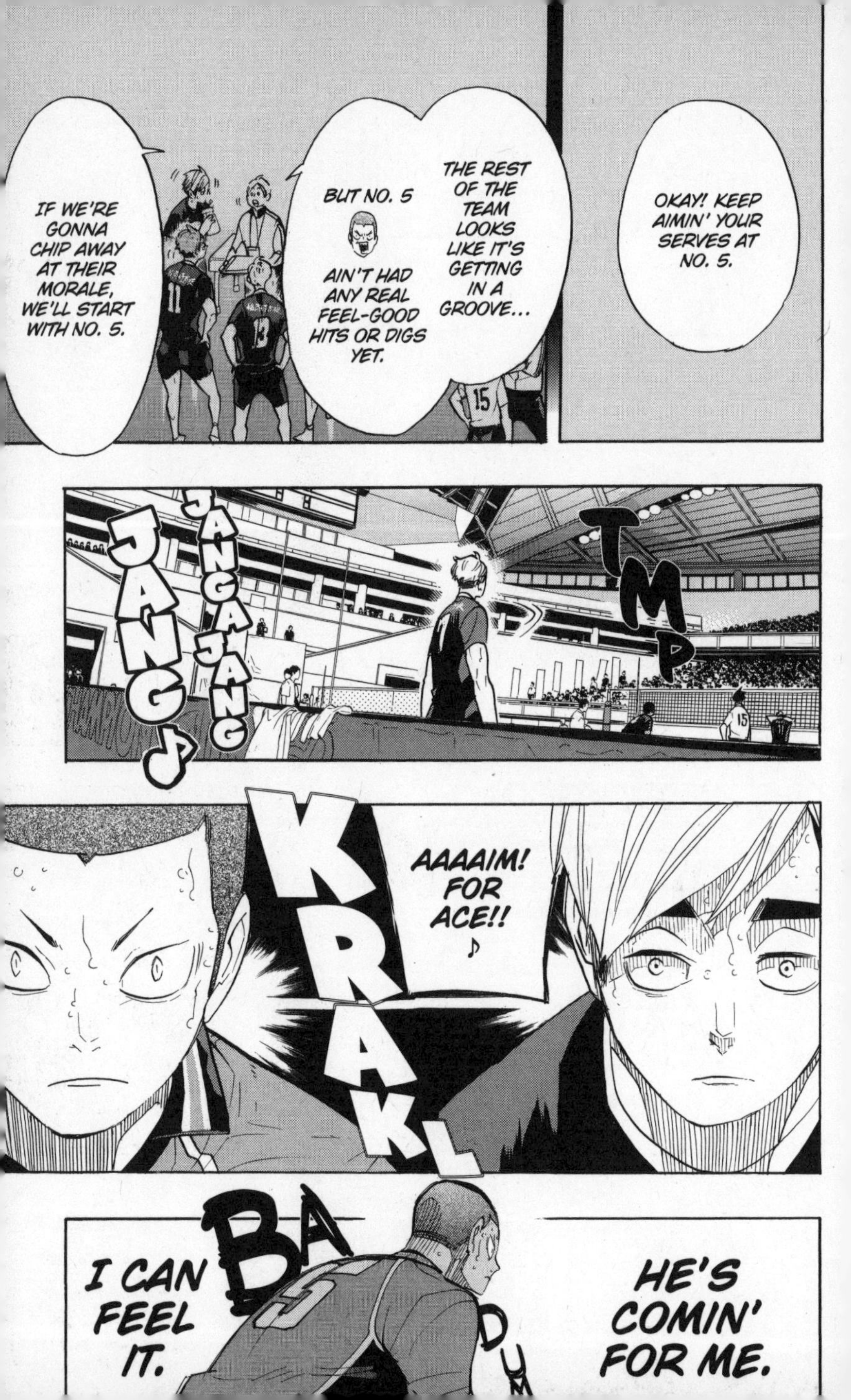
OKAY! KEEP AIMIN' YOUR SERVES AT NO. 5.
THE REST OF THE TEAM LOOKS LIKE IT'S GETTING IN A GROOVE...
BUT NO. 5 AIN'T HAD ANY REAL FEEL-GOOD HITS OR DIGS YET.
IF WE'RE GONNA CHIP AWAY AT THEIR MORALE, WE'LL START WITH NO. 5.
TMP
JANGAJANG
JANG♪
AAAAIM! FOR ACE!! ♪
KRAKL
HE'S COMIN' FOR ME.
BA DUM
I CAN FEEL IT.

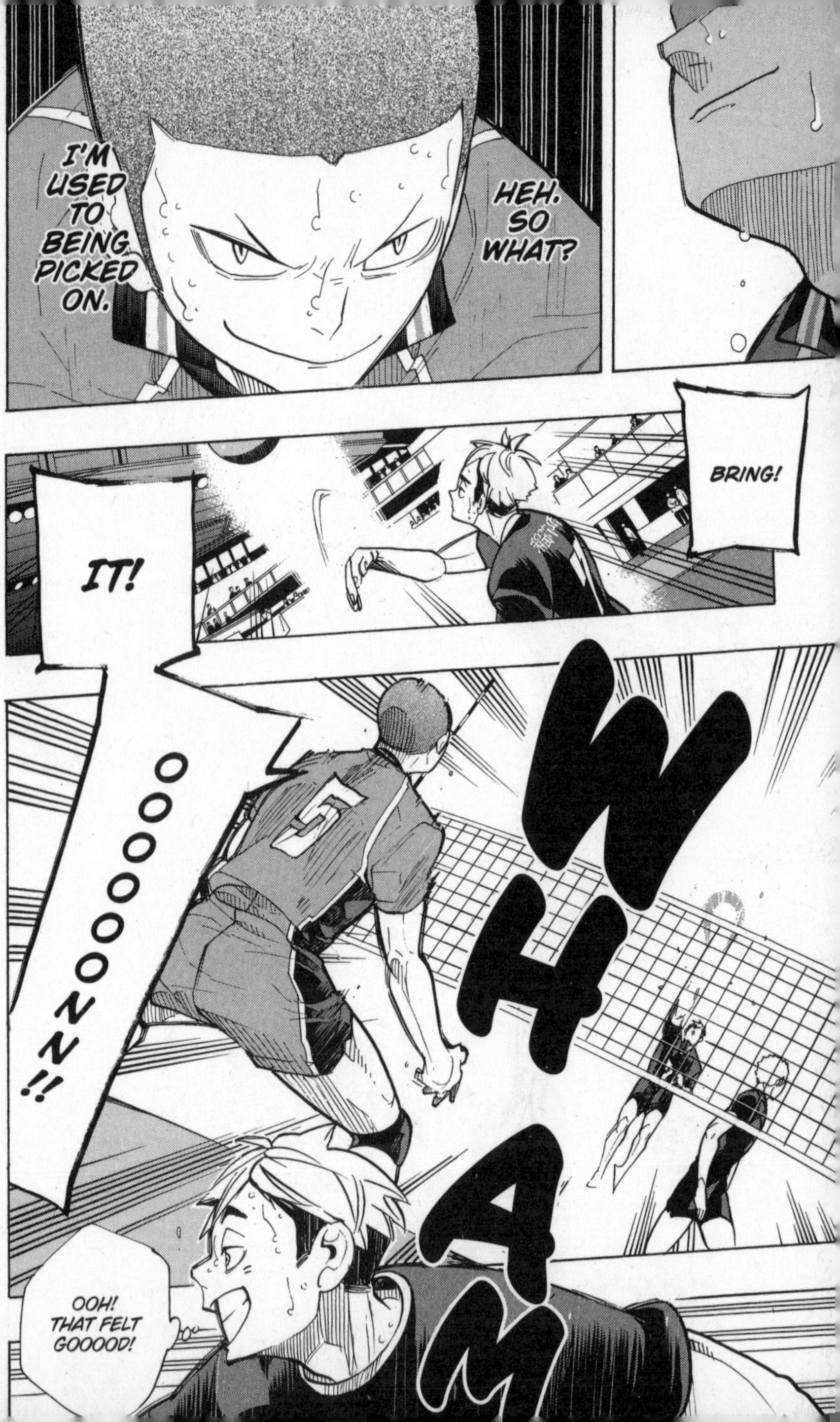
HEH. SO WHAT?
I'M USED TO BEING PICKED ON.
BRING!
IT!
OOOOOONN!!
WHAM
OOH! THAT FELT GOOOOD!

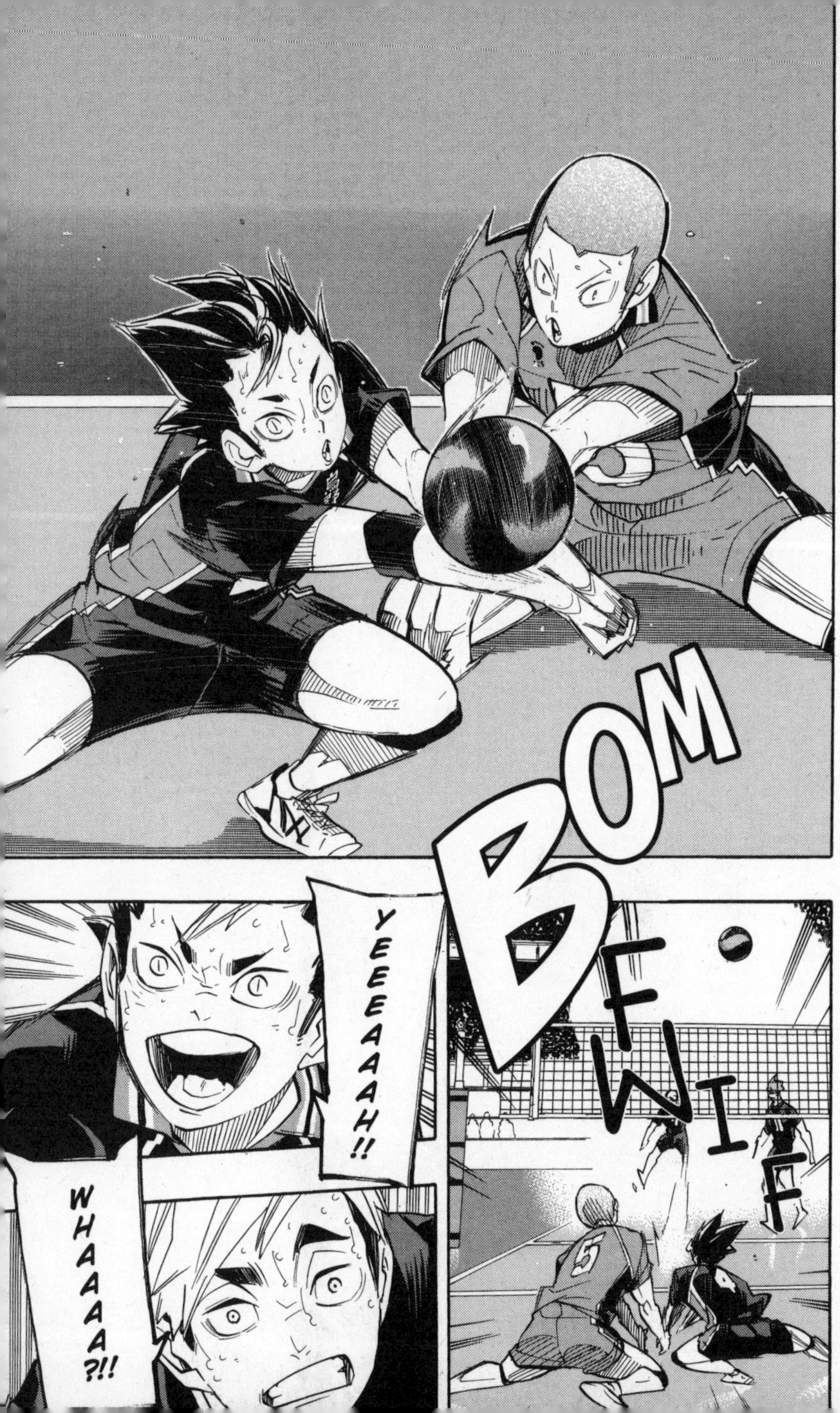
BOM
FWIF
YEEEAAAAH!!
WHAAAAA?!!

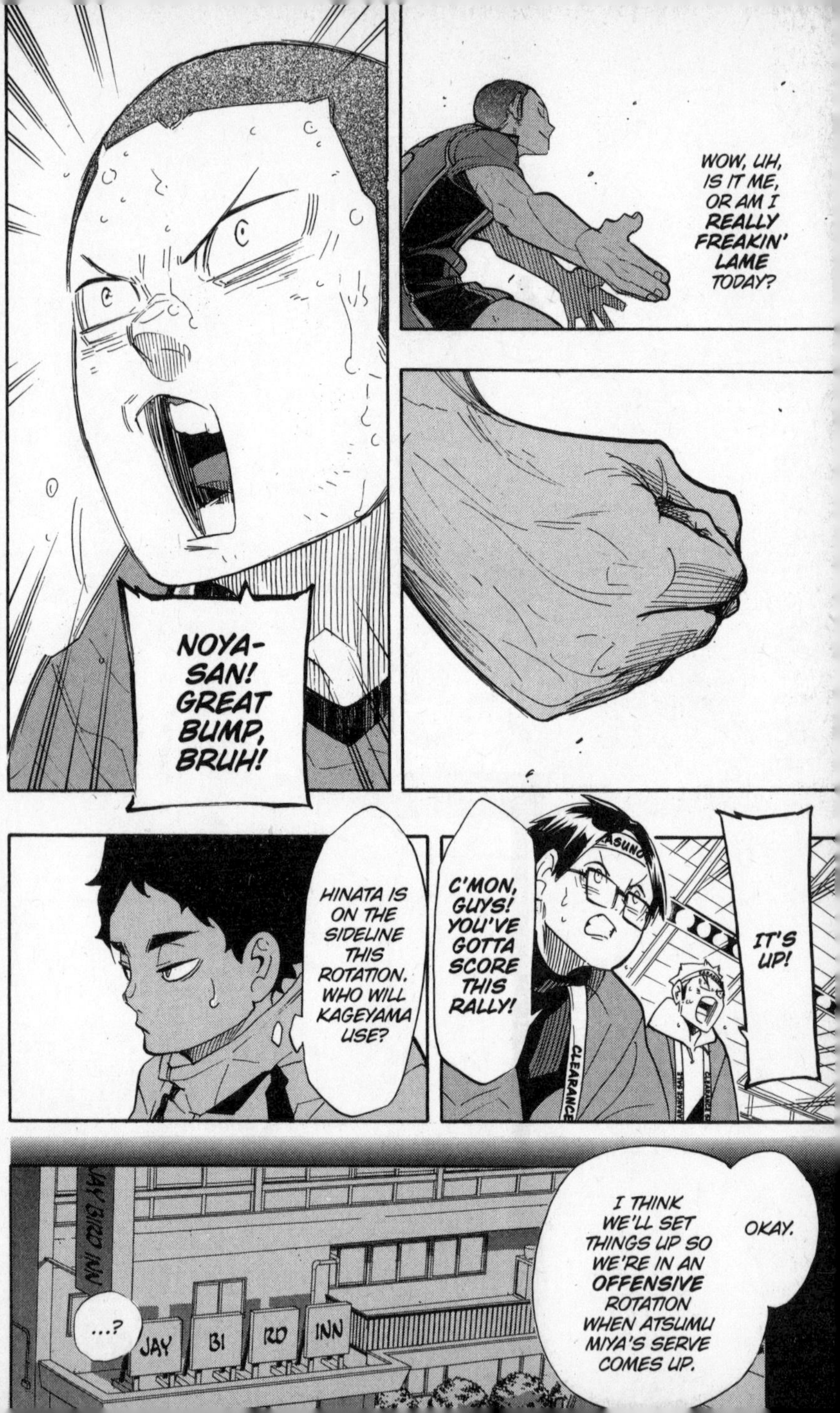

WOW, UH, IS IT ME, OR AM I REALLY FREAKIN' LAME TODAY?
NOYA-SAN! GREAT BUMP, BRUH!
IT'S UP!
C'MON, GUYS! YOU'VE GOTTA SCORE THIS RALLY!
HINATA IS ON THE SIDELINE THIS ROTATION. WHO WILL KAGEYAMA USE?
OKAY.
I THINK WE'LL SET THINGS UP SO WE'RE IN AN OFFENSIVE ROTATION WHEN ATSUMU MIYA'S SERVE COMES UP.
JAY BI RO INN
...?

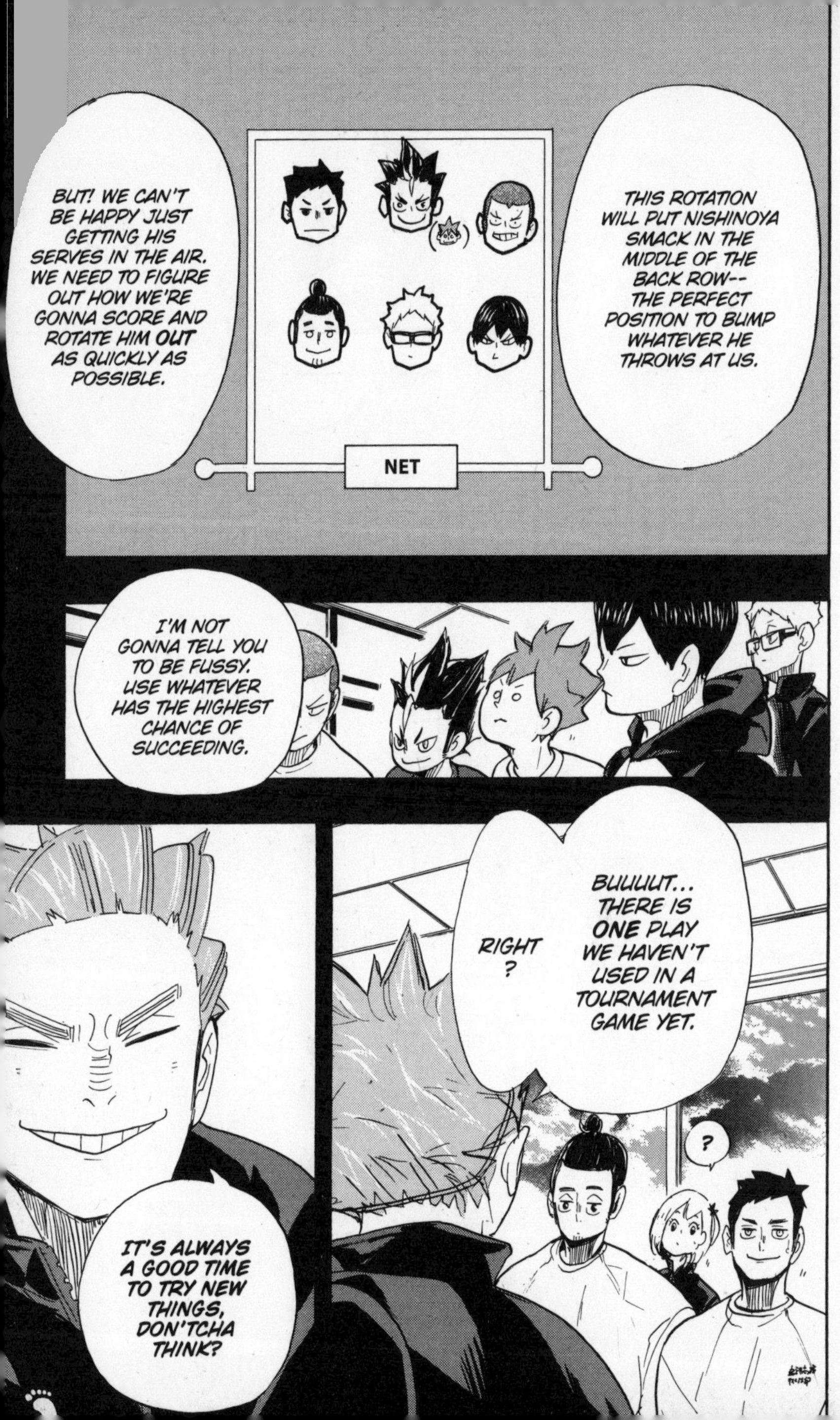
THIS ROTATION WILL PUT NISHINOYA SMACK IN THE MIDDLE OF THE BACK ROW-- THE PERFECT POSITION TO BUMP WHATEVER HE THROWS AT US.
BUT! WE CAN'T BE HAPPY JUST GETTING HIS SERVES IN THE AIR. WE NEED TO FIGURE OUT HOW WE'RE GONNA SCORE AND ROTATE HIM **OUT** AS QUICKLY AS POSSIBLE.
NET
I'M NOT GONNA TELL YOU TO BE FUSSY. USE WHATEVER HAS THE HIGHEST CHANCE OF SUCCEEDING.
BUUUUT... THERE IS **ONE** PLAY WE HAVEN'T USED IN A TOURNAMENT GAME YET.
RIGHT ?
?
IT'S ALWAYS A GOOD TIME TO TRY NEW THINGS, DON'TCHA THINK?

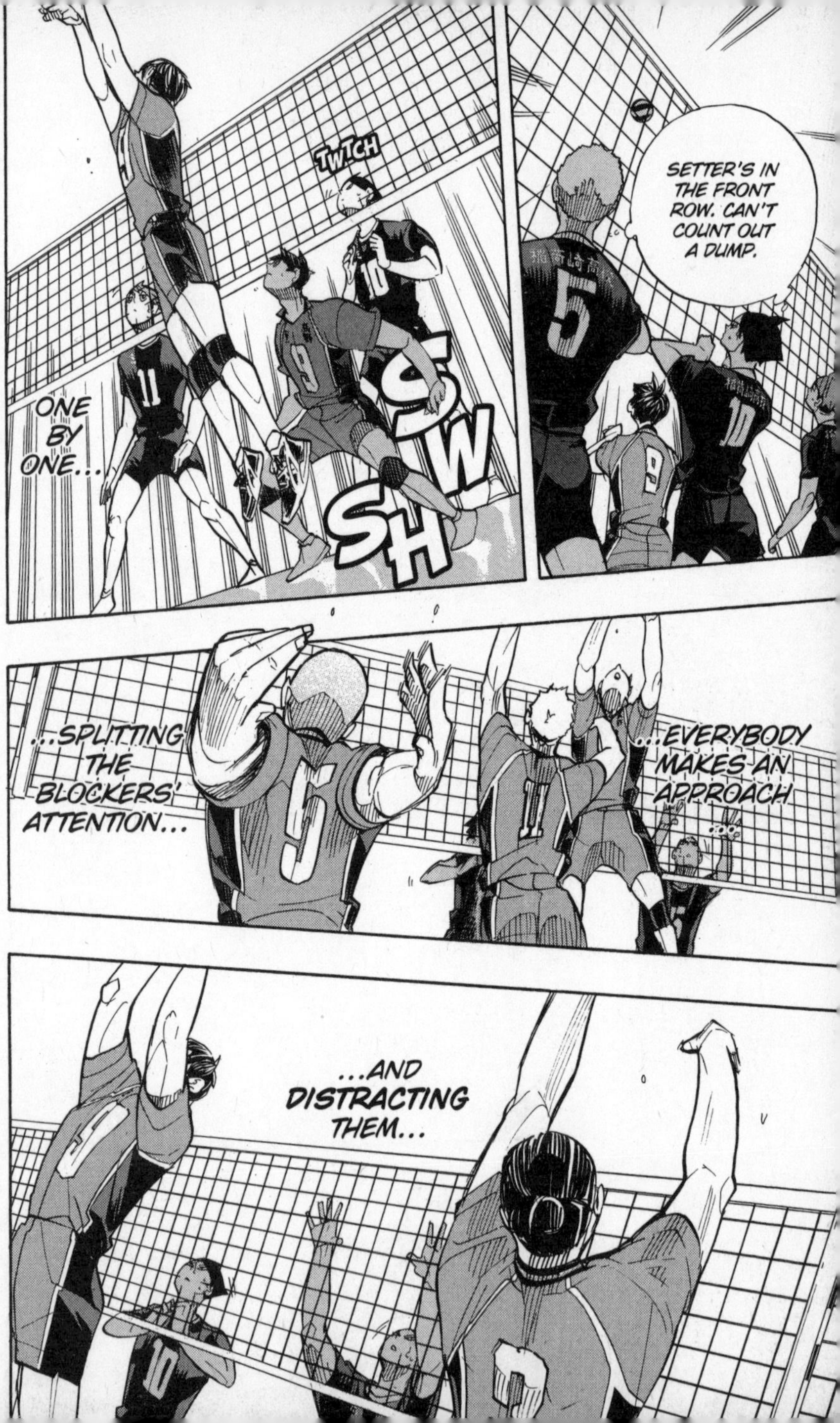

SETTER'S IN THE FRONT ROW. CAN'T COUNT OUT A DUMP.
TWITCH
SWSH
ONE BY ONE...
...EVERYBODY MAKES AN APPROACH...
...SPLITTING THE BLOCKERS' ATTENTION...
...AND DISTRACTING THEM...

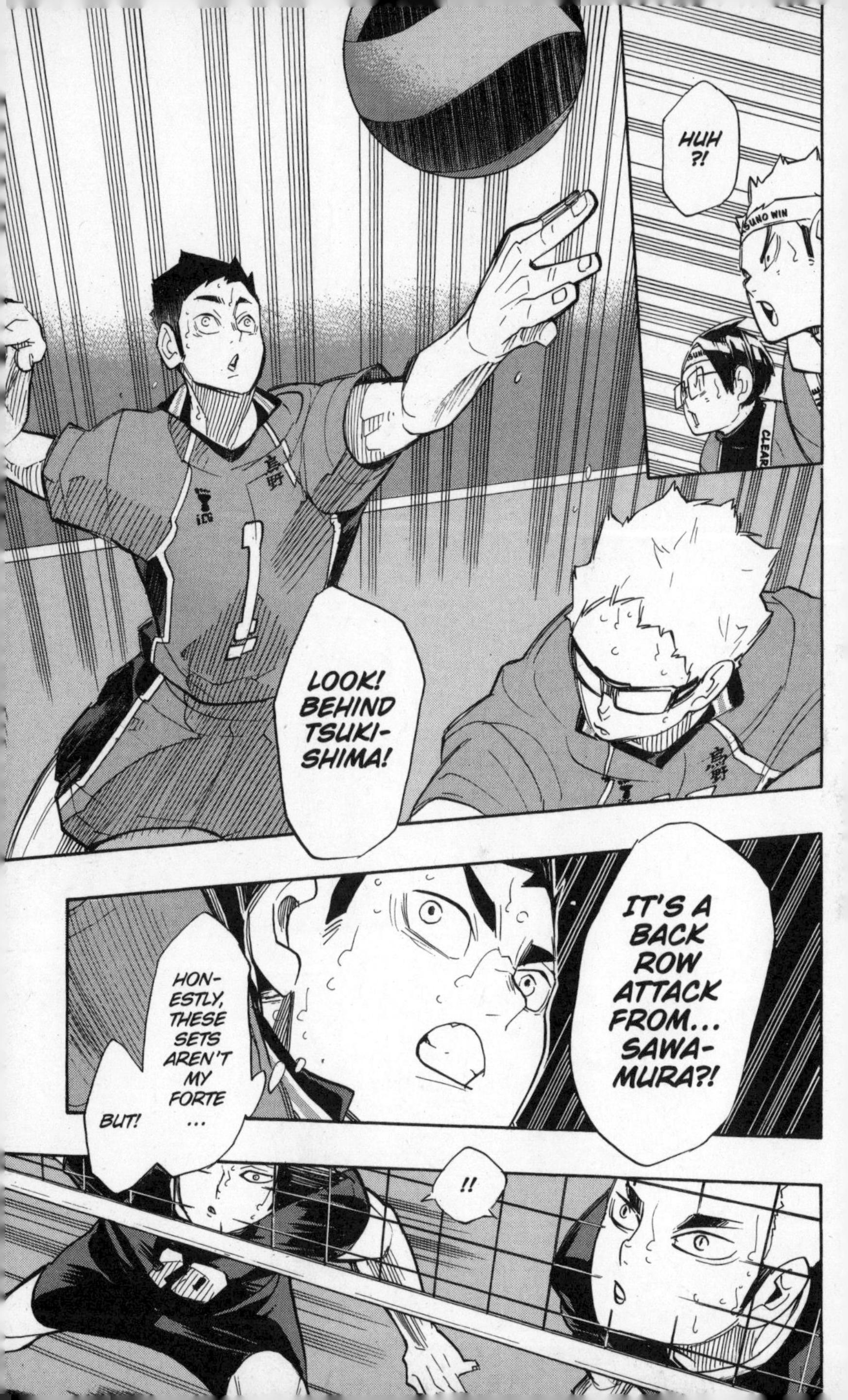
HUH?!
LOOK! BEHIND TSUKI-SHIMA!
IT'S A BACK ROW ATTACK FROM... SAWA-MURA?!
HON-ESTLY, THESE SETS AREN'T MY FORTE... BUT!
!!

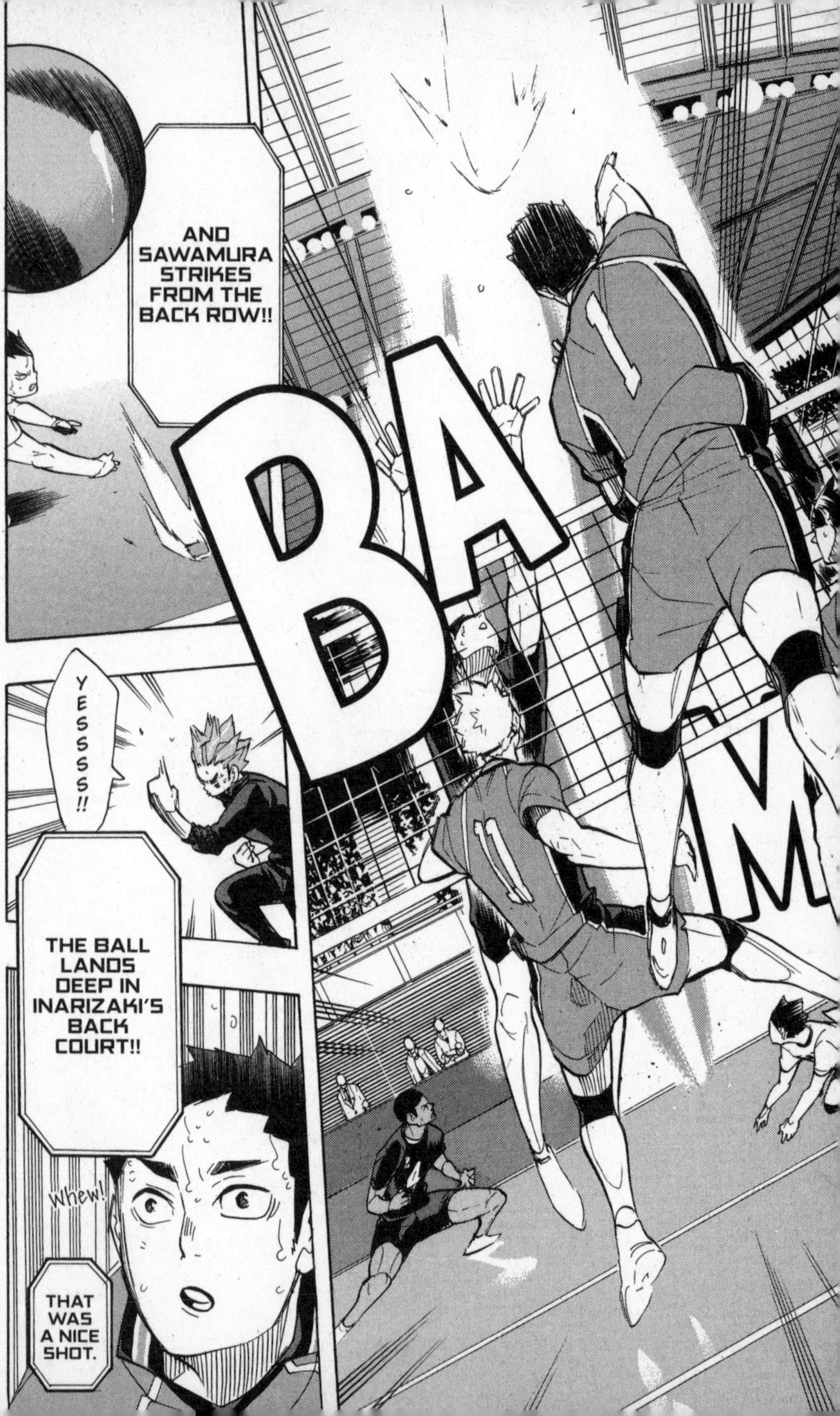
BAMM
AND SAWAMURA STRIKES FROM THE BACK ROW!!
YESSSS!!
THE BALL LANDS DEEP IN INARIZAKI'S BACK COURT!!
Whew!
THAT WAS A NICE SHOT.

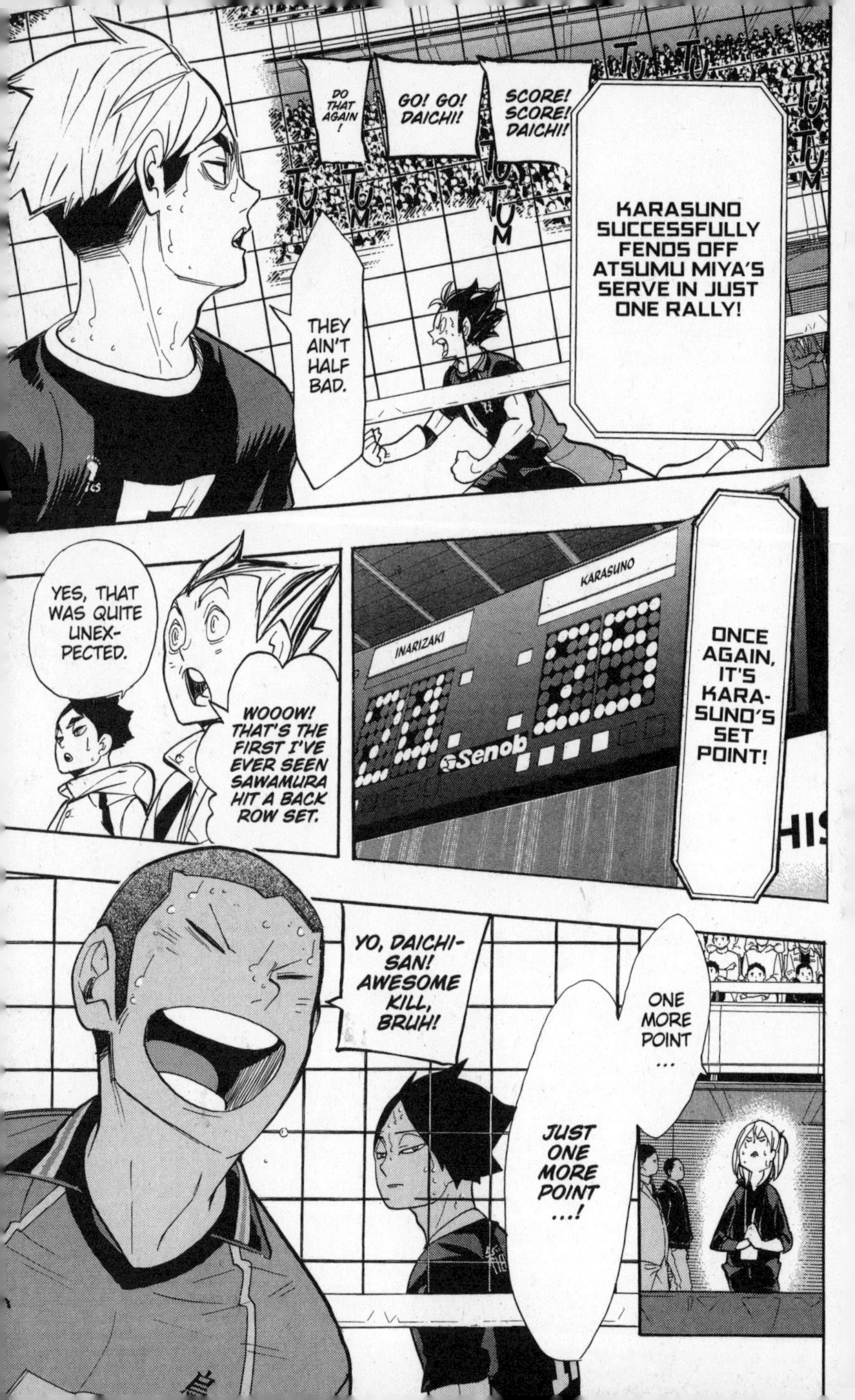
KARASUNO SUCCESSFULLY FENDS OFF ATSUMU MIYA'S SERVE IN JUST ONE RALLY!
TU TU TUM
SCORE! SCORE! DAICHI!
TU TUM
GO! GO! DAICHI!
DO THAT AGAIN!
TU TUM TU TUM
THEY AIN'T HALF BAD.
ONCE AGAIN, IT'S KARASUNO'S SET POINT!
KARASUNO
INARIZAKI
Senob
WOOOW! THAT'S THE FIRST I'VE EVER SEEN SAWAMURA HIT A BACK ROW SET.
YES, THAT WAS QUITE UNEXPECTED.
ONE MORE POINT...
JUST ONE MORE POINT...!
YO, DAICHI-SAN! AWESOME KILL, BRUH!

RINTARO SUNA

INARIZAKI HIGH SCHOOL
CLASS 2-1

POSITION:
MIDDLE BLOCKER

HEIGHT: 6'1"

WEIGHT: 161 LBS.
(AS OF JANUARY, 2ND YEAR
OF HIGH SCHOOL)

BIRTHDAY: JANUARY 25

FAVORITE FOOD:
CHUPPET ICE POPS

CURRENT WORRY:
HE'S NOT EVEN GOING
TO BOTHER CALLING THE
TWINS OUT EVERY TIME
THEY DO SOMETHING NUTS.

ABILITY PARAMETERS
(5-POINT SCALE)

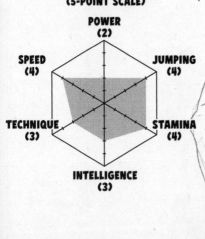

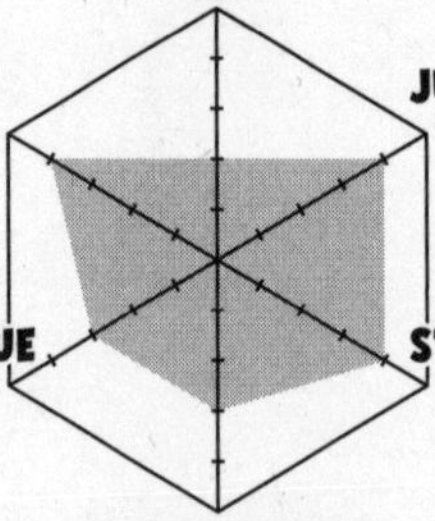
POWER (2)
JUMPING (4)
STAMINA (4)
INTELLIGENCE (3)
TECHNIQUE (3)
SPEED (4)

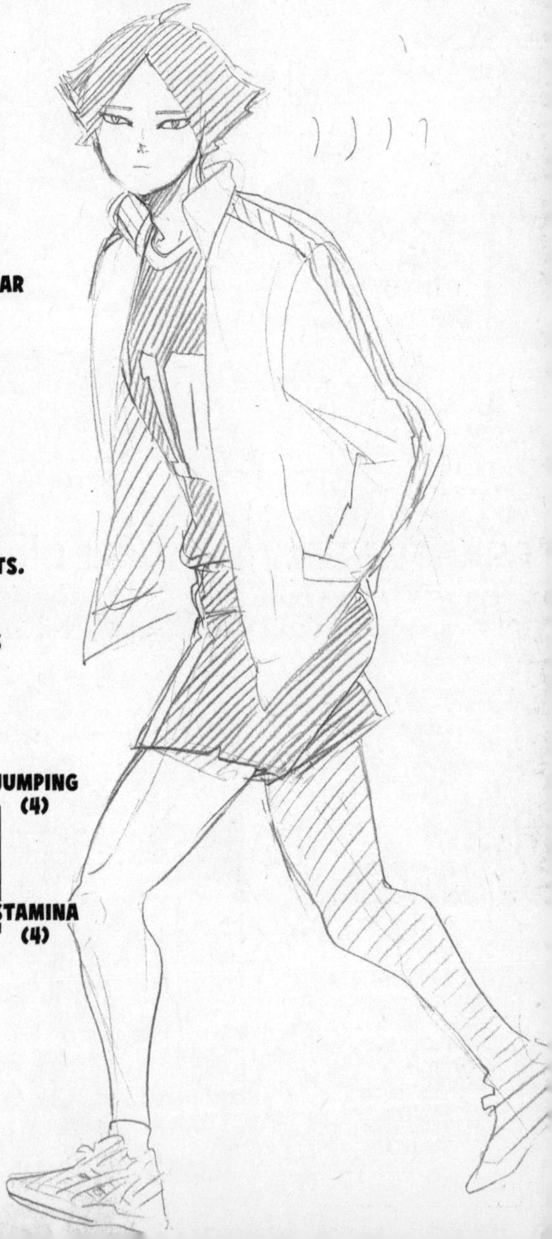

CHAPTER 262: Always Fall Forward

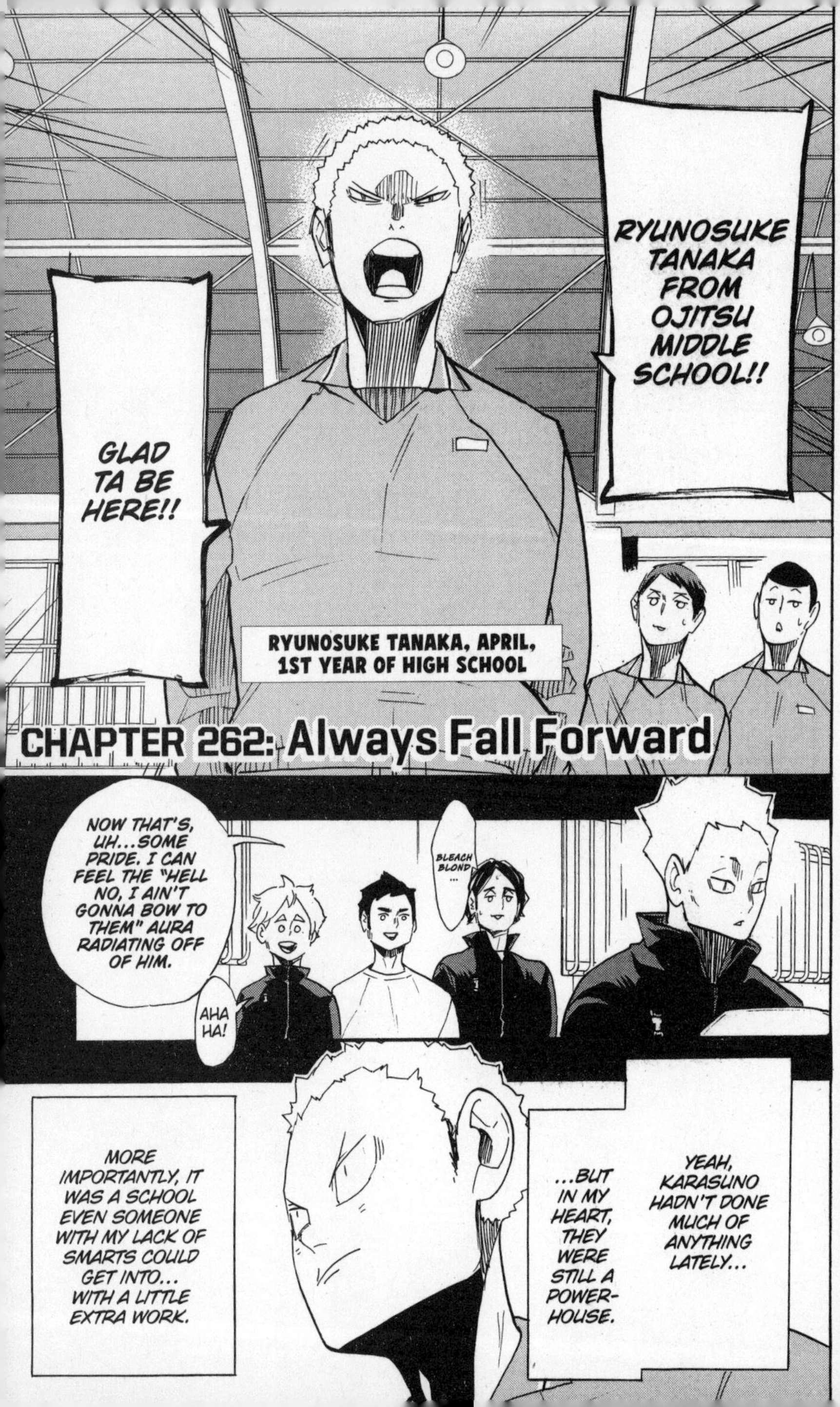

RYUNOSUKE TANAKA FROM OJITSU MIDDLE SCHOOL!!
GLAD TA BE HERE!!
RYUNOSUKE TANAKA, APRIL, 1ST YEAR OF HIGH SCHOOL
BLEACH BLOND ...
NOW THAT'S, UH...SOME PRIDE. I CAN FEEL THE "HELL NO, I AIN'T GONNA BOW TO THEM" AURA RADIATING OFF OF HIM.
AHA HA!
YEAH, KARASUNO HADN'T DONE MUCH OF ANYTHING LATELY...
...BUT IN MY HEART, THEY WERE STILL A POWER-HOUSE.
MORE IMPORTANTLY, IT WAS A SCHOOL EVEN SOMEONE WITH MY LACK OF SMARTS COULD GET INTO... WITH A LITTLE EXTRA WORK.

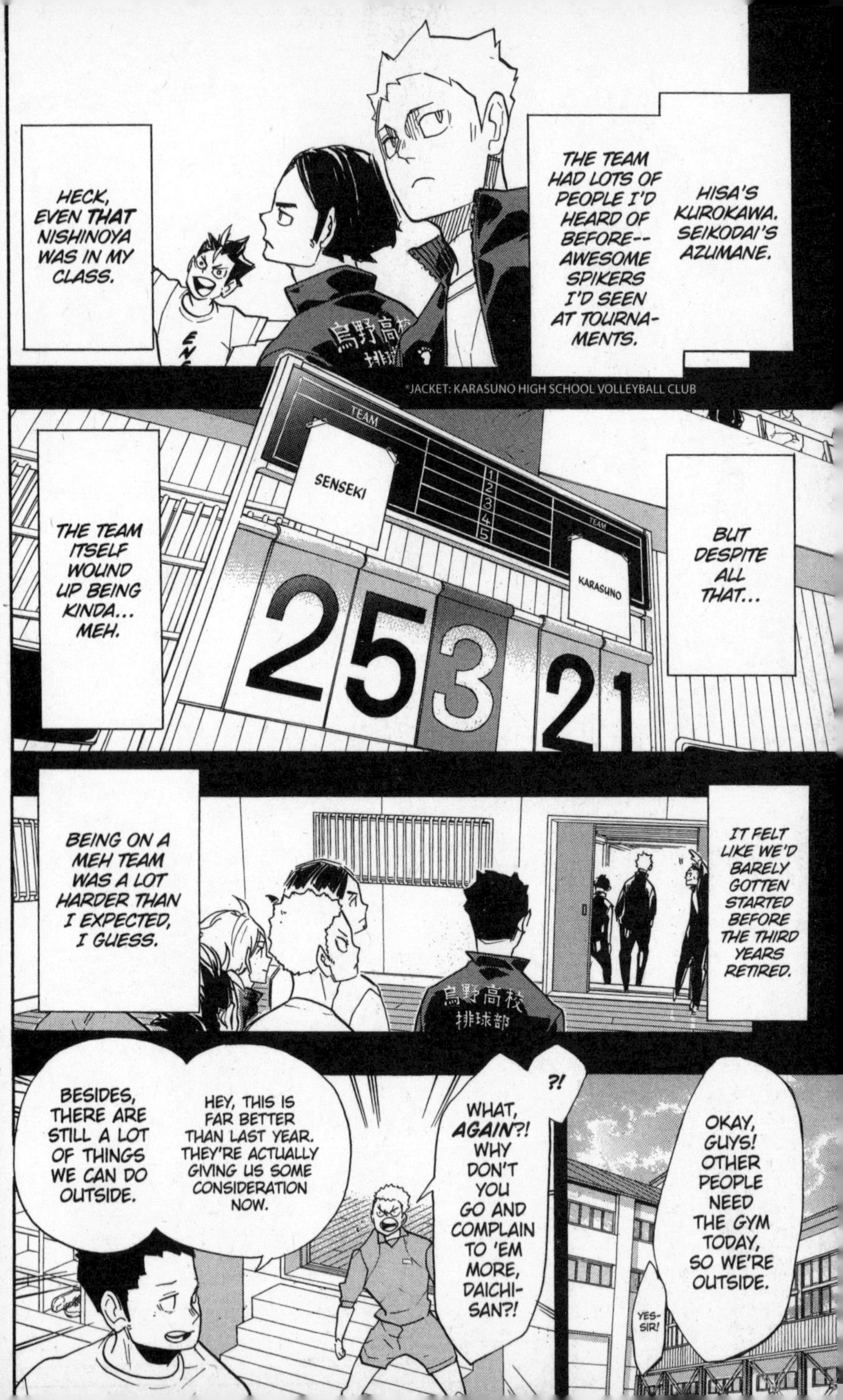
THE TEAM HAD LOTS OF PEOPLE I'D HEARD OF BEFORE-- AWESOME SPIKERS I'D SEEN AT TOURNAMENTS.
HISA'S KUROKAWA. SEIKODAI'S AZUMANE.
烏野高校 排球部
HECK, EVEN THAT NISHINOYA WAS IN MY CLASS.
*JACKET: KARASUNO HIGH SCHOOL VOLLEYBALL CLUB
BUT DESPITE ALL THAT...
TEAM
SENSEKI
KARASUNO
1 2 3 4 5
25 3 21
THE TEAM ITSELF WOUND UP BEING KINDA... MEH.
IT FELT LIKE WE'D BARELY GOTTEN STARTED BEFORE THE THIRD YEARS RETIRED.
烏野高校 排球部
BEING ON A MEH TEAM WAS A LOT HARDER THAN I EXPECTED, I GUESS.
OKAY, GUYS! OTHER PEOPLE NEED THE GYM TODAY, SO WE'RE OUTSIDE.
YES-SIR!
?!
WHAT, AGAIN?! WHY DON'T YOU GO AND COMPLAIN TO 'EM MORE, DAICHI-SAN?!
HEY, THIS IS FAR BETTER THAN LAST YEAR. THEY'RE ACTUALLY GIVING US SOME CONSIDERATION NOW.
BESIDES, THERE ARE STILL A LOT OF THINGS WE CAN DO OUTSIDE.

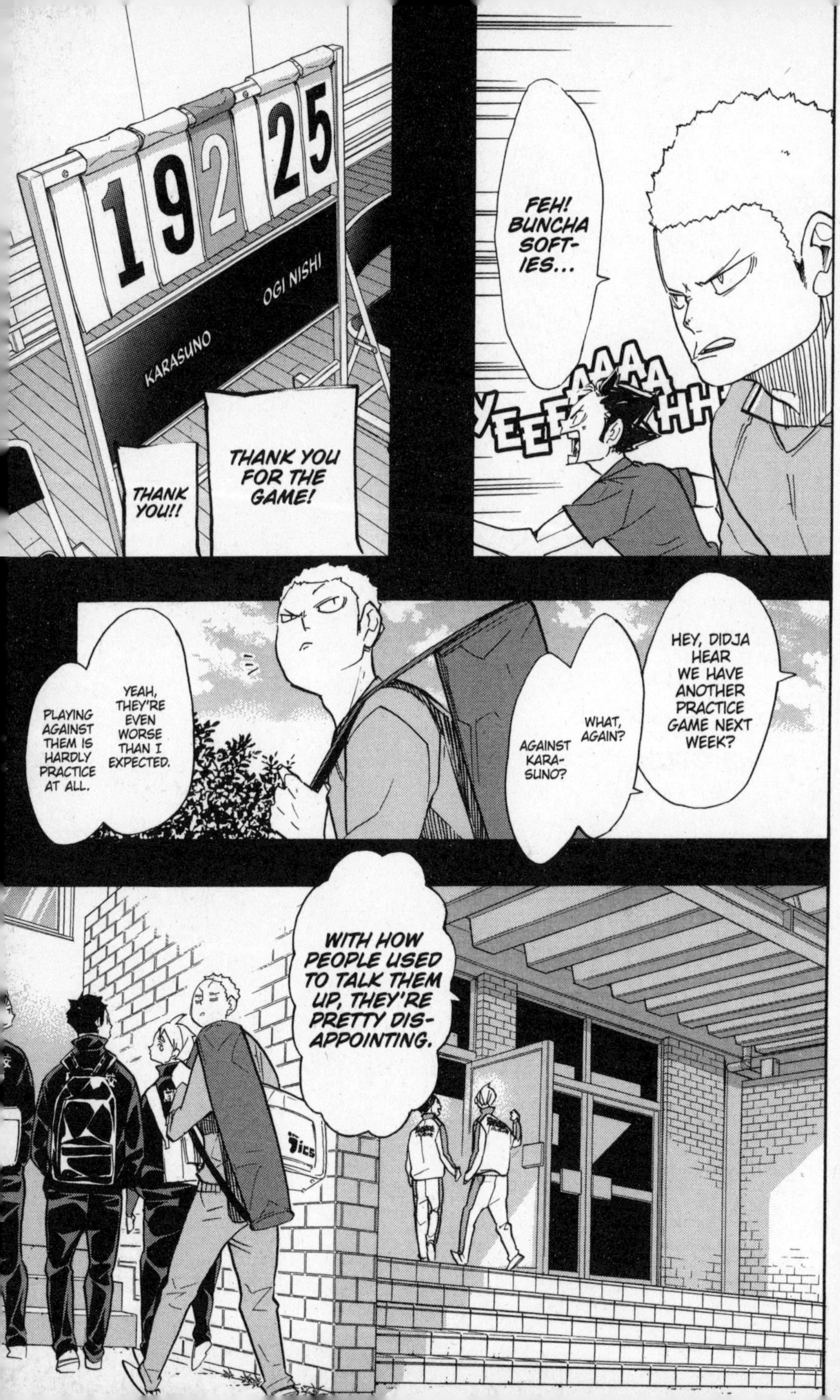
FEH! BUNCHA SOFT-IES...
19
2
25
OGI NISHI
KARASUNO
THANK YOU FOR THE GAME!
THANK YOU!!
HEY, DIDJA HEAR WE HAVE ANOTHER PRACTICE GAME NEXT WEEK?
WHAT, AGAIN?
AGAINST KARA-SUNO?
YEAH, THEY'RE EVEN WORSE THAN I EXPECTED.
PLAYING AGAINST THEM IS HARDLY PRACTICE AT ALL.
WITH HOW PEOPLE USED TO TALK THEM UP, THEY'RE PRETTY DIS-APPOINTING.

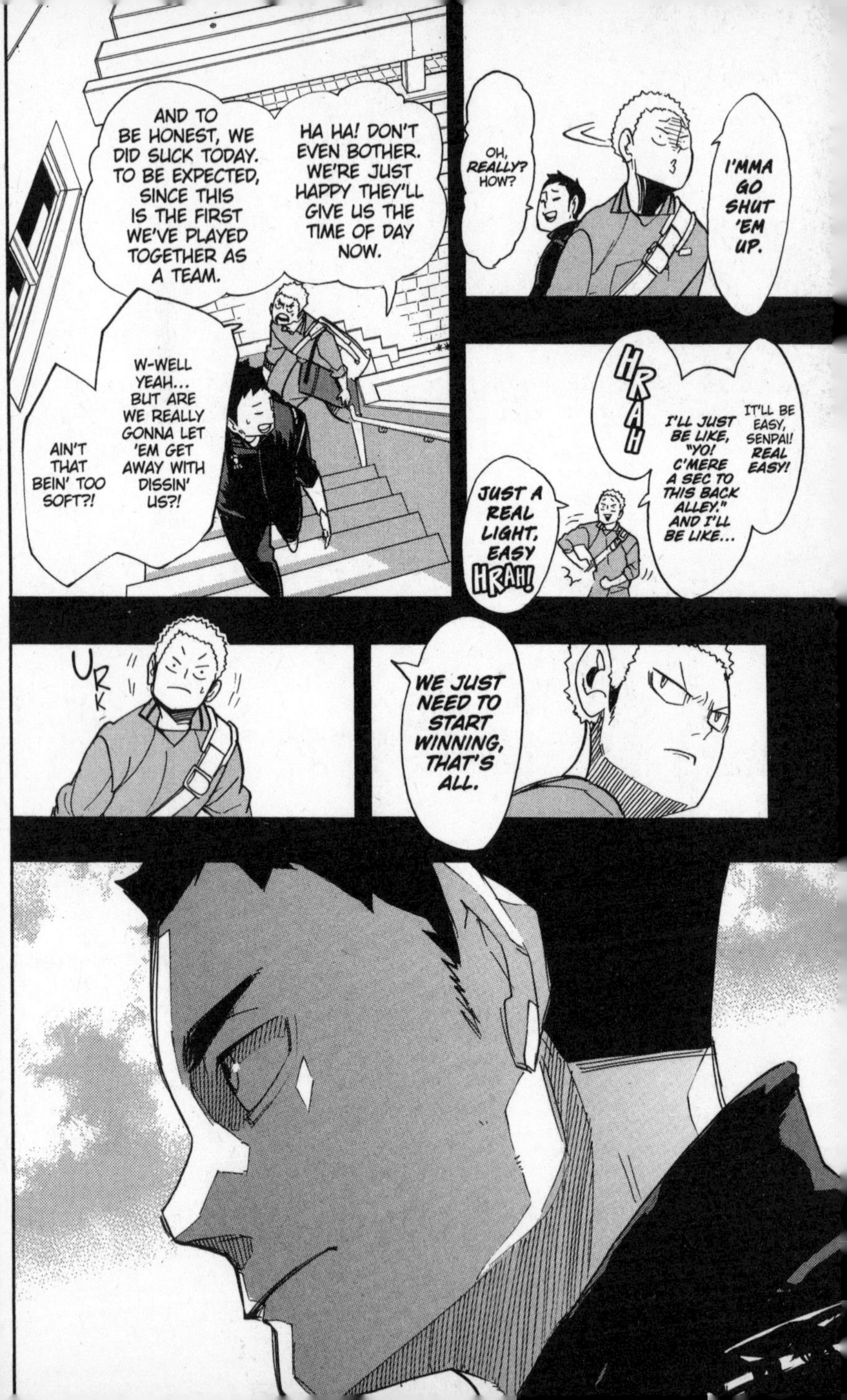

I'MMA GO SHUT 'EM UP.
OH, REALLY? HOW?
IT'LL BE EASY, SENPAI! REAL EASY!
I'LL JUST BE LIKE, "YO! C'MERE A SEC TO THIS BACK ALLEY." AND I'LL BE LIKE...
HRAH
JUST A REAL LIGHT, EASY HRAH!
HA HA! DON'T EVEN BOTHER. WE'RE JUST HAPPY THEY'LL GIVE US THE TIME OF DAY NOW.
AND TO BE HONEST, WE DID SUCK TODAY. TO BE EXPECTED, SINCE THIS IS THE FIRST WE'VE PLAYED TOGETHER AS A TEAM.
W-WELL YEAH... BUT ARE WE REALLY GONNA LET 'EM GET AWAY WITH DISSIN' US?!
AIN'T THAT BEIN' TOO SOFT?!
WE JUST NEED TO START WINNING, THAT'S ALL.
URK

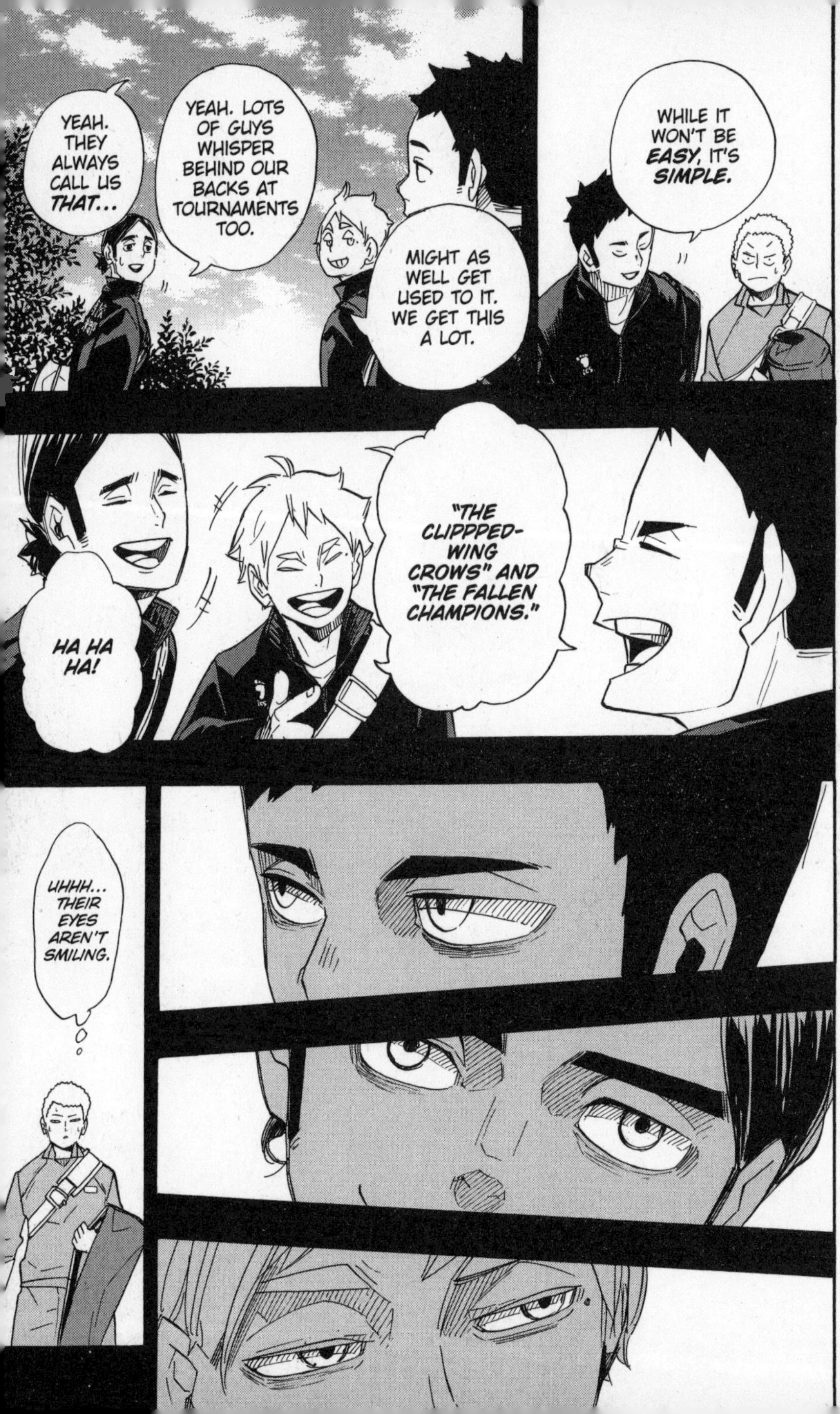
WHILE IT WON'T BE EASY, IT'S SIMPLE.
MIGHT AS WELL GET USED TO IT. WE GET THIS A LOT.
YEAH. LOTS OF GUYS WHISPER BEHIND OUR BACKS AT TOURNAMENTS TOO.
YEAH. THEY ALWAYS CALL US THAT...
"THE CLIPPPED-WING CROWS" AND "THE FALLEN CHAMPIONS."
HA HA HA!
UHHH... THEIR EYES AREN'T SMILING.

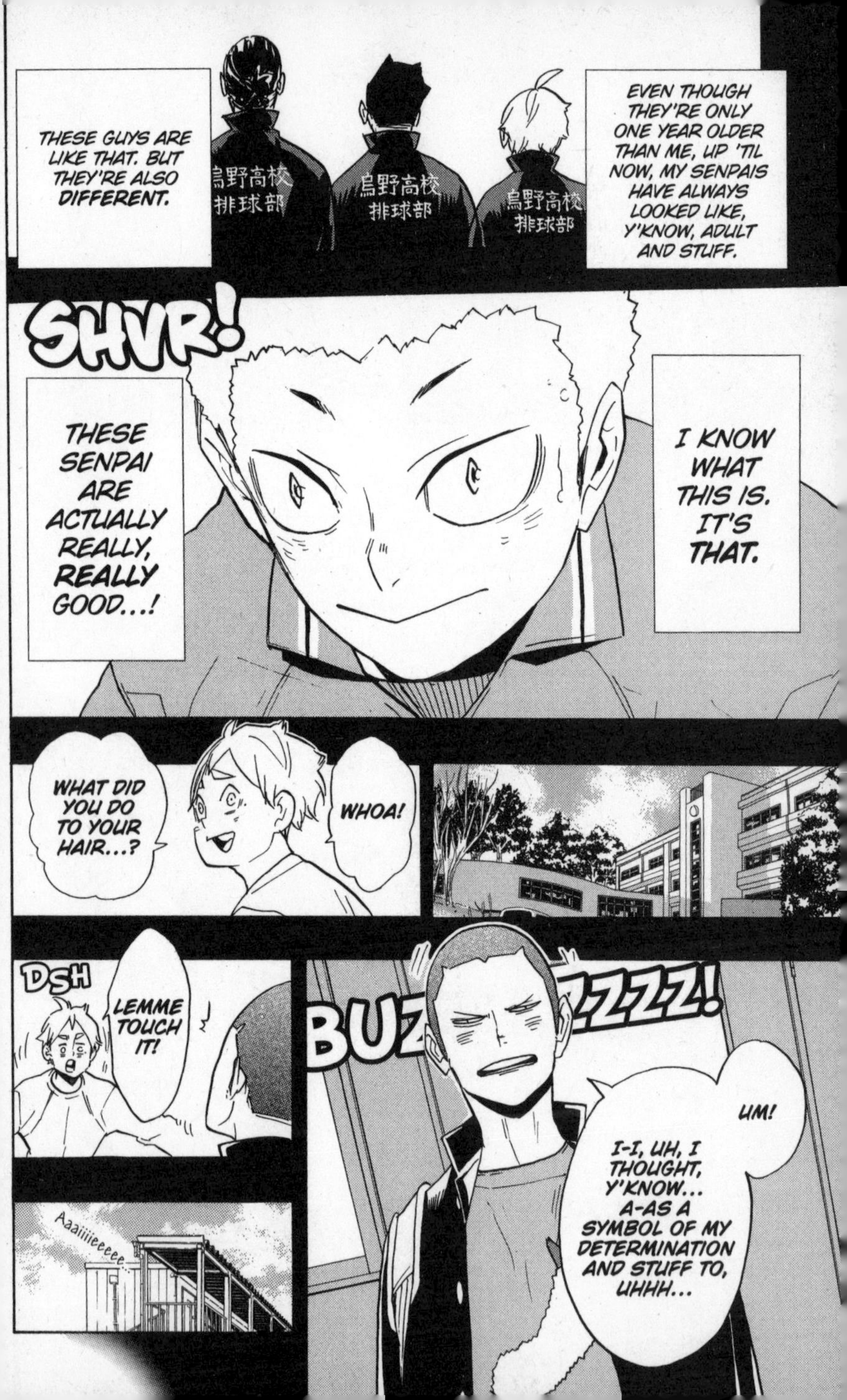

EVEN THOUGH THEY'RE ONLY ONE YEAR OLDER THAN ME, UP 'TIL NOW, MY SENPAIS HAVE ALWAYS LOOKED LIKE, Y'KNOW, ADULT AND STUFF.
烏野高校 排球部
烏野高校 排球部
烏野高校 排球部
THESE GUYS ARE LIKE THAT. BUT THEY'RE ALSO DIFFERENT.
SHVR!
I KNOW WHAT THIS IS. IT'S THAT.
THESE SENPAI ARE ACTUALLY REALLY, REALLY GOOD...!
WHOA!
WHAT DID YOU DO TO YOUR HAIR...?
BUZZZZZ!
UM!
I-I, UH, I THOUGHT, Y'KNOW... A-AS A SYMBOL OF MY DETERMINATION AND STUFF TO, UHHH...
DSH
LEMME TOUCH IT!
Aaaiiiieeeee...

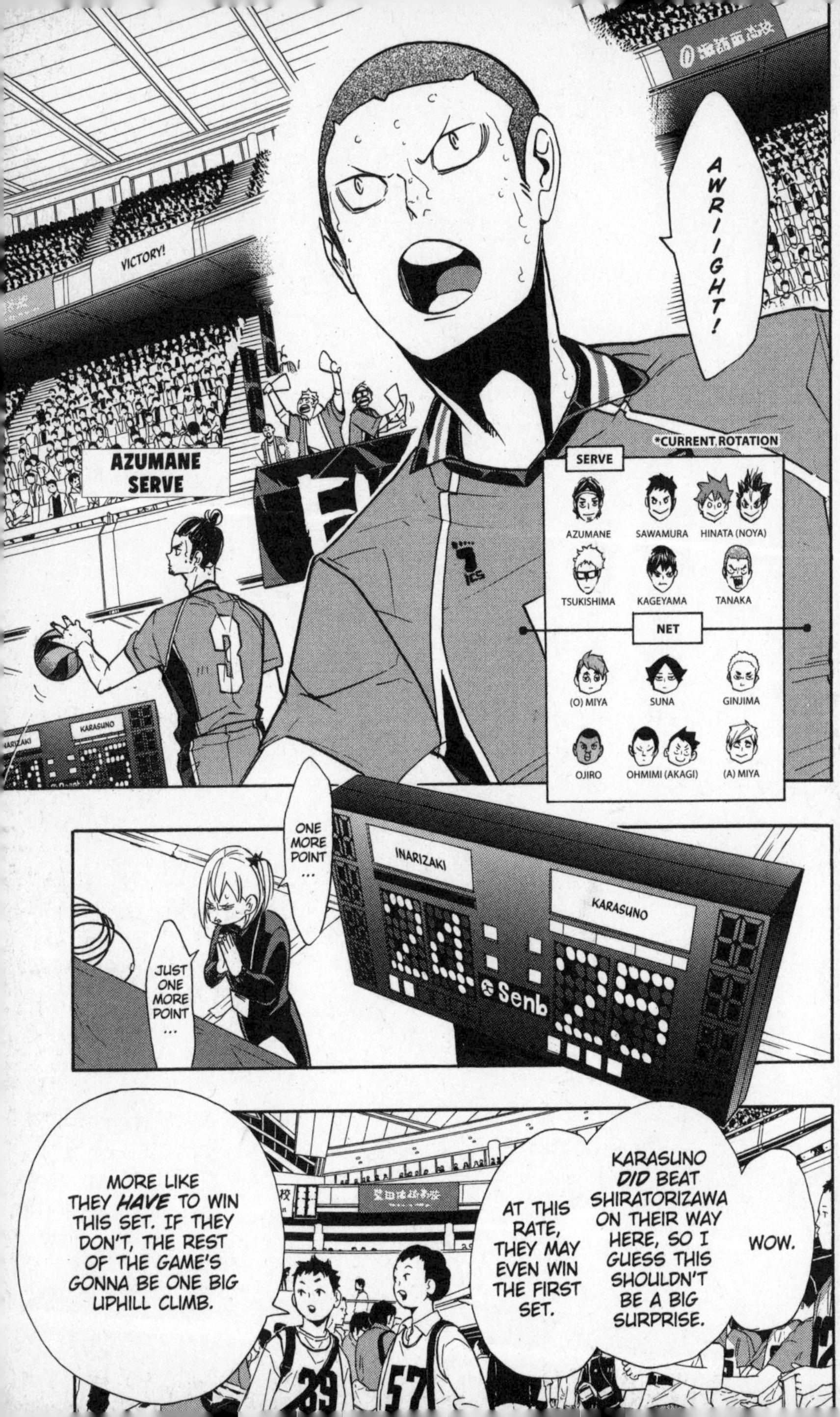

AWRIGHT!
*CURRENT ROTATION
SERVE
AZUMANE
SAWAMURA
HINATA (NOYA)
TSUKISHIMA
KAGEYAMA
TANAKA
NET
(O) MIYA
SUNA
GINJIMA
OJIRO
OHMIMI (AKAGI)
(A) MIYA
AZUMANE SERVE
VICTORY!
INARIZAKI
KARASUNO
ONE MORE POINT...
JUST ONE MORE POINT...
WOW.
KARASUNO DID BEAT SHIRATORIZAWA ON THEIR WAY HERE, SO I GUESS THIS SHOULDN'T BE A BIG SURPRISE.
AT THIS RATE, THEY MAY EVEN WIN THE FIRST SET.
MORE LIKE THEY HAVE TO WIN THIS SET. IF THEY DON'T, THE REST OF THE GAME'S GONNA BE ONE BIG UPHILL CLIMB.

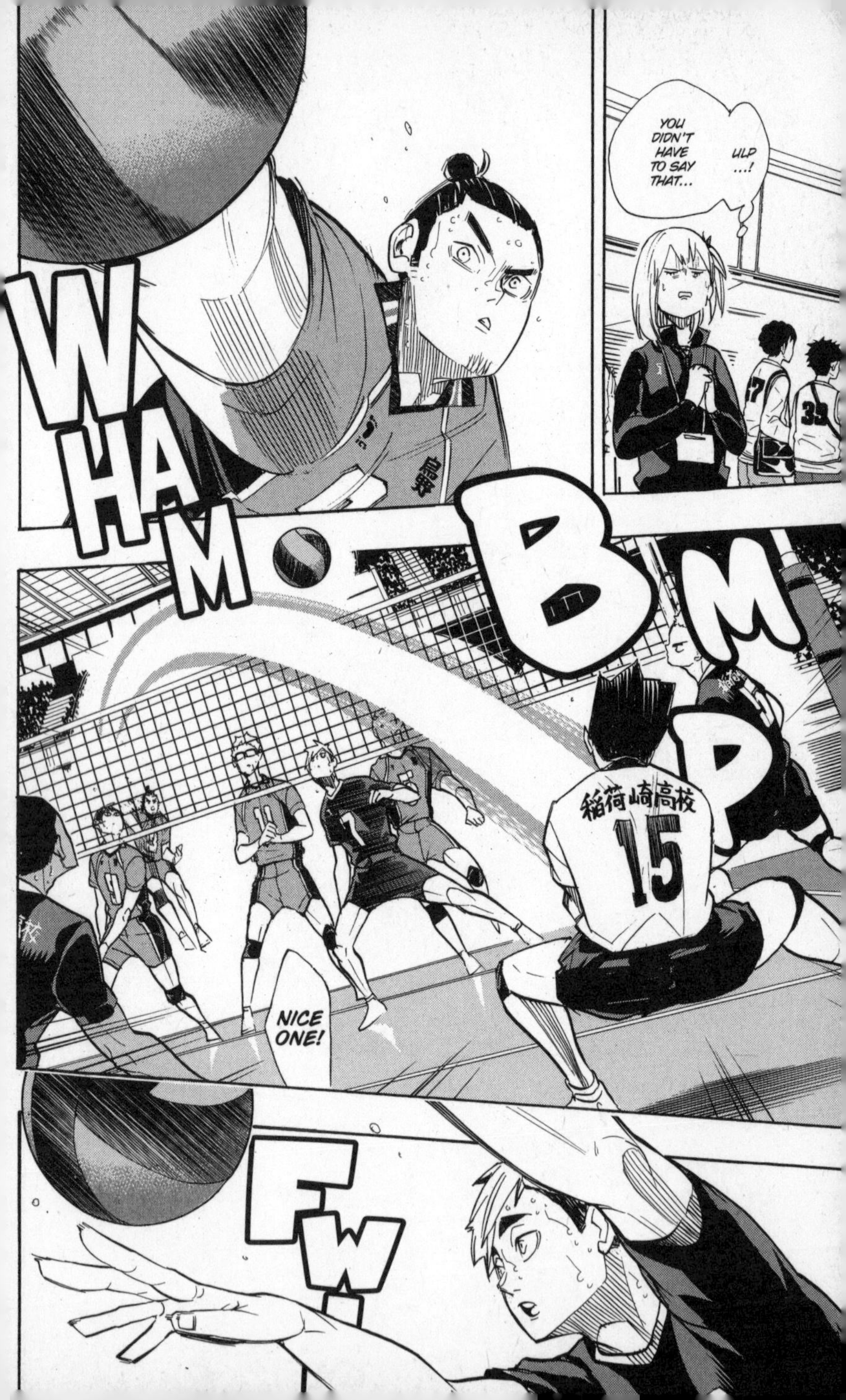
YOU DIDN'T HAVE TO SAY THAT...
ULP ...!
WHAM
BMP
稲荷崎高校
15
NICE ONE!
FW

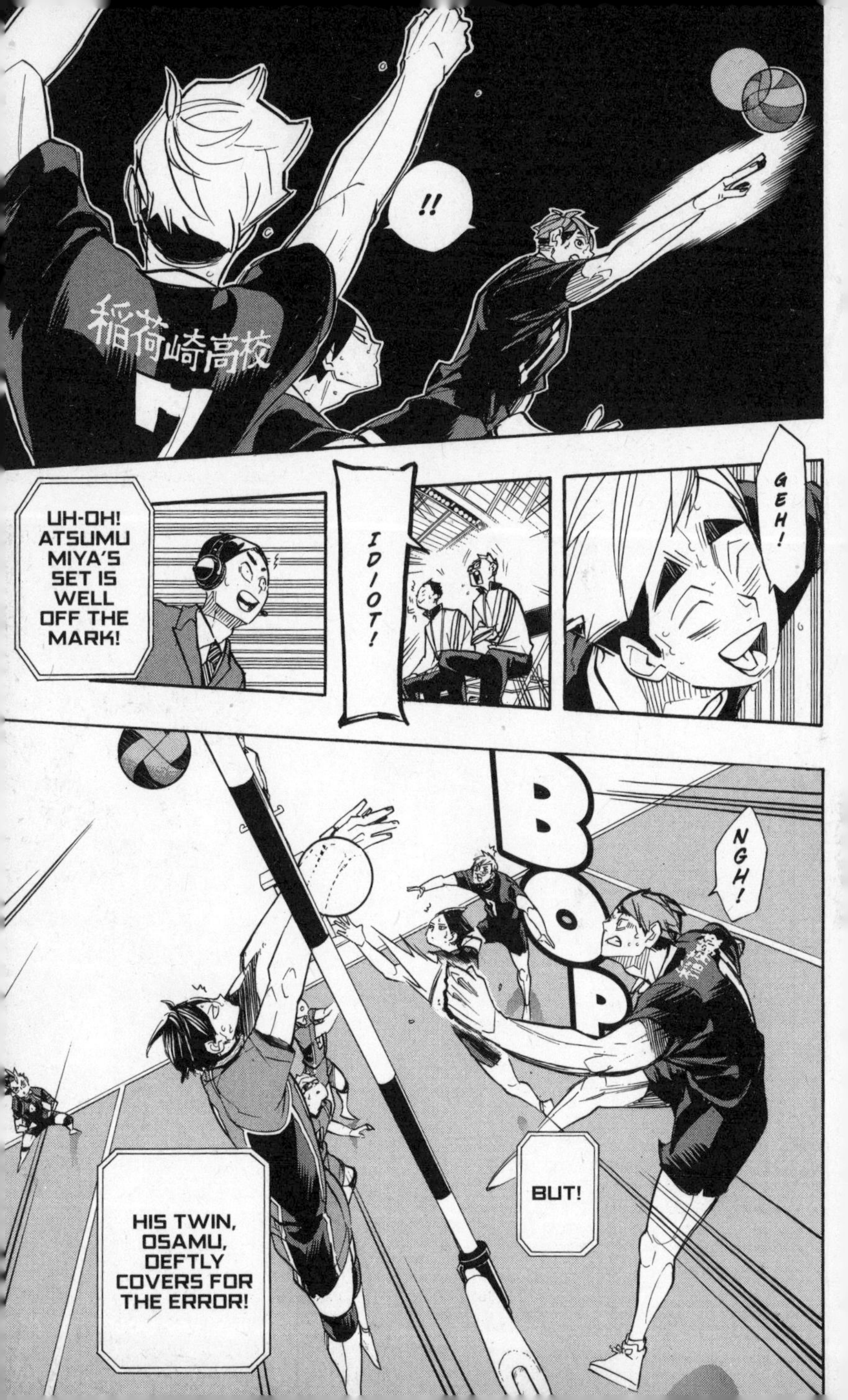
稲荷崎高校
!!
GEH!
IDIOT!
UH-OH! ATSUMU MIYA'S SET IS WELL OFF THE MARK!
NGH!
BOOP
BUT!
HIS TWIN, OSAMU, DEFTLY COVERS FOR THE ERROR!

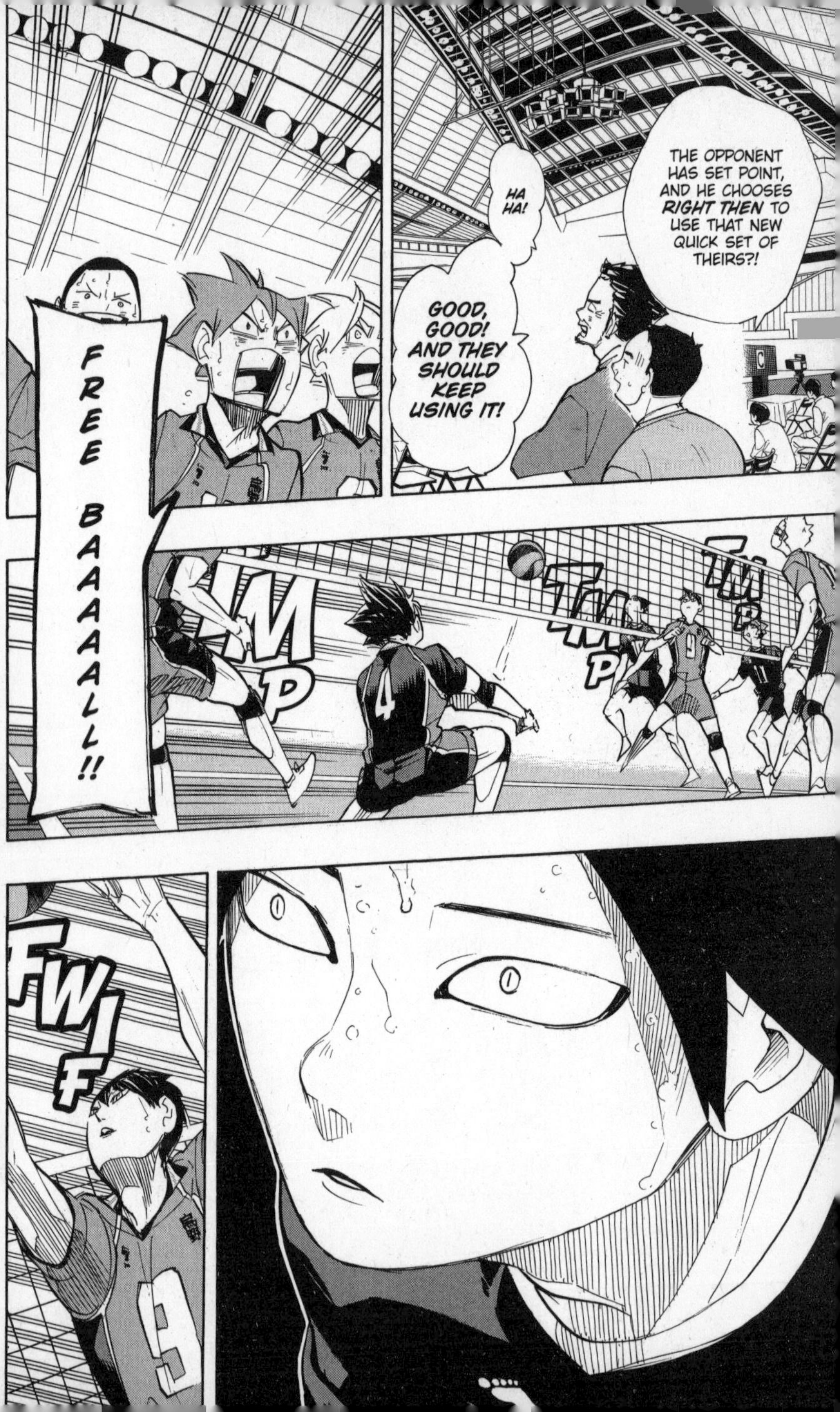

THE OPPONENT HAS SET POINT, AND HE CHOOSES *RIGHT THEN* TO USE THAT NEW QUICK SET OF THEIRS?!
HA HA!
GOOD, GOOD! AND THEY SHOULD KEEP USING IT!
FREE BAAAAAALL!!
TMP
TMP
FWIF

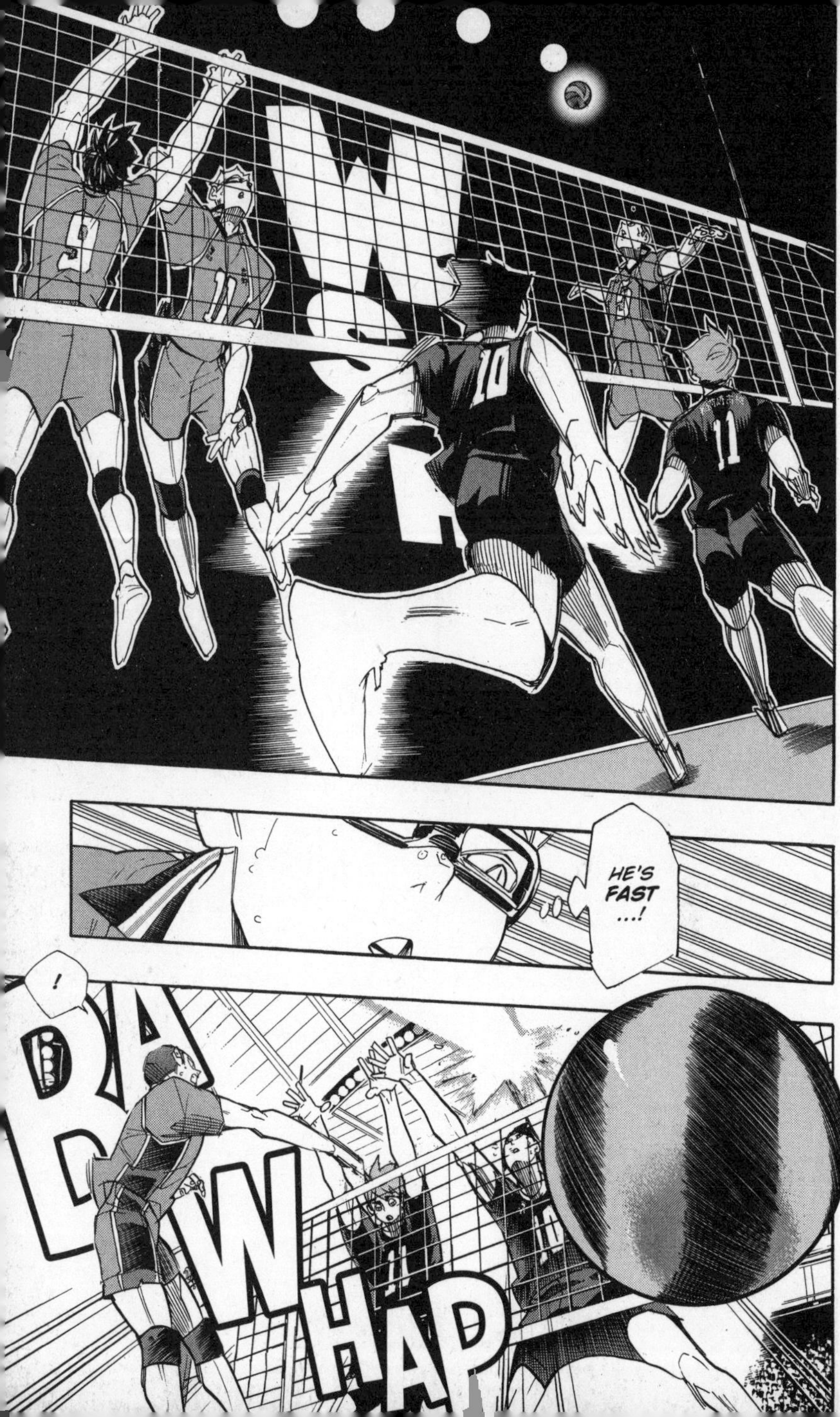

WHS
HE'S FAST ...!
!
BADWHAP

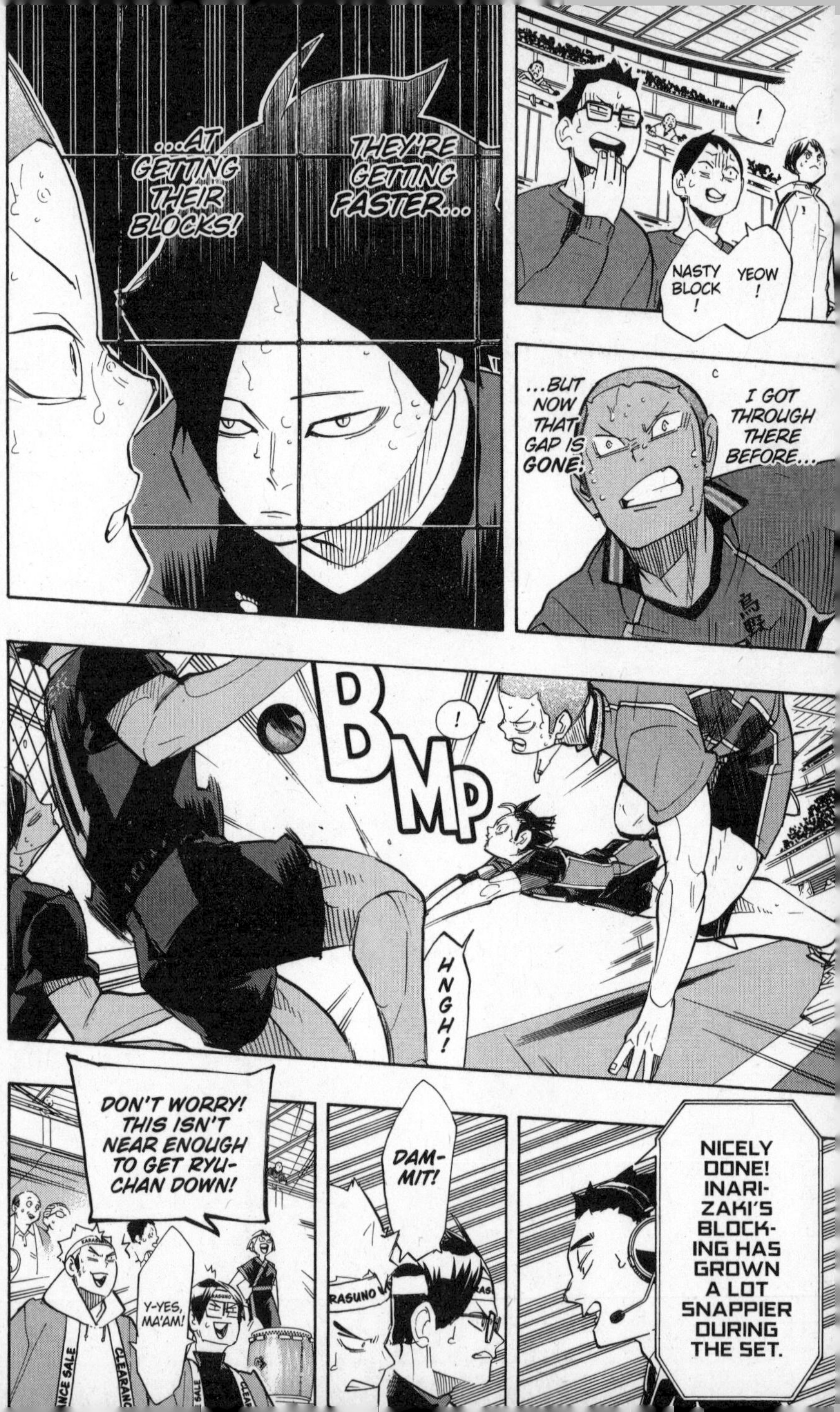
!
YEOW!
NASTY BLOCK!
I GOT THROUGH THERE BEFORE...
...BUT NOW THAT GAP IS GONE.
THEY'RE GETTING FASTER...
...AT GETTING THEIR BLOCKS!
!
BMP
HNGH!
NICELY DONE! INARIZAKI'S BLOCKING HAS GROWN A LOT SNAPPIER DURING THE SET.
DAMMIT!
DON'T WORRY! THIS ISN'T NEAR ENOUGH TO GET RYU-CHAN DOWN!
Y-YES, MA'AM!

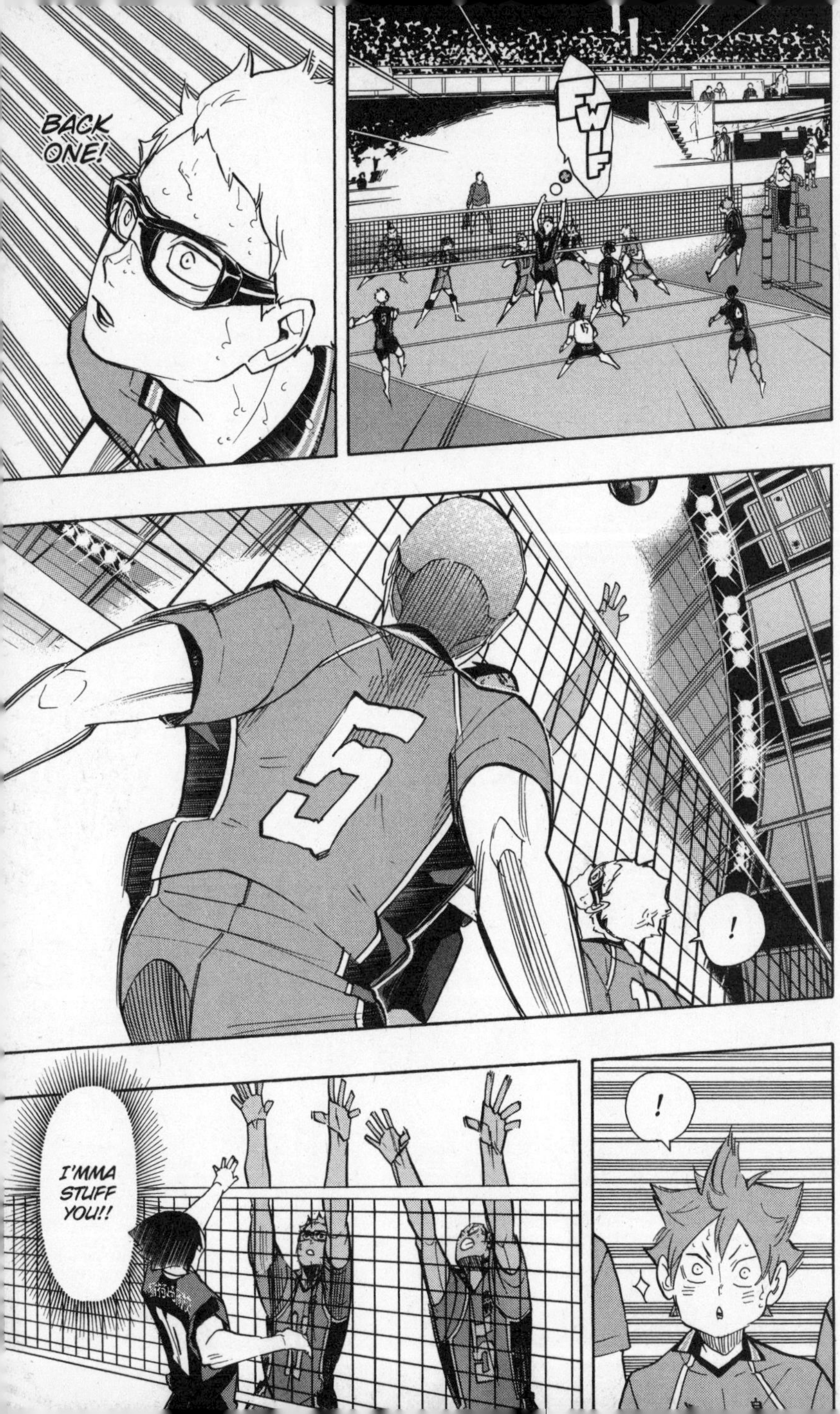
FWIF
BACK ONE!
!
!
I'MMA STUFF YOU!!

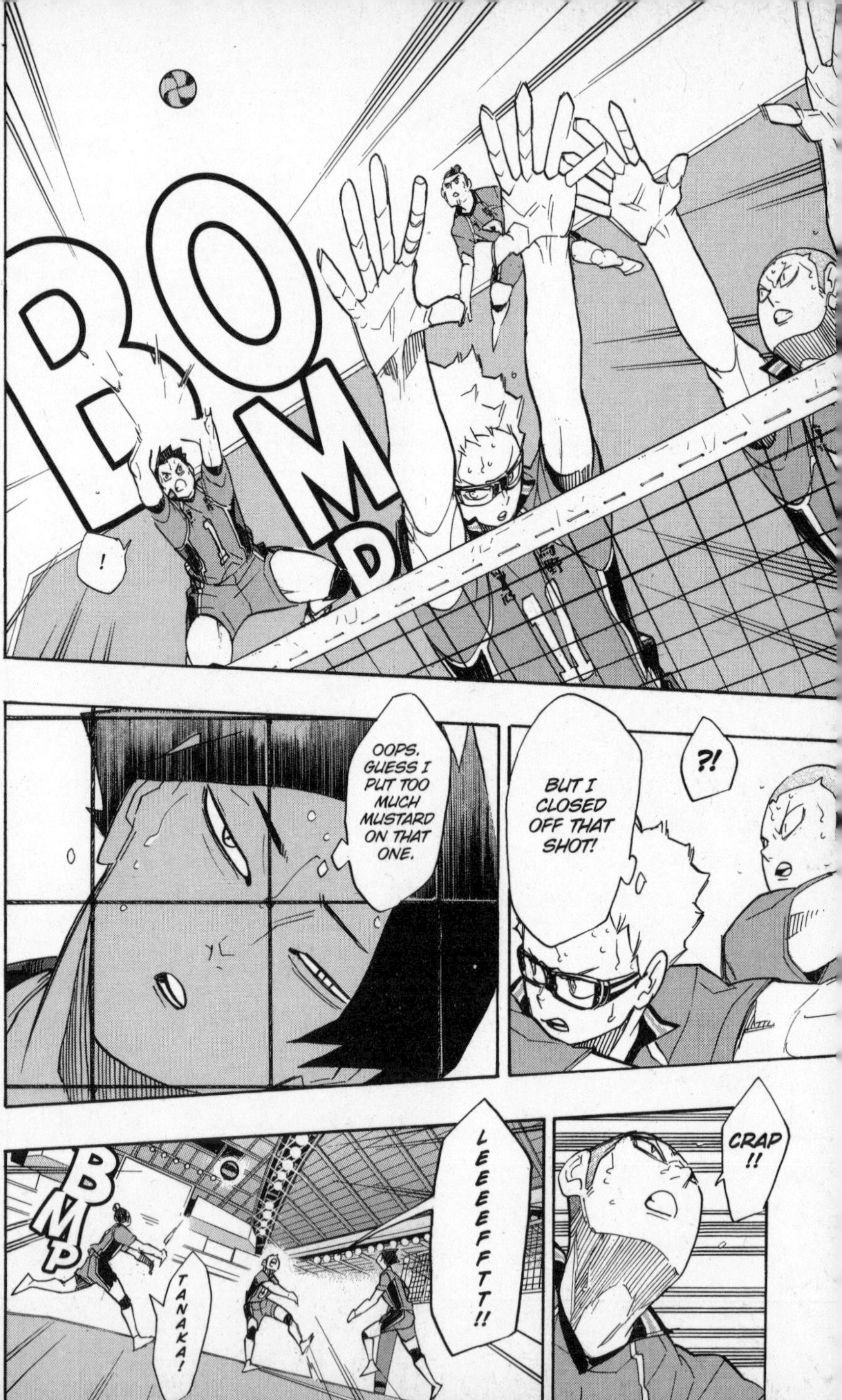
BOMD
!
?!
BUT I CLOSED OFF THAT SHOT!
OOPS. GUESS I PUT TOO MUCH MUSTARD ON THAT ONE.
CRAP!!
LEEEEFFTT!!
TANAKA!
BMP

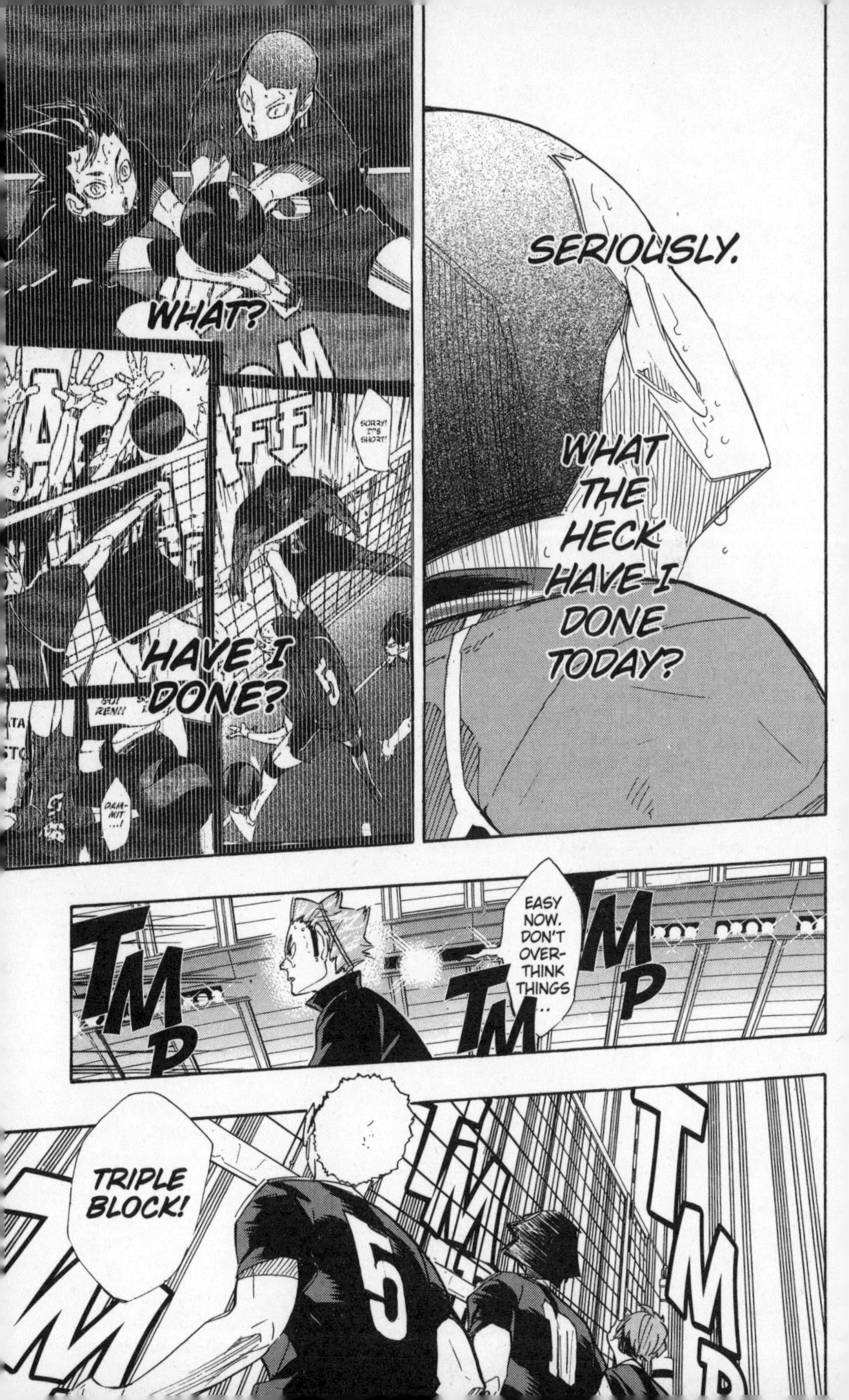
SERIOUSLY.
WHAT THE HECK HAVE I DONE TODAY?
WHAT?
SORRY! IT'S SHORT!
HAVE I DONE?
GO! REN!!
DAM-MIT...!
EASY NOW. DON'T OVER-THINK THINGS...
TMP
TMP
TMP
TRIPLE BLOCK!

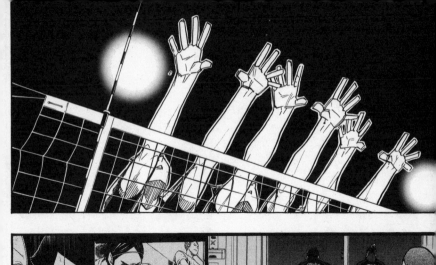

HA HA
HA!

"THE CLIPPED-
WING
CROWS" AND
"THE FALLEN
CHAMPIONS."

NN...

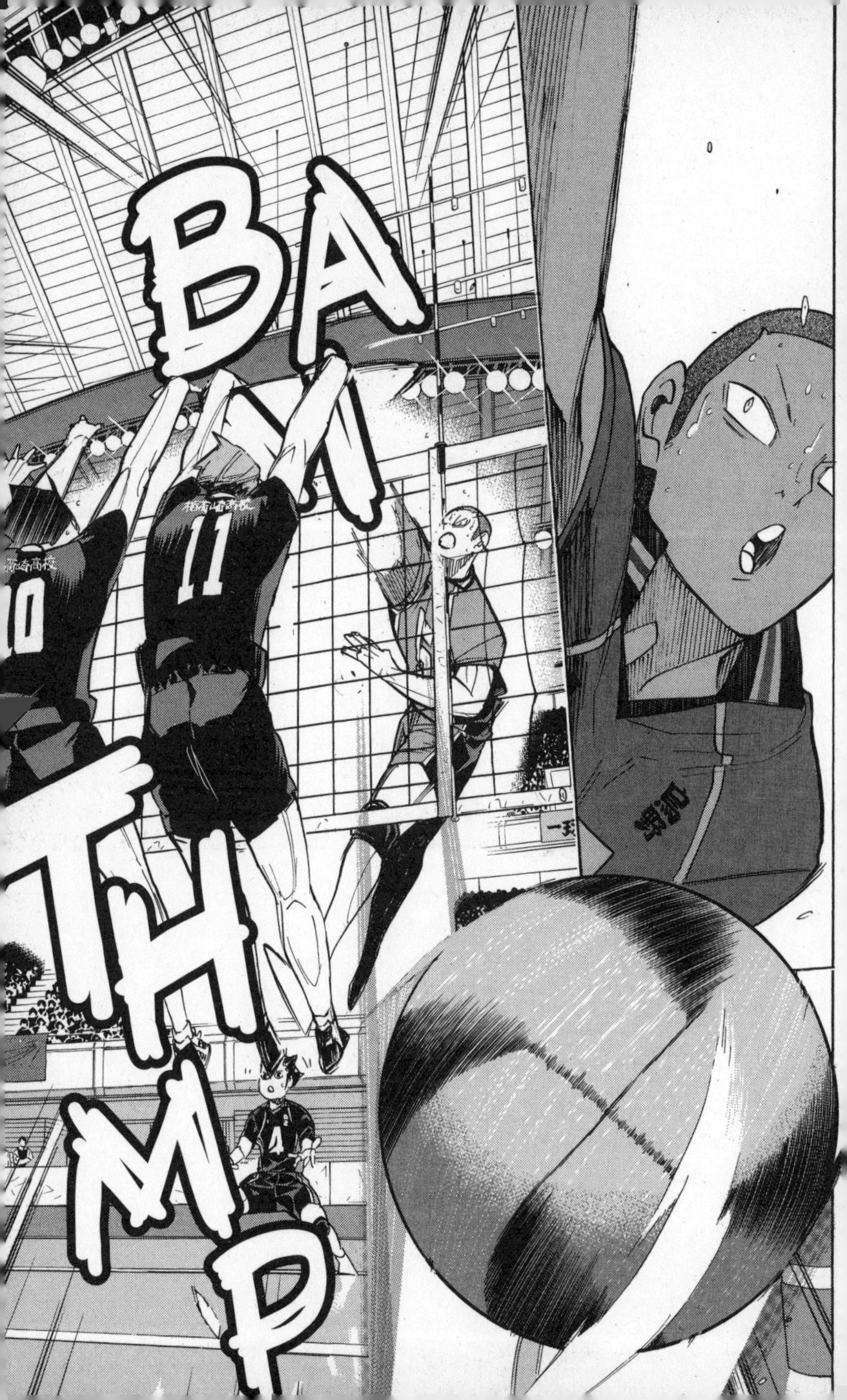
BAMTHMP

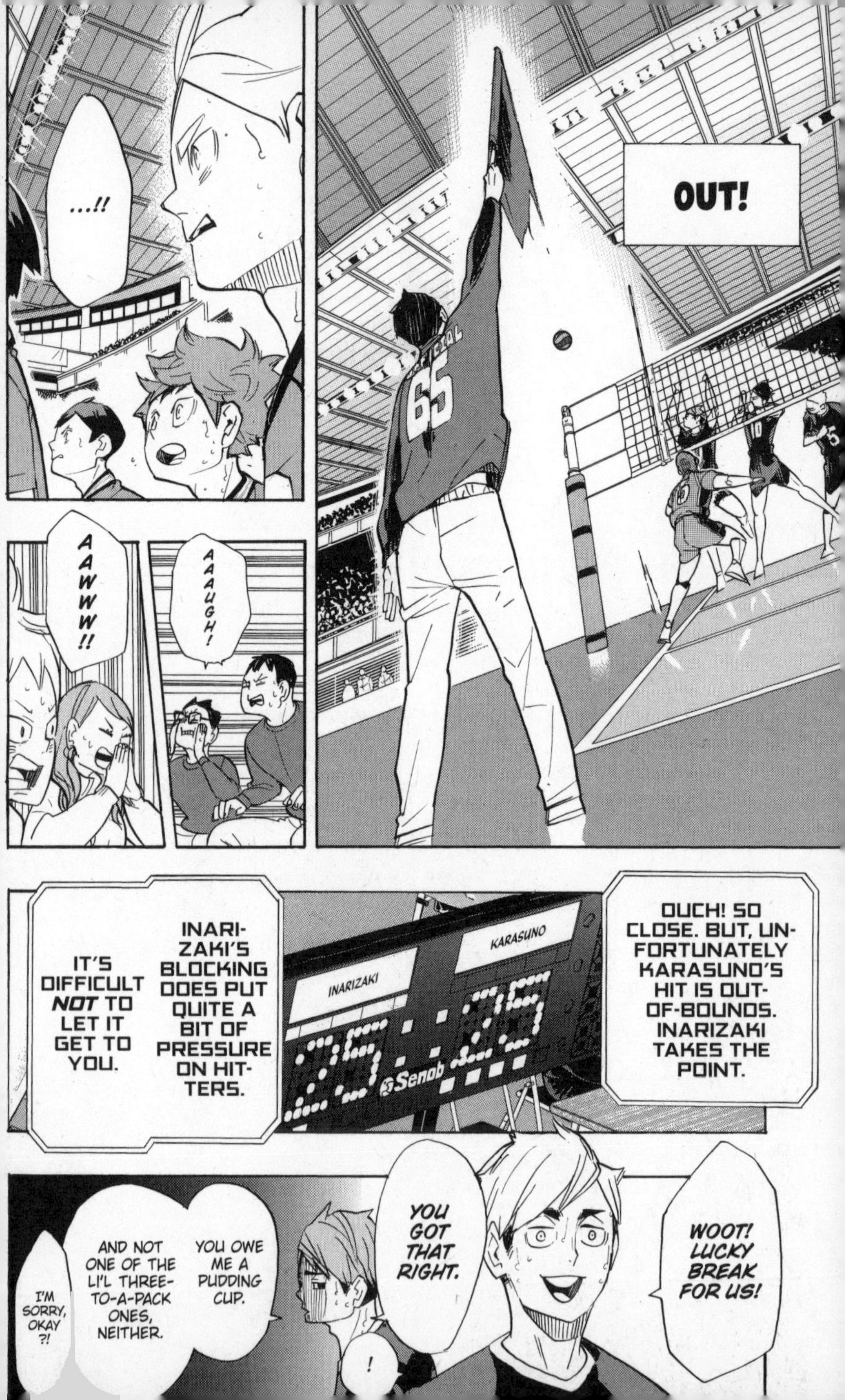
OUT!
...!!
AAAUGH!
AAWWW!!
OUCH! SO CLOSE. BUT, UNFORTUNATELY KARASUNO'S HIT IS OUT-OF-BOUNDS. INARIZAKI TAKES THE POINT.
KARASUNO
INARIZAKI
Senob
INARIZAKI'S BLOCKING DOES PUT QUITE A BIT OF PRESSURE ON HITTERS.
IT'S DIFFICULT NOT TO LET IT GET TO YOU.
WOOT! LUCKY BREAK FOR US!
YOU GOT THAT RIGHT.
YOU OWE ME A PUDDING CUP.
AND NOT ONE OF THE LI'L THREE-TO-A-PACK ONES, NEITHER.
!
I'M SORRY, OKAY?!

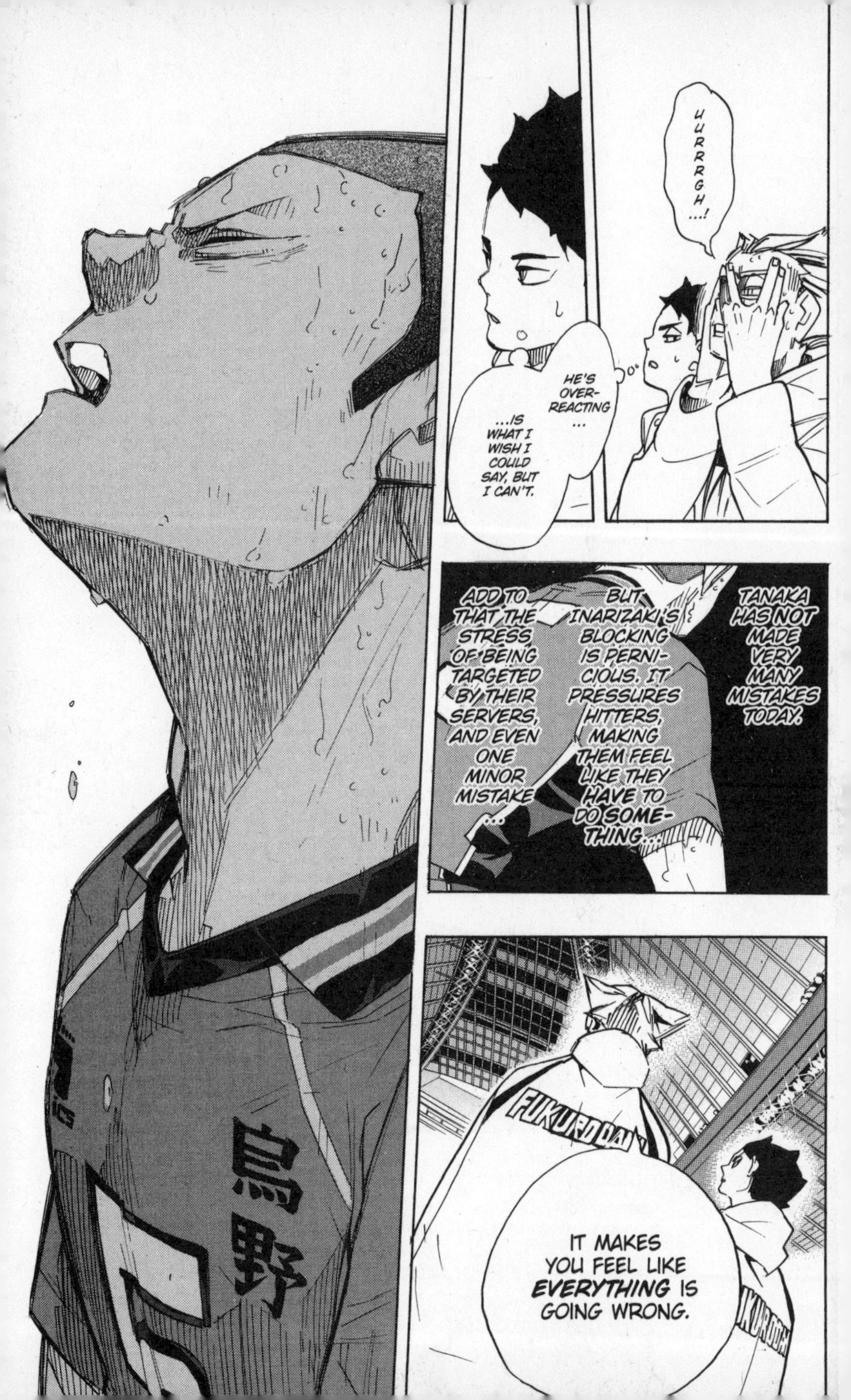
URRRGH...!
HE'S OVER-REACTING...
...IS WHAT I WISH I COULD SAY, BUT I CAN'T.
TANAKA HAS NOT MADE VERY MANY MISTAKES TODAY.
BUT INARIZAKI'S BLOCKING IS PERNICIOUS. IT PRESSURES HITTERS, MAKING THEM FEEL LIKE THEY HAVE TO DO SOMETHING...
ADD TO THAT THE STRESS OF BEING TARGETED BY THEIR SERVERS, AND EVEN ONE MINOR MISTAKE...
FUKURODANI
IT MAKES YOU FEEL LIKE **EVERYTHING** IS GOING WRONG.
烏野

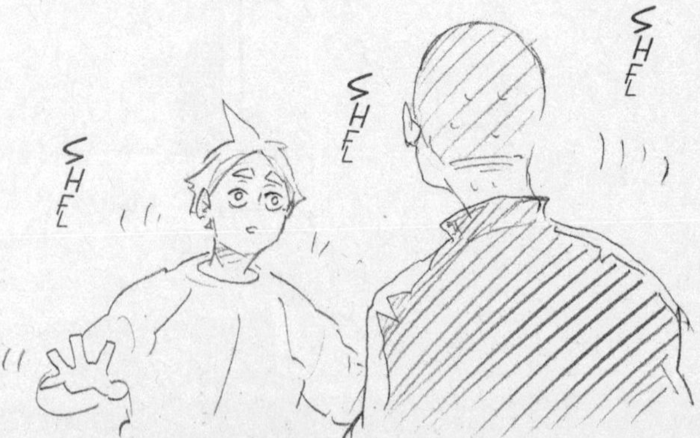
SHE
SHE
SHE

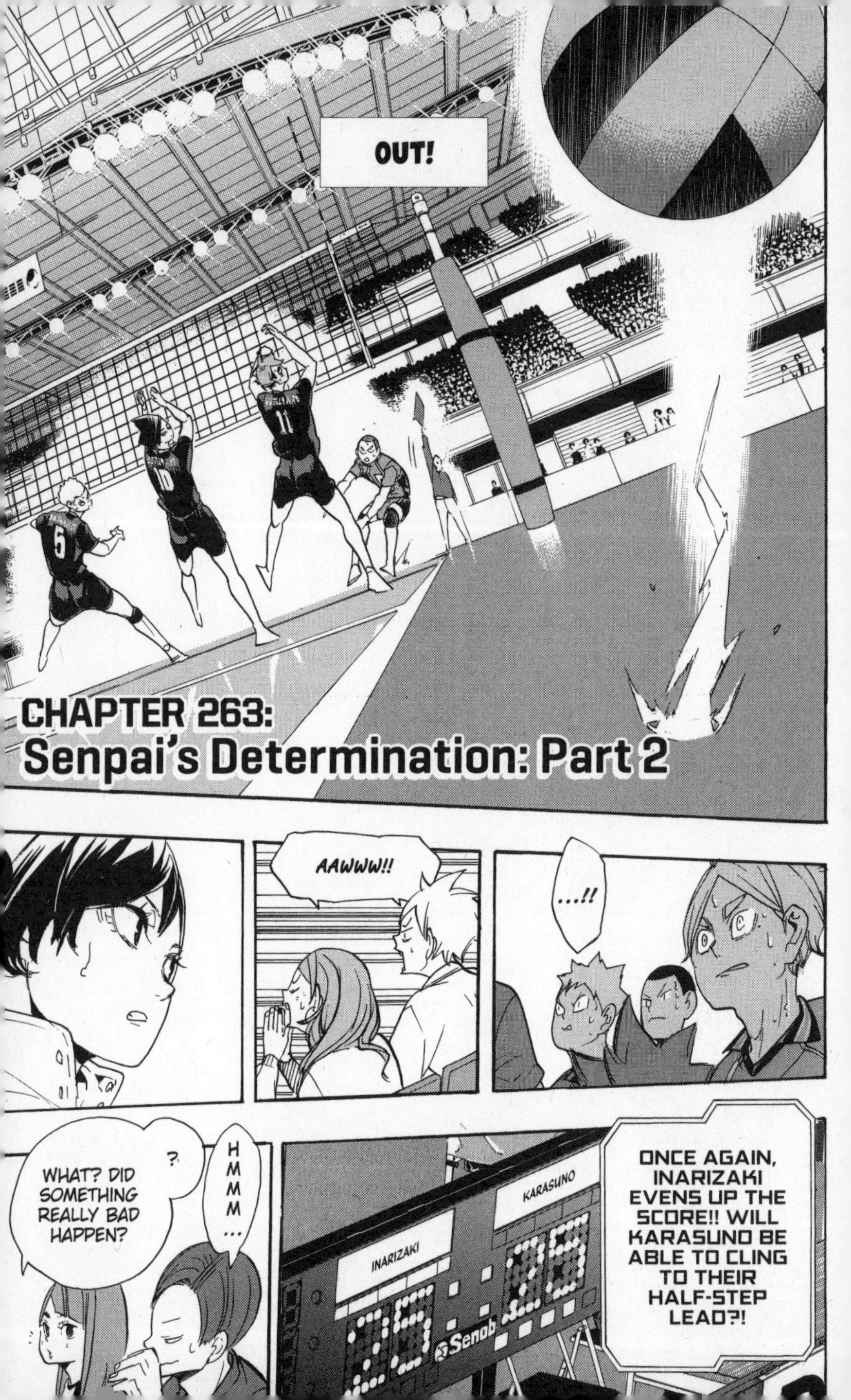
OUT!
CHAPTER 263:
Senpai's Determination: Part 2
...!!
AAWWW!!
ONCE AGAIN, INARIZAKI EVENS UP THE SCORE!! WILL KARASUNO BE ABLE TO CLING TO THEIR HALF-STEP LEAD?!
KARASUNO
INARIZAKI
HMMM...
?
WHAT? DID SOMETHING REALLY BAD HAPPEN?

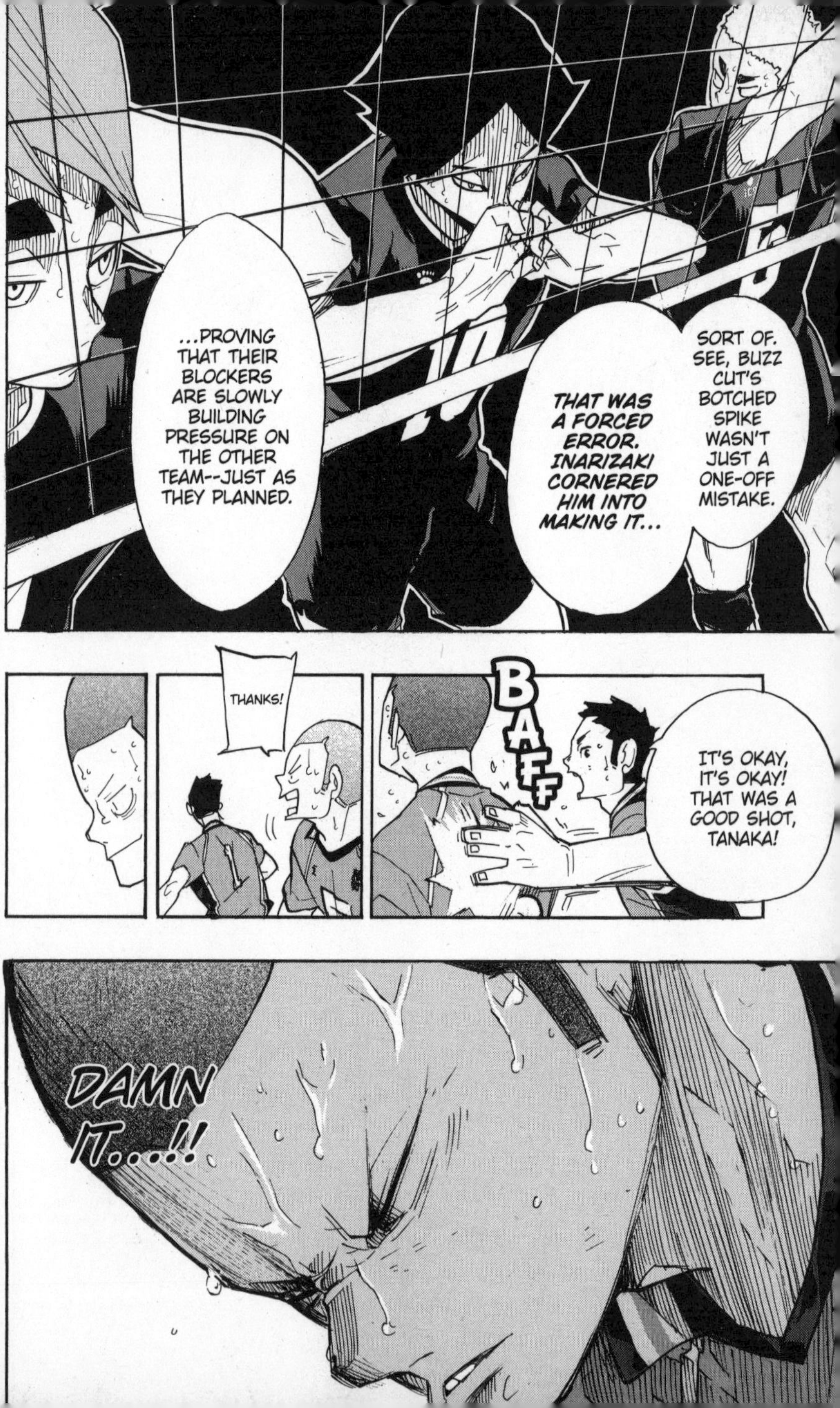
SORT OF. SEE, BUZZ CUT'S BOTCHED SPIKE WASN'T JUST A ONE-OFF MISTAKE.
THAT WAS A FORCED ERROR. INARIZAKI CORNERED HIM INTO MAKING IT...
...PROVING THAT THEIR BLOCKERS ARE SLOWLY BUILDING PRESSURE ON THE OTHER TEAM--JUST AS THEY PLANNED.
IT'S OKAY, IT'S OKAY! THAT WAS A GOOD SHOT, TANAKA!
BAFF
THANKS!
DAMN IT...!!

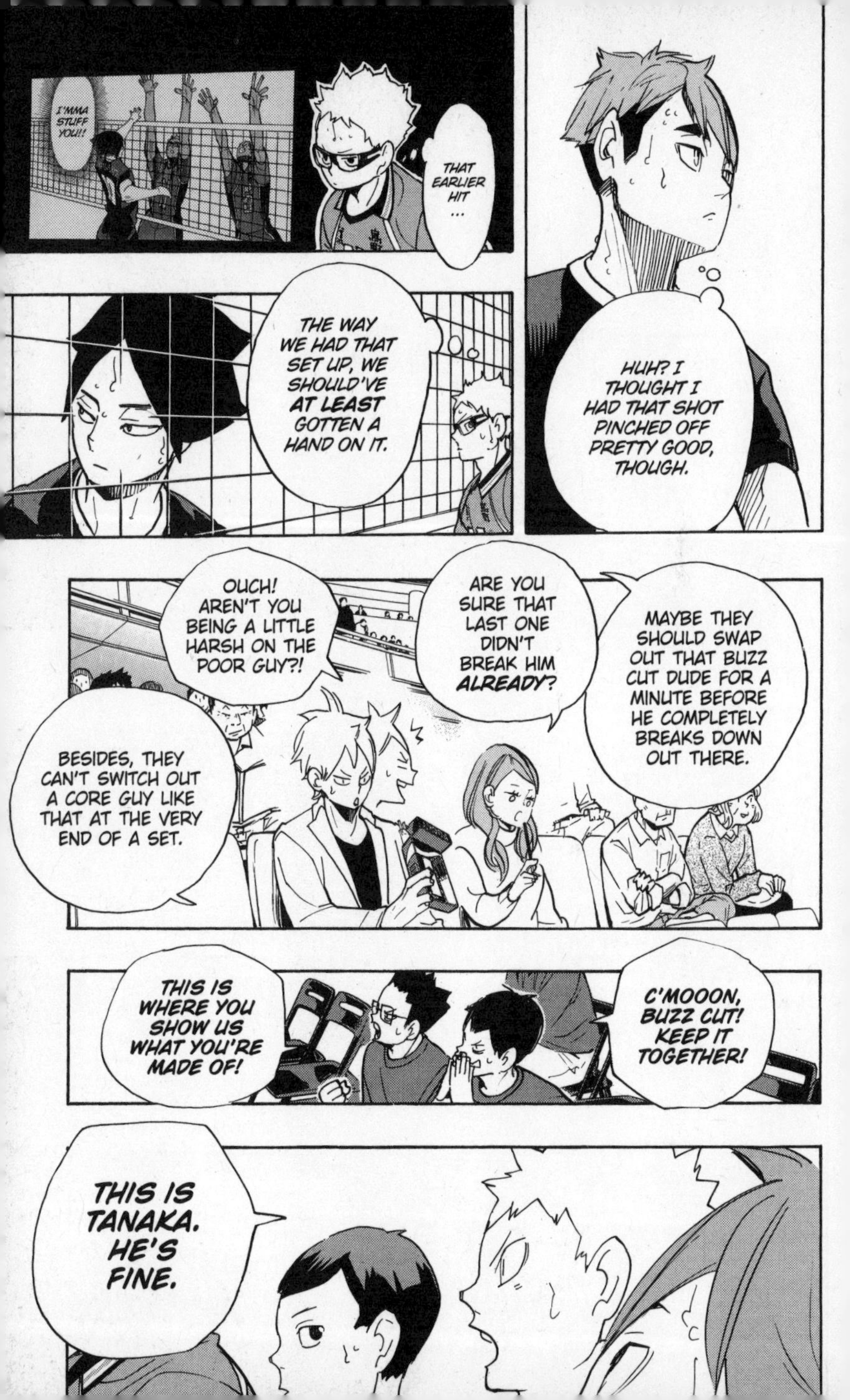
HUH? I THOUGHT I HAD THAT SHOT PINCHED OFF PRETTY GOOD, THOUGH.
THAT EARLIER HIT ...
I'MMA STUFF YOU!!
THE WAY WE HAD THAT SET UP, WE SHOULD'VE **AT LEAST** GOTTEN A HAND ON IT.
MAYBE THEY SHOULD SWAP OUT THAT BUZZ CUT DUDE FOR A MINUTE BEFORE HE COMPLETELY BREAKS DOWN OUT THERE.
ARE YOU SURE THAT LAST ONE DIDN'T BREAK HIM **ALREADY**?
OUCH! AREN'T YOU BEING A LITTLE HARSH ON THE POOR GUY?!
BESIDES, THEY CAN'T SWITCH OUT A CORE GUY LIKE THAT AT THE VERY END OF A SET.
C'MOOON, BUZZ CUT! KEEP IT TOGETHER!
THIS IS WHERE YOU SHOW US WHAT YOU'RE MADE OF!
THIS IS TANAKA. HE'S FINE.

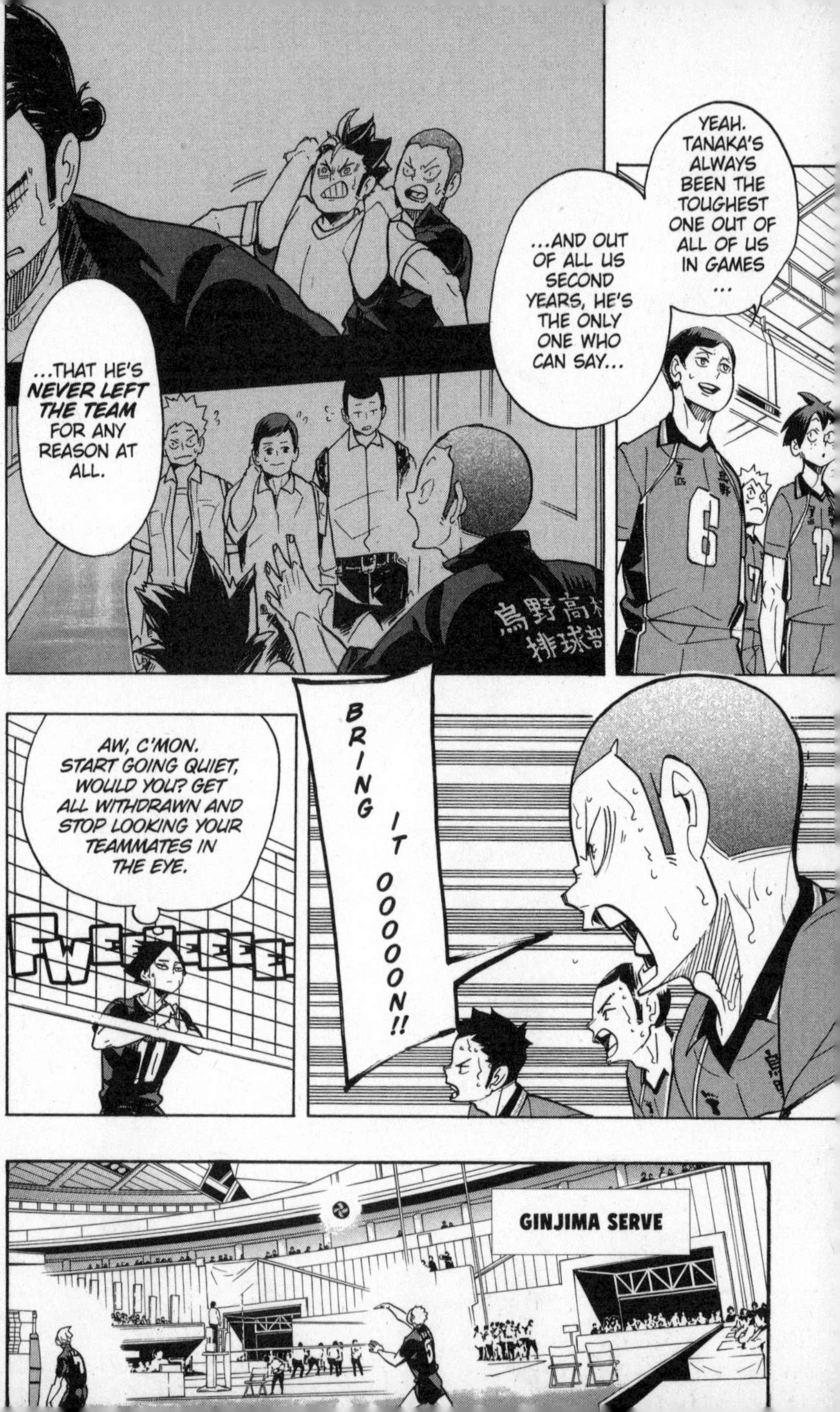
YEAH. TANAKA'S ALWAYS BEEN THE TOUGHEST ONE OUT OF ALL OF US IN GAMES ...
...AND OUT OF ALL US SECOND YEARS, HE'S THE ONLY ONE WHO CAN SAY...
...THAT HE'S NEVER LEFT THE TEAM FOR ANY REASON AT ALL.
鳥野高校 排球部
BRING IT OOOOOON!!
AW, C'MON. START GOING QUIET, WOULD YOU? GET ALL WITHDRAWN AND STOP LOOKING YOUR TEAMMATES IN THE EYE.
FWEEEEE
GINJIMA SERVE

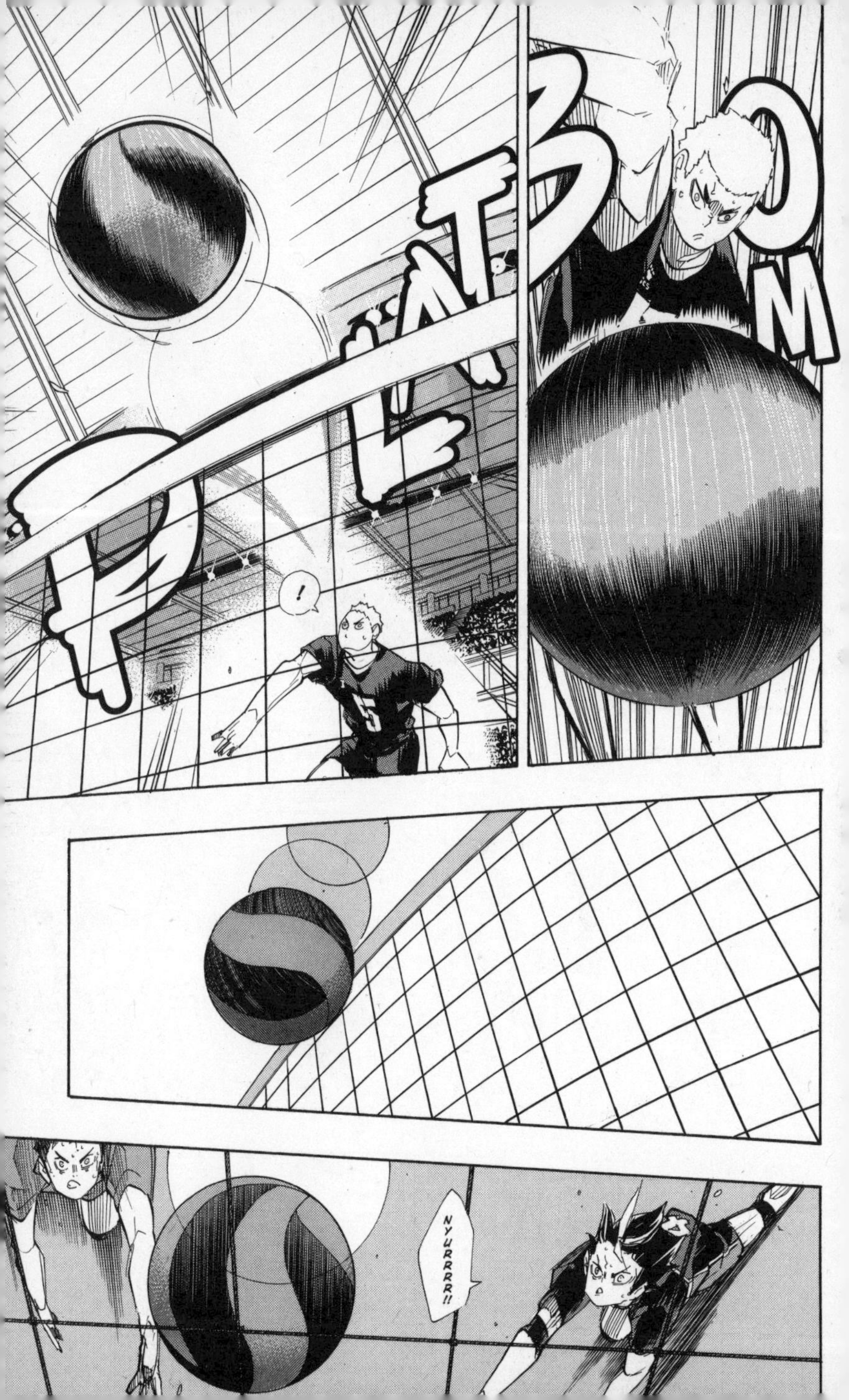

BOOM
PLAT
!
NYURRRR!!

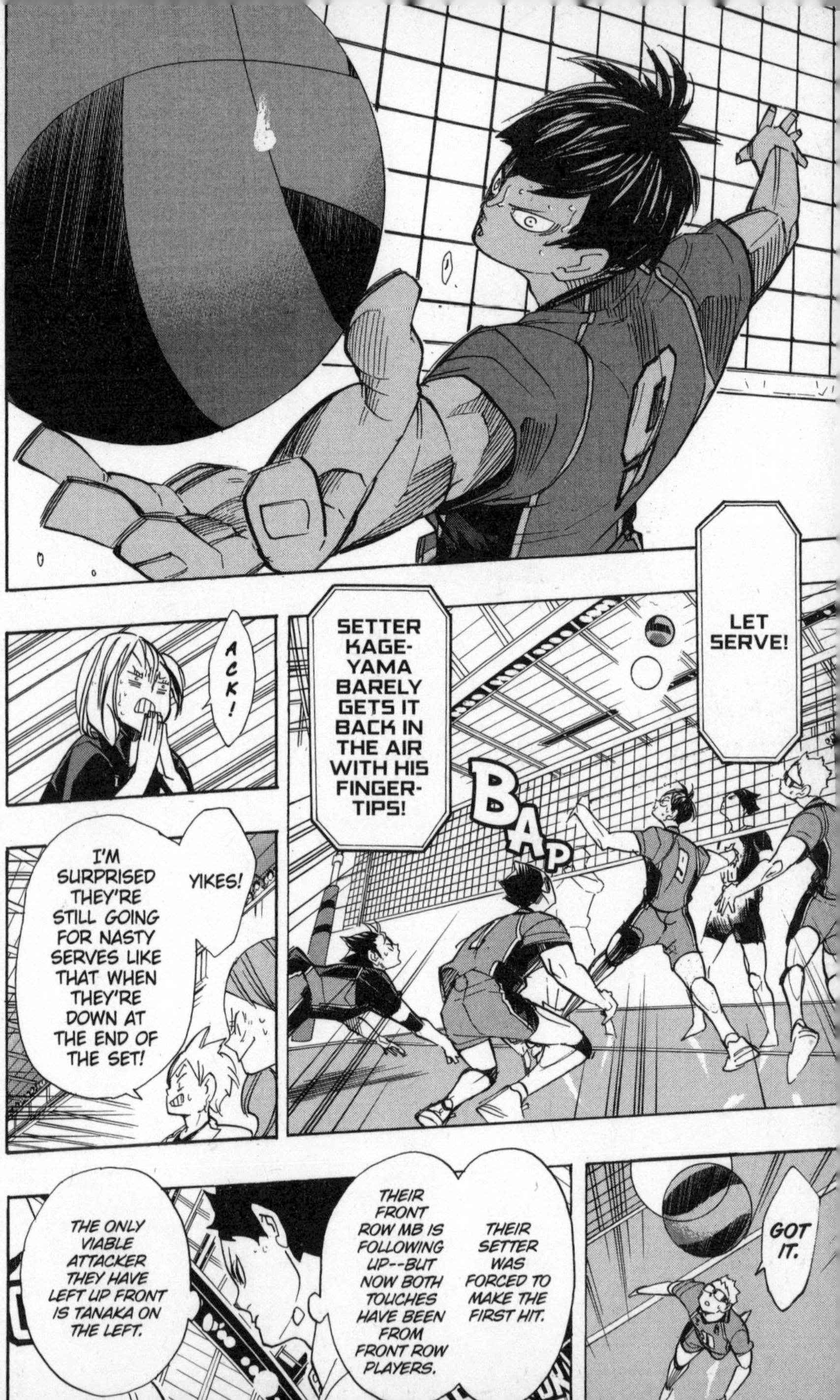
LET SERVE!
SETTER KAGEYAMA BARELY GETS IT BACK IN THE AIR WITH HIS FINGERTIPS!
BAP
ACK!
YIKES!
I'M SURPRISED THEY'RE STILL GOING FOR NASTY SERVES LIKE THAT WHEN THEY'RE DOWN AT THE END OF THE SET!
GOT IT.
THEIR SETTER WAS FORCED TO MAKE THE FIRST HIT.
THEIR FRONT ROW MB IS FOLLOWING UP--BUT NOW BOTH TOUCHES HAVE BEEN FROM FRONT ROW PLAYERS.
THE ONLY VIABLE ATTACKER THEY HAVE LEFT UP FRONT IS TANAKA ON THE LEFT.

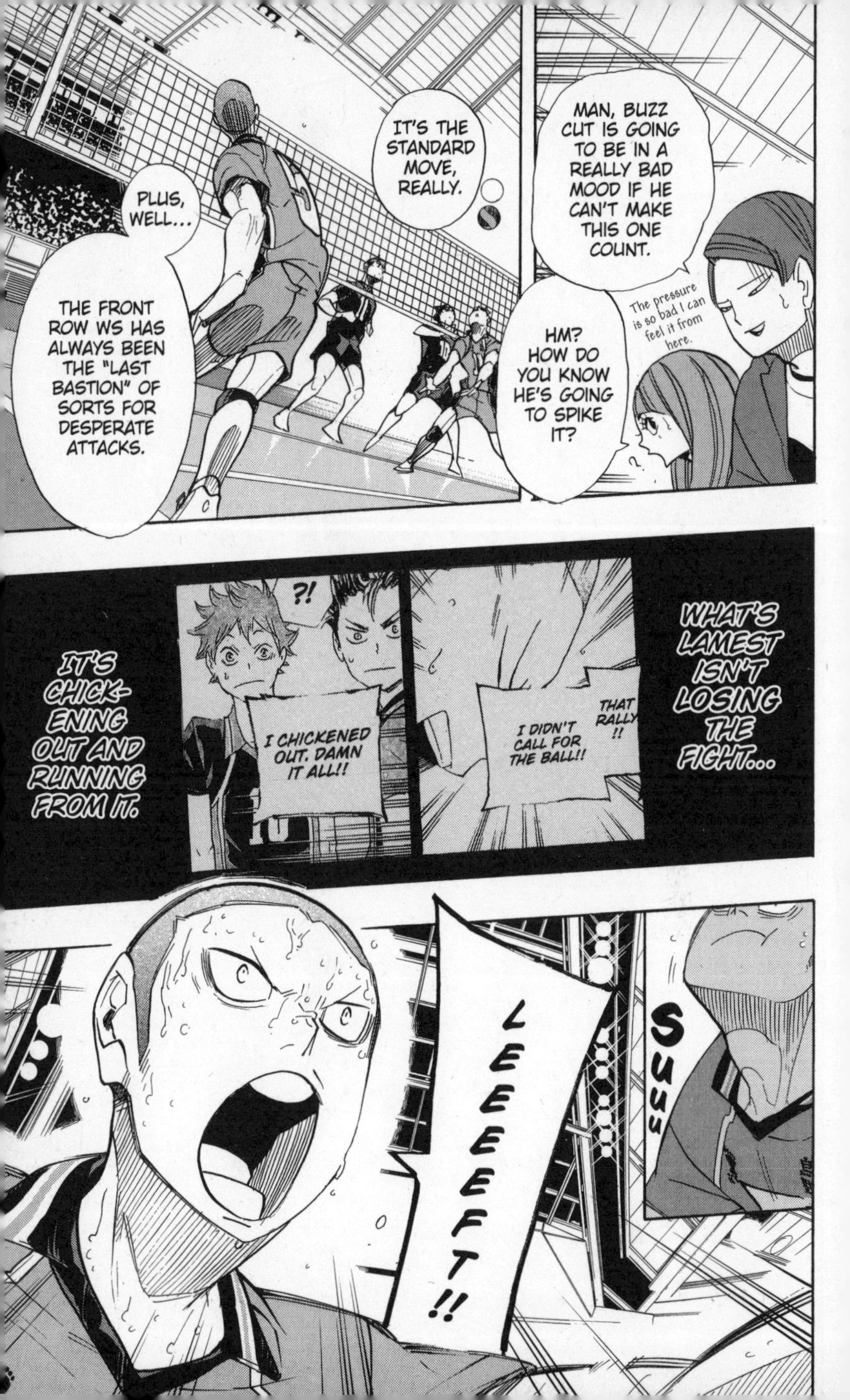
MAN, BUZZ CUT IS GOING TO BE IN A REALLY BAD MOOD IF HE CAN'T MAKE THIS ONE COUNT.
The pressure is so bad I can feel it from here.
HM? HOW DO YOU KNOW HE'S GOING TO SPIKE IT?
IT'S THE STANDARD MOVE, REALLY.
PLUS, WELL...
THE FRONT ROW WS HAS ALWAYS BEEN THE "LAST BASTION" OF SORTS FOR DESPERATE ATTACKS.
WHAT'S LAMEST ISN'T LOSING THE FIGHT...
THAT RALLY!!
I DIDN'T CALL FOR THE BALL!!
?!
I CHICKENED OUT. DAMN IT ALL!!
IT'S CHICK-ENING OUT AND RUNNING FROM IT.
SUUU
LEEEEEFT!!

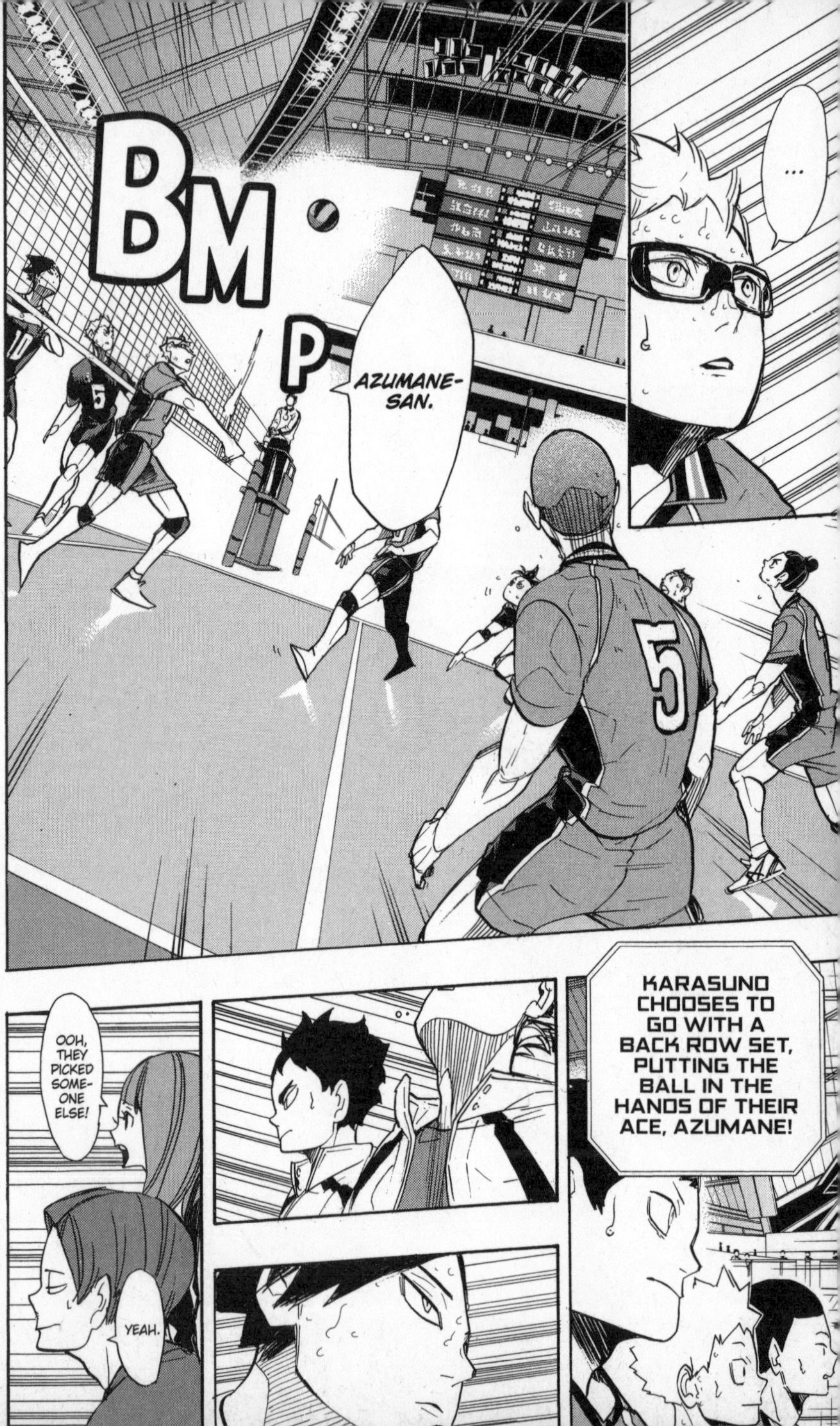
...
BMP
AZUMANE-SAN.
KARASUNO CHOOSES TO GO WITH A BACK ROW SET, PUTTING THE BALL IN THE HANDS OF THEIR ACE, AZUMANE!
OOH, THEY PICKED SOME-ONE ELSE!
YEAH.

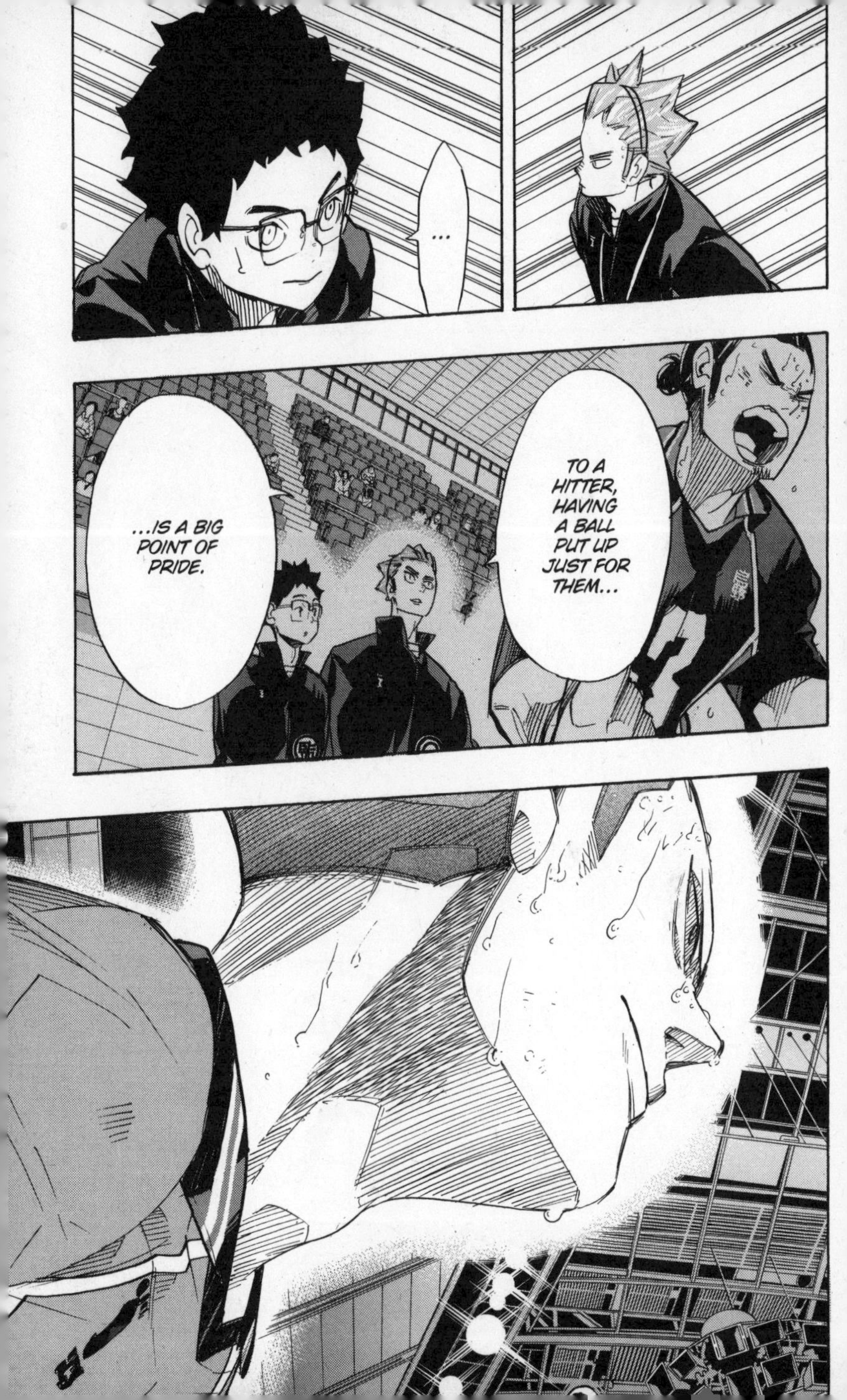
...
TO A HITTER, HAVING A BALL PUT UP JUST FOR THEM...
...IS A BIG POINT OF PRIDE.

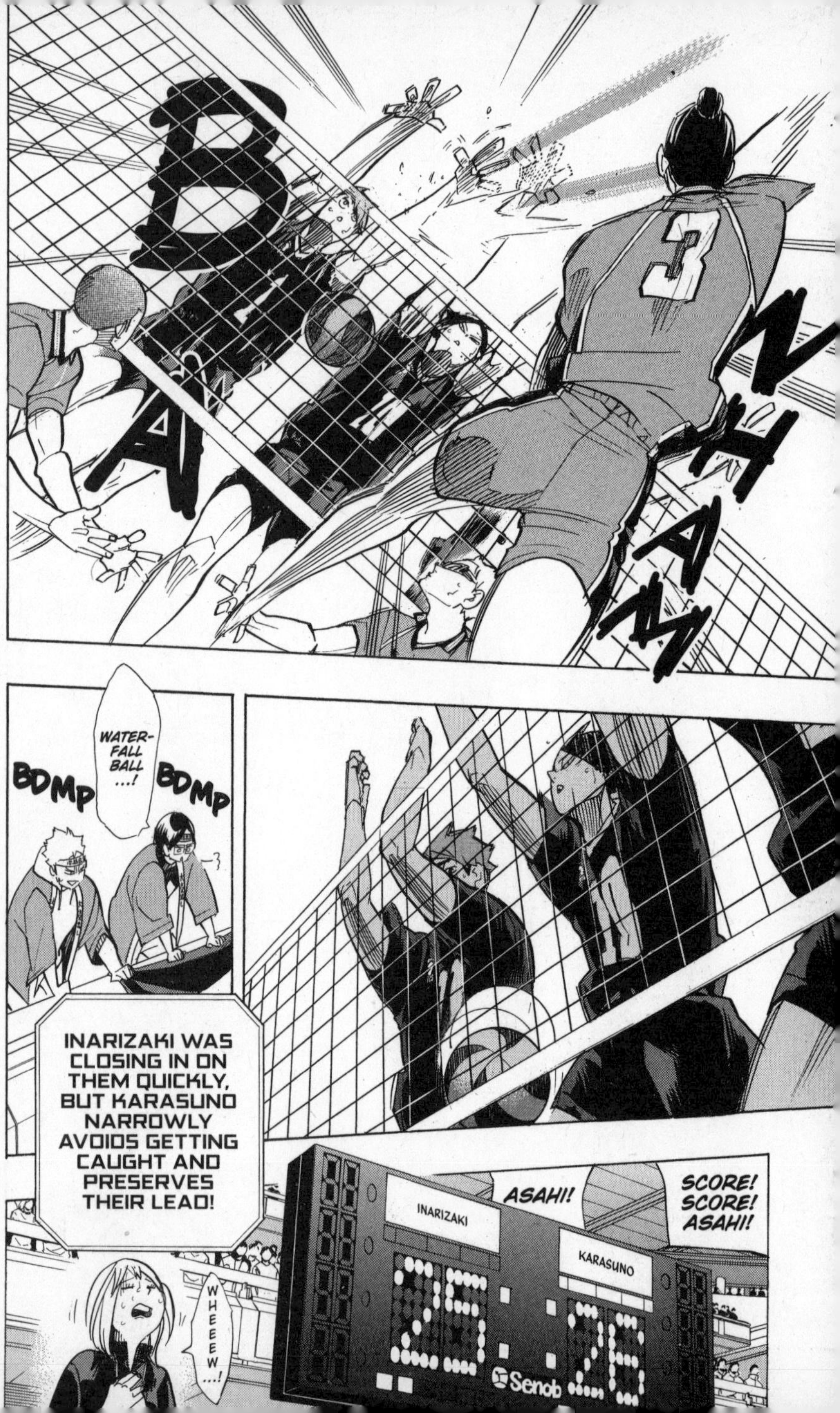
WHAM
WATER-FALL BALL ...!
BDMP
BDMP
SCORE! SCORE! ASAHI!
ASAHI!
INARIZAKI
KARASUNO
25
26
INARIZAKI WAS CLOSING IN ON THEM QUICKLY, BUT KARASUNO NARROWLY AVOIDS GETTING CAUGHT AND PRESERVES THEIR LEAD!
WHEEEW...!

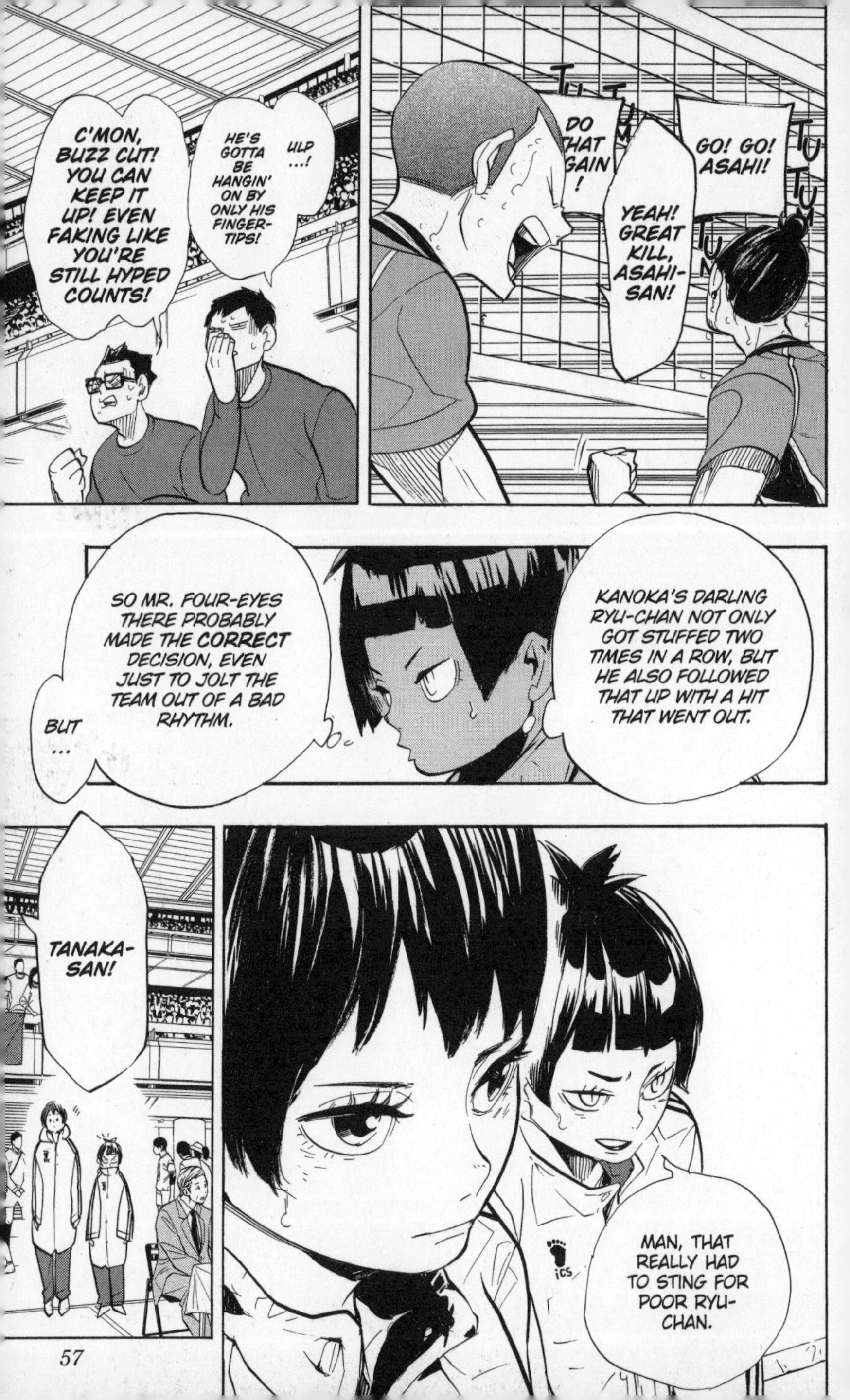
TUTUM
GO! GO! ASAHI!
YEAH! GREAT KILL, ASAHI-SAN!
DO THAT AGAIN!
TUTUM
ULP ...!
HE'S GOTTA BE HANGIN' ON BY ONLY HIS FINGER-TIPS!
C'MON, BUZZ CUT! YOU CAN KEEP IT UP! EVEN FAKING LIKE YOU'RE STILL HYPED COUNTS!
KANOKA'S DARLING RYU-CHAN NOT ONLY GOT STUFFED TWO TIMES IN A ROW, BUT HE ALSO FOLLOWED THAT UP WITH A HIT THAT WENT OUT.
SO MR. FOUR-EYES THERE PROBABLY MADE THE CORRECT DECISION, EVEN JUST TO JOLT THE TEAM OUT OF A BAD RHYTHM.
BUT ...
MAN, THAT REALLY HAD TO STING FOR POOR RYU-CHAN.
TANAKA-SAN!

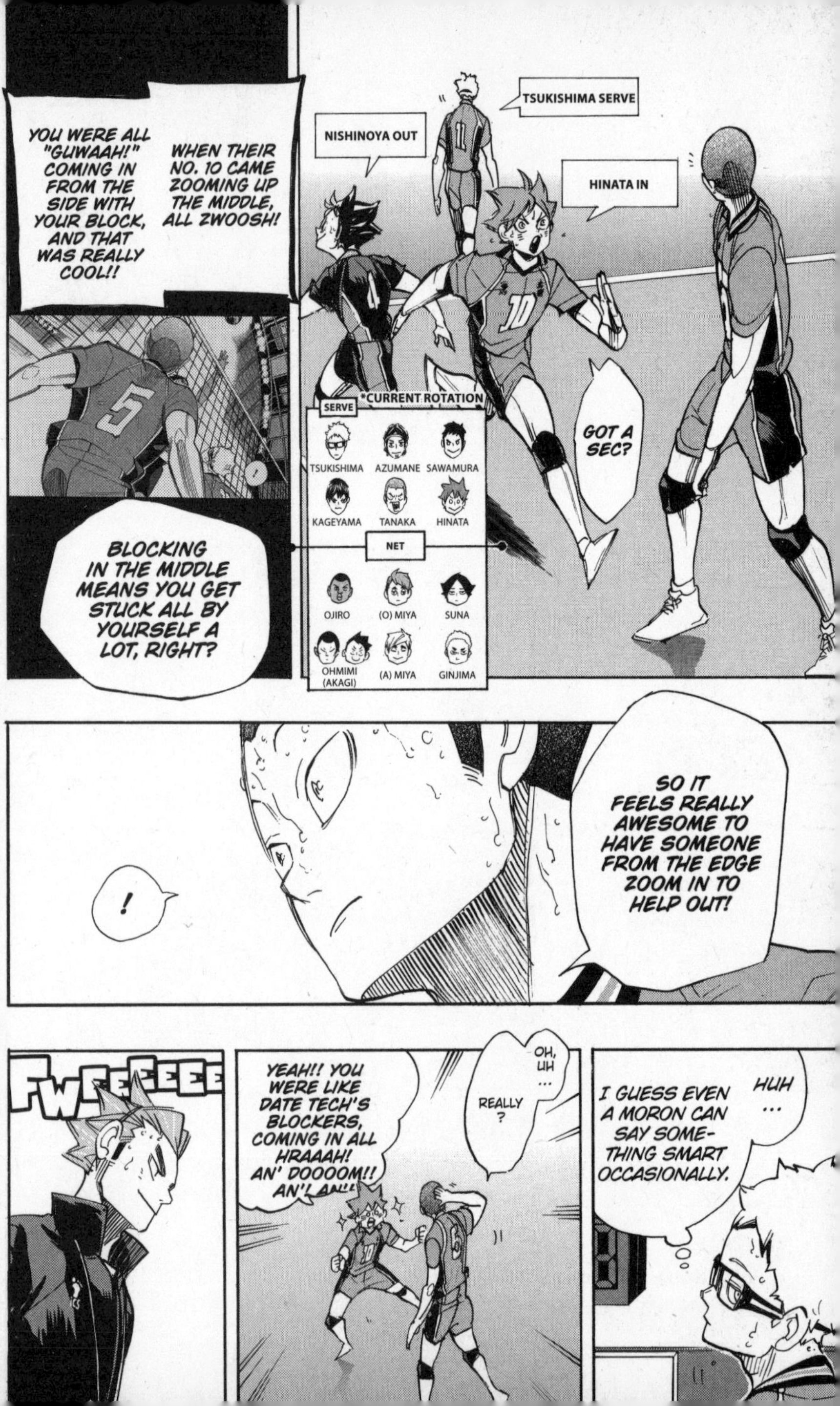
TSUKISHIMA SERVE
HINATA IN
NISHINOYA OUT
GOT A SEC?
*CURRENT ROTATION
SERVE
TSUKISHIMA AZUMANE SAWAMURA
KAGEYAMA TANAKA HINATA
NET
OJIRO (O) MIYA SUNA
OHMIMI (AKAGI) (A) MIYA GINJIMA
WHEN THEIR NO. 10 CAME ZOOMING UP THE MIDDLE, ALL ZWOOSH!
YOU WERE ALL "GUWAAH!" COMING IN FROM THE SIDE WITH YOUR BLOCK, AND THAT WAS REALLY COOL!!
!
BLOCKING IN THE MIDDLE MEANS YOU GET STUCK ALL BY YOURSELF A LOT, RIGHT?
SO IT FEELS REALLY AWESOME TO HAVE SOMEONE FROM THE EDGE ZOOM IN TO HELP OUT!
!
HUH ...
I GUESS EVEN A MORON CAN SAY SOME-THING SMART OCCASIONALLY.
OH, UH ...
REALLY ?
YEAH!! YOU WERE LIKE DATE TECH'S BLOCKERS, COMING IN ALL HRAAAH! AN' DOOOOM!! AN' I AN'...
FWEEEEEE

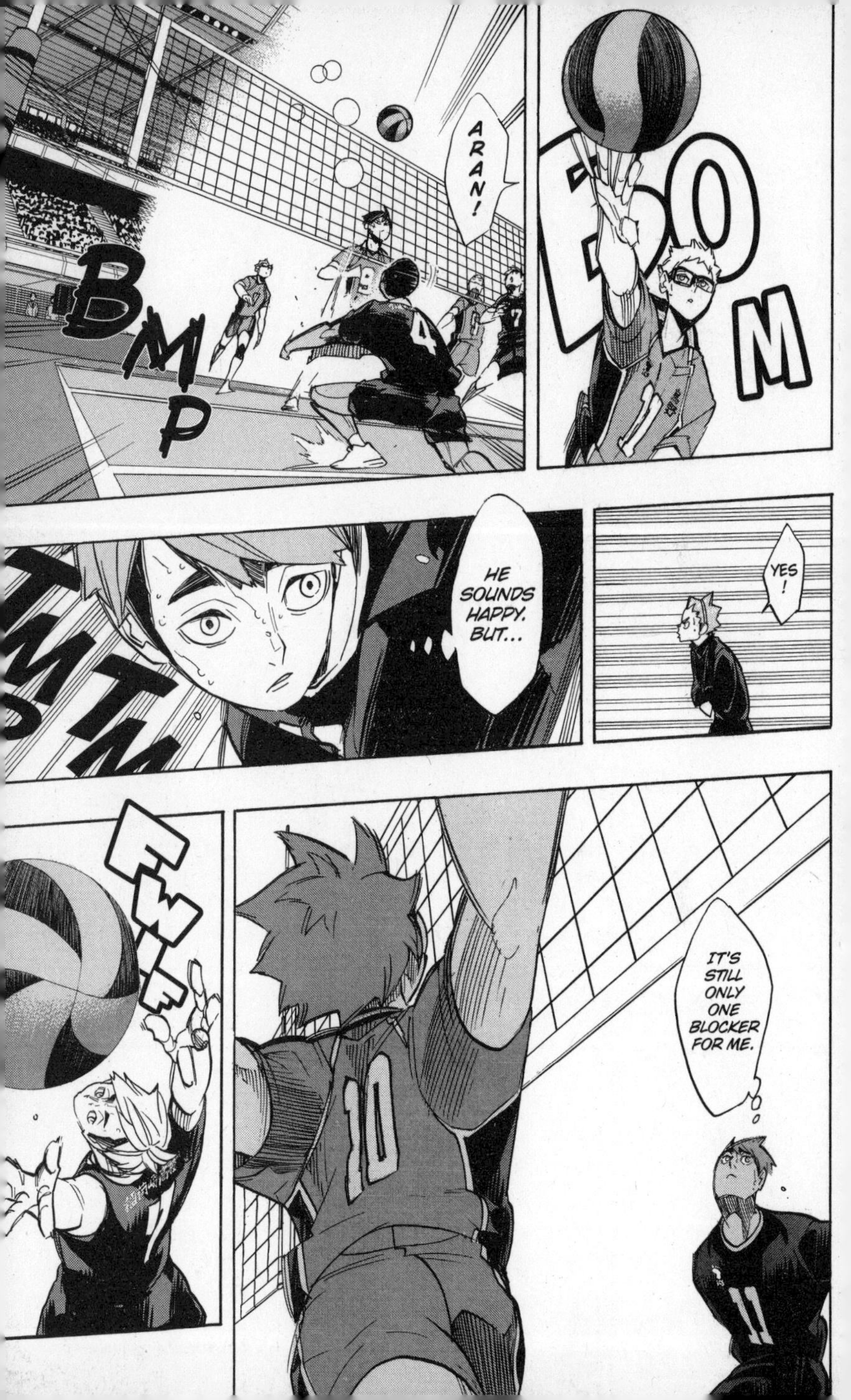
BOM
ARAN!
BMMP
YES!
HE SOUNDS HAPPY. BUT...
IT'S STILL ONLY ONE BLOCKER FOR ME.
FWIF

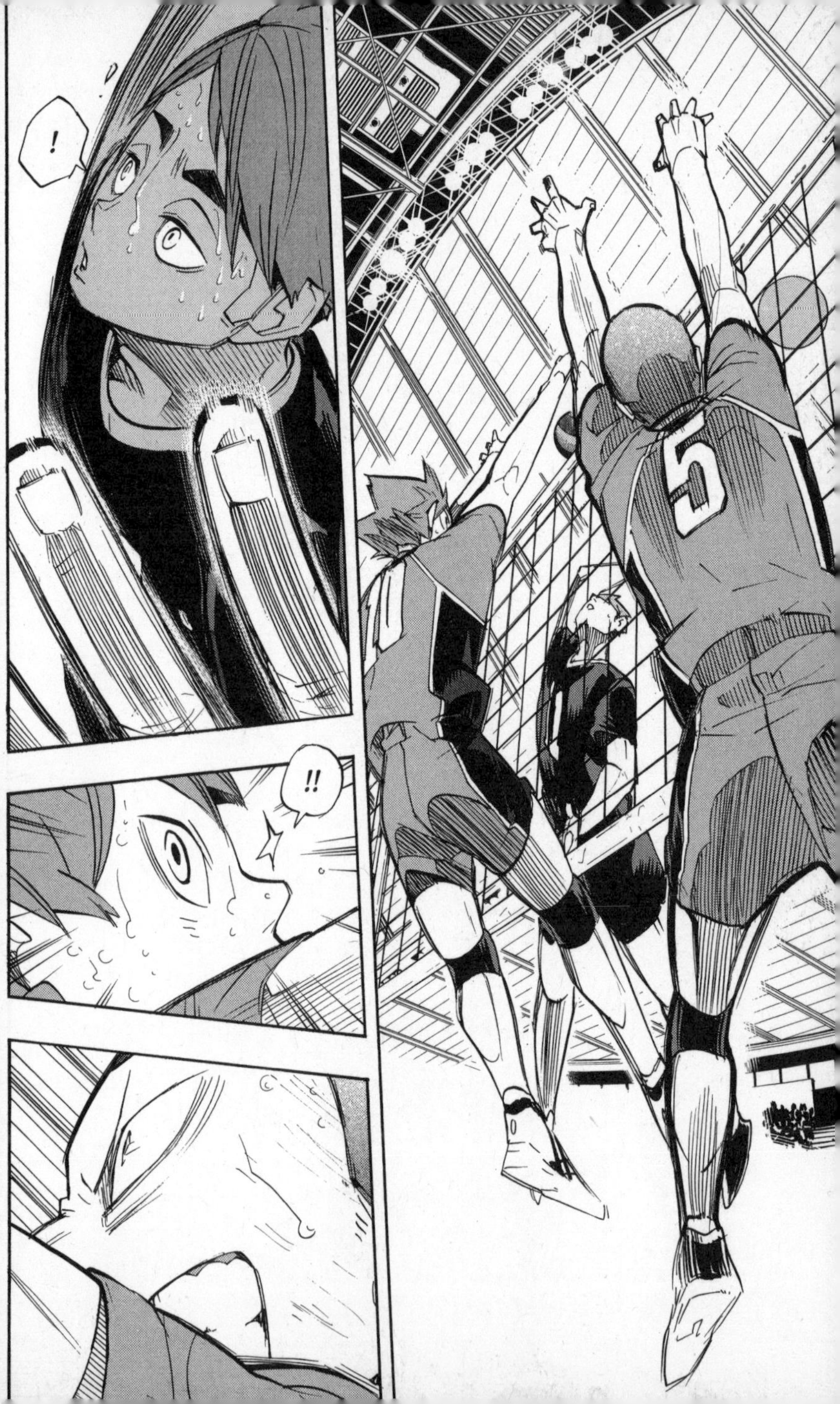
!
!!

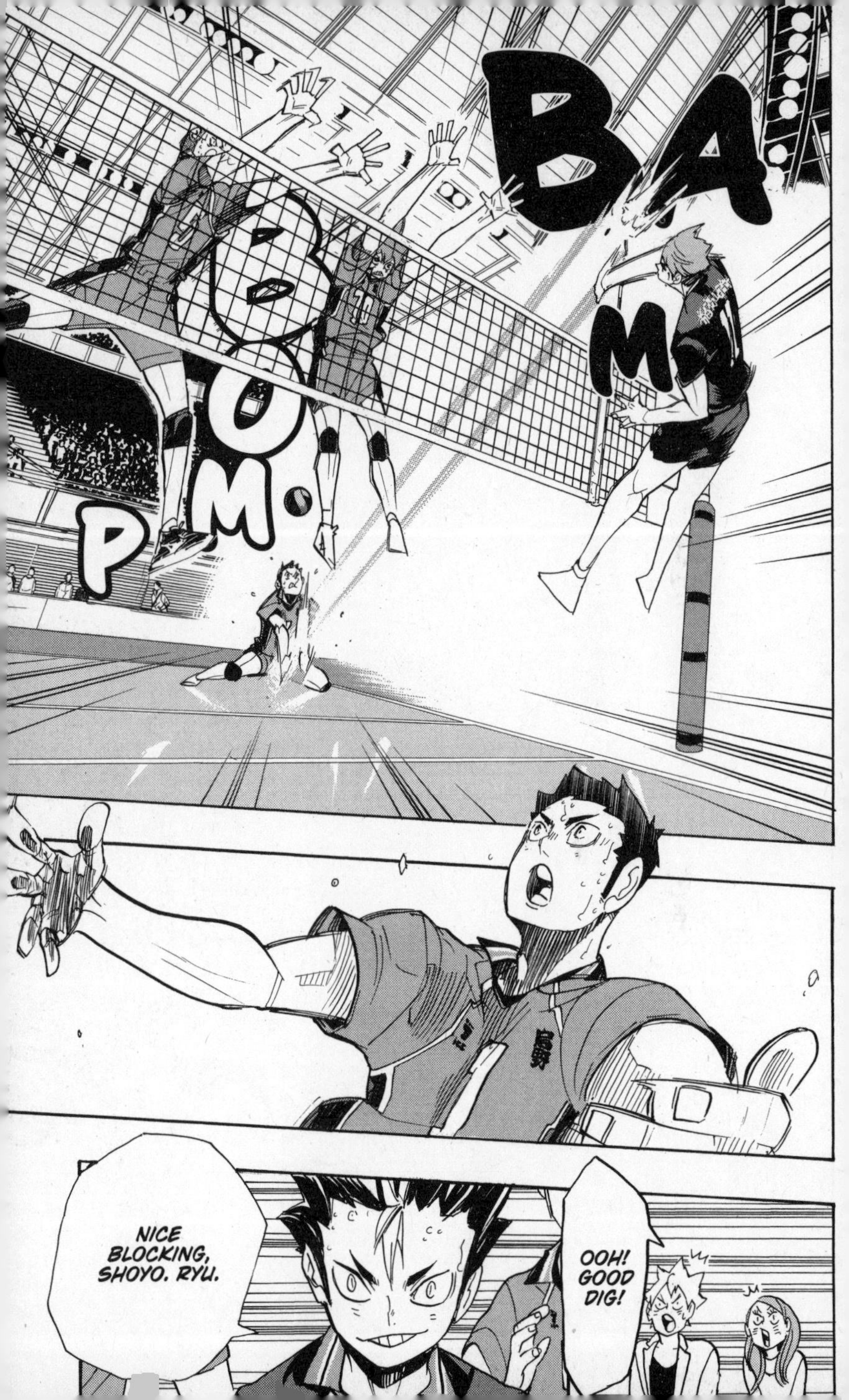
BAM
BOMP
OOH! GOOD DIG!
NICE BLOCKING, SHOYO. RYU.

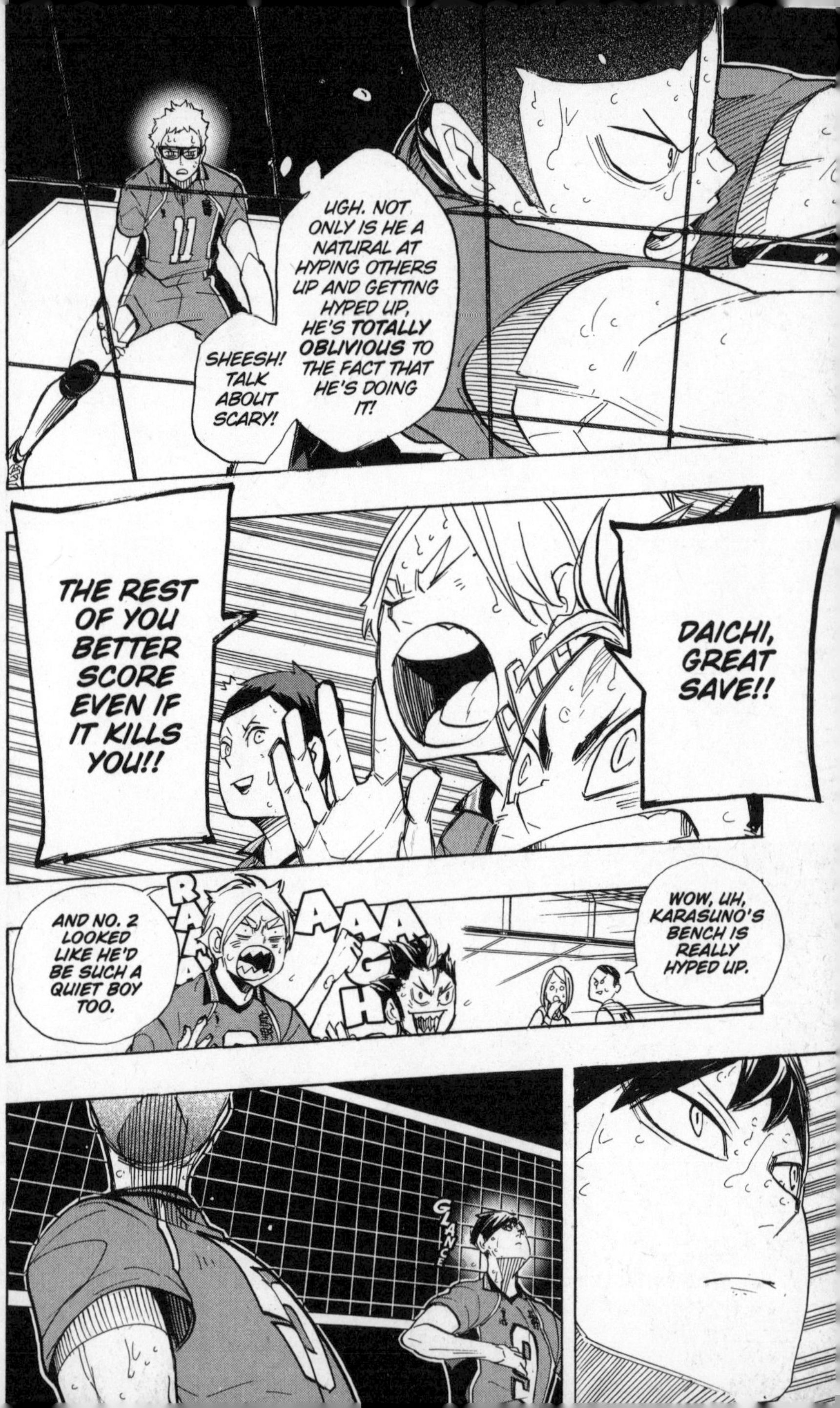
UGH. NOT ONLY IS HE A NATURAL AT HYPING OTHERS UP AND GETTING HYPED UP, HE'S TOTALLY OBLIVIOUS TO THE FACT THAT HE'S DOING IT!
SHEESH! TALK ABOUT SCARY!
DAICHI, GREAT SAVE!!
THE REST OF YOU BETTER SCORE EVEN IF IT KILLS YOU!!
WOW, UH, KARASUNO'S BENCH IS REALLY HYPED UP.
RAAAAAGH
AND NO. 2 LOOKED LIKE HE'D BE SUCH A QUIET BOY TOO.
GLANCE

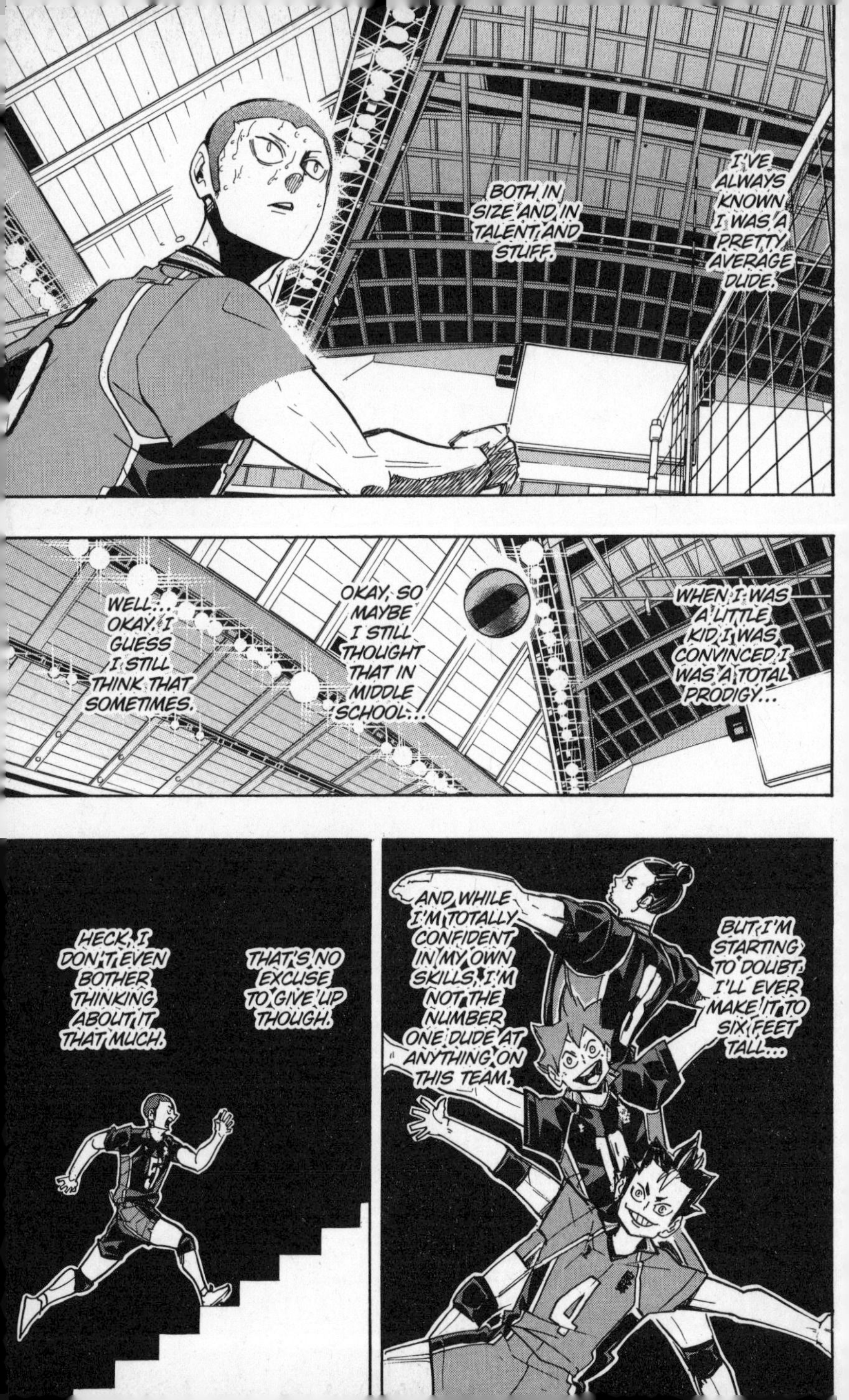
I'VE ALWAYS KNOWN I WAS A PRETTY AVERAGE DUDE.
BOTH IN SIZE AND IN TALENT AND STUFF.
WHEN I WAS A LITTLE KID I WAS CONVINCED I WAS A TOTAL PRODIGY...
OKAY, SO MAYBE I STILL THOUGHT THAT IN MIDDLE SCHOOL...
WELL... OKAY, I GUESS I STILL THINK THAT SOMETIMES.
BUT I'M STARTING TO DOUBT I'LL EVER MAKE IT TO SIX FEET TALL...
AND WHILE I'M TOTALLY CONFIDENT IN MY OWN SKILLS, I'M NOT THE NUMBER ONE DUDE AT ANYTHING ON THIS TEAM.
THAT'S NO EXCUSE TO GIVE UP THOUGH.
HECK, I DON'T EVEN BOTHER THINKING ABOUT IT THAT MUCH.

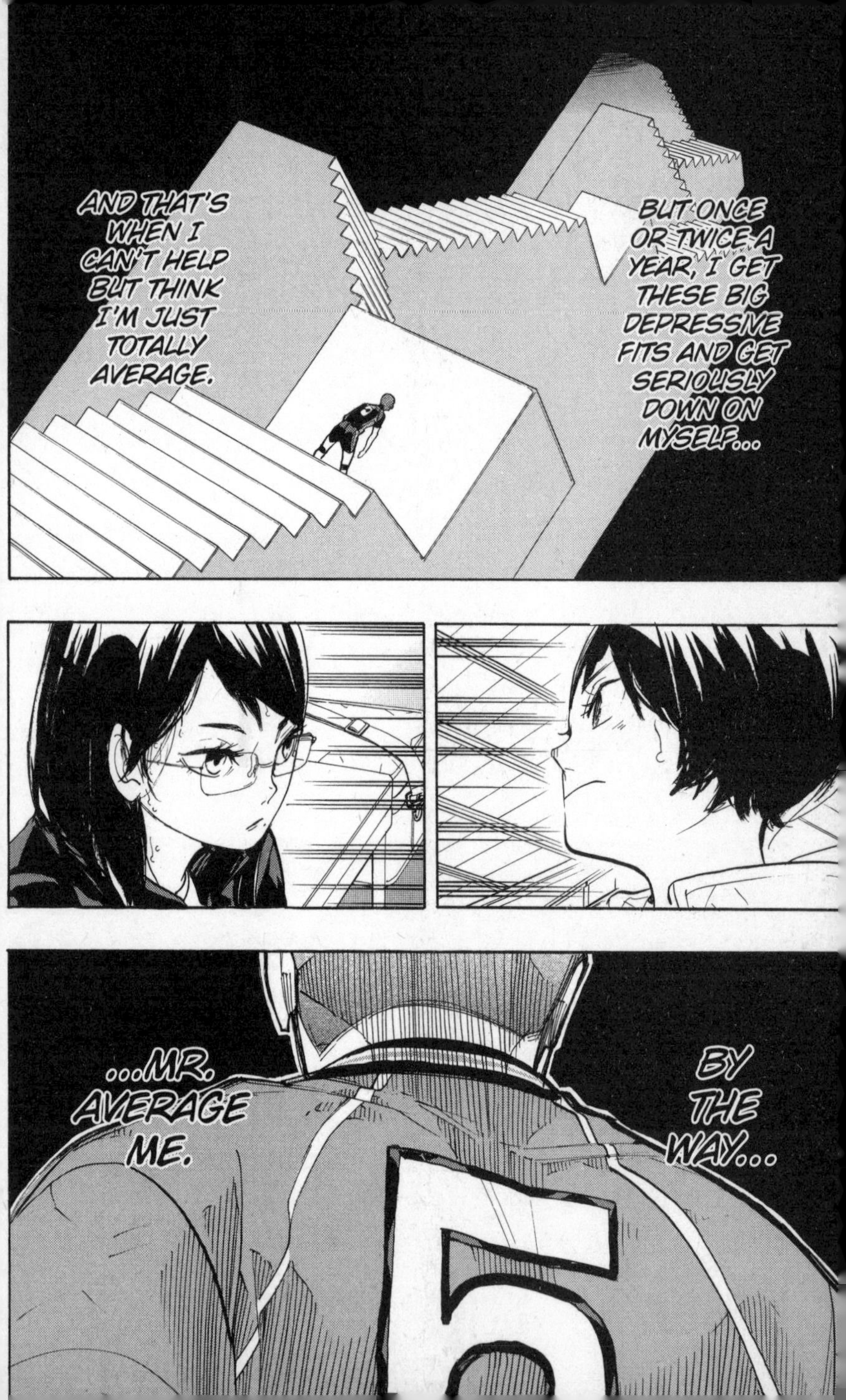
BUT ONCE OR TWICE A YEAR, I GET THESE BIG DEPRESSIVE FITS AND GET SERIOUSLY DOWN ON MYSELF...
AND THAT'S WHEN I CAN'T HELP BUT THINK I'M JUST TOTALLY AVERAGE.
BY THE WAY...
...MR. AVERAGE ME.

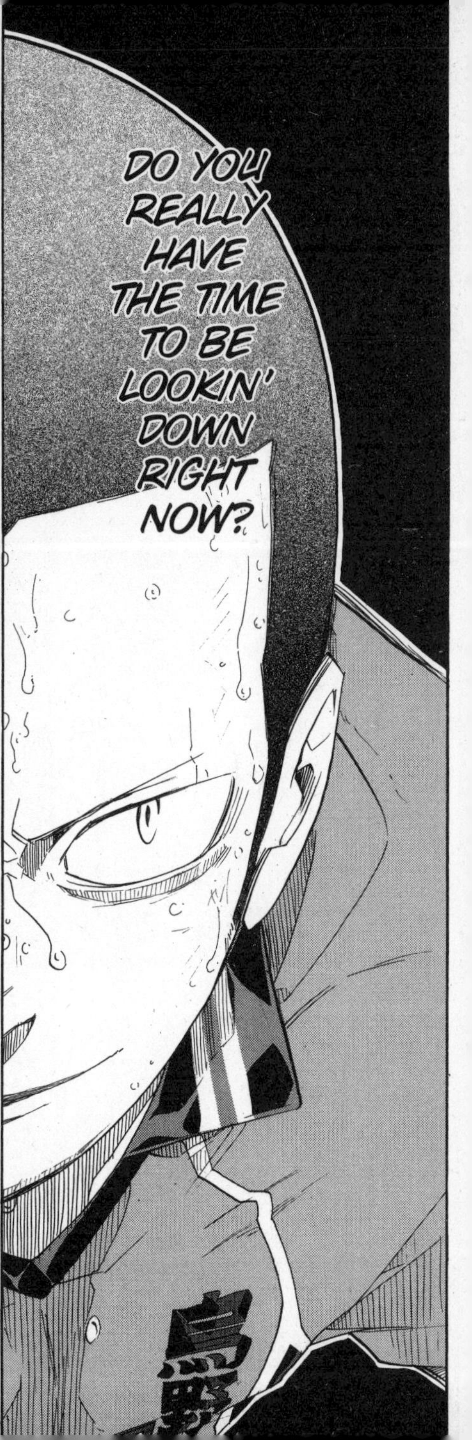
DO YOU REALLY HAVE THE TIME TO BE LOOKIN' DOWN RIGHT NOW?
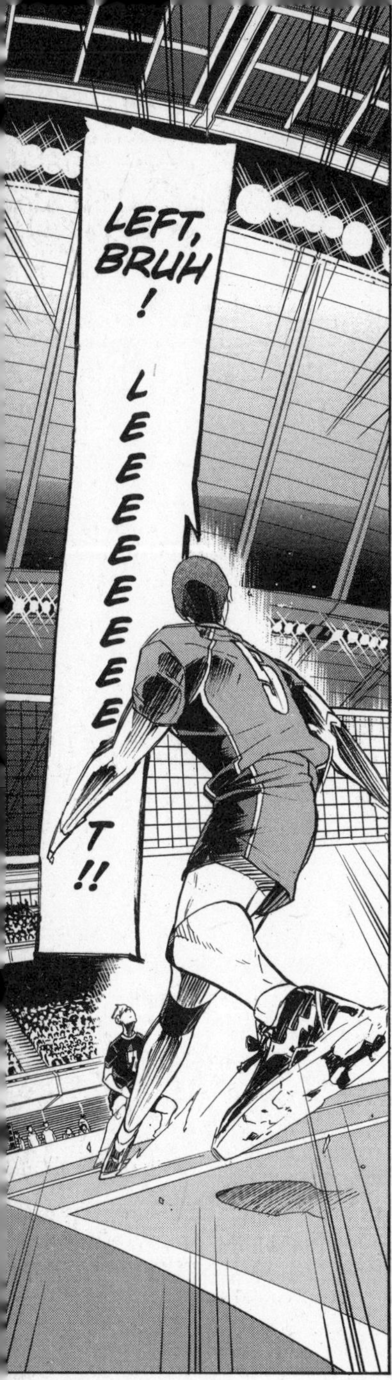
LEFT, BRUH!
LEEEEEEEEET!!

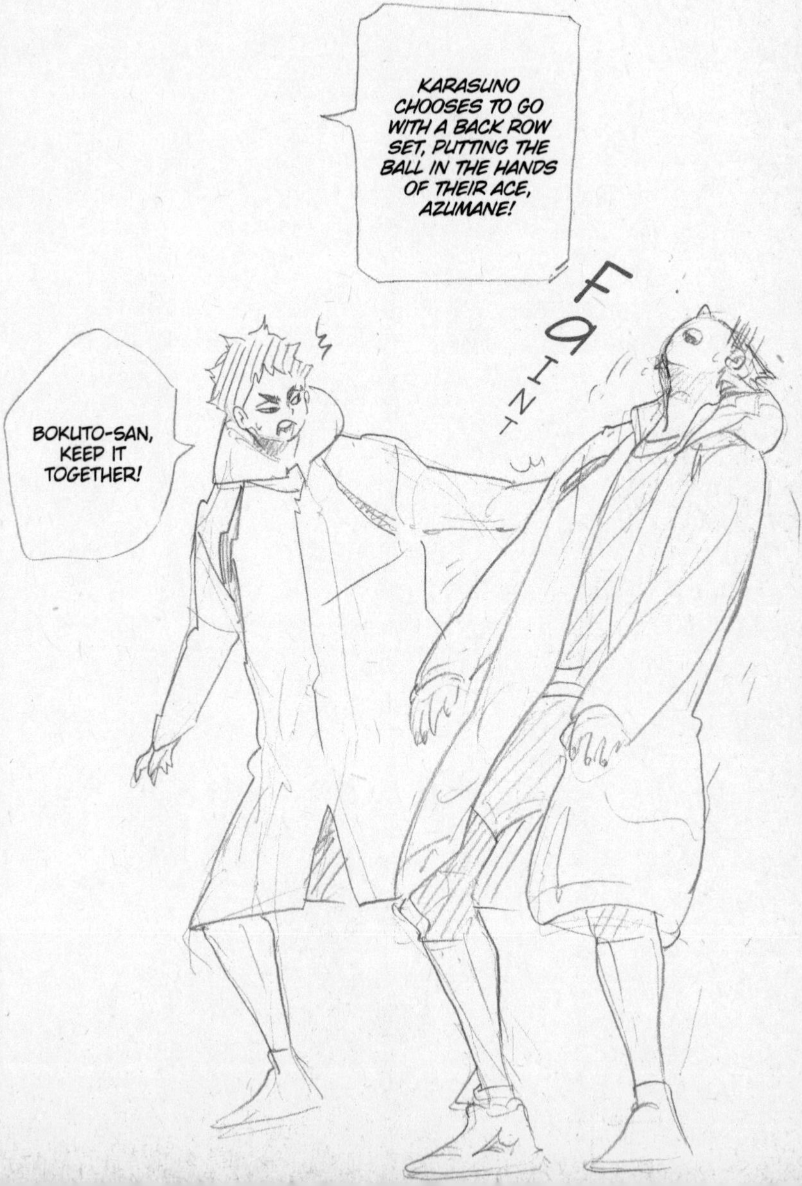
KARASUNO CHOOSES TO GO WITH A BACK ROW SET, PUTTING THE BALL IN THE HANDS OF THEIR ACE, AZUMANE!
FAINT
BOKUTO-SAN, KEEP IT TOGETHER!

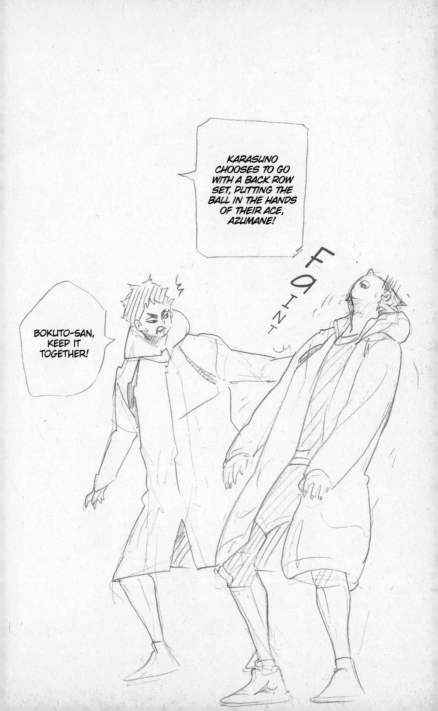

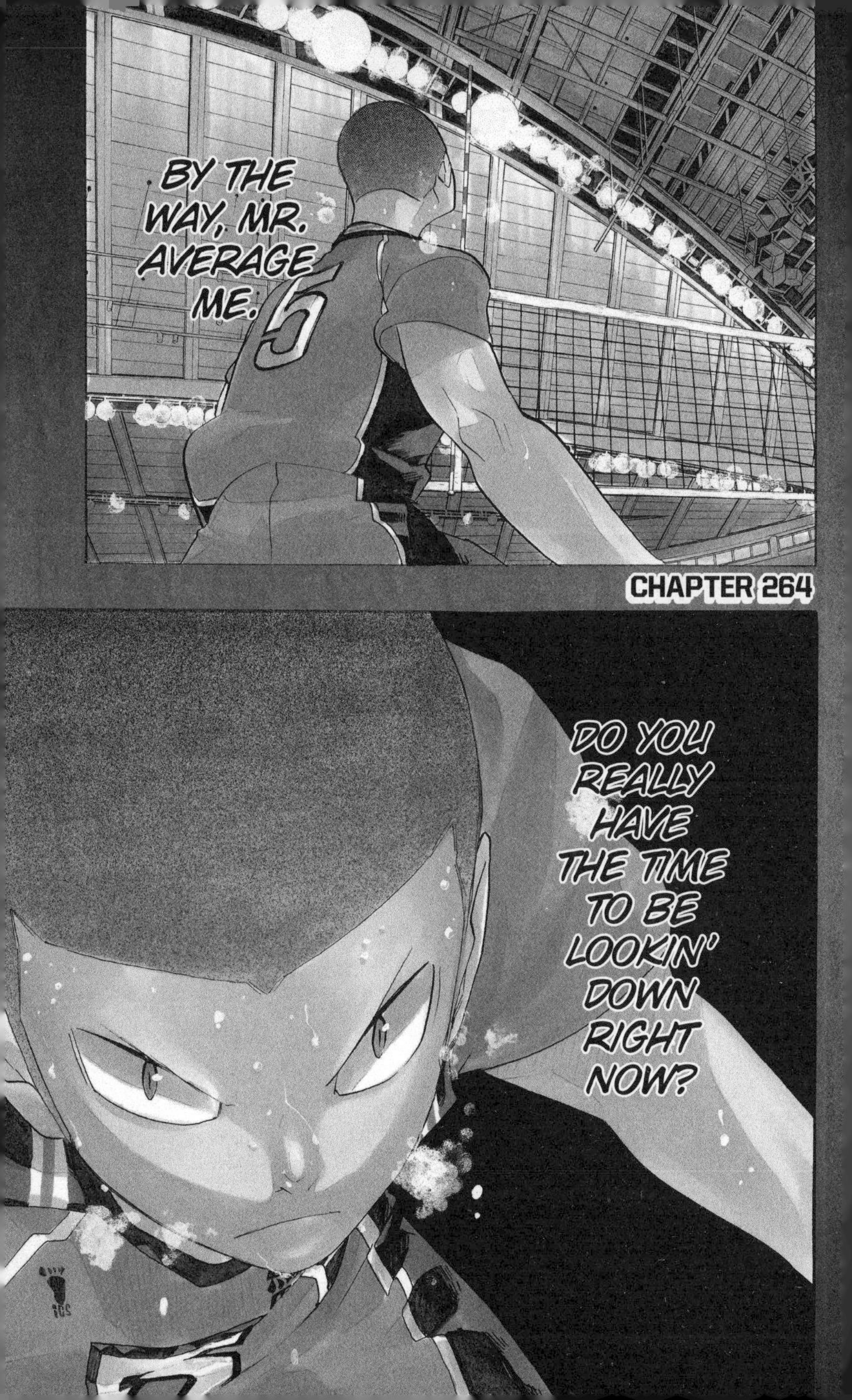
BY THE WAY, MR. AVERAGE ME.
CHAPTER 264
DO YOU REALLY HAVE THE TIME TO BE LOOKIN' DOWN RIGHT NOW?

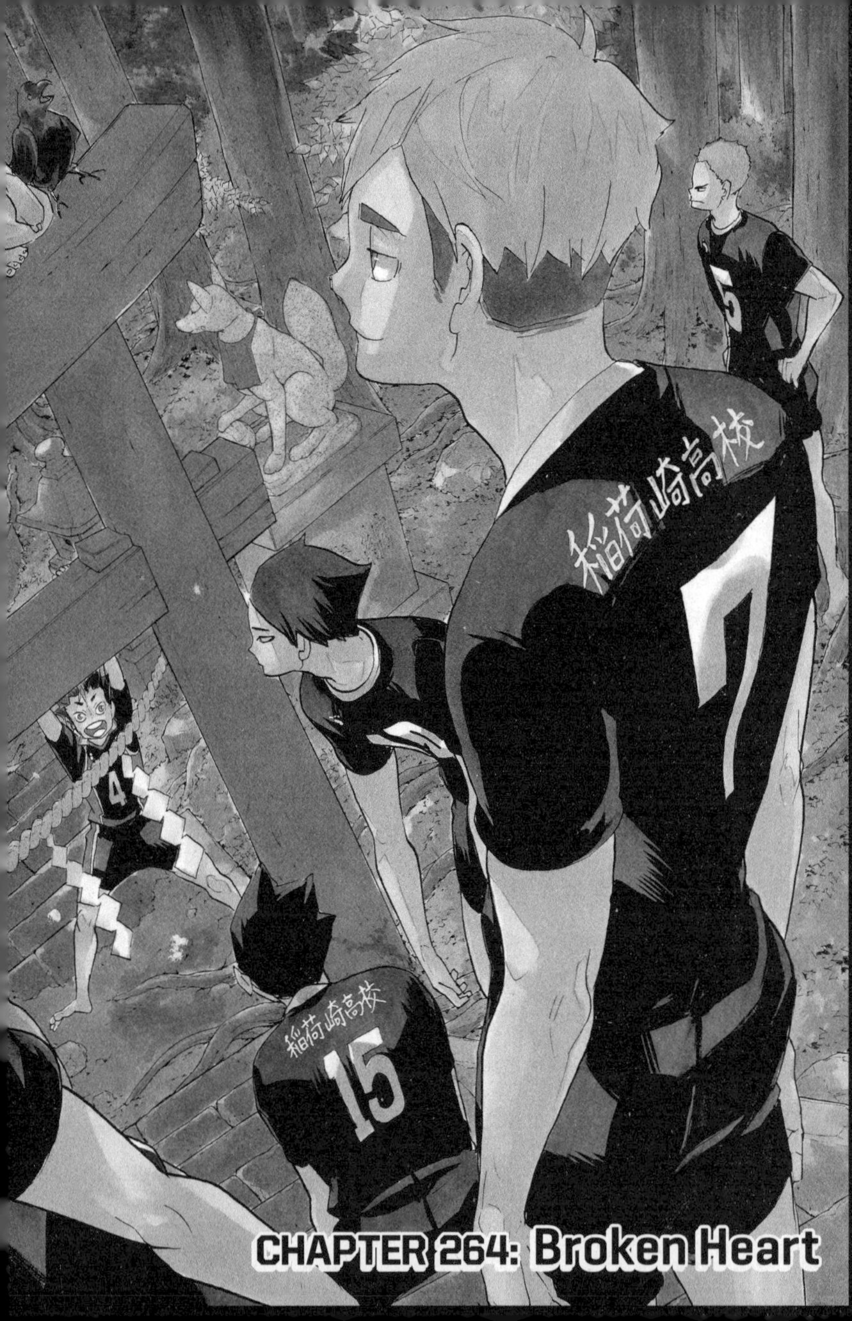
稲荷崎高校
稲荷崎高校
CHAPTER 264: Broken Heart

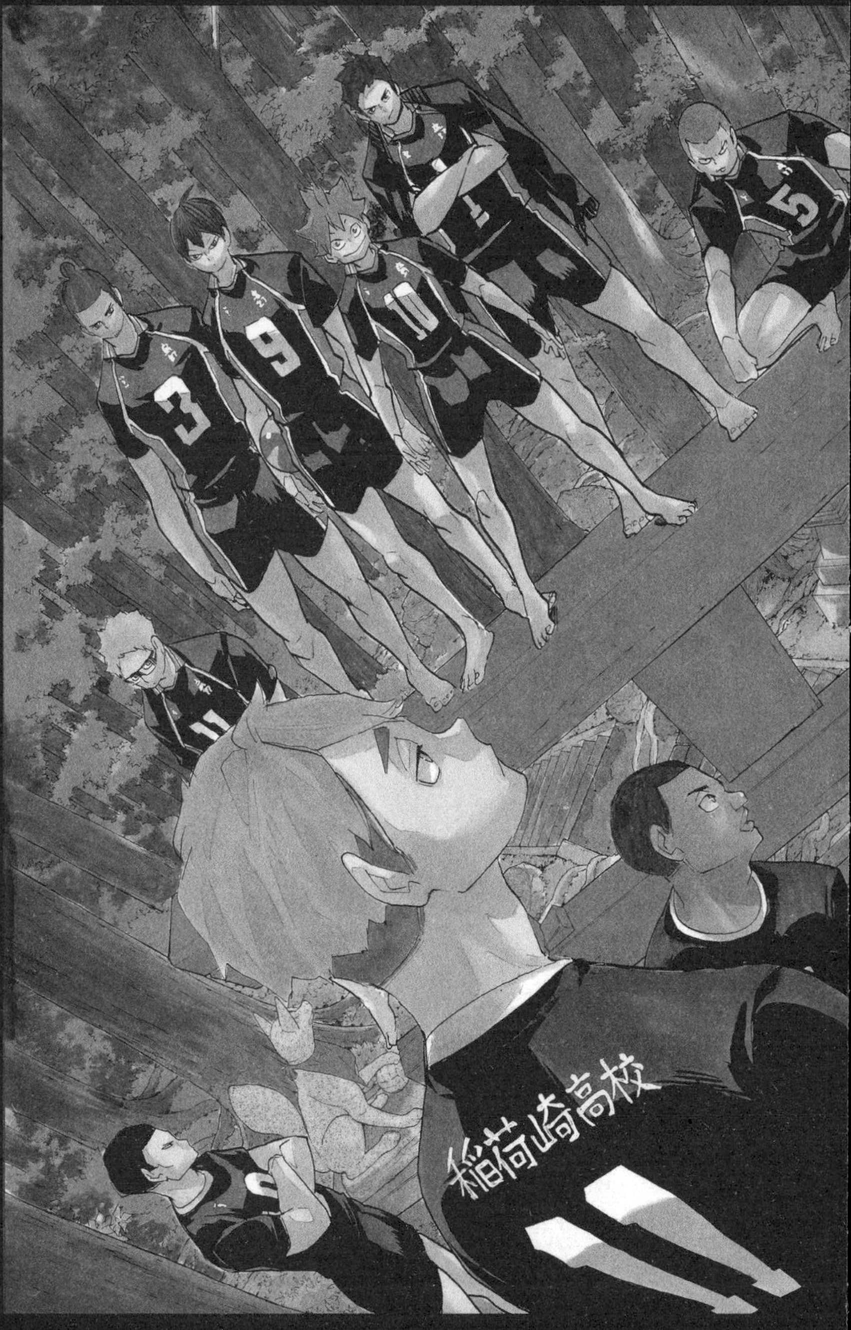
稲荷崎高校

HAIKYU!!

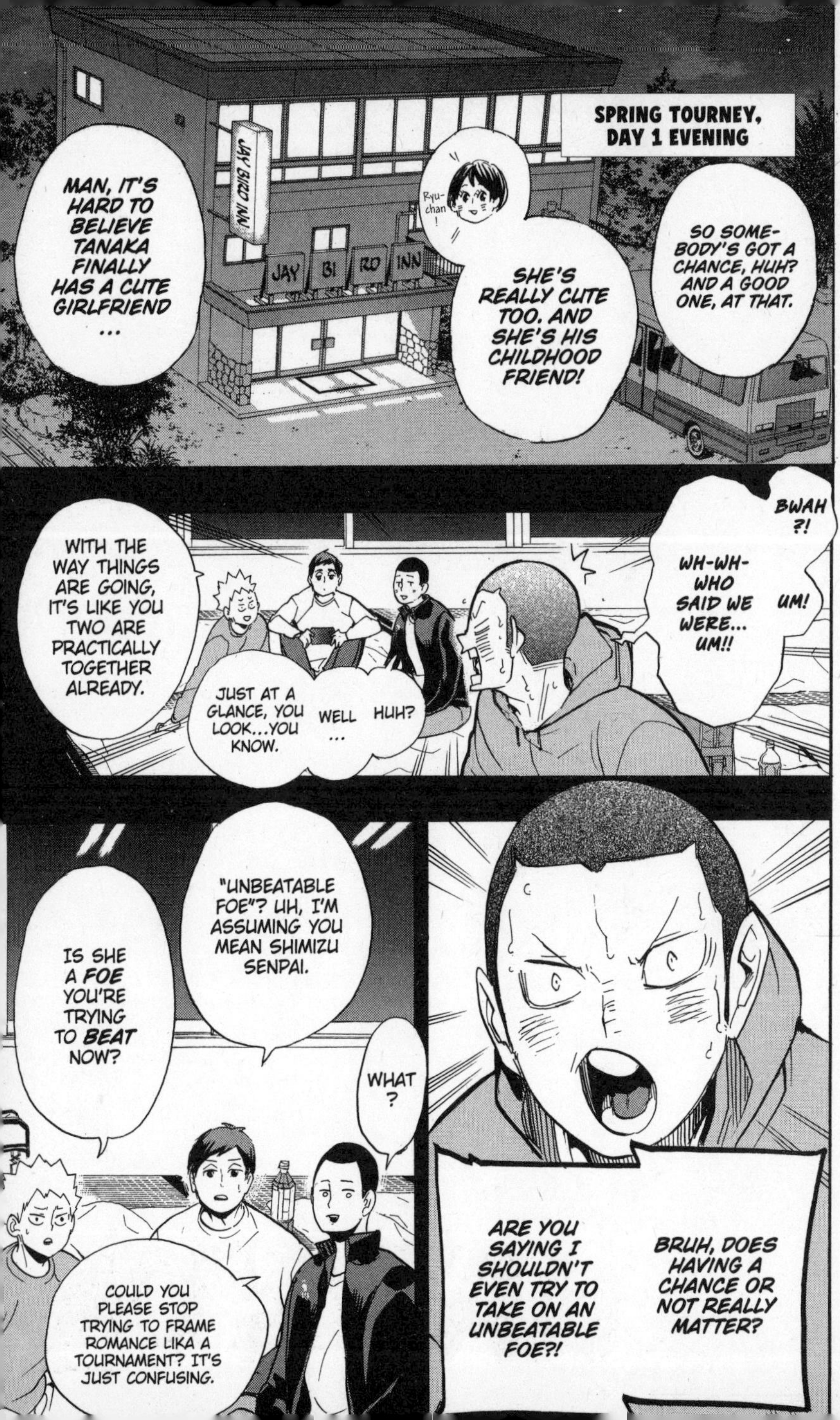
SPRING TOURNEY, DAY 1 EVENING
JAY BIRD INN
JAY BI RD INN
SO SOME-BODY'S GOT A CHANCE, HUH? AND A GOOD ONE, AT THAT.
Ryu-chan!
SHE'S REALLY CUTE TOO. AND SHE'S HIS CHILDHOOD FRIEND!
MAN, IT'S HARD TO BELIEVE TANAKA FINALLY HAS A CUTE GIRLFRIEND...
BWAH?!
WH-WH-WHO SAID WE WERE... UM!!
UM!
HUH?
WELL...
JUST AT A GLANCE, YOU LOOK...YOU KNOW.
WITH THE WAY THINGS ARE GOING, IT'S LIKE YOU TWO ARE PRACTICALLY TOGETHER ALREADY.
BRUH, DOES HAVING A CHANCE OR NOT REALLY MATTER?
ARE YOU SAYING I SHOULDN'T EVEN TRY TO TAKE ON AN UNBEATABLE FOE?!
WHAT?
"UNBEATABLE FOE"? UH, I'M ASSUMING YOU MEAN SHIMIZU SENPAI.
IS SHE A *FOE* YOU'RE TRYING TO *BEAT* NOW?
COULD YOU PLEASE STOP TRYING TO FRAME ROMANCE LIKA A TOURNAMENT? IT'S JUST CONFUSING.

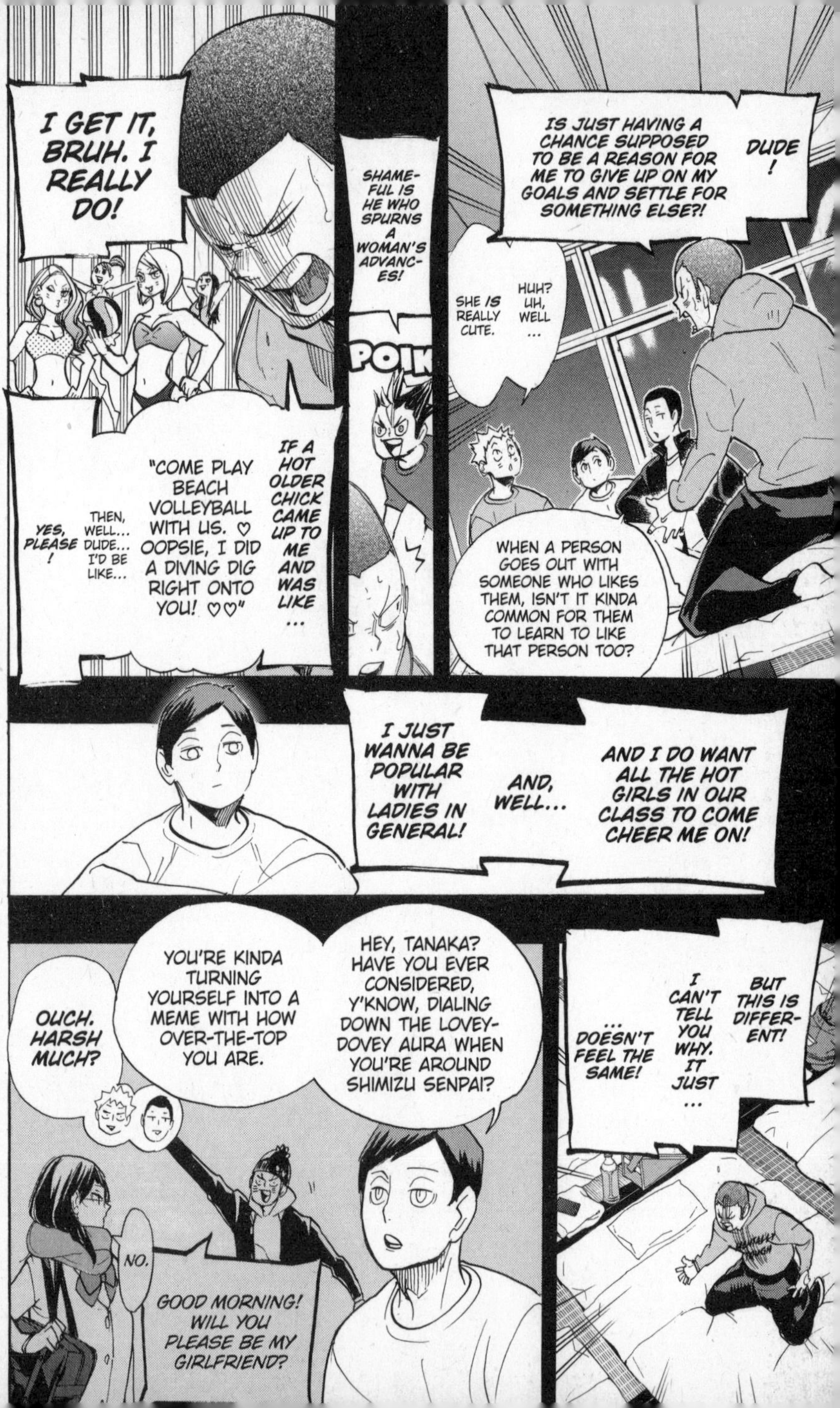
DUDE!
IS JUST HAVING A CHANCE SUPPOSED TO BE A REASON FOR ME TO GIVE UP ON MY GOALS AND SETTLE FOR SOMETHING ELSE?!
HUH? UH, WELL...
SHE IS REALLY CUTE.
WHEN A PERSON GOES OUT WITH SOMEONE WHO LIKES THEM, ISN'T IT KINDA COMMON FOR THEM TO LEARN TO LIKE THAT PERSON TOO?
SHAME-FUL IS HE WHO SPURNS A WOMAN'S ADVANC-ES!
POIK
I GET IT, BRUH. I REALLY DO!
IF A HOT OLDER CHICK CAME UP TO ME AND WAS LIKE...
"COME PLAY BEACH VOLLEYBALL WITH US. ♡ OOPSIE, I DID A DIVING DIG RIGHT ONTO YOU! ♡♡"
THEN, WELL... DUDE... I'D BE LIKE...
YES, PLEASE!
I JUST WANNA BE POPULAR WITH LADIES IN GENERAL! AND, WELL... AND I DO WANT ALL THE HOT GIRLS IN OUR CLASS TO COME CHEER ME ON!
BUT THIS IS DIFFER-ENT!
I CAN'T TELL YOU WHY. IT JUST...
...DOESN'T FEEL THE SAME!
HEY, TANAKA? HAVE YOU EVER CONSIDERED, Y'KNOW, DIALING DOWN THE LOVEY-DOVEY AURA WHEN YOU'RE AROUND SHIMIZU SENPAI?
YOU'RE KINDA TURNING YOURSELF INTO A MEME WITH HOW OVER-THE-TOP YOU ARE.
OUCH. HARSH MUCH?
GOOD MORNING! WILL YOU PLEASE BE MY GIRLFRIEND?
NO.

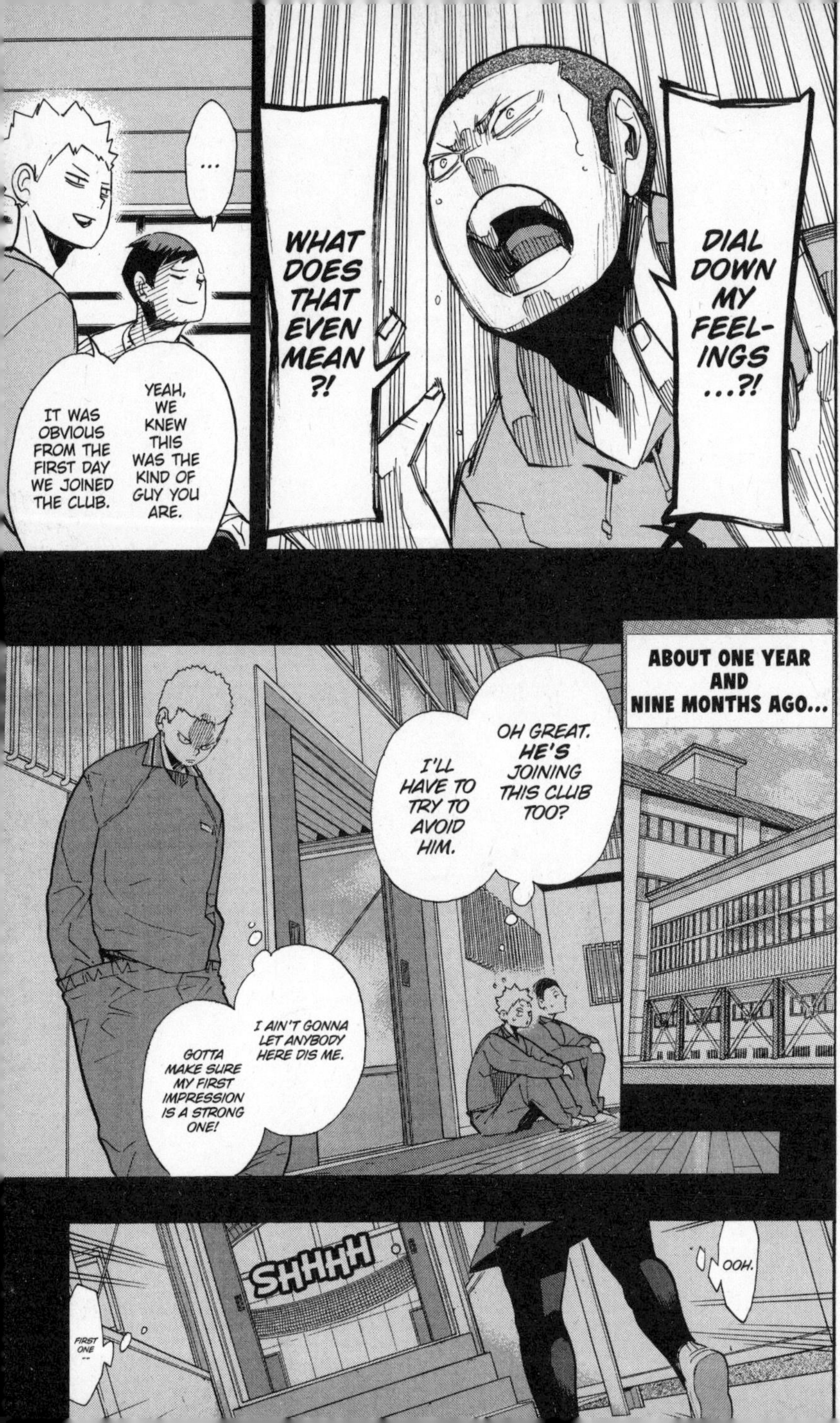
DIAL DOWN MY FEELINGS...?!
WHAT DOES THAT EVEN MEAN?!
...
YEAH, WE KNEW THIS WAS THE KIND OF GUY YOU ARE.
IT WAS OBVIOUS FROM THE FIRST DAY WE JOINED THE CLUB.
ABOUT ONE YEAR AND NINE MONTHS AGO...
OH GREAT. HE'S JOINING THIS CLUB TOO?
I'LL HAVE TO TRY TO AVOID HIM.
I AIN'T GONNA LET ANYBODY HERE DIS ME.
GOTTA MAKE SURE MY FIRST IMPRESSION IS A STRONG ONE!
OOH.
SHHHH
FIRST ONE --

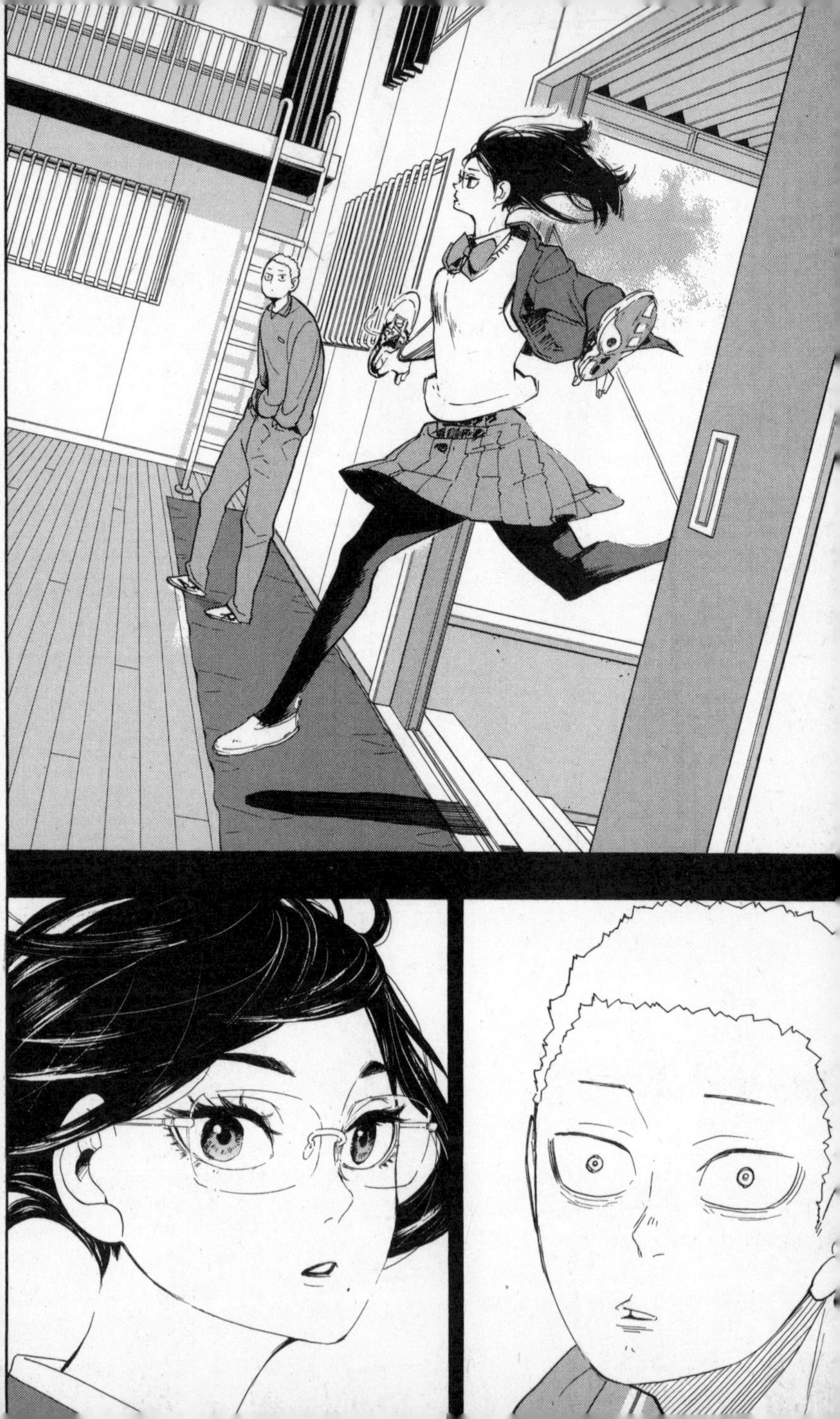

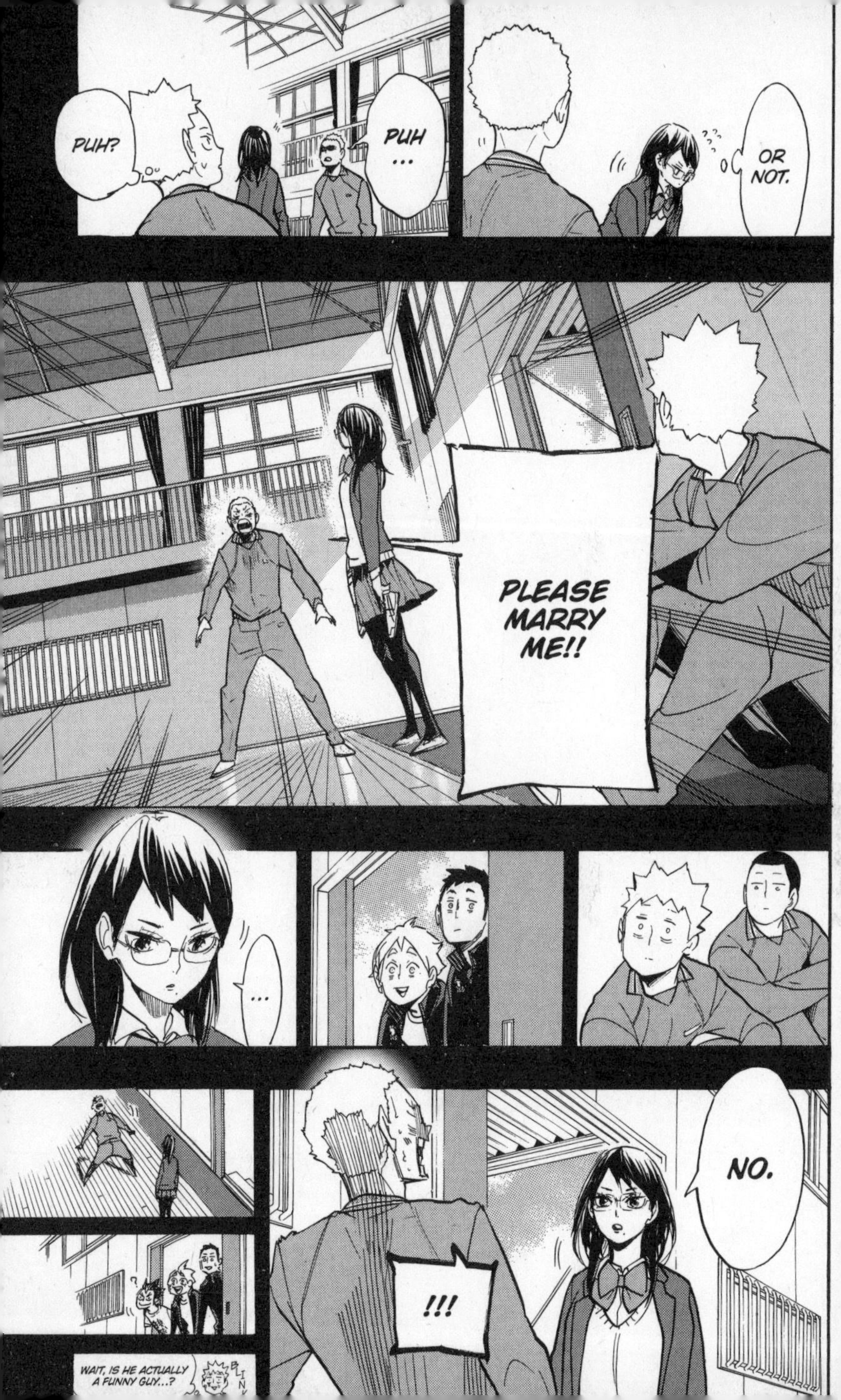
OR NOT.
PUH ...
PUH?
PLEASE MARRY ME!!
...
NO.
!!!
WAIT, IS HE ACTUALLY A FUNNY GUY...?
BLINK

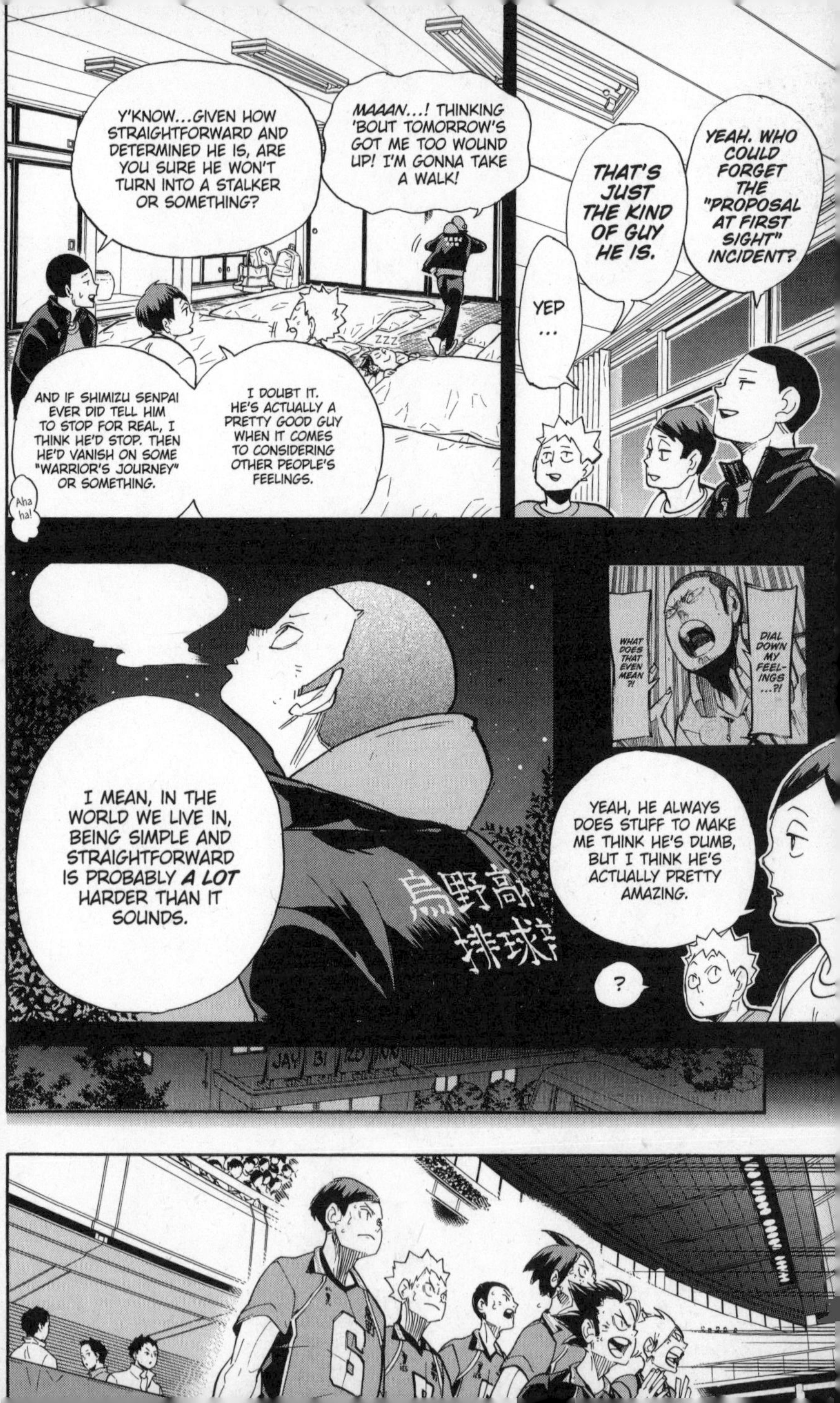
YEAH. WHO COULD FORGET THE "PROPOSAL AT FIRST SIGHT" INCIDENT?
THAT'S JUST THE KIND OF GUY HE IS.
YEP ...
MAAAN...! THINKING 'BOUT TOMORROW'S GOT ME TOO WOUND UP! I'M GONNA TAKE A WALK!
Y'KNOW...GIVEN HOW STRAIGHTFORWARD AND DETERMINED HE IS, ARE YOU SURE HE WON'T TURN INTO A STALKER OR SOMETHING?
I DOUBT IT. HE'S ACTUALLY A PRETTY GOOD GUY WHEN IT COMES TO CONSIDERING OTHER PEOPLE'S FEELINGS.
AND IF SHIMIZU SENPAI EVER DID TELL HIM TO STOP FOR REAL, I THINK HE'D STOP. THEN HE'D VANISH ON SOME "WARRIOR'S JOURNEY" OR SOMETHING.
Aha ha!
DIAL DOWN MY FEEL-INGS ...?!
WHAT DOES THAT EVEN MEAN ?!
YEAH, HE ALWAYS DOES STUFF TO MAKE ME THINK HE'S DUMB, BUT I THINK HE'S ACTUALLY PRETTY AMAZING.
?
I MEAN, IN THE WORLD WE LIVE IN, BEING SIMPLE AND STRAIGHTFORWARD IS PROBABLY *A LOT* HARDER THAN IT SOUNDS.
烏野高
排球

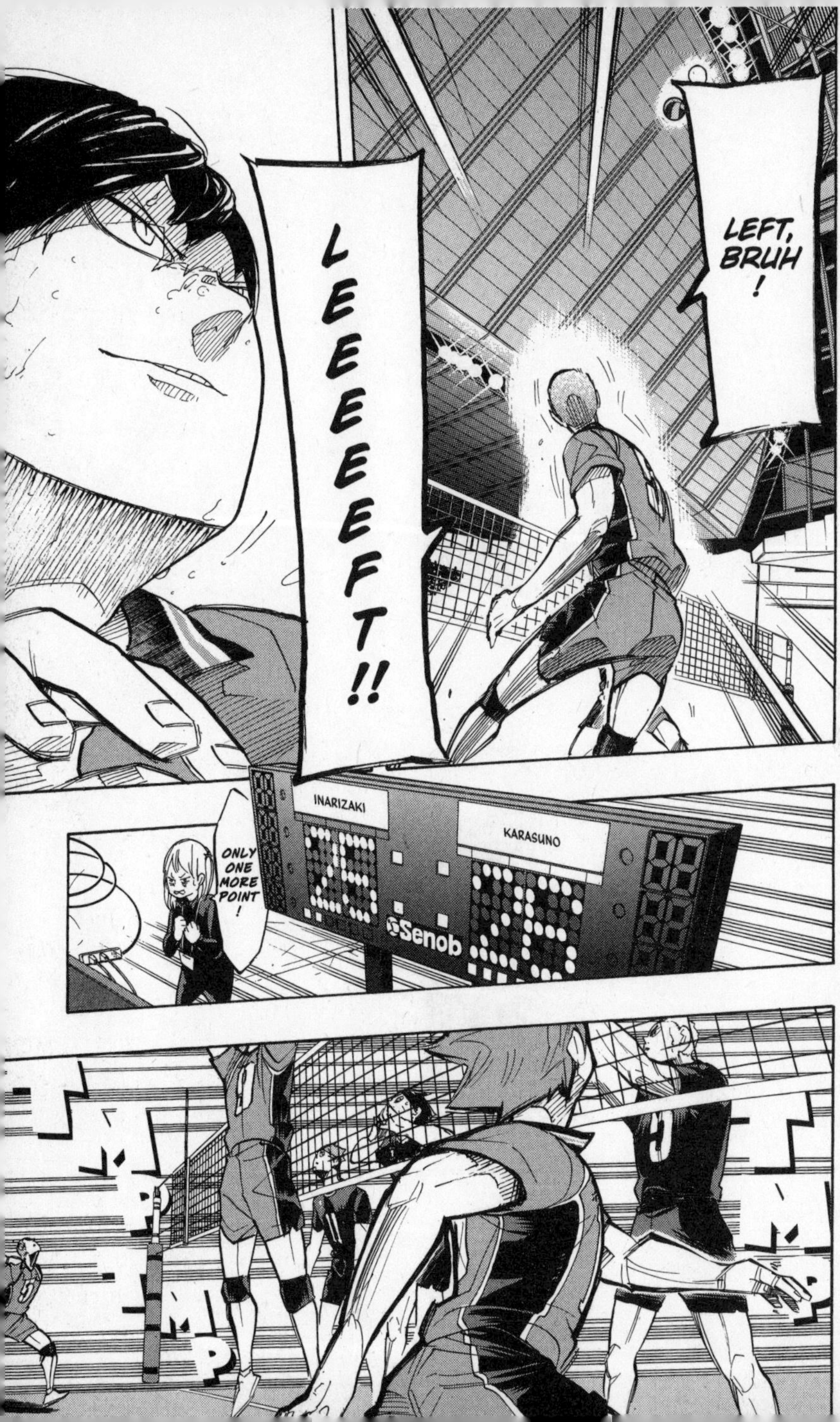
LEFT, BRUH!
LEEEEEFT!!
INARIZAKI
KARASUNO
Senob
ONLY ONE MORE POINT!

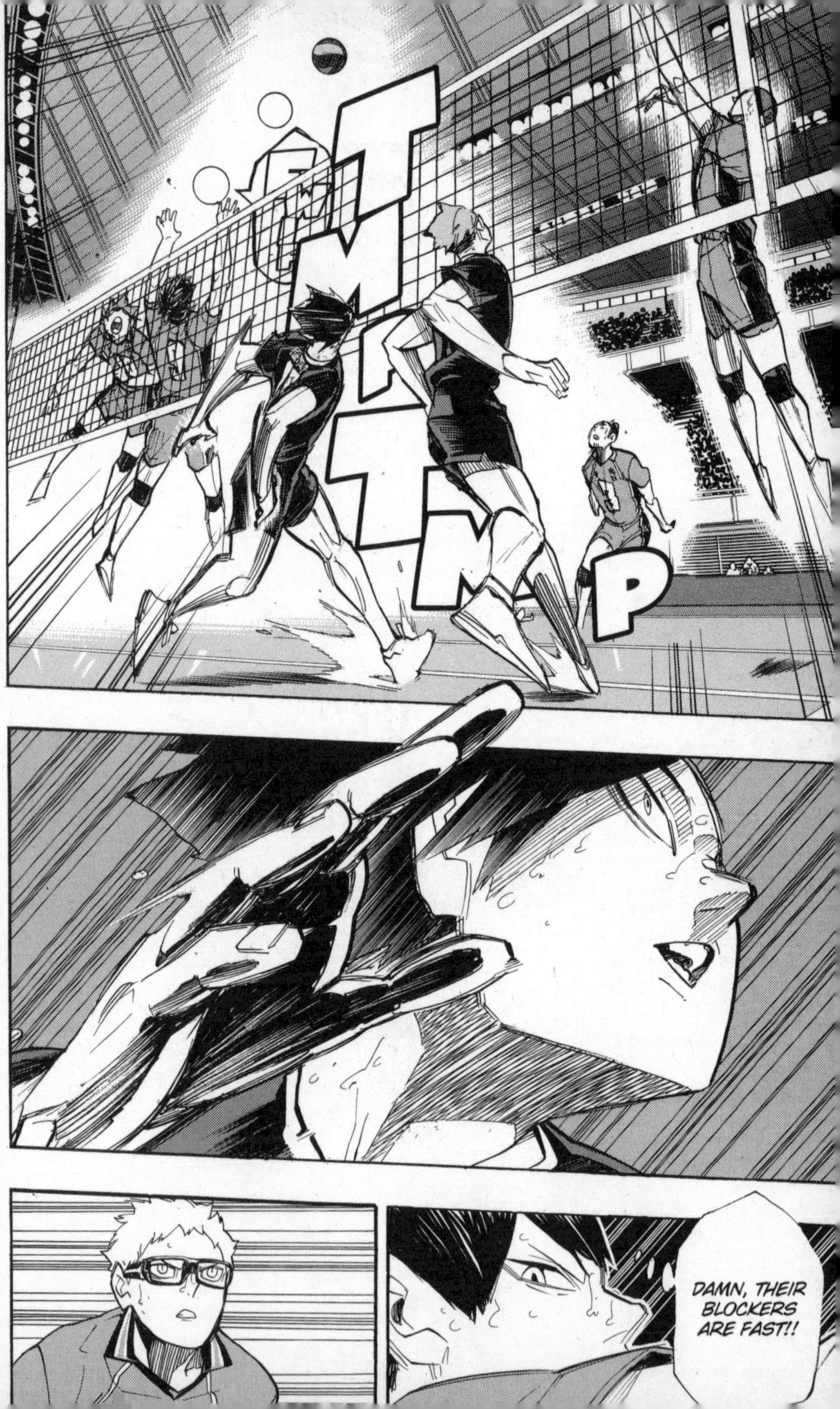
DAMN, THEIR BLOCKERS ARE FAST!!

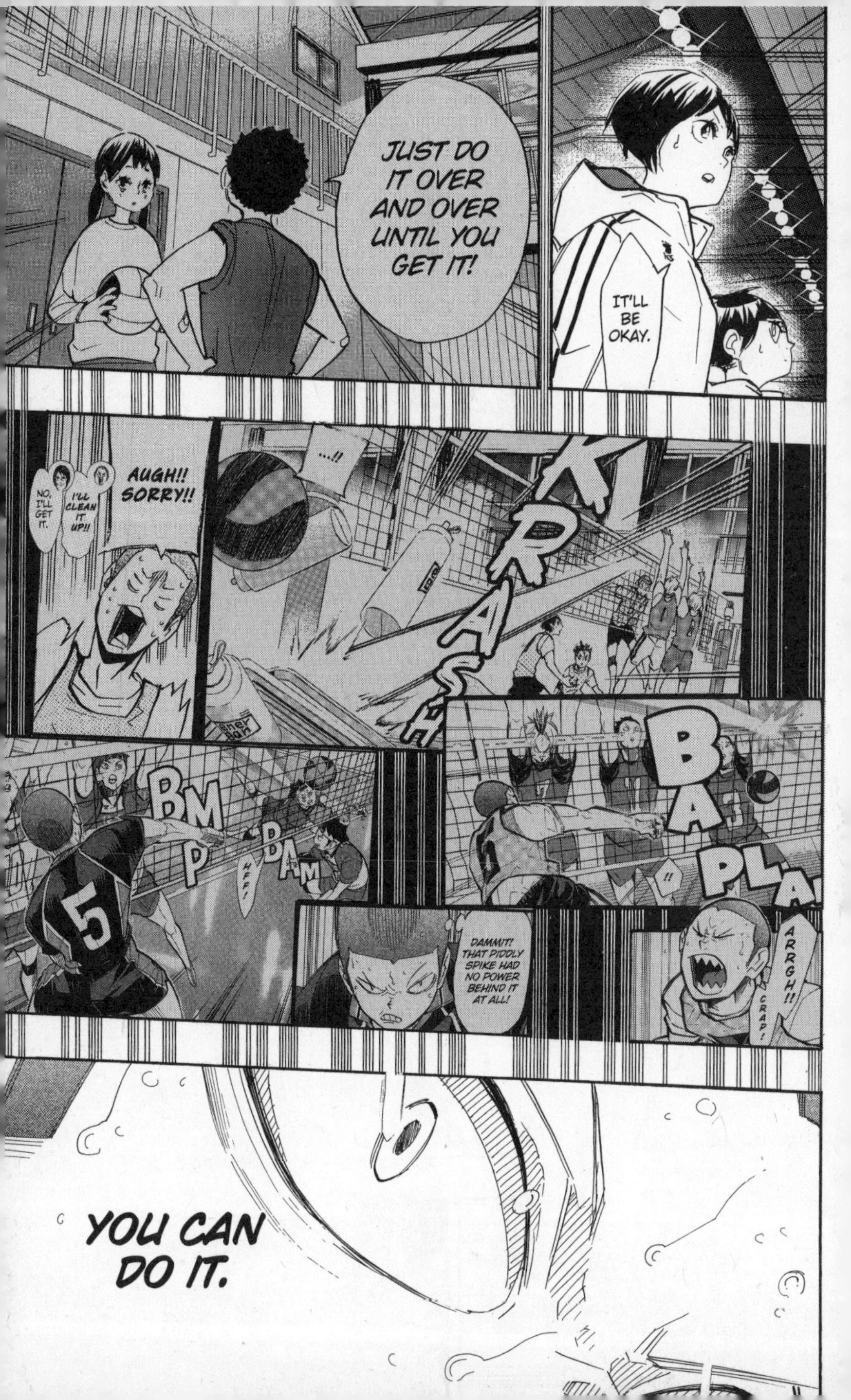

IT'LL BE OKAY.
JUST DO IT OVER AND OVER UNTIL YOU GET IT!
...!!
KRASH
AUGH!! SORRY!!
I'LL CLEAN IT UP!!
NO, I'LL GET IT.
BA
PLA
!!
BMP
BAM
HFF!
ARRGH!!
CRAP!
DAMMIT! THAT PIDDLY SPIKE HAD NO POWER BEHIND IT AT ALL!
YOU CAN DO IT.

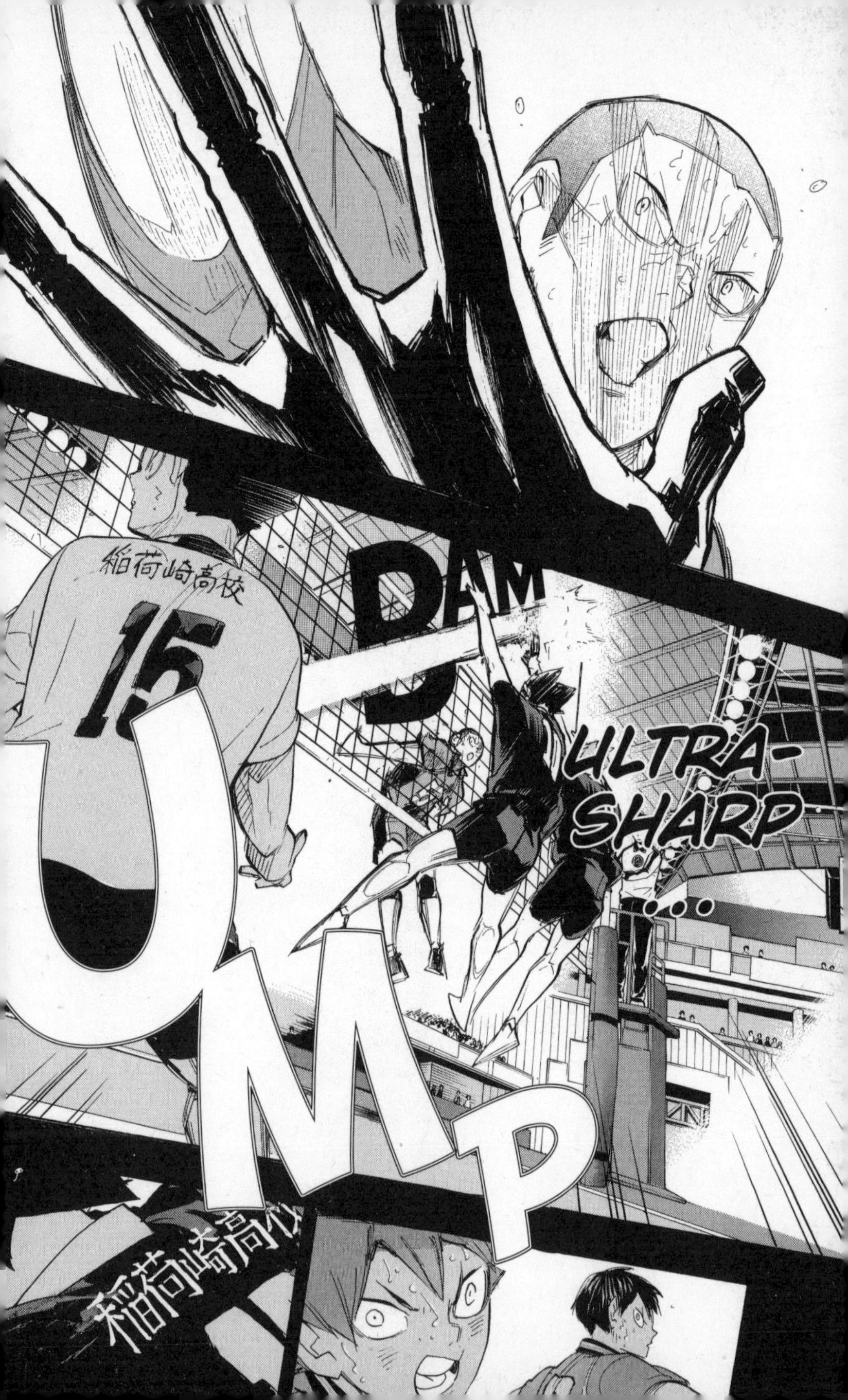
DAM
UMP
稲荷崎高校
15
ULTRA-SHARP...

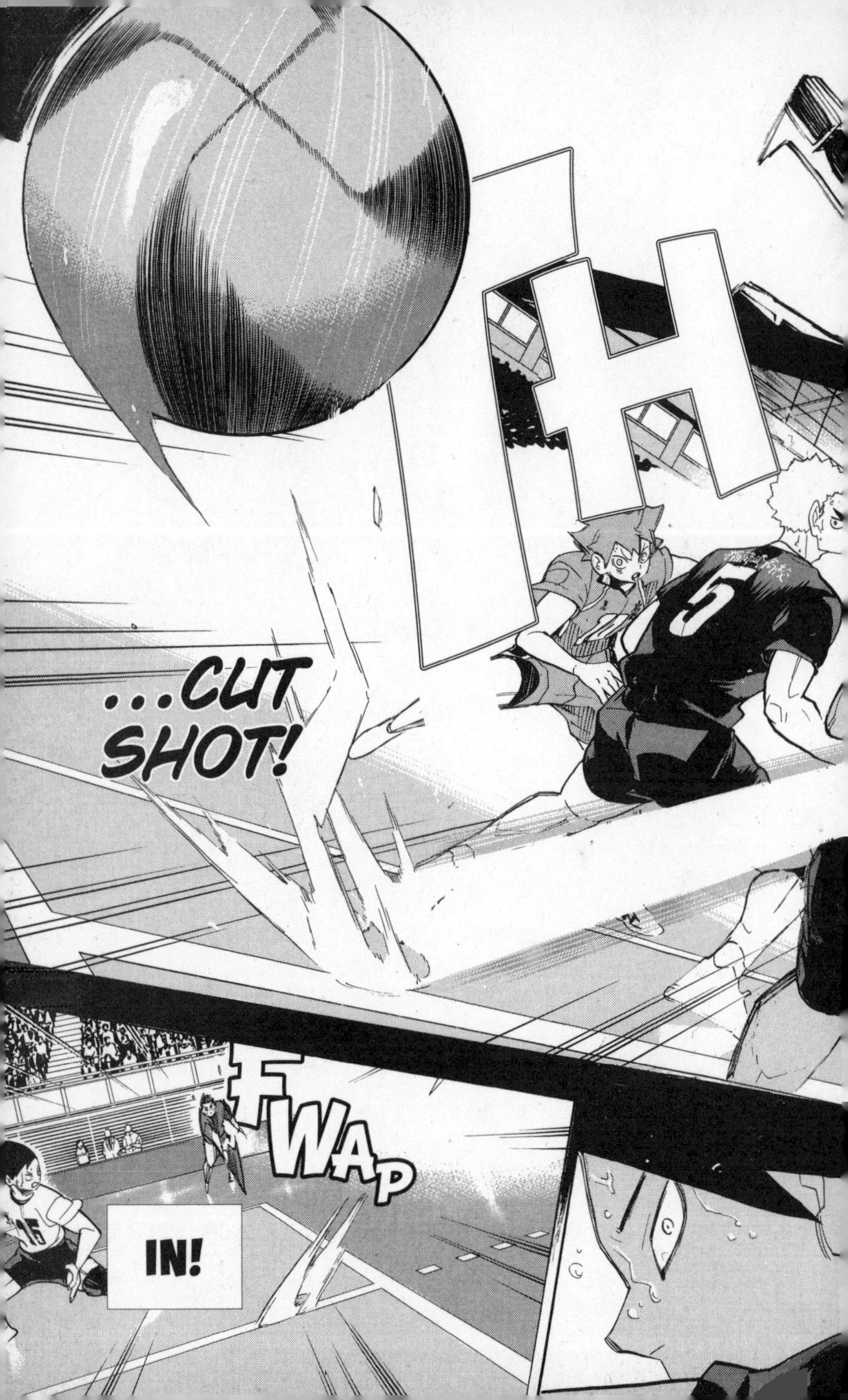
...CUT SHOT!
FWAP
IN!

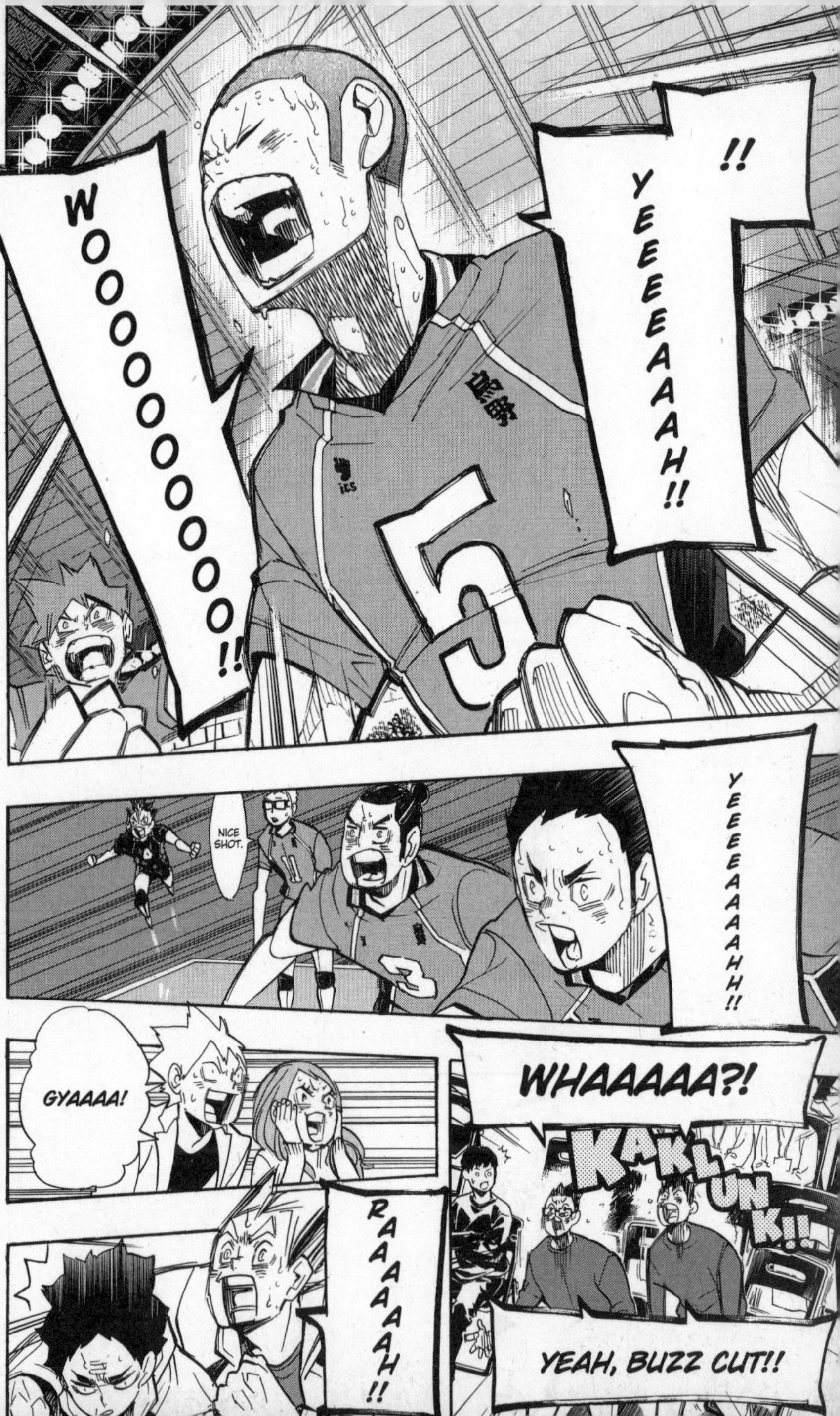
YEEEEAAAAH!!
WOOOOOOOOOO!!
YEEEEAAAAAAH!!
NICE SHOT.
WHAAAAAA?!
KAKLUNK!!
GYAAAA!
YEAH, BUZZ CUT!!
RAAAAAAAH!!

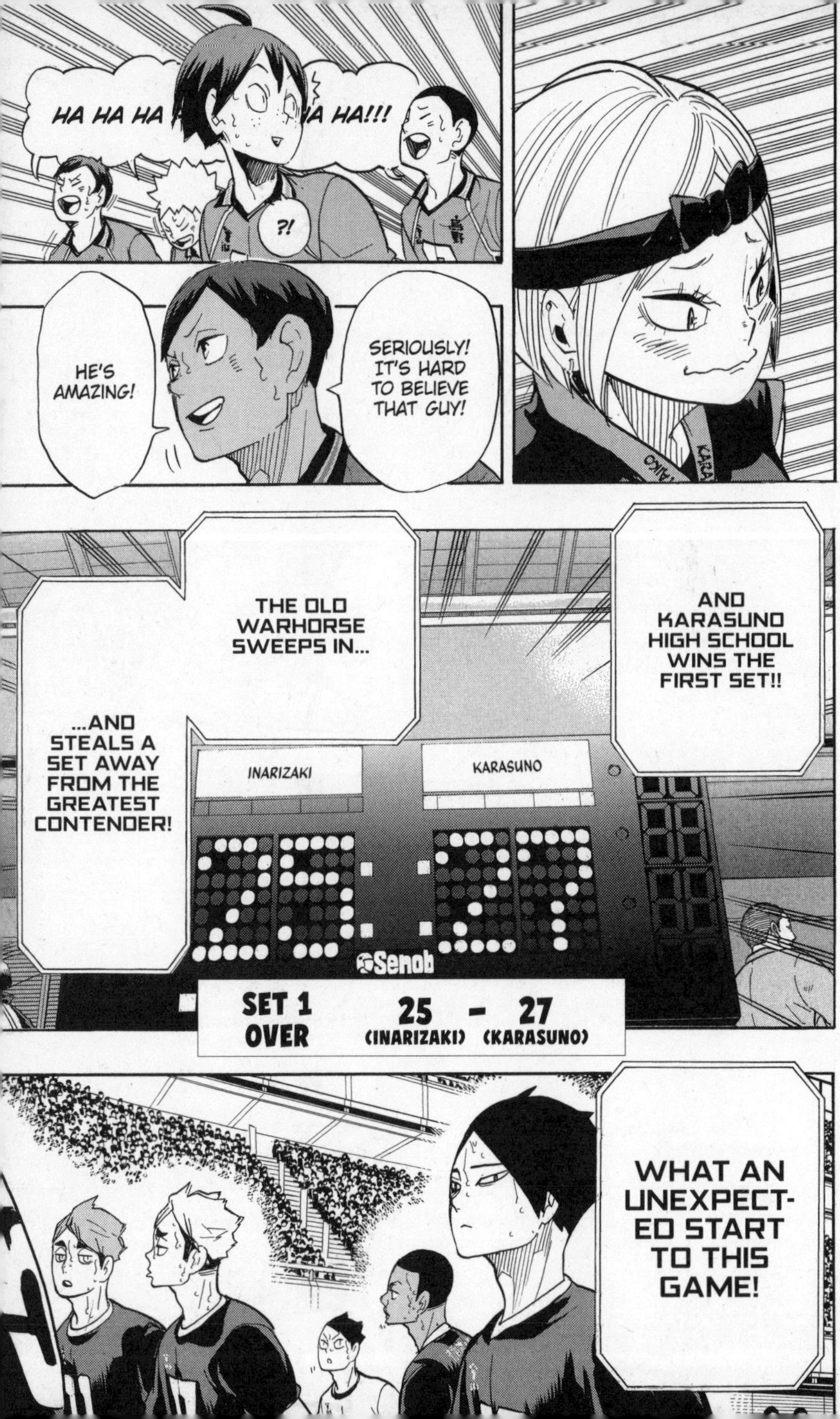
HA HA HA
A HA!!!
?!
SERIOUSLY! IT'S HARD TO BELIEVE THAT GUY!
HE'S AMAZING!
AND KARASUNO HIGH SCHOOL WINS THE FIRST SET!!
THE OLD WARHORSE SWEEPS IN...
...AND STEALS A SET AWAY FROM THE GREATEST CONTENDER!
INARIZAKI
KARASUNO
Senob
SET 1 OVER
25 - 27
(INARIZAKI) (KARASUNO)
WHAT AN UNEXPECT-ED START TO THIS GAME!

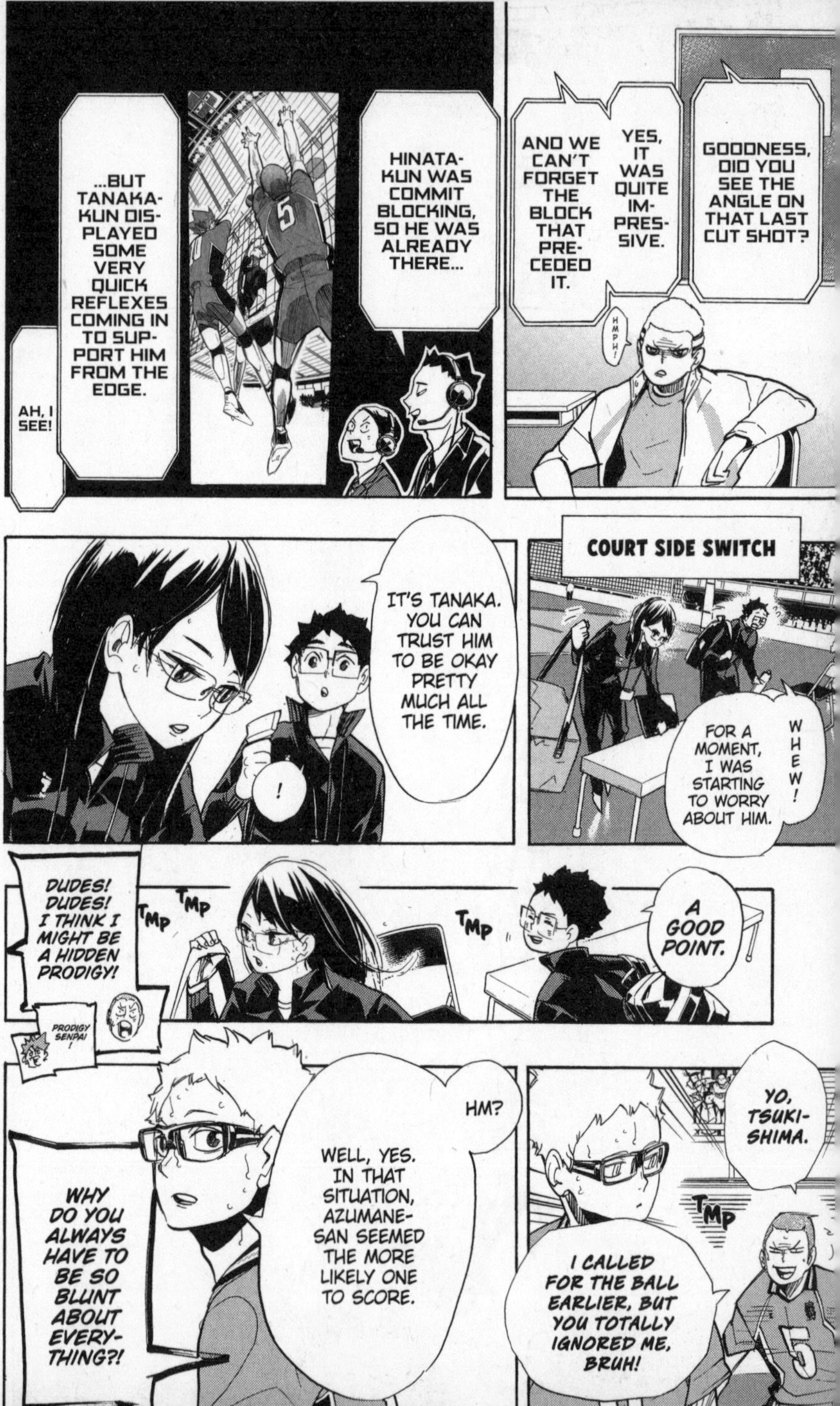
GOODNESS, DID YOU SEE THE ANGLE ON THAT LAST CUT SHOT?
YES, IT WAS QUITE IMPRESSIVE.
AND WE CAN'T FORGET THE BLOCK THAT PRECEDED IT.
HMPH!
HINATA-KUN WAS COMMIT BLOCKING, SO HE WAS ALREADY THERE...
...BUT TANAKA-KUN DISPLAYED SOME VERY QUICK REFLEXES COMING IN TO SUPPORT HIM FROM THE EDGE.
AH, I SEE!
COURT SIDE SWITCH
WHEW!
FOR A MOMENT, I WAS STARTING TO WORRY ABOUT HIM.
IT'S TANAKA. YOU CAN TRUST HIM TO BE OKAY PRETTY MUCH ALL THE TIME.
!
A GOOD POINT.
TMP
TMP
TMP
DUDES! DUDES! I THINK I MIGHT BE A HIDDEN PRODIGY!
PRODIGY SENPAI!
YO, TSUKISHIMA.
TMP
I CALLED FOR THE BALL EARLIER, BUT YOU TOTALLY IGNORED ME, BRUH!
HM?
WELL, YES. IN THAT SITUATION, AZUMANE-SAN SEEMED THE MORE LIKELY ONE TO SCORE.
WHY DO YOU ALWAYS HAVE TO BE SO BLUNT ABOUT EVERYTHING?!

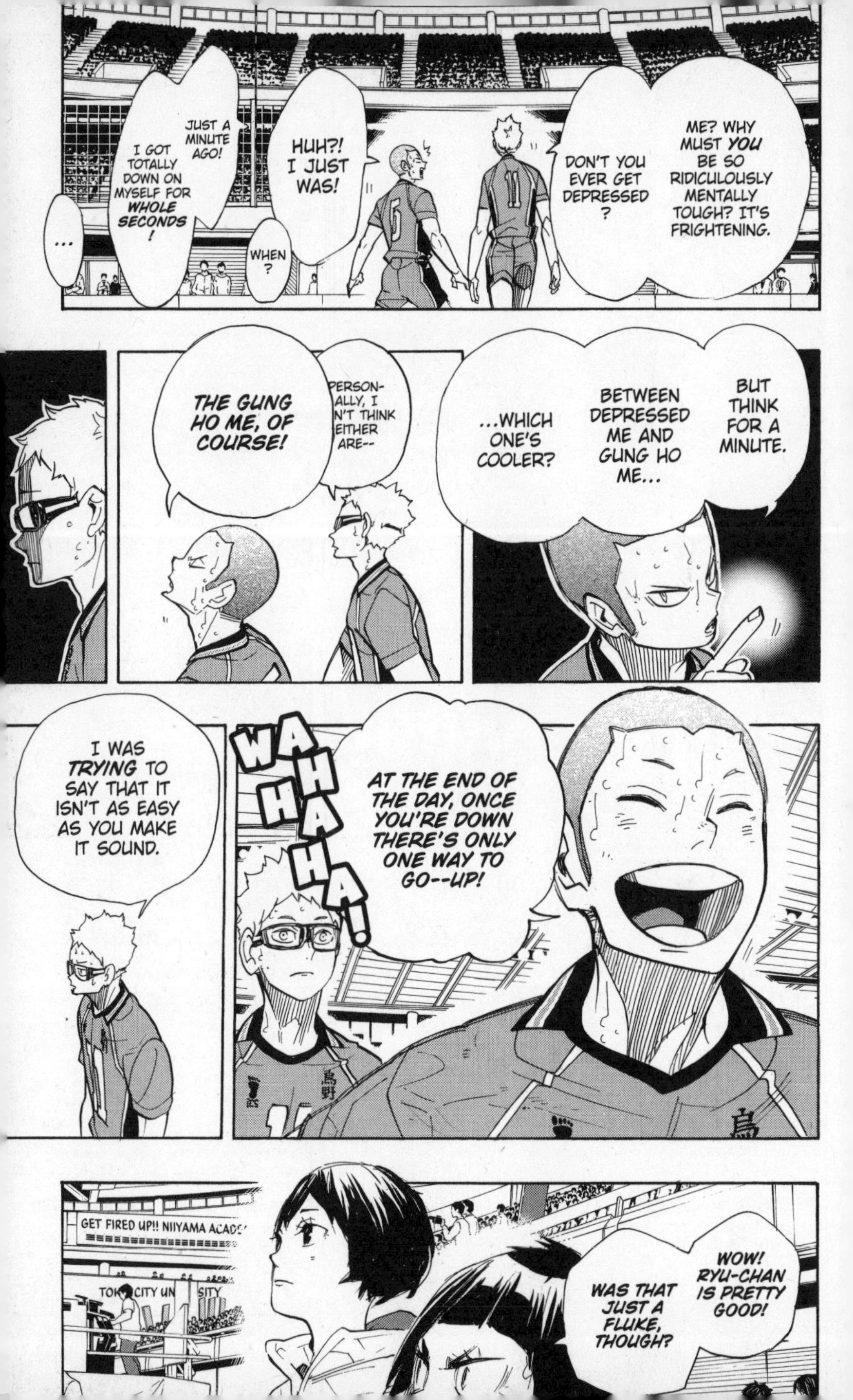
ME? WHY MUST YOU BE SO RIDICULOUSLY MENTALLY TOUGH? IT'S FRIGHTENING.
DON'T YOU EVER GET DEPRESSED?
HUH?! I JUST WAS!
WHEN?
JUST A MINUTE AGO!
I GOT TOTALLY DOWN ON MYSELF FOR WHOLE SECONDS!
...
BUT THINK FOR A MINUTE.
BETWEEN DEPRESSED ME AND GUNG HO ME...
...WHICH ONE'S COOLER?
PERSON- ALLY, I N'T THINK EITHER ARE--
THE GUNG HO ME, OF COURSE!
WAHAHAHA!
AT THE END OF THE DAY, ONCE YOU'RE DOWN THERE'S ONLY ONE WAY TO GO--UP!
I WAS TRYING TO SAY THAT IT ISN'T AS EASY AS YOU MAKE IT SOUND.
WOW! RYU-CHAN IS PRETTY GOOD!
WAS THAT JUST A FLUKE, THOUGH?
GET FIRED UP!! NIIYAMA ACAD
TOK CITY UN SITY

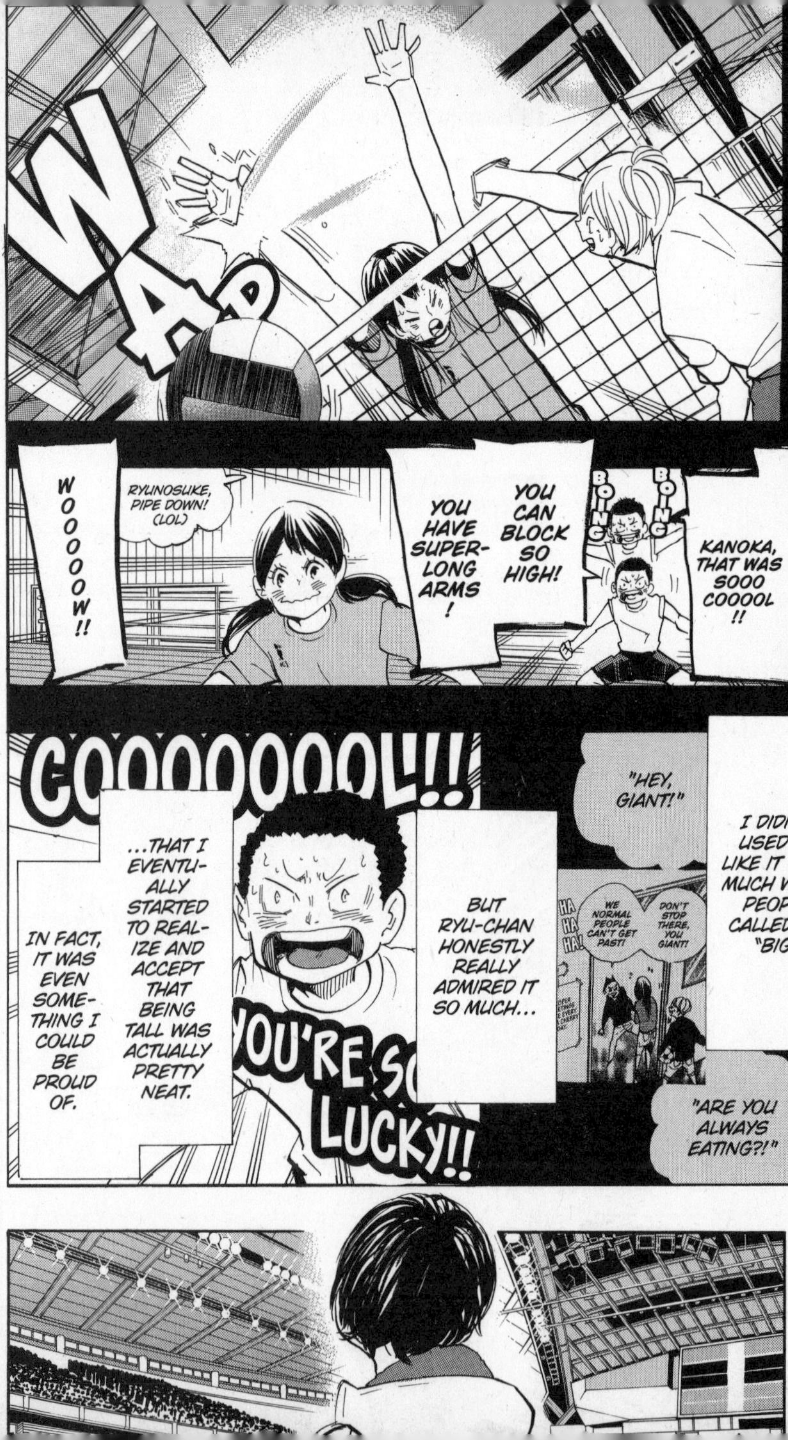
WAP
WHOOOOOAAAA!!
KANOKA, THAT WAS SOOO COOOOL!!
BOING
BOING
YOU CAN BLOCK SO HIGH!
YOU HAVE SUPER-LONG ARMS!
RYUNOSUKE, PIPE DOWN! (LOL)
WOOOOOOW!!
I DIDN'T USED TO LIKE IT VERY MUCH WHEN PEOPLE CALLED ME "BIG."
"HEY, GIANT!"
HA HA HA!
DON'T STOP THERE, YOU GIANT!
WE NORMAL PEOPLE CAN'T GET PAST!
"ARE YOU ALWAYS EATING?!"
BUT RYU-CHAN HONESTLY REALLY ADMIRED IT SO MUCH...
COOOOOOOL!!
YOU'RE SO LUCKY!!
...THAT I EVENTUALLY STARTED TO REALIZE AND ACCEPT THAT BEING TALL WAS ACTUALLY PRETTY NEAT.
IN FACT, IT WAS EVEN SOMETHING I COULD BE PROUD OF.

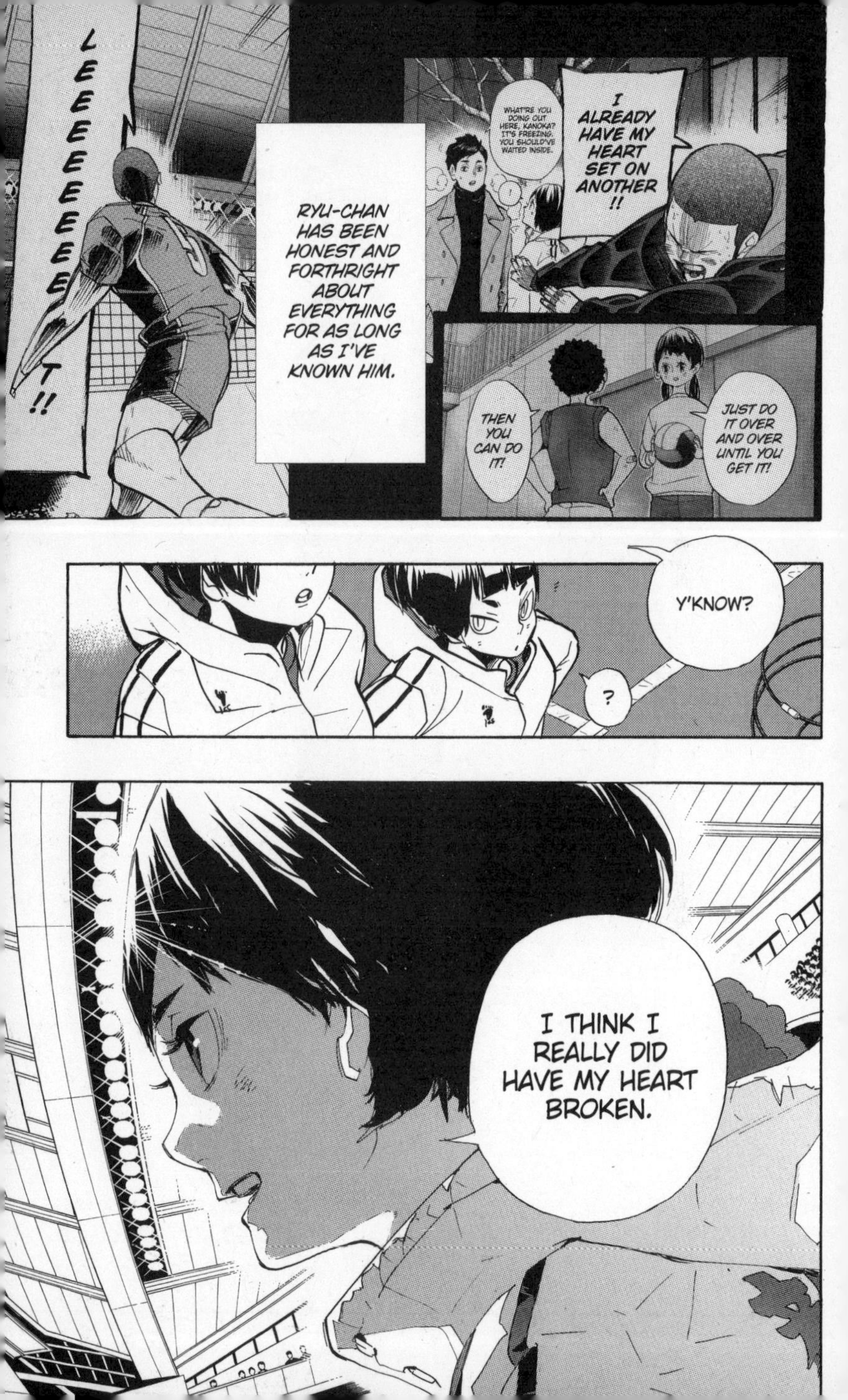
I ALREADY HAVE MY HEART SET ON ANOTHER!!
WHAT'RE YOU DOING OUT HERE, KANOKA? IT'S FREEZING. YOU SHOULD'VE WAITED INSIDE.
JUST DO IT OVER AND OVER UNTIL YOU GET IT!
THEN YOU CAN DO IT!
RYU-CHAN HAS BEEN HONEST AND FORTHRIGHT ABOUT EVERYTHING FOR AS LONG AS I'VE KNOWN HIM.
LEEEEEEEET!!
Y'KNOW?
?
I THINK I REALLY DID HAVE MY HEART BROKEN.

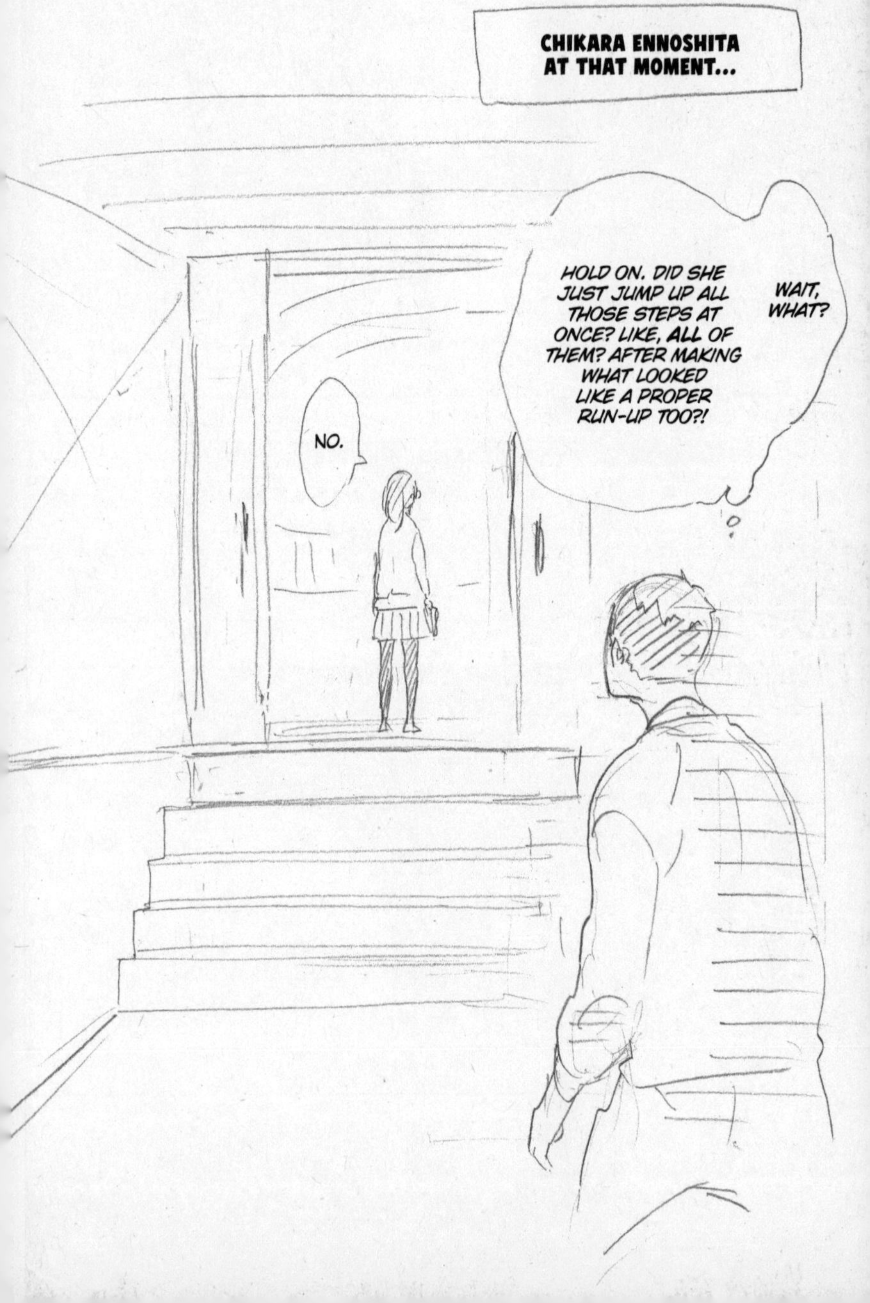
CHIKARA ENNOSHITA AT THAT MOMENT...
WAIT, WHAT?
HOLD ON. DID SHE JUST JUMP UP ALL THOSE STEPS AT ONCE? LIKE, ALL OF THEM? AFTER MAKING WHAT LOOKED LIKE A PROPER RUN-UP TOO?!
NO.

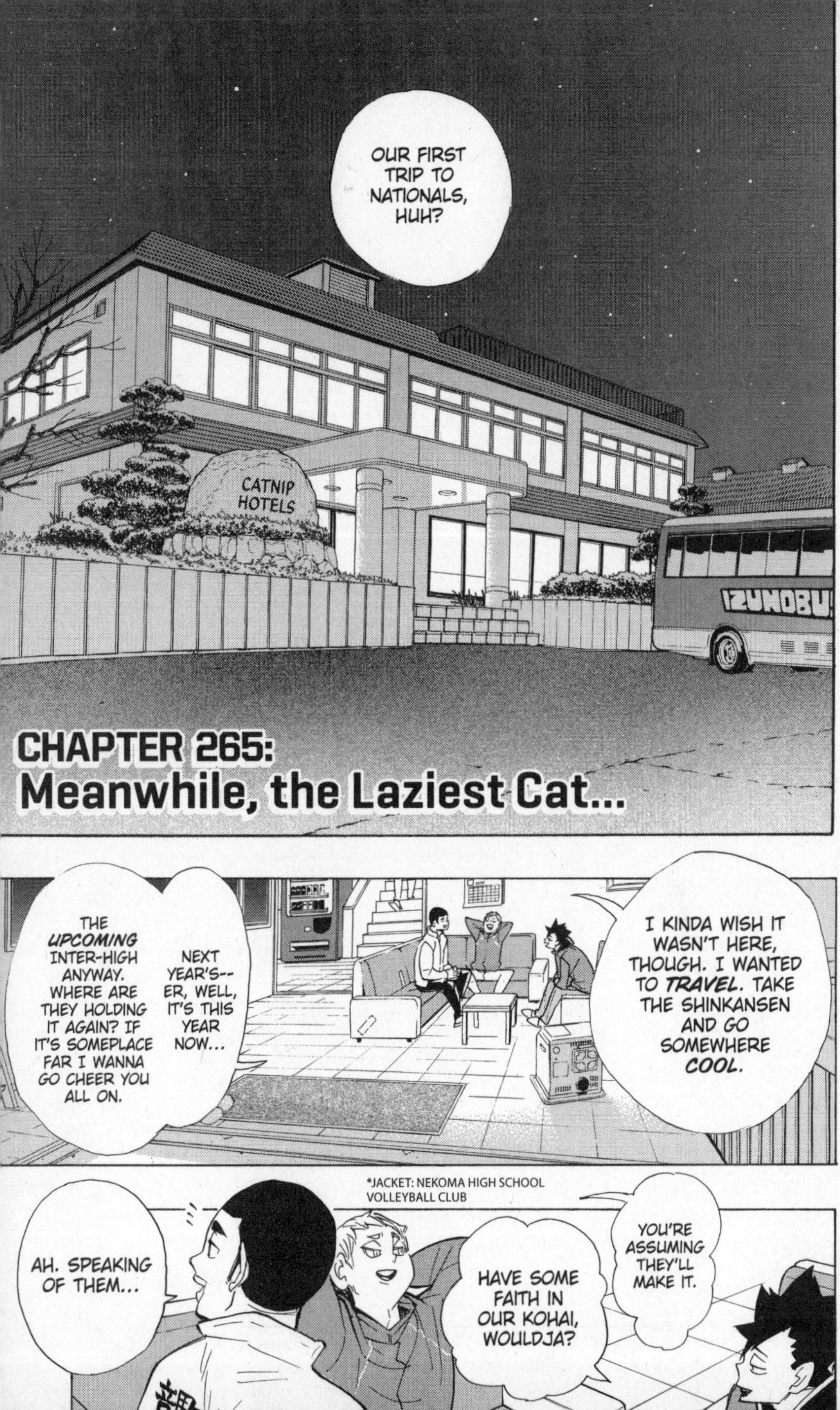
OUR FIRST TRIP TO NATIONALS, HUH?
CATNIP HOTELS
IZUNOBU
CHAPTER 265:
Meanwhile, the Laziest Cat...
I KINDA WISH IT WASN'T HERE, THOUGH. I WANTED TO *TRAVEL*. TAKE THE SHINKANSEN AND GO SOMEWHERE *COOL*.
NEXT YEAR'S-- ER, WELL, IT'S THIS YEAR NOW...
THE *UPCOMING* INTER-HIGH ANYWAY. WHERE ARE THEY HOLDING IT AGAIN? IF IT'S SOMEPLACE FAR I WANNA GO CHEER YOU ALL ON.
YOU'RE ASSUMING THEY'LL MAKE IT.
HAVE SOME FAITH IN OUR KOHAI, WOULDJA?
AH. SPEAKING OF THEM...
*JACKET: NEKOMA HIGH SCHOOL VOLLEYBALL CLUB

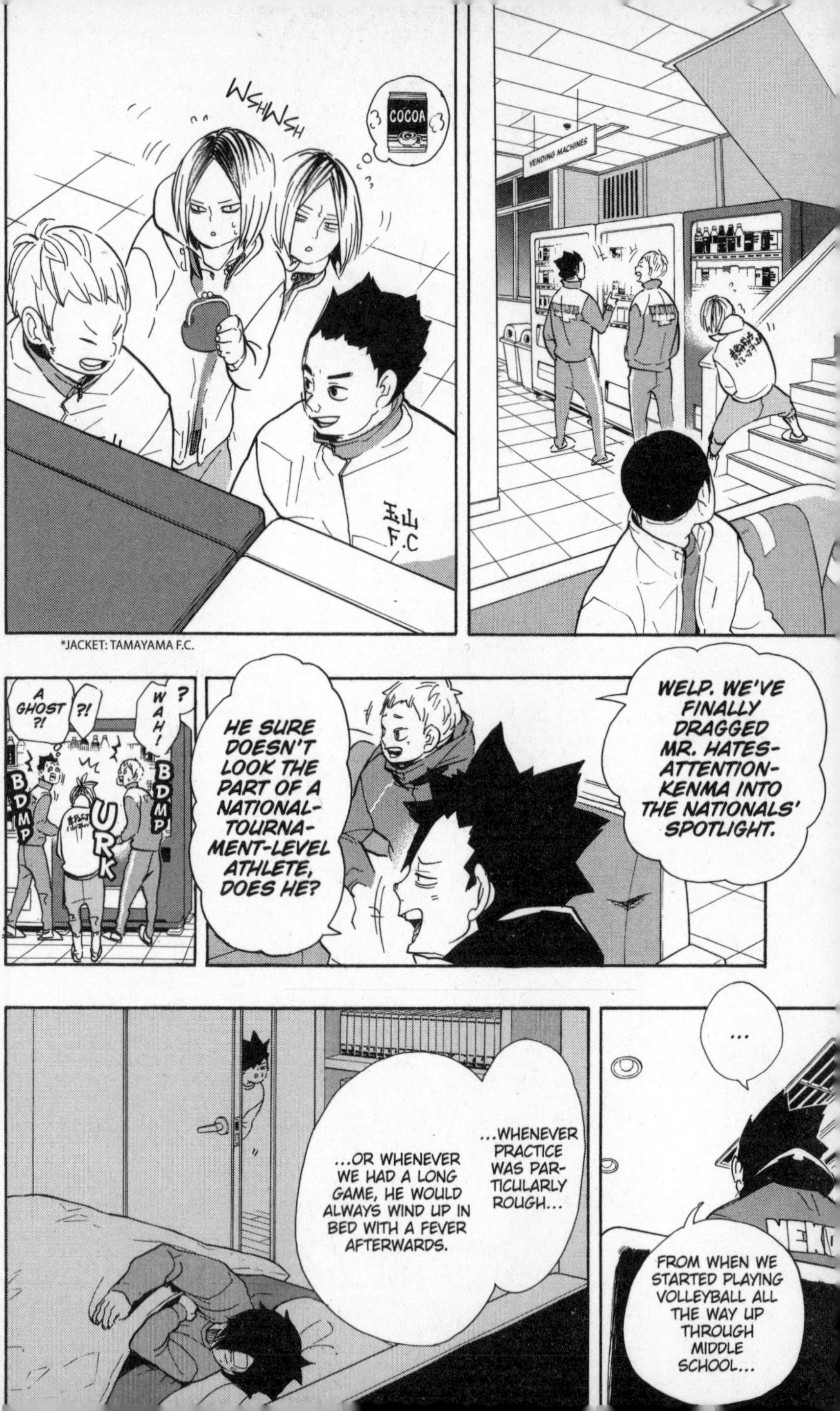
VENDING MACHINES
WSHWSH
COCOA
玉山
F.C
WELP. WE'VE FINALLY DRAGGED MR. HATES-ATTENTION-KENMA INTO THE NATIONALS' SPOTLIGHT.
HE SURE DOESN'T LOOK THE PART OF A NATIONAL-TOURNAMENT-LEVEL ATHLETE, DOES HE?
?
WAH!
?!
A GHOST ?!
BDMP
URK
BDMP
...
FROM WHEN WE STARTED PLAYING VOLLEYBALL ALL THE WAY UP THROUGH MIDDLE SCHOOL...
NEKO
...WHENEVER PRACTICE WAS PARTICULARLY ROUGH...
...OR WHENEVER WE HAD A LONG GAME, HE WOULD ALWAYS WIND UP IN BED WITH A FEVER AFTERWARDS.

*JACKET: TAMAYAMA F.C.

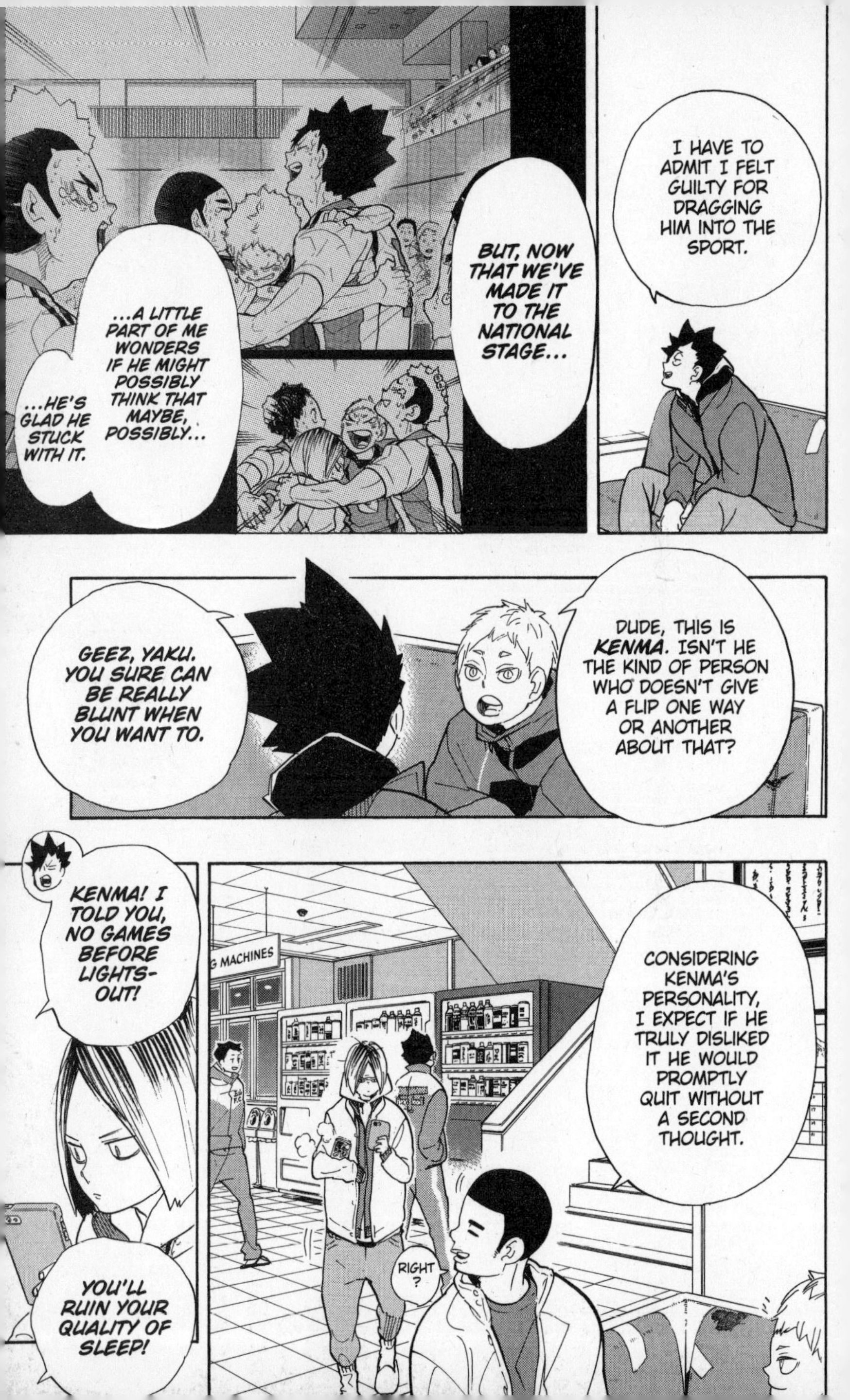
I HAVE TO ADMIT I FELT GUILTY FOR DRAGGING HIM INTO THE SPORT.
BUT, NOW THAT WE'VE MADE IT TO THE NATIONAL STAGE...
...A LITTLE PART OF ME WONDERS IF HE MIGHT POSSIBLY THINK THAT MAYBE, POSSIBLY...
...HE'S GLAD HE STUCK WITH IT.
DUDE, THIS IS KENMA. ISN'T HE THE KIND OF PERSON WHO DOESN'T GIVE A FLIP ONE WAY OR ANOTHER ABOUT THAT?
GEEZ, YAKU. YOU SURE CAN BE REALLY BLUNT WHEN YOU WANT TO.
CONSIDERING KENMA'S PERSONALITY, I EXPECT IF HE TRULY DISLIKED IT HE WOULD PROMPTLY QUIT WITHOUT A SECOND THOUGHT.
RIGHT?
KENMA! I TOLD YOU, NO GAMES BEFORE LIGHTS-OUT!
YOU'LL RUIN YOUR QUALITY OF SLEEP!

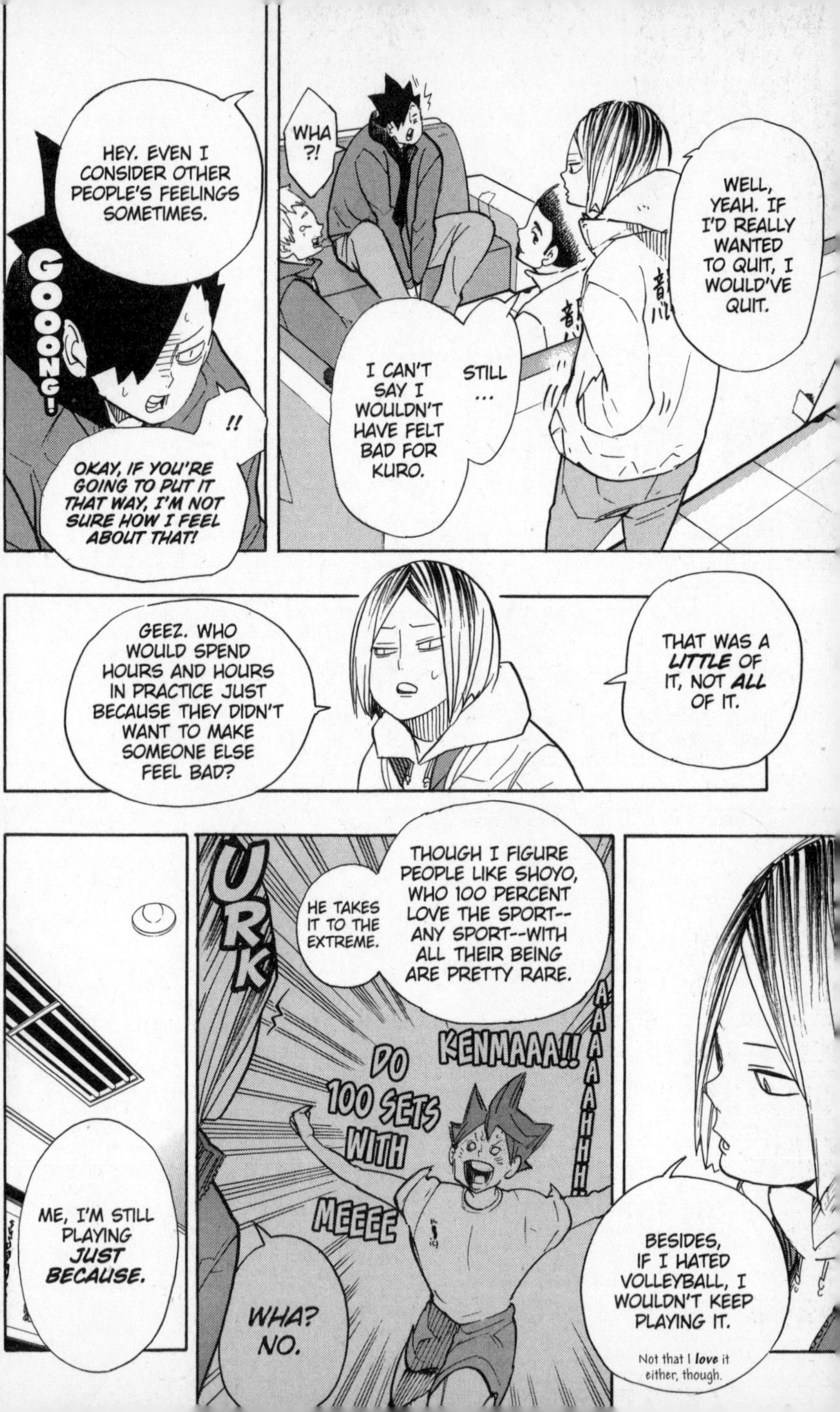
WELL, YEAH. IF I'D REALLY WANTED TO QUIT, I WOULD'VE QUIT.
WHA ?!
STILL ...
I CAN'T SAY I WOULDN'T HAVE FELT BAD FOR KURO.
HEY. EVEN I CONSIDER OTHER PEOPLE'S FEELINGS SOMETIMES.
GOOOONG!
!!
OKAY, IF YOU'RE GOING TO PUT IT THAT WAY, I'M NOT SURE HOW I FEEL ABOUT THAT!
THAT WAS A *LITTLE* OF IT, NOT *ALL* OF IT.
GEEZ. WHO WOULD SPEND HOURS AND HOURS IN PRACTICE JUST BECAUSE THEY DIDN'T WANT TO MAKE SOMEONE ELSE FEEL BAD?
BESIDES, IF I HATED VOLLEYBALL, I WOULDN'T KEEP PLAYING IT.
Not that I *love* it either, though.
THOUGH I FIGURE PEOPLE LIKE SHOYO, WHO 100 PERCENT LOVE THE SPORT-- ANY SPORT--WITH ALL THEIR BEING ARE PRETTY RARE.
HE TAKES IT TO THE EXTREME.
URK
KENMAAA!!
AAAAAHHH!
DO 100 SETS WITH MEEEE
WHA? NO.
ME, I'M STILL PLAYING *JUST BECAUSE.*

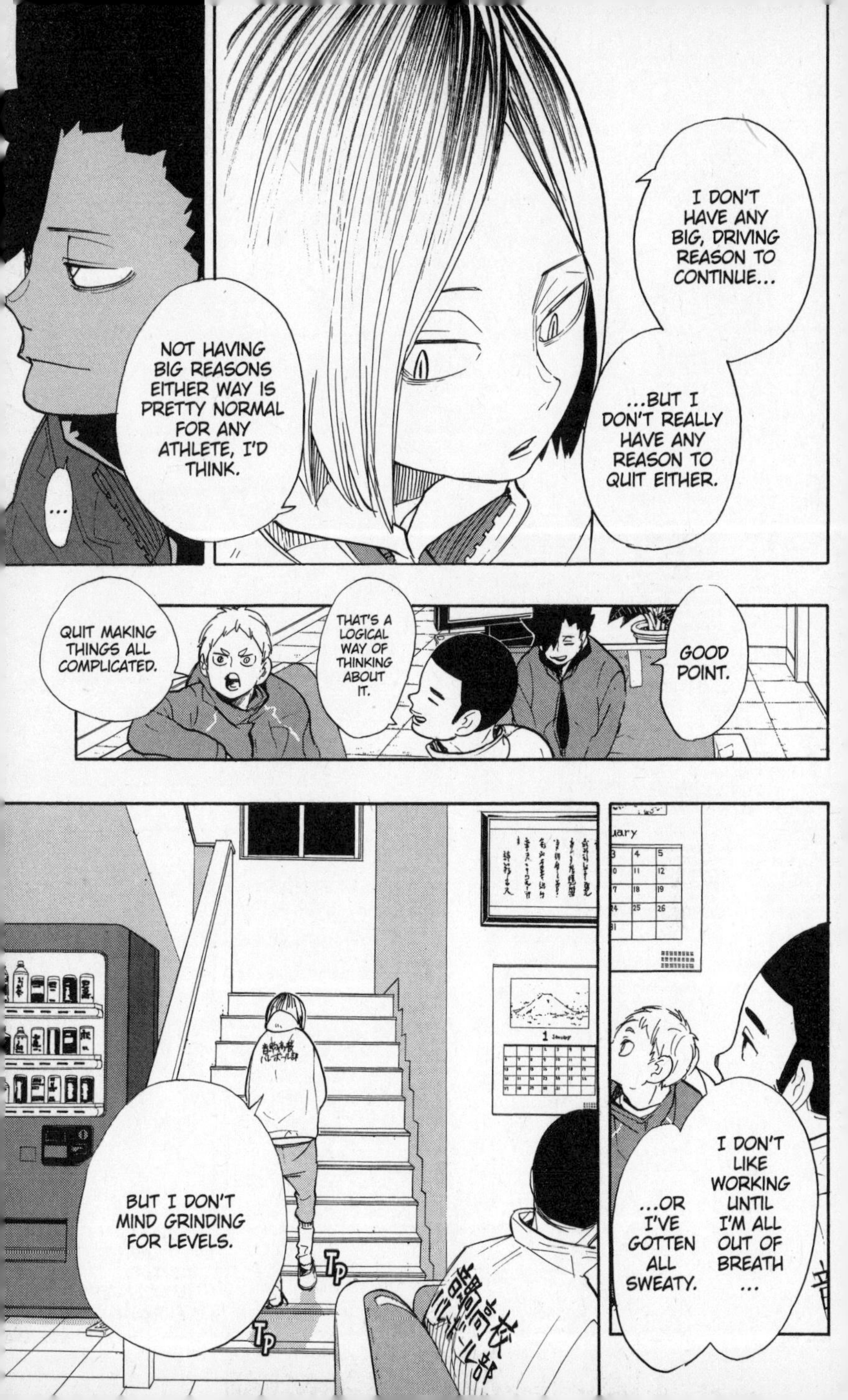
I DON'T HAVE ANY BIG, DRIVING REASON TO CONTINUE...
...BUT I DON'T REALLY HAVE ANY REASON TO QUIT EITHER.
NOT HAVING BIG REASONS EITHER WAY IS PRETTY NORMAL FOR ANY ATHLETE, I'D THINK.
...
GOOD POINT.
THAT'S A LOGICAL WAY OF THINKING ABOUT IT.
QUIT MAKING THINGS ALL COMPLICATED.
I DON'T LIKE WORKING UNTIL I'M ALL OUT OF BREATH...
...OR I'VE GOTTEN ALL SWEATY.
BUT I DON'T MIND GRINDING FOR LEVELS.
Tp
Tp

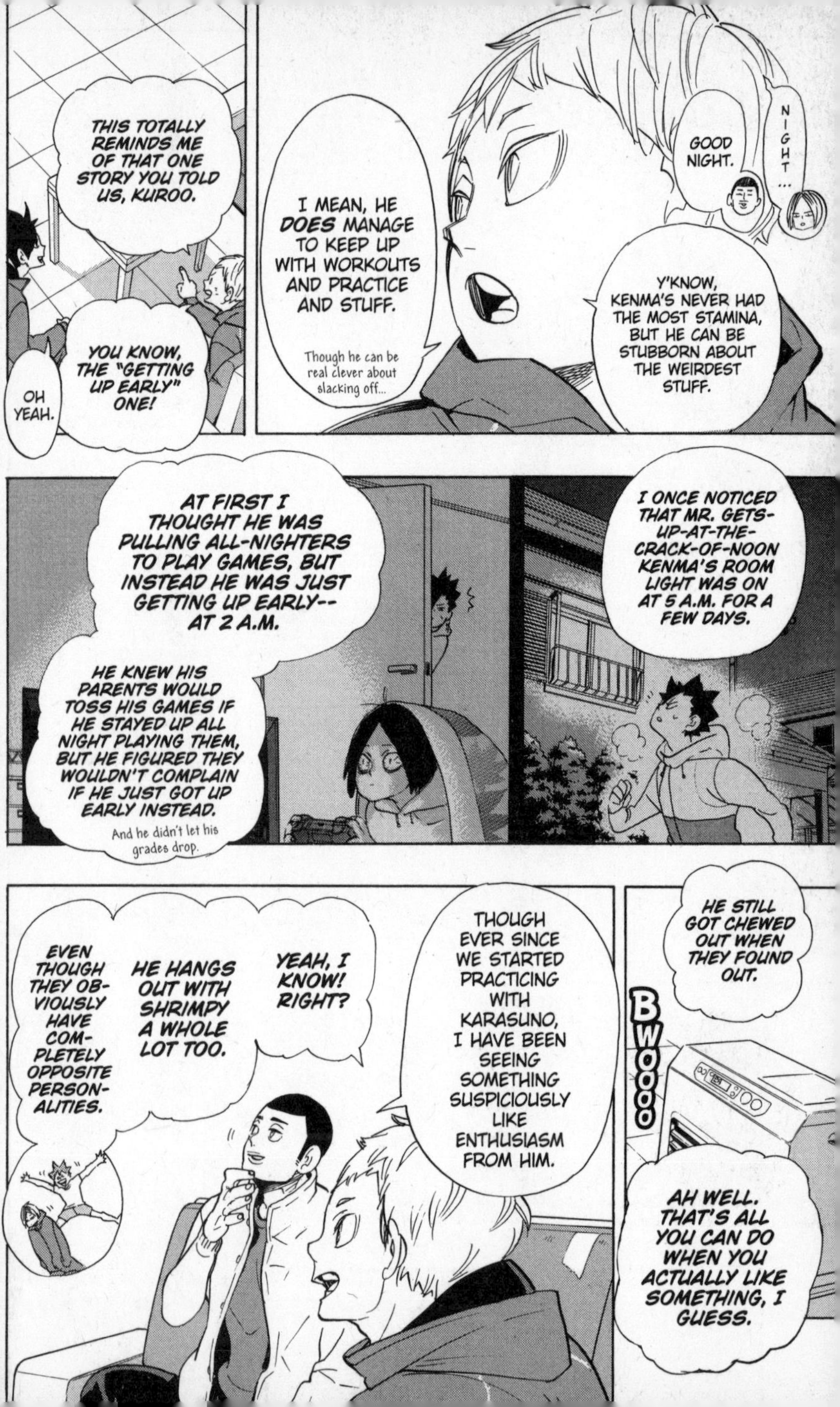
NIGHT...
GOOD NIGHT.
Y'KNOW, KENMA'S NEVER HAD THE MOST STAMINA, BUT HE CAN BE STUBBORN ABOUT THE WEIRDEST STUFF.
I MEAN, HE DOES MANAGE TO KEEP UP WITH WORKOUTS AND PRACTICE AND STUFF.
Though he can be real clever about slacking off...
THIS TOTALLY REMINDS ME OF THAT ONE STORY YOU TOLD US, KUROO.
YOU KNOW, THE "GETTING UP EARLY" ONE!
OH YEAH.
I ONCE NOTICED THAT MR. GETS-UP-AT-THE-CRACK-OF-NOON KENMA'S ROOM LIGHT WAS ON AT 5 A.M. FOR A FEW DAYS.
AT FIRST I THOUGHT HE WAS PULLING ALL-NIGHTERS TO PLAY GAMES, BUT INSTEAD HE WAS JUST GETTING UP EARLY--AT 2 A.M.
HE KNEW HIS PARENTS WOULD TOSS HIS GAMES IF HE STAYED UP ALL NIGHT PLAYING THEM, BUT HE FIGURED THEY WOULDN'T COMPLAIN IF HE JUST GOT UP EARLY INSTEAD.
And he didn't let his grades drop.
HE STILL GOT CHEWED OUT WHEN THEY FOUND OUT.
BWOOOO
AH WELL. THAT'S ALL YOU CAN DO WHEN YOU ACTUALLY LIKE SOMETHING, I GUESS.
THOUGH EVER SINCE WE STARTED PRACTICING WITH KARASUNO, I HAVE BEEN SEEING SOMETHING SUSPICIOUSLY LIKE ENTHUSIASM FROM HIM.
YEAH, I KNOW! RIGHT?
HE HANGS OUT WITH SHRIMPY A WHOLE LOT TOO.
EVEN THOUGH THEY OBVIOUSLY HAVE COMPLETELY OPPOSITE PERSONALITIES.

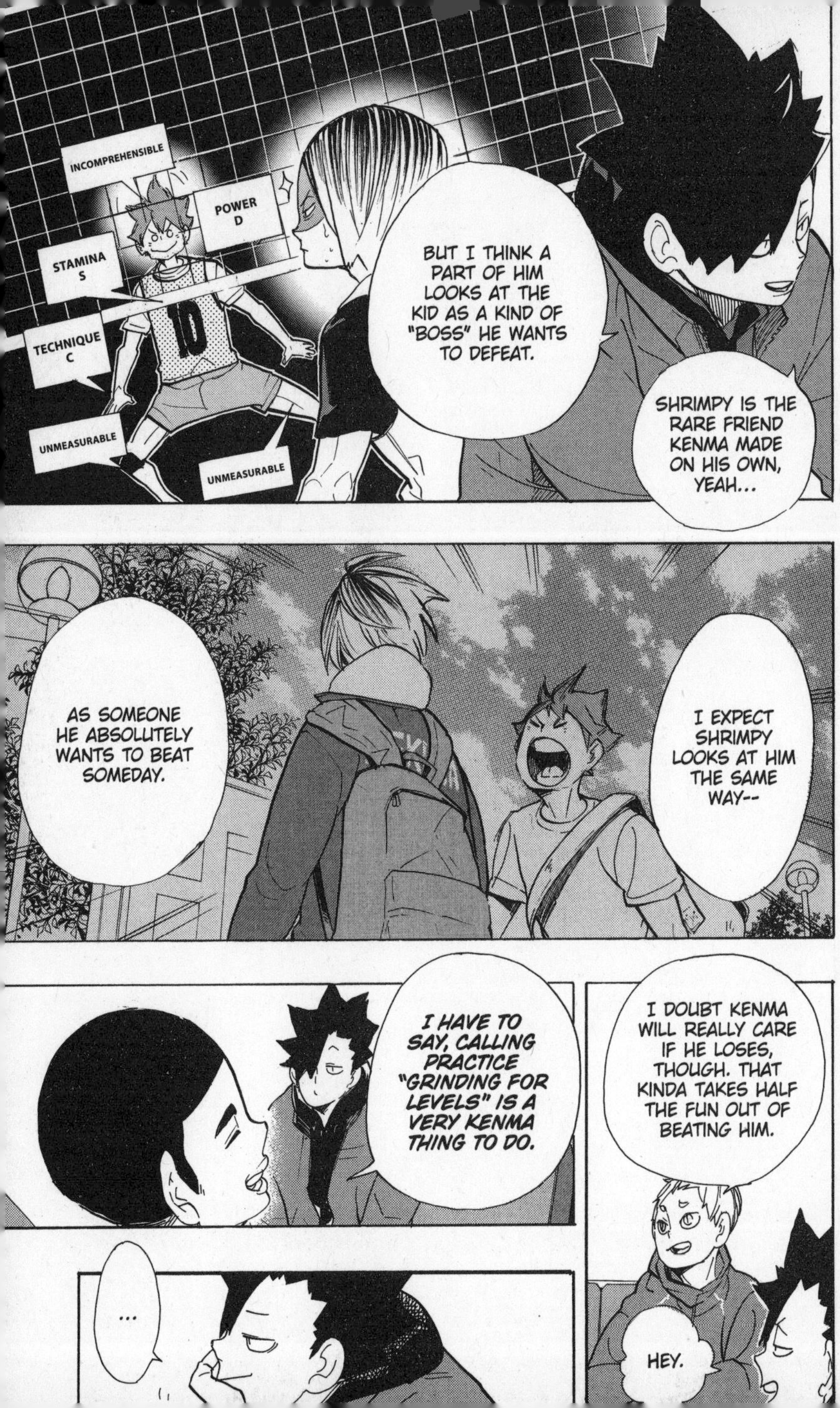

SHRIMPY IS THE RARE FRIEND KENMA MADE ON HIS OWN, YEAH...
BUT I THINK A PART OF HIM LOOKS AT THE KID AS A KIND OF "BOSS" HE WANTS TO DEFEAT.
POWER D
INCOMPREHENSIBLE
STAMINA S
TECHNIQUE C
UNMEASURABLE
UNMEASURABLE
I EXPECT SHRIMPY LOOKS AT HIM THE SAME WAY--
AS SOMEONE HE ABSOLUTELY WANTS TO BEAT SOMEDAY.
I DOUBT KENMA WILL REALLY CARE IF HE LOSES, THOUGH. THAT KINDA TAKES HALF THE FUN OUT OF BEATING HIM.
HEY.
I HAVE TO SAY, CALLING PRACTICE "GRINDING FOR LEVELS" IS A VERY KENMA THING TO DO.
...

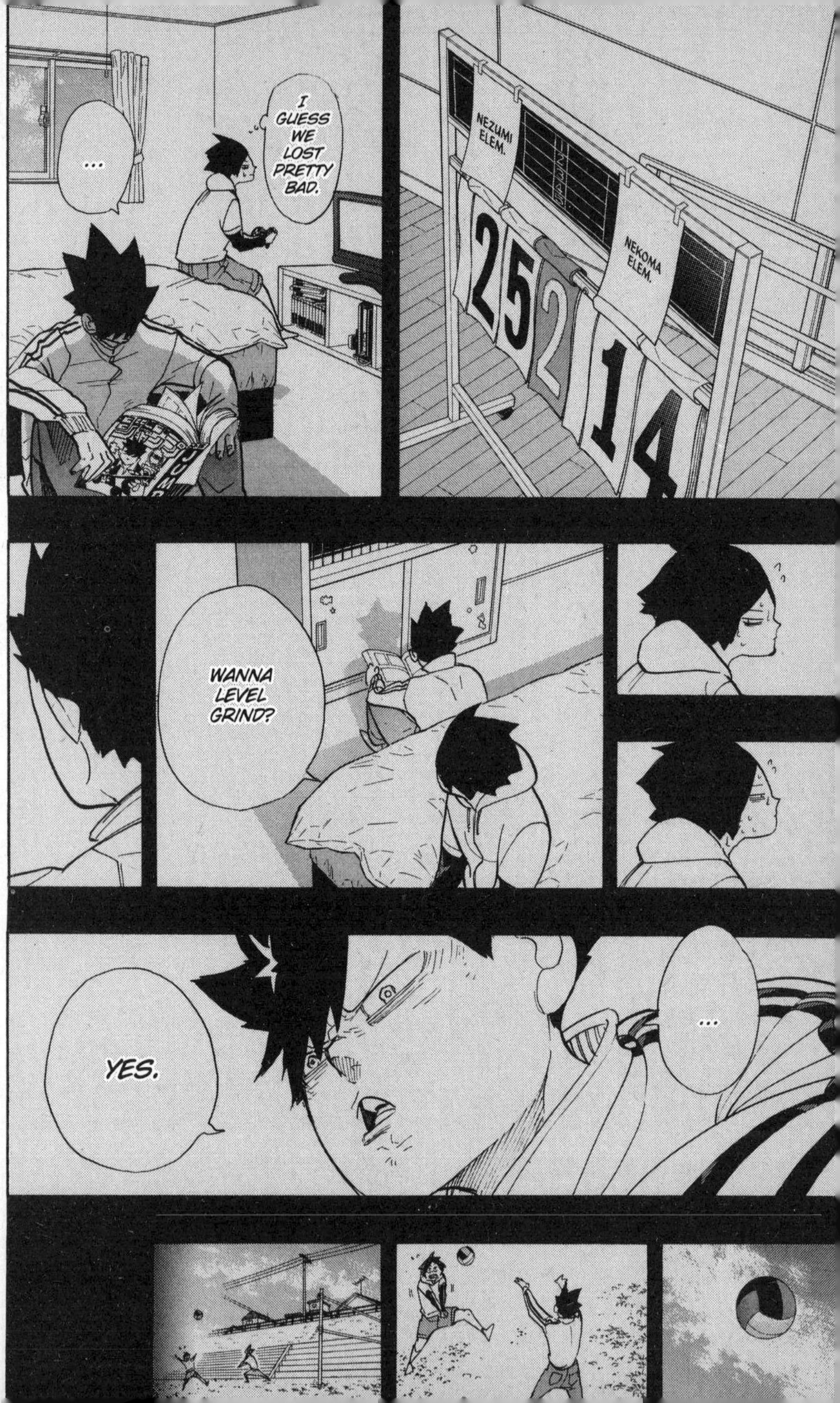
NEZUMI ELEM.
NEKOMA ELEM.
25
2
14
I GUESS WE LOST PRETTY BAD.
...
WANNA LEVEL GRIND?
...
YES.

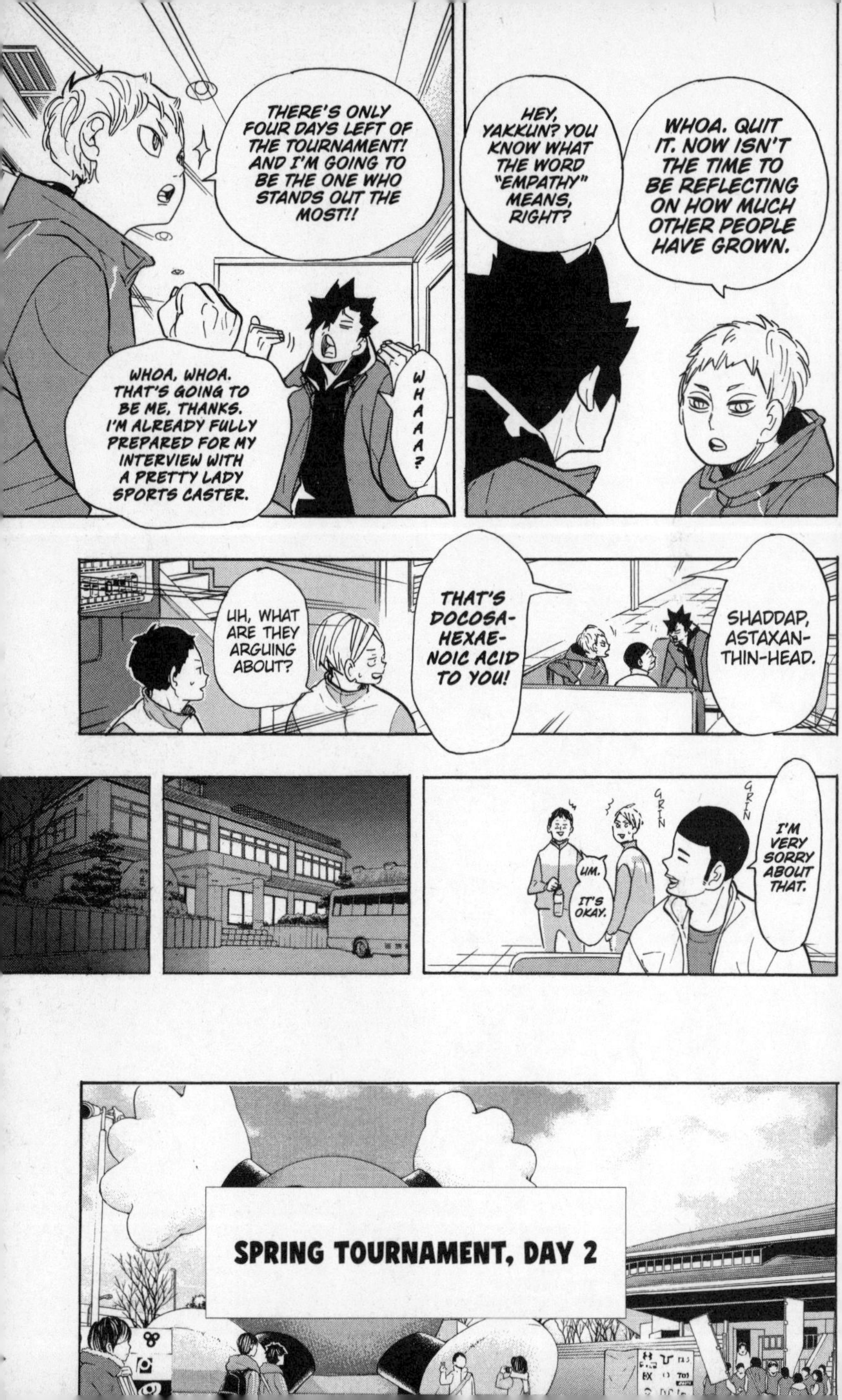
WHOA. QUIT IT. NOW ISN'T THE TIME TO BE REFLECTING ON HOW MUCH OTHER PEOPLE HAVE GROWN.
HEY, YAKKUN? YOU KNOW WHAT THE WORD "EMPATHY" MEANS, RIGHT?
THERE'S ONLY FOUR DAYS LEFT OF THE TOURNAMENT! AND I'M GOING TO BE THE ONE WHO STANDS OUT THE MOST!!
WHOA, WHOA. THAT'S GOING TO BE ME, THANKS. I'M ALREADY FULLY PREPARED FOR MY INTERVIEW WITH A PRETTY LADY SPORTS CASTER.
WHAAAA?
SHADDAP, ASTAXAN-THIN-HEAD.
THAT'S DOCOSA-HEXAE-NOIC ACID TO YOU!
UH, WHAT ARE THEY ARGUING ABOUT?
GRIN
I'M VERY SORRY ABOUT THAT.
GRIN
UM.
IT'S OKAY.
SPRING TOURNAMENT, DAY 2

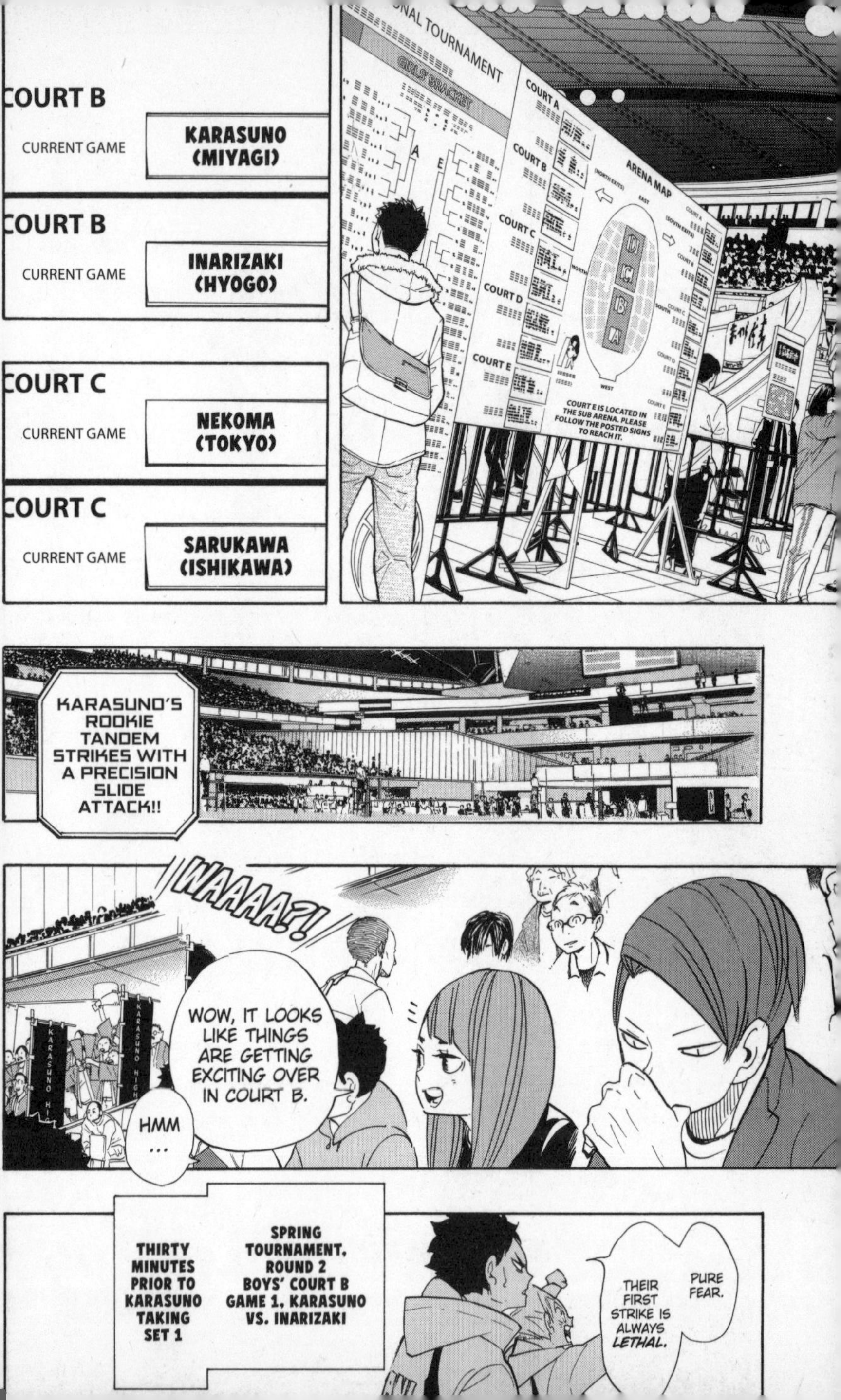
NAL TOURNAMENT
GIRLS' BRACKET
COURT A
COURT B
COURT C
COURT D
COURT E
ARENA MAP
(NORTH EXITS)
(SOUTH EXITS)
COURT E IS LOCATED IN THE SUB ARENA. PLEASE FOLLOW THE POSTED SIGNS TO REACH IT.
COURT B
CURRENT GAME
KARASUNO (MIYAGI)
COURT B
CURRENT GAME
INARIZAKI (HYOGO)
COURT C
CURRENT GAME
NEKOMA (TOKYO)
COURT C
CURRENT GAME
SARUKAWA (ISHIKAWA)
KARASUNO'S ROOKIE TANDEM STRIKES WITH A PRECISION SLIDE ATTACK!!
WAAAA?!
WOW, IT LOOKS LIKE THINGS ARE GETTING EXCITING OVER IN COURT B.
HMM...
SPRING TOURNAMENT, ROUND 2 BOYS' COURT B GAME 1, KARASUNO VS. INARIZAKI
THIRTY MINUTES PRIOR TO KARASUNO TAKING SET 1
PURE FEAR.
THEIR FIRST STRIKE IS ALWAYS *LETHAL.*

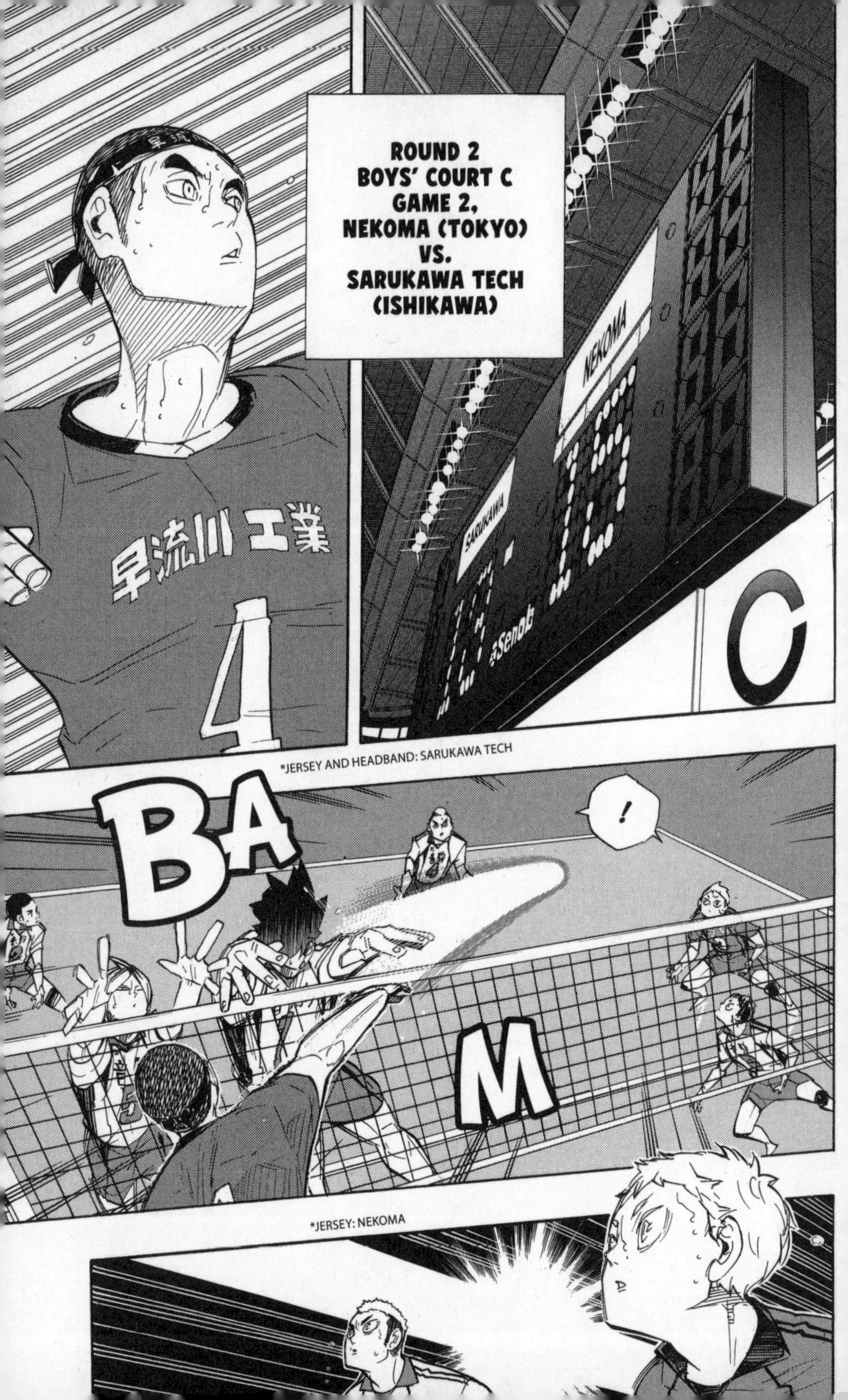
ROUND 2
BOYS' COURT C
GAME 2,
NEKOMA (TOKYO)
VS.
SARUKAWA TECH
(ISHIKAWA)
NEKOMA
SARUKAWA
C
早流川 工業
4
*JERSEY AND HEADBAND: SARUKAWA TECH
!
BAM
*JERSEY: NEKOMA

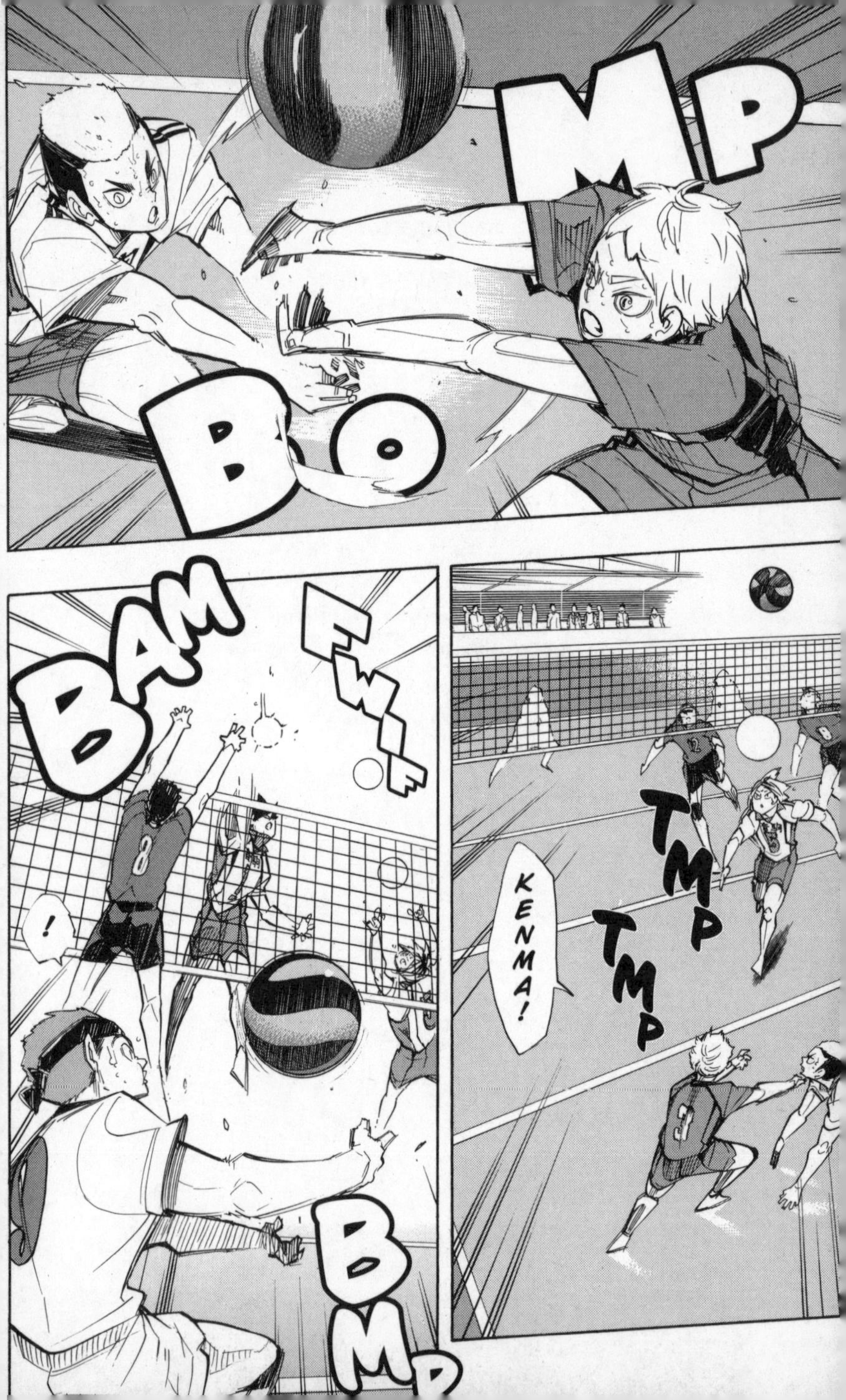
BOMP
TMP
TMP
KENMA!
FWIF
BAM
!
BMP

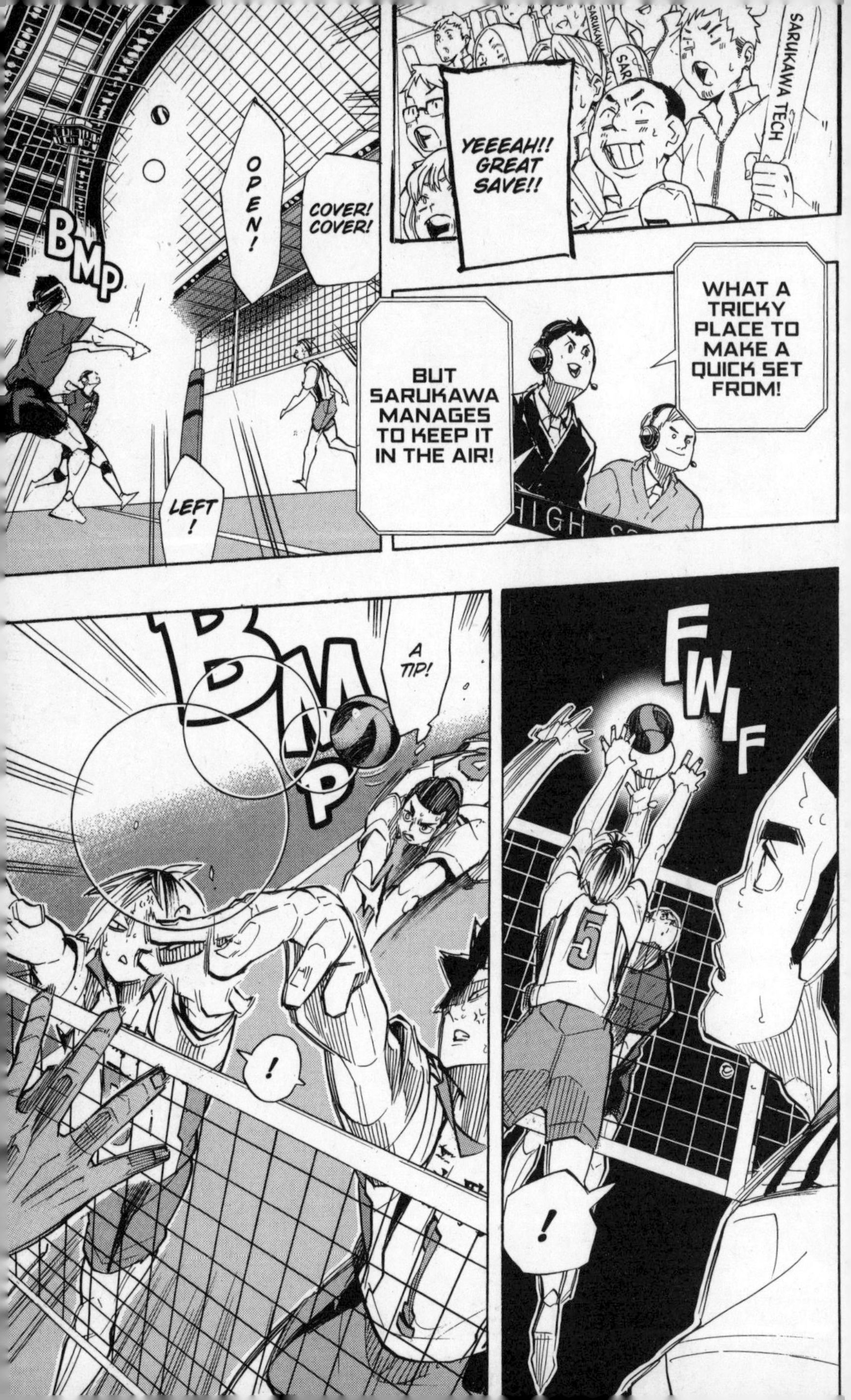

SARUKAWA TECH
SARUKAWA
YEEEAH!! GREAT SAVE!!
WHAT A TRICKY PLACE TO MAKE A QUICK SET FROM!
BUT SARUKAWA MANAGES TO KEEP IT IN THE AIR!
OPEN!
COVER! COVER!
BMP
LEFT!
FWIF
!
A TIP!
BMP
!

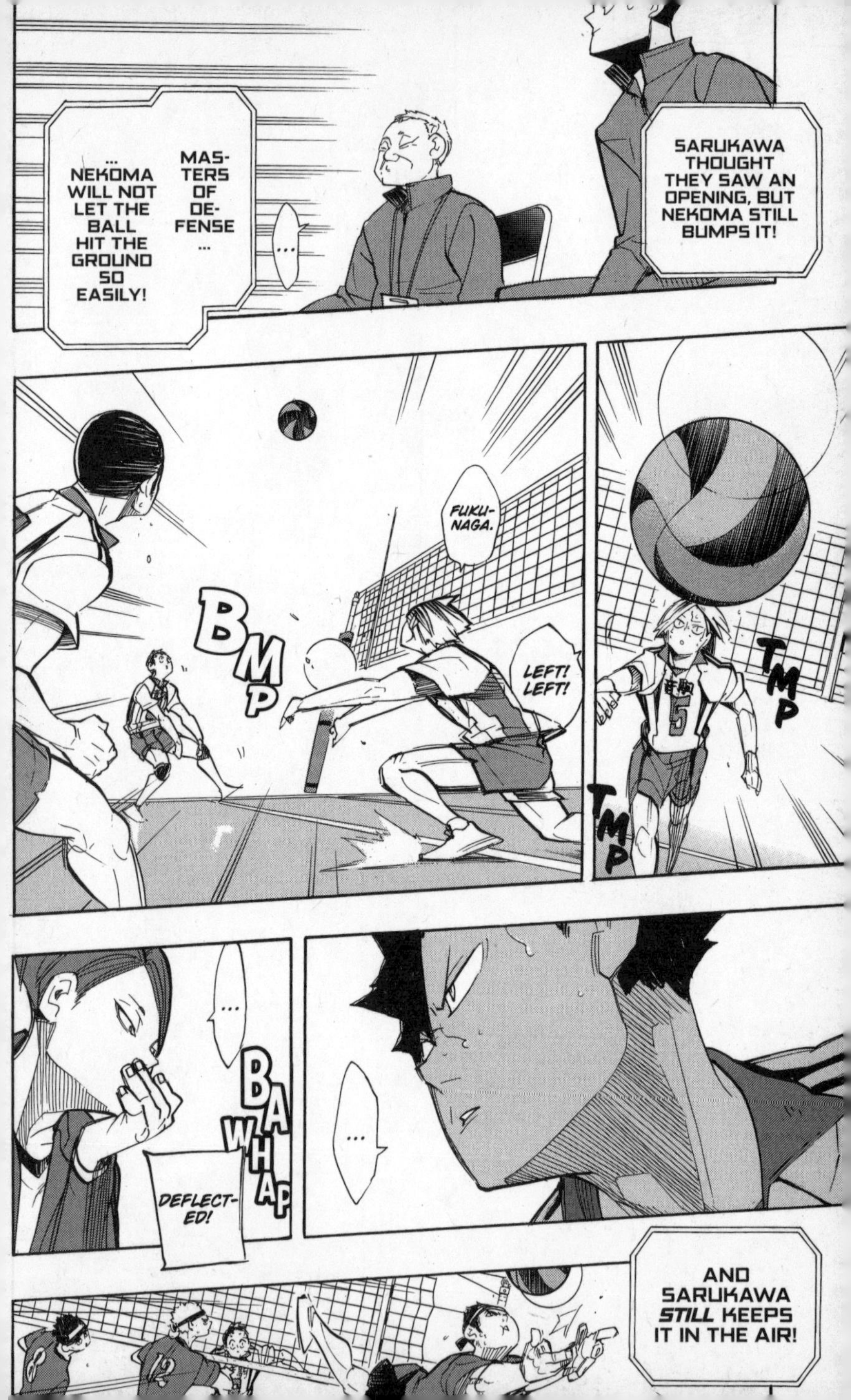

SARUKAWA THOUGHT THEY SAW AN OPENING, BUT NEKOMA STILL BUMPS IT!
...
MAS-TERS OF DE-FENSE ...
... NEKOMA WILL NOT LET THE BALL HIT THE GROUND SO EASILY!
TMP
TMP
FUKU-NAGA.
LEFT! LEFT!
BMP
...
...
BAWHAP
DEFLECT-ED!
AND SARUKAWA *STILL* KEEPS IT IN THE AIR!

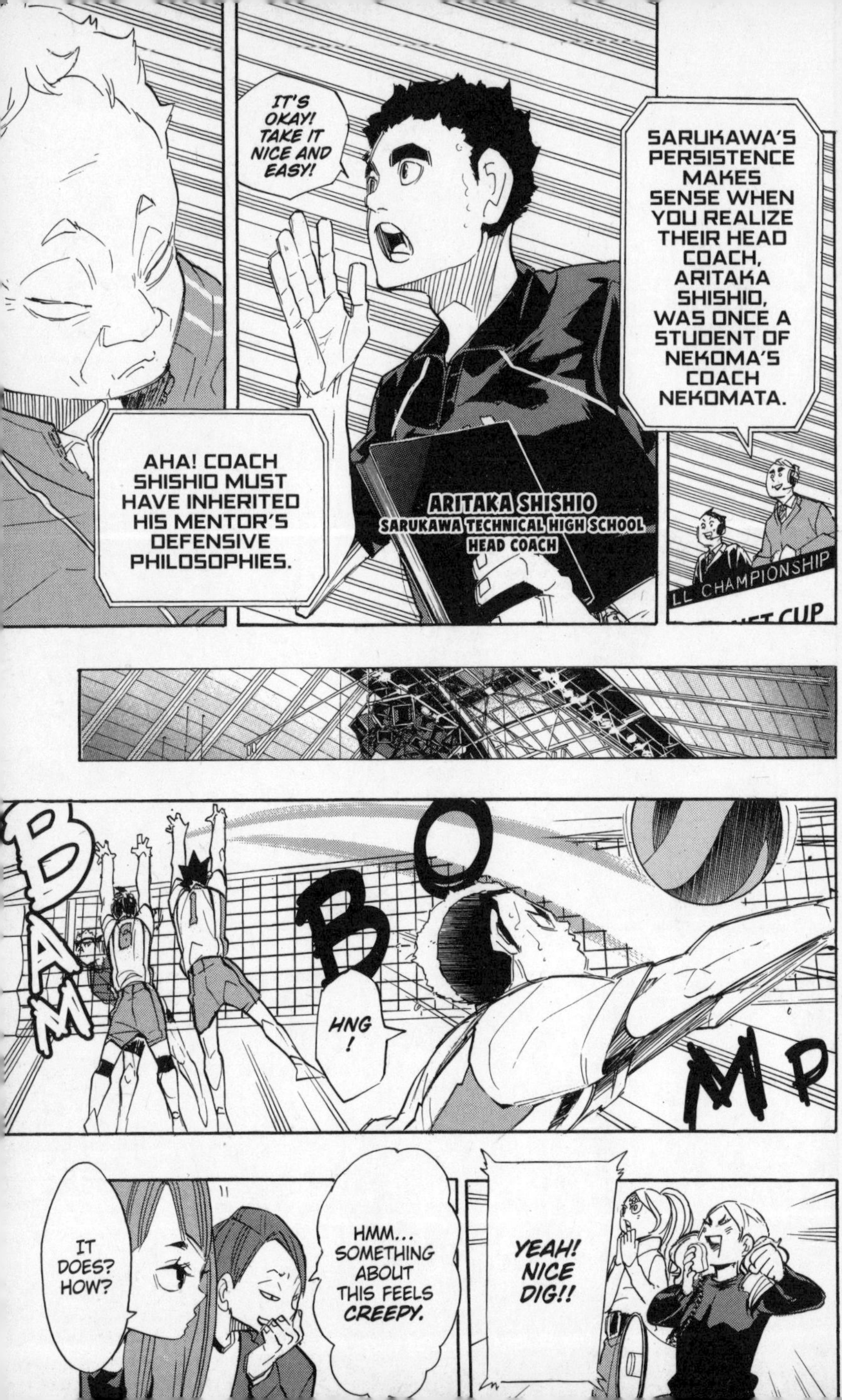
SARUKAWA'S PERSISTENCE MAKES SENSE WHEN YOU REALIZE THEIR HEAD COACH, ARITAKA SHISHIO, WAS ONCE A STUDENT OF NEKOMA'S COACH NEKOMATA.
LL CHAMPIONSHIP
IT'S OKAY! TAKE IT NICE AND EASY!
ARITAKA SHISHIO
SARUKAWA TECHNICAL HIGH SCHOOL
HEAD COACH
AHA! COACH SHISHIO MUST HAVE INHERITED HIS MENTOR'S DEFENSIVE PHILOSOPHIES.
BOMP
HNG!
BAM
YEAH! NICE DIG!!
HMM... SOMETHING ABOUT THIS FEELS CREEPY.
IT DOES? HOW?

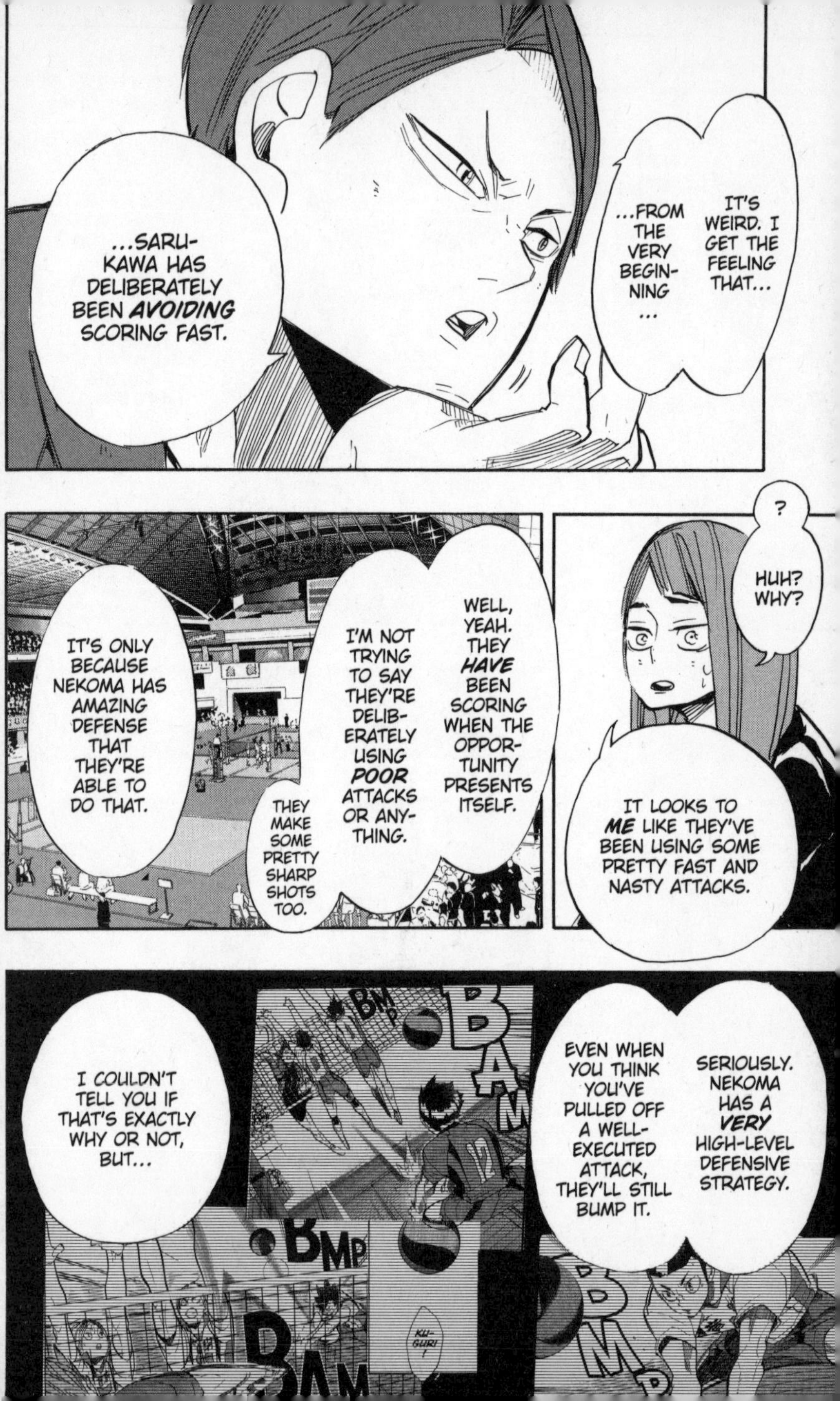
IT'S WEIRD. I GET THE FEELING THAT...
...FROM THE VERY BEGINNING...
...SARUKAWA HAS DELIBERATELY BEEN AVOIDING SCORING FAST.
?
HUH? WHY?
IT LOOKS TO ME LIKE THEY'VE BEEN USING SOME PRETTY FAST AND NASTY ATTACKS.
WELL, YEAH. THEY HAVE BEEN SCORING WHEN THE OPPORTUNITY PRESENTS ITSELF.
I'M NOT TRYING TO SAY THEY'RE DELIBERATELY USING POOR ATTACKS OR ANYTHING.
THEY MAKE SOME PRETTY SHARP SHOTS TOO.
IT'S ONLY BECAUSE NEKOMA HAS AMAZING DEFENSE THAT THEY'RE ABLE TO DO THAT.
SERIOUSLY. NEKOMA HAS A VERY HIGH-LEVEL DEFENSIVE STRATEGY.
EVEN WHEN YOU THINK YOU'VE PULLED OFF A WELL-EXECUTED ATTACK, THEY'LL STILL BUMP IT.
BAM
BMP
I COULDN'T TELL YOU IF THAT'S EXACTLY WHY OR NOT, BUT...
BMP
BMP
KUGURI!
BAM

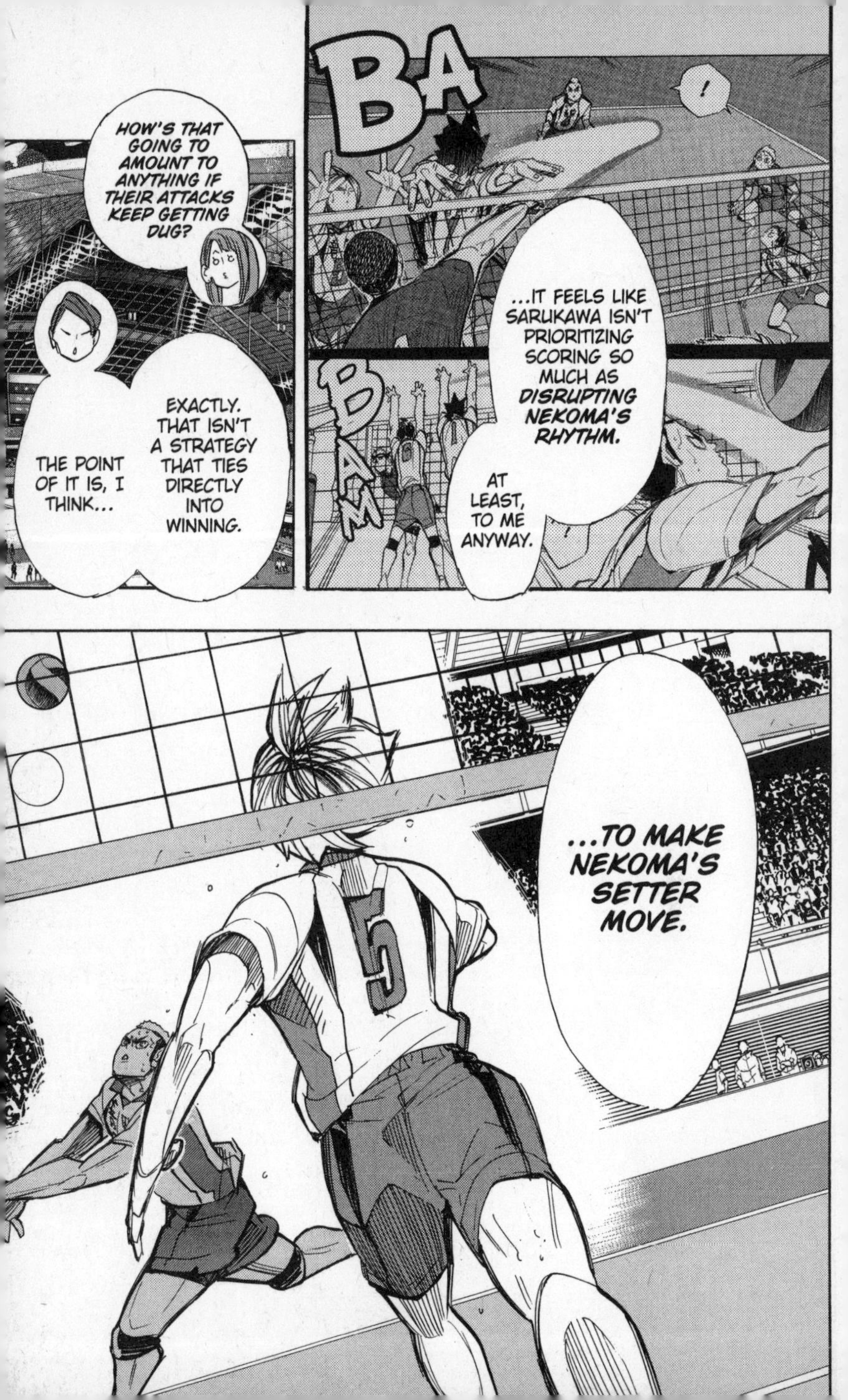
BA
!
BAM
...IT FEELS LIKE SARUKAWA ISN'T PRIORITIZING SCORING SO MUCH AS DISRUPTING NEKOMA'S RHYTHM.
AT LEAST, TO ME ANYWAY.
HOW'S THAT GOING TO AMOUNT TO ANYTHING IF THEIR ATTACKS KEEP GETTING DUG?
EXACTLY. THAT ISN'T A STRATEGY THAT TIES DIRECTLY INTO WINNING.
THE POINT OF IT IS, I THINK...
...TO MAKE NEKOMA'S SETTER MOVE.

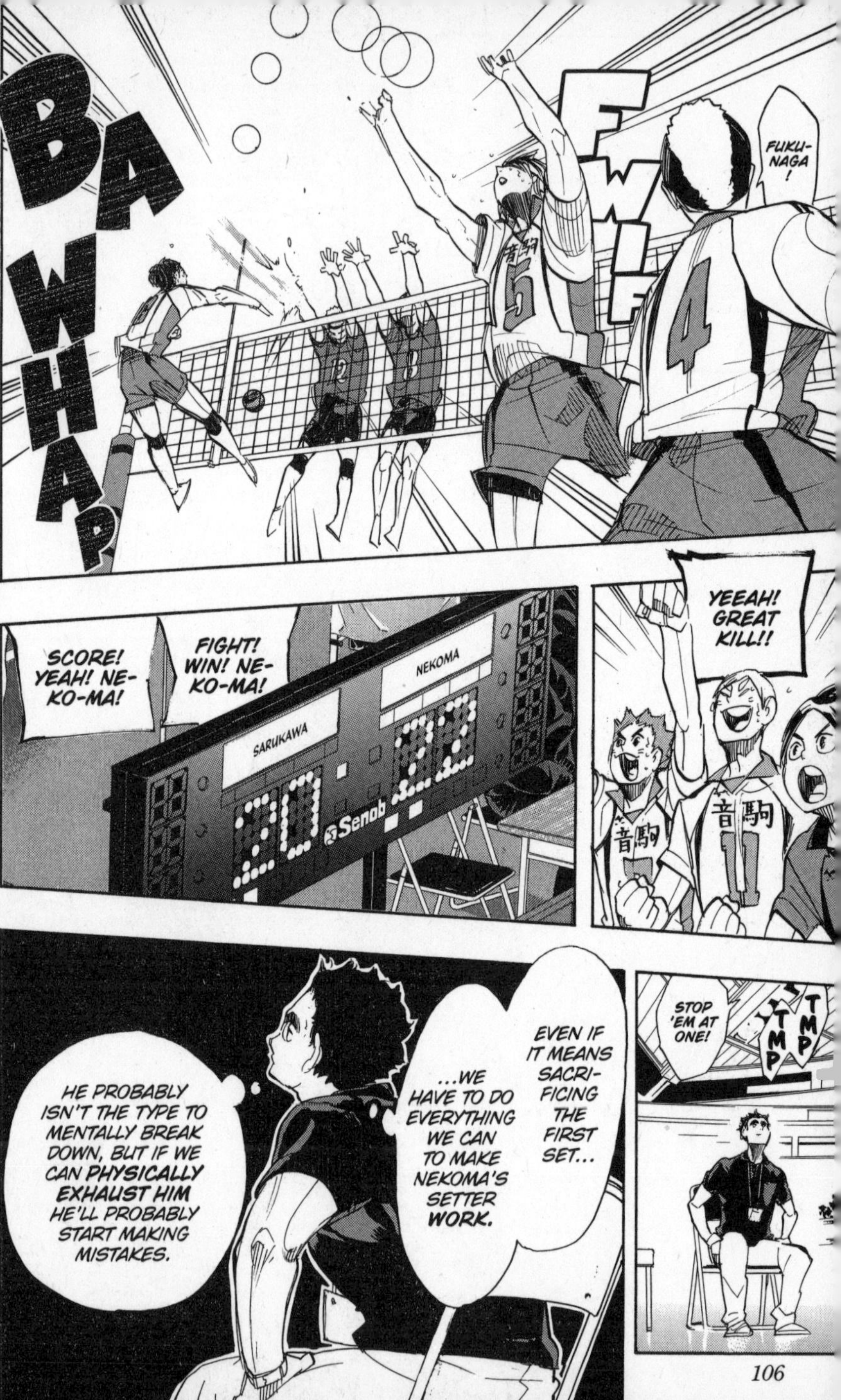
FUKU-NAGA!
FWIF
BAWHAP
YEEAH! GREAT KILL!!
FIGHT! WIN! NE-KO-MA!
SCORE! YEAH! NE-KO-MA!
NEKOMA
SARUKAWA
Senob
STOP 'EM AT ONE!
TMP TMP TMP
EVEN IF IT MEANS SACRIFICING THE FIRST SET...
...WE HAVE TO DO EVERYTHING WE CAN TO MAKE NEKOMA'S SETTER WORK.
HE PROBABLY ISN'T THE TYPE TO MENTALLY BREAK DOWN, BUT IF WE CAN PHYSICALLY EXHAUST HIM HE'LL PROBABLY START MAKING MISTAKES.

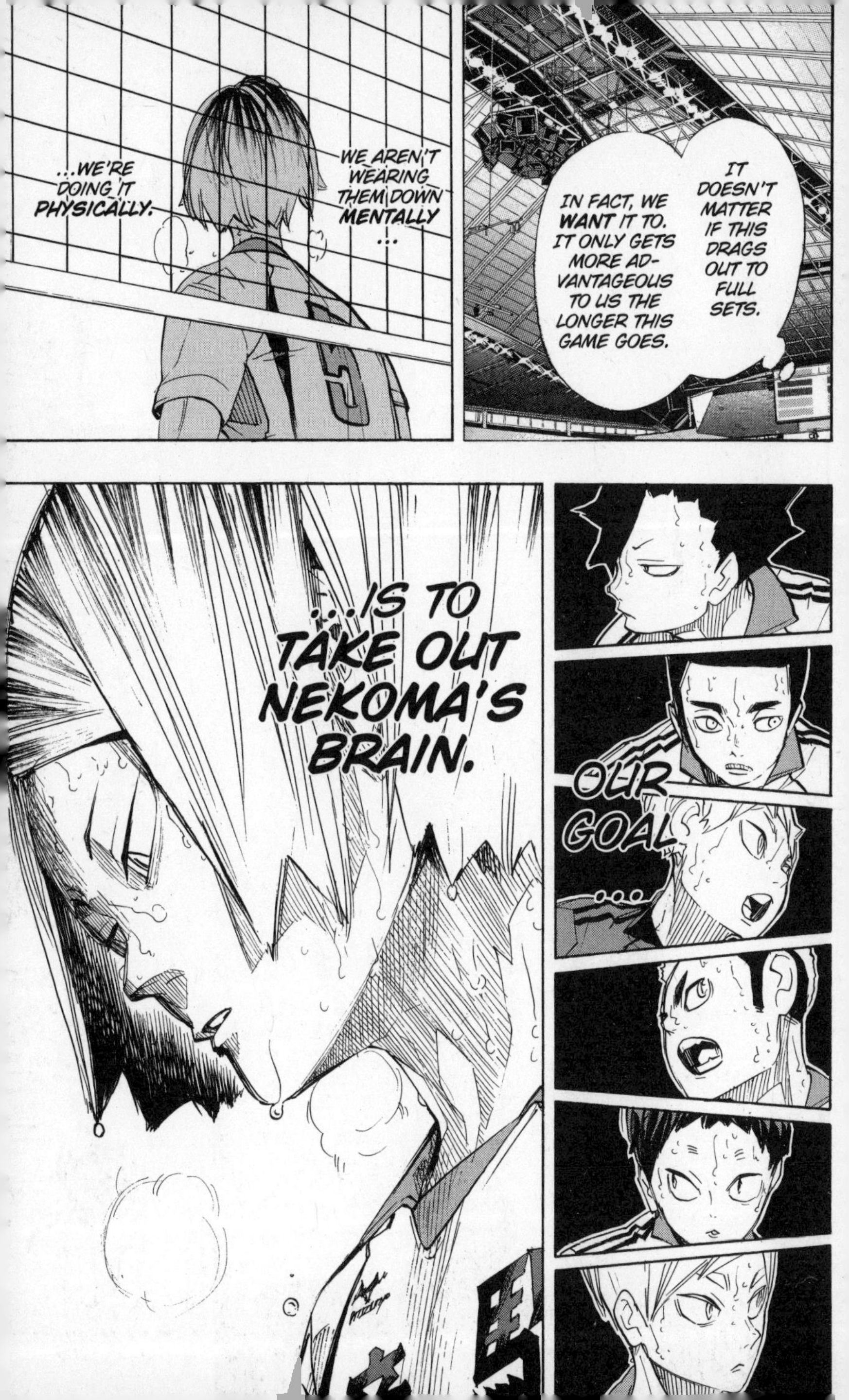
IT DOESN'T MATTER IF THIS DRAGS OUT TO FULL SETS.
IN FACT, WE WANT IT TO. IT ONLY GETS MORE ADVANTAGEOUS TO US THE LONGER THIS GAME GOES.
WE AREN'T WEARING THEM DOWN MENTALLY...
...WE'RE DOING IT PHYSICALLY.
OUR GOAL
...IS TO TAKE OUT NEKOMA'S BRAIN.

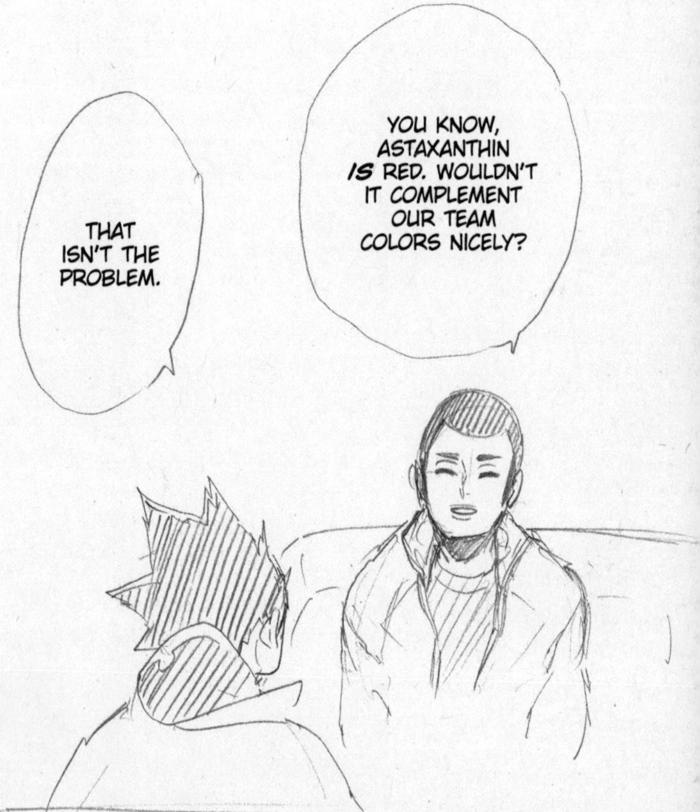
YOU KNOW, ASTAXANTHIN *IS* RED. WOULDN'T IT COMPLEMENT OUR TEAM COLORS NICELY?
THAT ISN'T THE PROBLEM.

CHAPTER 266: Cats vs. Monkeys

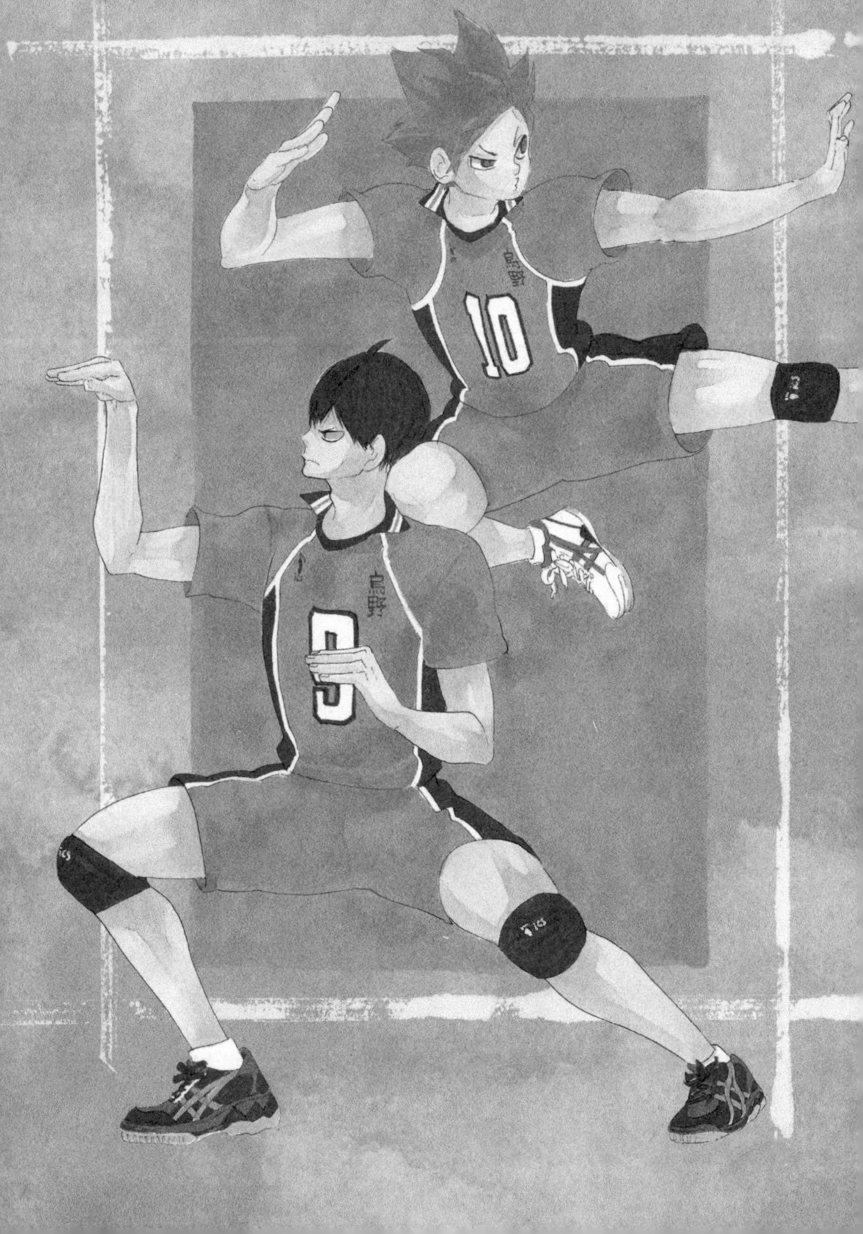

HAIKYU!!

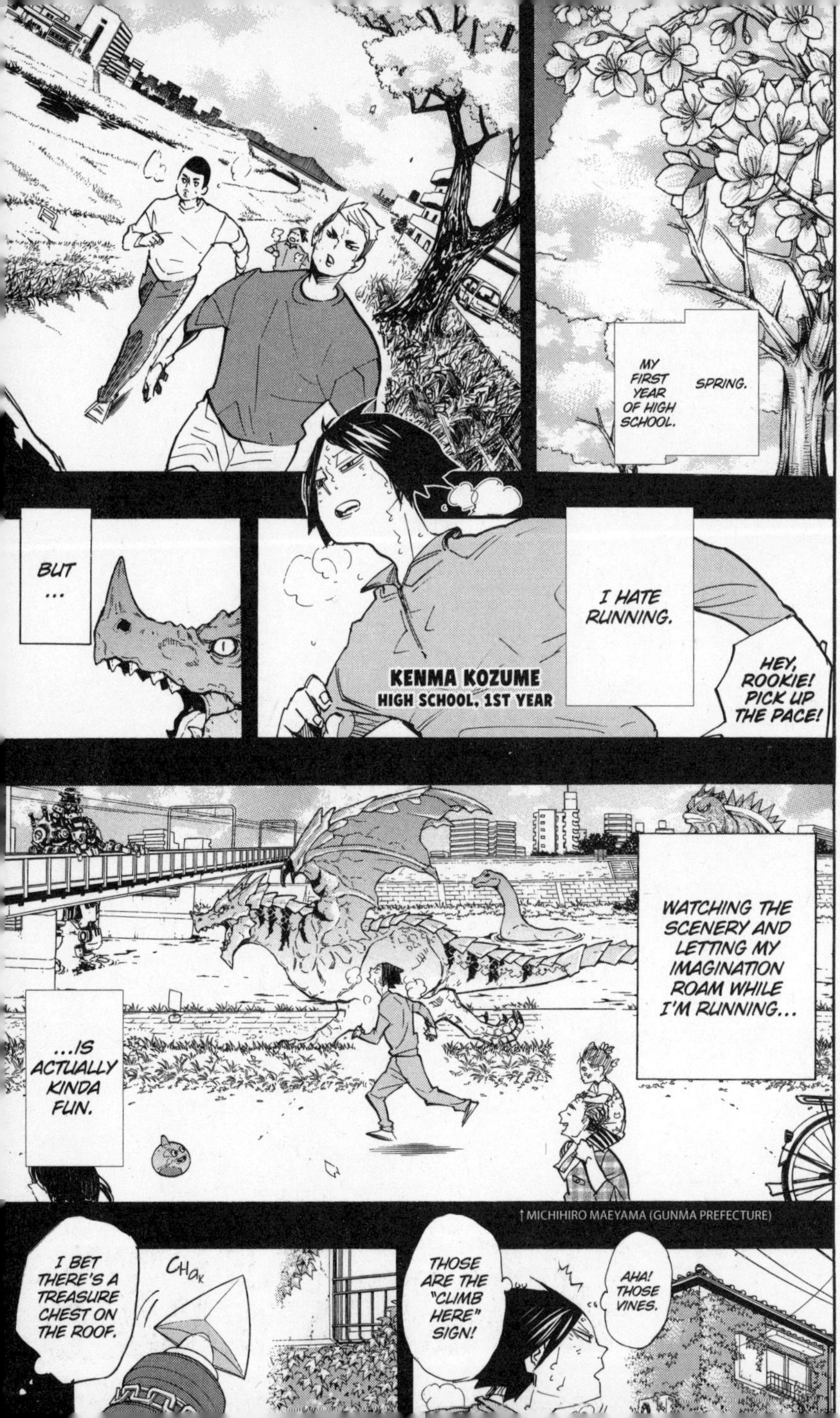
SPRING.
MY FIRST YEAR OF HIGH SCHOOL.
HEY, ROOKIE! PICK UP THE PACE!
I HATE RUNNING.
KENMA KOZUME
HIGH SCHOOL, 1ST YEAR
BUT ...
WATCHING THE SCENERY AND LETTING MY IMAGINATION ROAM WHILE I'M RUNNING...
...IS ACTUALLY KINDA FUN.
↑MICHIHIRO MAEYAMA (GUNMA PREFECTURE)
AHA! THOSE VINES.
THOSE ARE THE "CLIMB HERE" SIGN!
CHAK
I BET THERE'S A TREASURE CHEST ON THE ROOF.

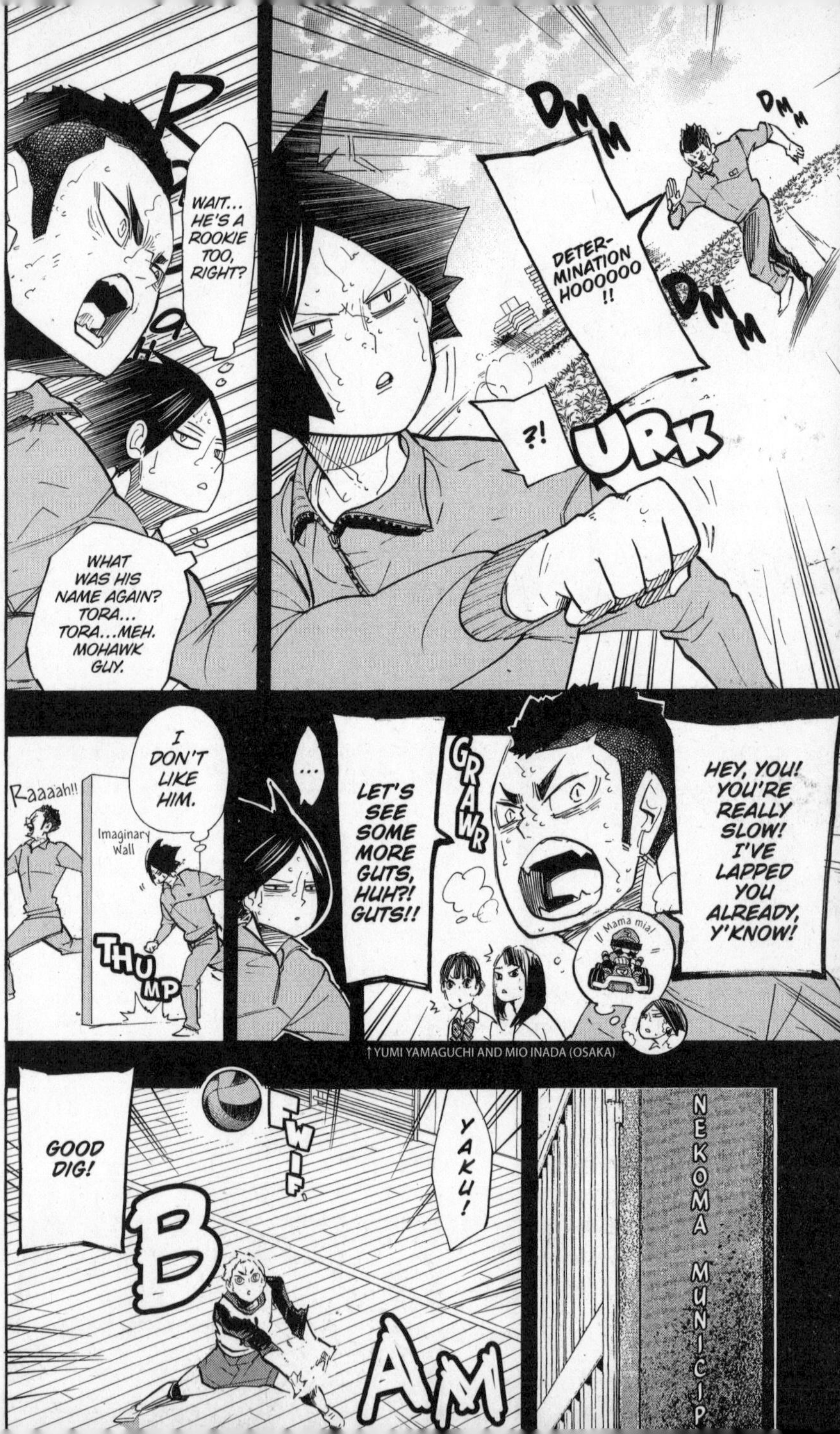
DMM
DMM
DETERMINATION HOOOOOO !!
DMM
?!
URK
WAIT... HE'S A ROOKIE TOO, RIGHT?
WHAT WAS HIS NAME AGAIN? TORA... TORA...MEH. MOHAWK GUY.
HEY, YOU! YOU'RE REALLY SLOW! I'VE LAPPED YOU ALREADY, Y'KNOW!
GRAWR
Mama mia!
LET'S SEE SOME MORE GUTS, HUH?! GUTS!!
...
I DON'T LIKE HIM.
Raaaah!!
Imaginary Wall
THUMP
↑YUMI YAMAGUCHI AND MIO INADA (OSAKA)
NEKOMA MUNICIP
YAKU!
FWIF
GOOD DIG!
BAM

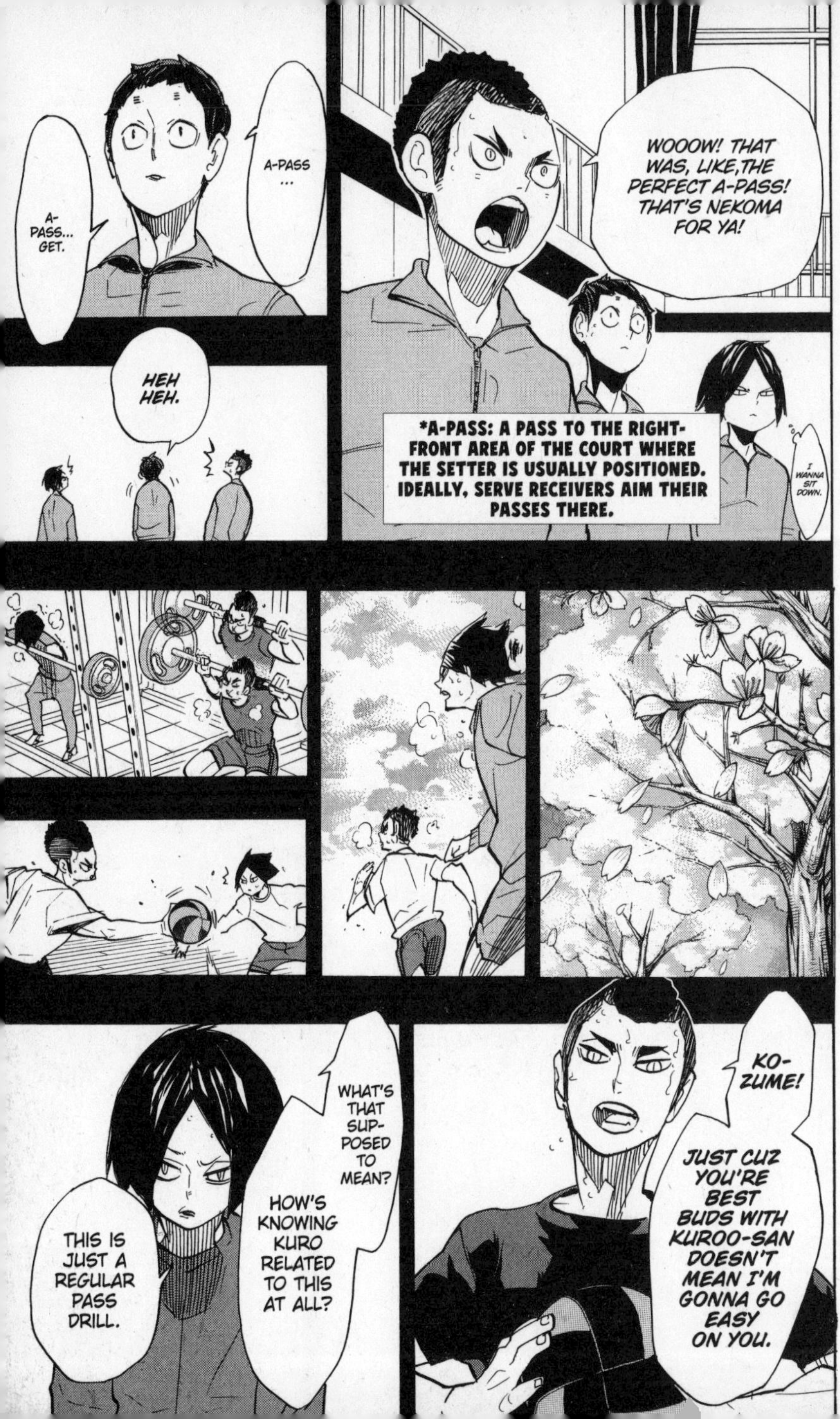
WOOOW! THAT WAS, LIKE,THE PERFECT A-PASS! THAT'S NEKOMA FOR YA!
*A-PASS: A PASS TO THE RIGHT-FRONT AREA OF THE COURT WHERE THE SETTER IS USUALLY POSITIONED. IDEALLY, SERVE RECEIVERS AIM THEIR PASSES THERE.
I WANNA SIT DOWN.
A-PASS ...
A-PASS... GET.
HEH HEH.
KO-ZUME!
JUST CUZ YOU'RE BEST BUDS WITH KUROO-SAN DOESN'T MEAN I'M GONNA GO EASY ON YOU.
WHAT'S THAT SUP-POSED TO MEAN?
HOW'S KNOWING KURO RELATED TO THIS AT ALL?
THIS IS JUST A REGULAR PASS DRILL.

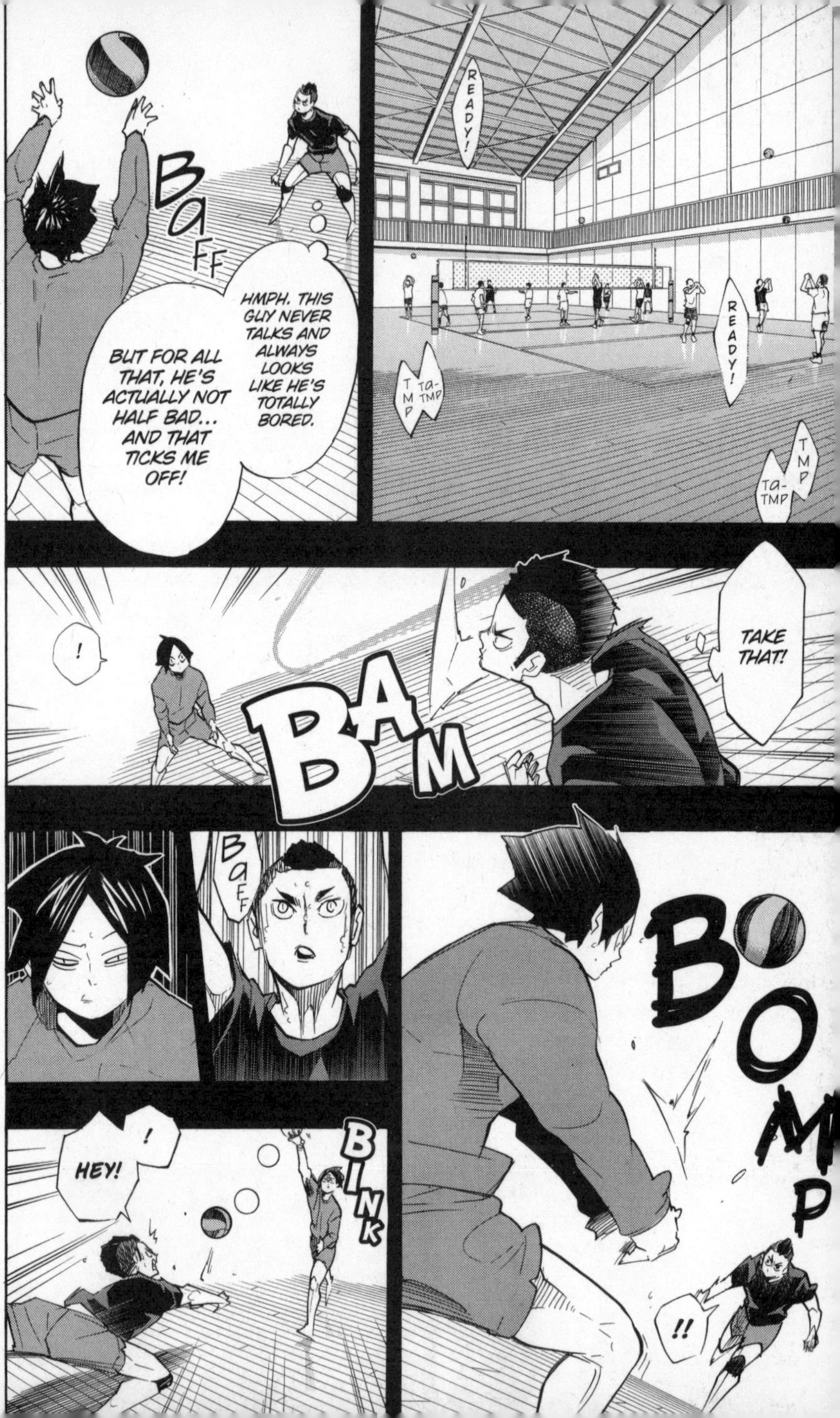
READY!
READY!
TMP
TA-TMP
TMP
TA-TMP
BAFF
HMPH. THIS GUY NEVER TALKS AND ALWAYS LOOKS LIKE HE'S TOTALLY BORED.
BUT FOR ALL THAT, HE'S ACTUALLY NOT HALF BAD... AND THAT TICKS ME OFF!
TAKE THAT!
BAM
!
BOOMP
!!
BAFF
!
HEY!
BLINK

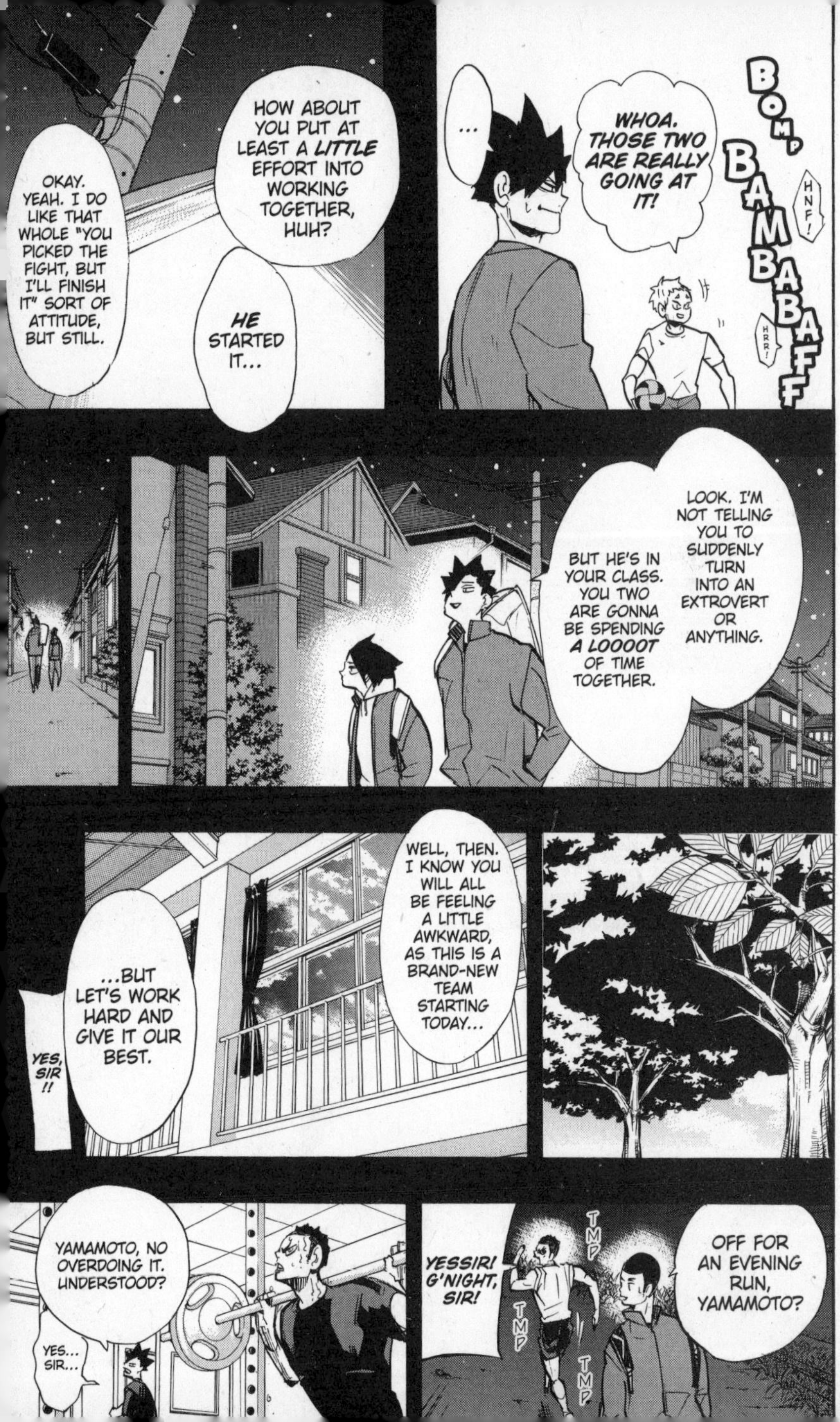
BOMP
BAMBABAFF
HNF!
HRR!
WHOA. THOSE TWO ARE REALLY GOING AT IT!
...
HOW ABOUT YOU PUT AT LEAST A *LITTLE* EFFORT INTO WORKING TOGETHER, HUH?
HE STARTED IT...
OKAY. YEAH. I DO LIKE THAT WHOLE "YOU PICKED THE FIGHT, BUT I'LL FINISH IT" SORT OF ATTITUDE, BUT STILL.
LOOK. I'M NOT TELLING YOU TO SUDDENLY TURN INTO AN EXTROVERT OR ANYTHING.
BUT HE'S IN YOUR CLASS. YOU TWO ARE GONNA BE SPENDING *A LOOOOT* OF TIME TOGETHER.
WELL, THEN. I KNOW YOU WILL ALL BE FEELING A LITTLE AWKWARD, AS THIS IS A BRAND-NEW TEAM STARTING TODAY...
...BUT LET'S WORK HARD AND GIVE IT OUR BEST.
YES, SIR!!
OFF FOR AN EVENING RUN, YAMAMOTO?
TMP
TMP
TMP
YESSIR! G'NIGHT, SIR!
YAMAMOTO, NO OVERDOING IT. UNDERSTOOD?
YES... SIR...

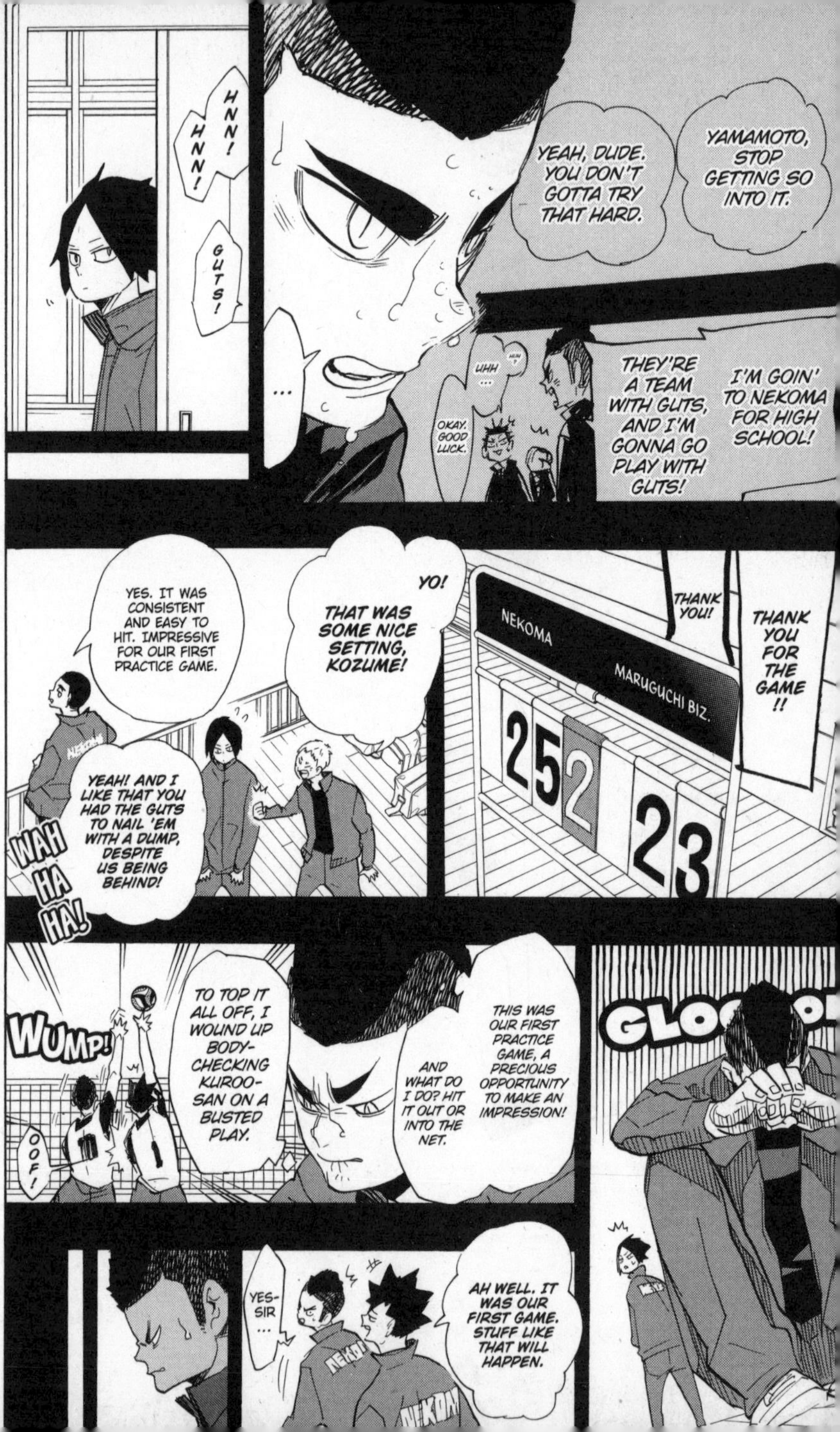
YAMAMOTO, STOP GETTING SO INTO IT.
YEAH, DUDE. YOU DON'T GOTTA TRY THAT HARD.
I'M GOIN' TO NEKOMA FOR HIGH SCHOOL!
THEY'RE A TEAM WITH GUTS, AND I'M GONNA GO PLAY WITH GUTS!
HUH?
UHH...
OKAY. GOOD LUCK.
...
HNN! HNN!
GUTS!
THANK YOU FOR THE GAME!!
THANK YOU!
NEKOMA
MARUGUCHI BIZ.
25 2
23
YO!
THAT WAS SOME NICE SETTING, KOZUME!
YES. IT WAS CONSISTENT AND EASY TO HIT. IMPRESSIVE FOR OUR FIRST PRACTICE GAME.
YEAH! AND I LIKE THAT YOU HAD THE GUTS TO NAIL 'EM WITH A DUMP, DESPITE US BEING BEHIND!
WAH HA HA!
GLOO
THIS WAS OUR FIRST PRACTICE GAME, A PRECIOUS OPPORTUNITY TO MAKE AN IMPRESSION!
AND WHAT DO I DO? HIT IT OUT OR INTO THE NET.
TO TOP IT ALL OFF, I WOUND UP BODY-CHECKING KUROO-SAN ON A BUSTED PLAY.
WUMP!
OOF!
AH WELL. IT WAS OUR FIRST GAME. STUFF LIKE THAT WILL HAPPEN.
YES-SIR...

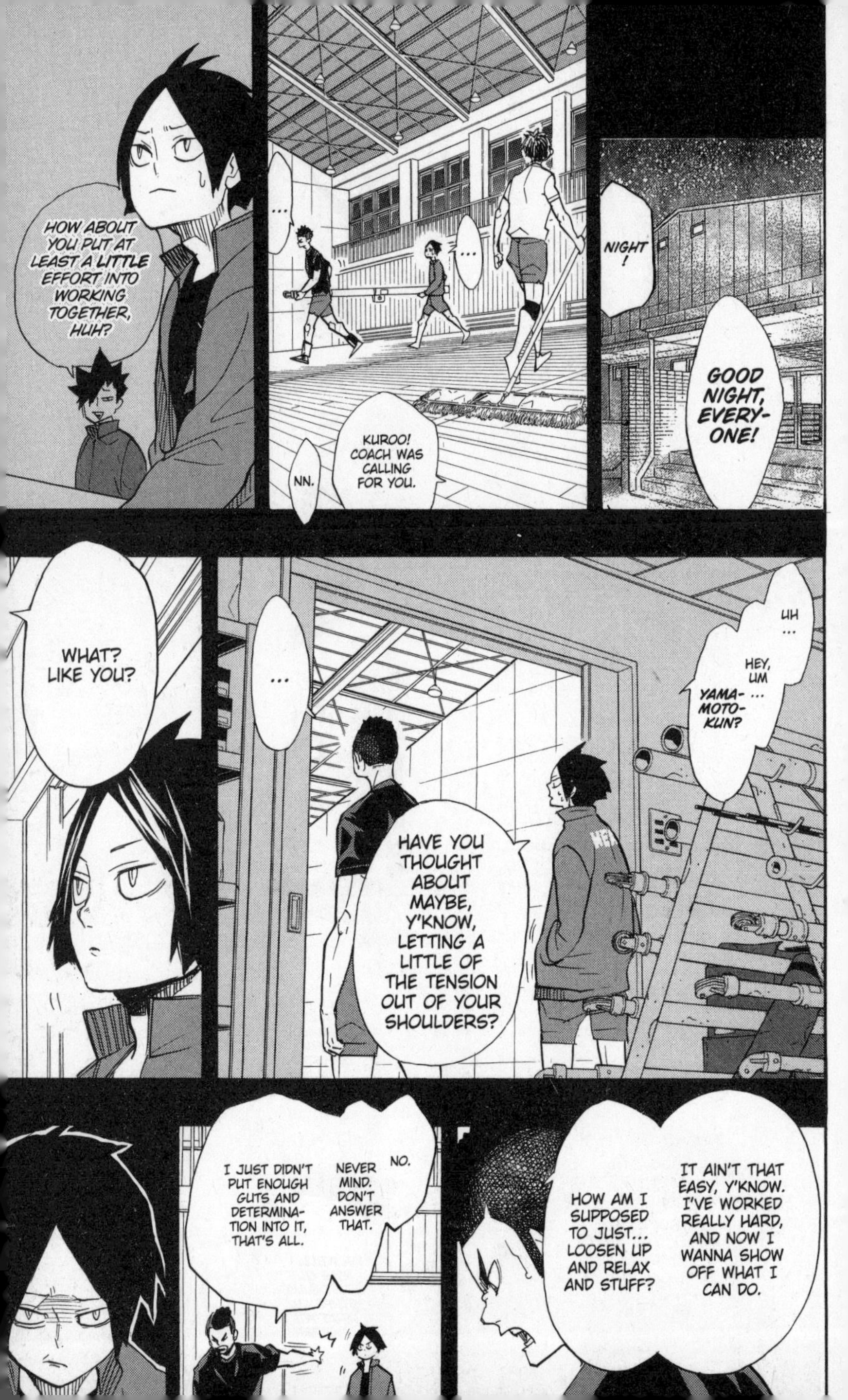
NIGHT!
GOOD NIGHT, EVERYONE!
...
...
KUROO! COACH WAS CALLING FOR YOU.
NN.
HOW ABOUT YOU PUT AT LEAST A LITTLE EFFORT INTO WORKING TOGETHER, HUH?
UH ...
HEY, UM ... YAMAMOTO-KUN?
...
HAVE YOU THOUGHT ABOUT MAYBE, Y'KNOW, LETTING A LITTLE OF THE TENSION OUT OF YOUR SHOULDERS?
WHAT? LIKE YOU?
IT AIN'T THAT EASY, Y'KNOW. I'VE WORKED REALLY HARD, AND NOW I WANNA SHOW OFF WHAT I CAN DO.
HOW AM I SUPPOSED TO JUST... LOOSEN UP AND RELAX AND STUFF?
NO.
NEVER MIND. DON'T ANSWER THAT.
I JUST DIDN'T PUT ENOUGH GUTS AND DETERMINATION INTO IT, THAT'S ALL.

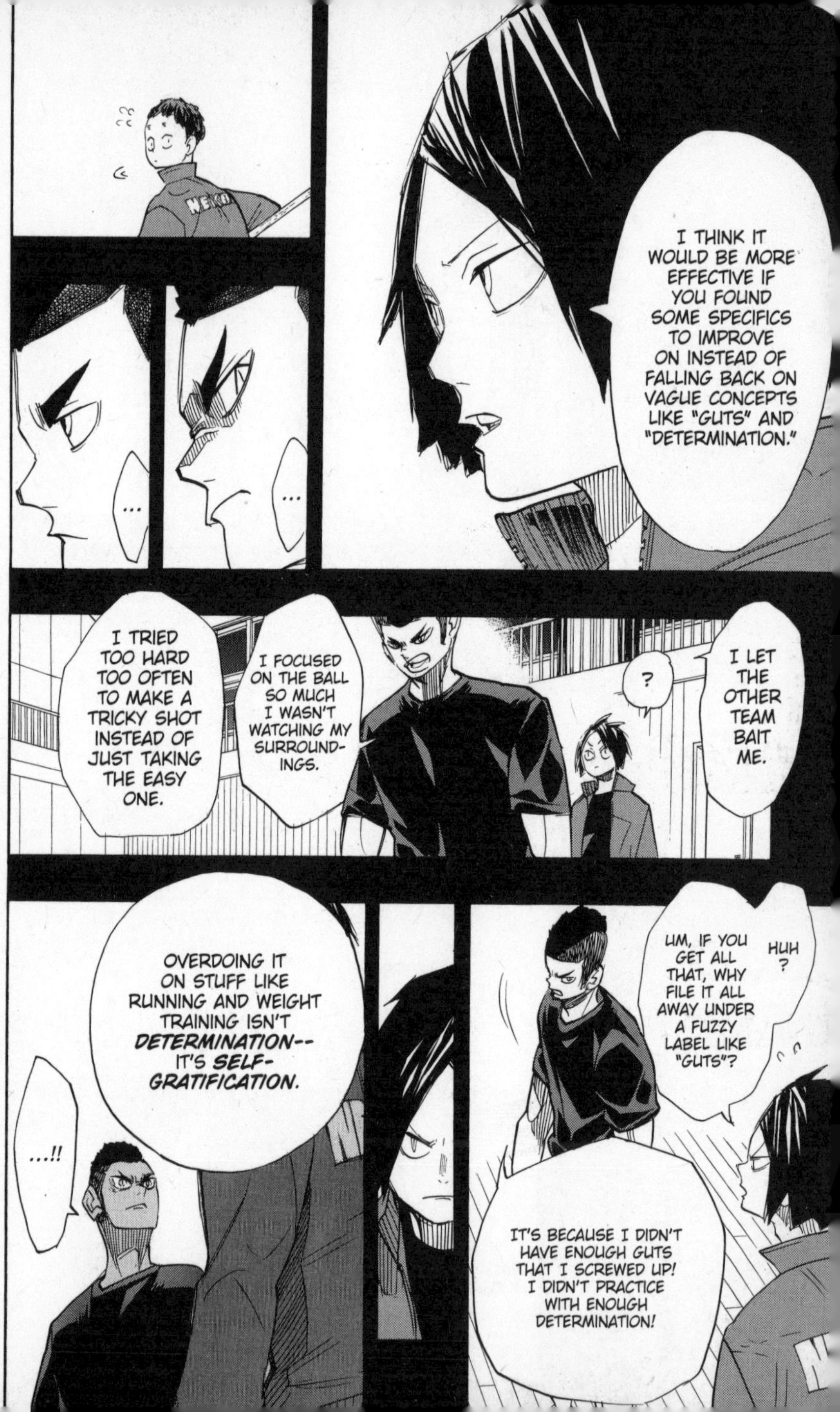
I THINK IT WOULD BE MORE EFFECTIVE IF YOU FOUND SOME SPECIFICS TO IMPROVE ON INSTEAD OF FALLING BACK ON VAGUE CONCEPTS LIKE "GUTS" AND "DETERMINATION."
...
...
I LET THE OTHER TEAM BAIT ME.
?
I FOCUSED ON THE BALL SO MUCH I WASN'T WATCHING MY SURROUND-INGS.
I TRIED TOO HARD TOO OFTEN TO MAKE A TRICKY SHOT INSTEAD OF JUST TAKING THE EASY ONE.
HUH?
UM, IF YOU GET ALL THAT, WHY FILE IT ALL AWAY UNDER A FUZZY LABEL LIKE "GUTS"?
IT'S BECAUSE I DIDN'T HAVE ENOUGH GUTS THAT I SCREWED UP! I DIDN'T PRACTICE WITH ENOUGH DETERMINATION!
OVERDOING IT ON STUFF LIKE RUNNING AND WEIGHT TRAINING ISN'T DETERMINATION-- IT'S SELF-GRATIFICATION.
...!!

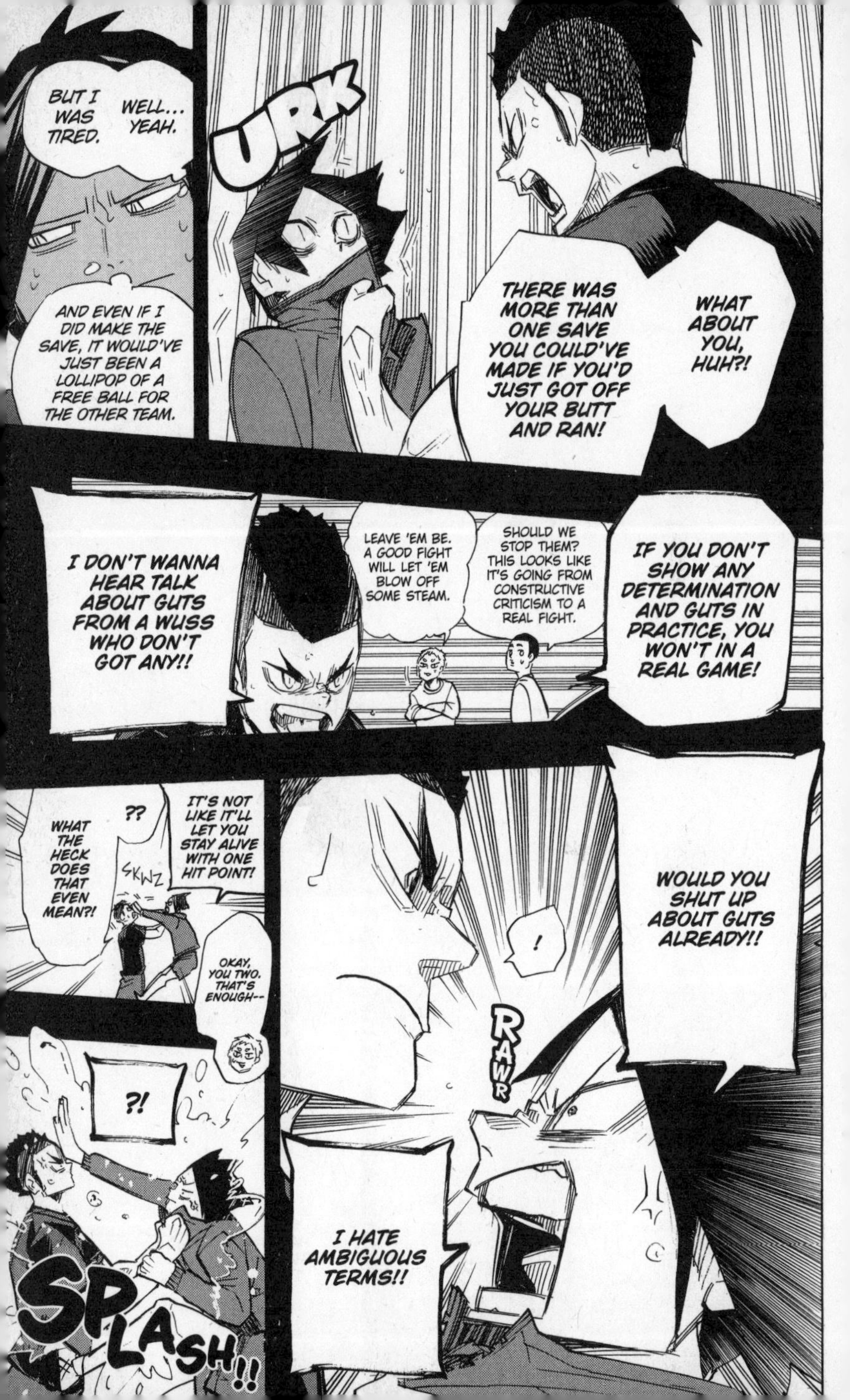
WHAT ABOUT YOU, HUH?!
THERE WAS MORE THAN ONE SAVE YOU COULD'VE MADE IF YOU'D JUST GOT OFF YOUR BUTT AND RAN!
URK
WELL... YEAH.
BUT I WAS TIRED.
AND EVEN IF I DID MAKE THE SAVE, IT WOULD'VE JUST BEEN A LOLLIPOP OF A FREE BALL FOR THE OTHER TEAM.
IF YOU DON'T SHOW ANY DETERMINATION AND GUTS IN PRACTICE, YOU WON'T IN A REAL GAME!
SHOULD WE STOP THEM? THIS LOOKS LIKE IT'S GOING FROM CONSTRUCTIVE CRITICISM TO A REAL FIGHT.
LEAVE 'EM BE. A GOOD FIGHT WILL LET 'EM BLOW OFF SOME STEAM.
I DON'T WANNA HEAR TALK ABOUT GUTS FROM A WUSS WHO DON'T GOT ANY!!
WOULD YOU SHUT UP ABOUT GUTS ALREADY!!
!
RAWR
I HATE AMBIGUOUS TERMS!!
IT'S NOT LIKE IT'LL LET YOU STAY ALIVE WITH ONE HIT POINT!
??
WHAT THE HECK DOES THAT EVEN MEAN?!
SKWZ
OKAY, YOU TWO. THAT'S ENOUGH--
?!
SPLASH!!

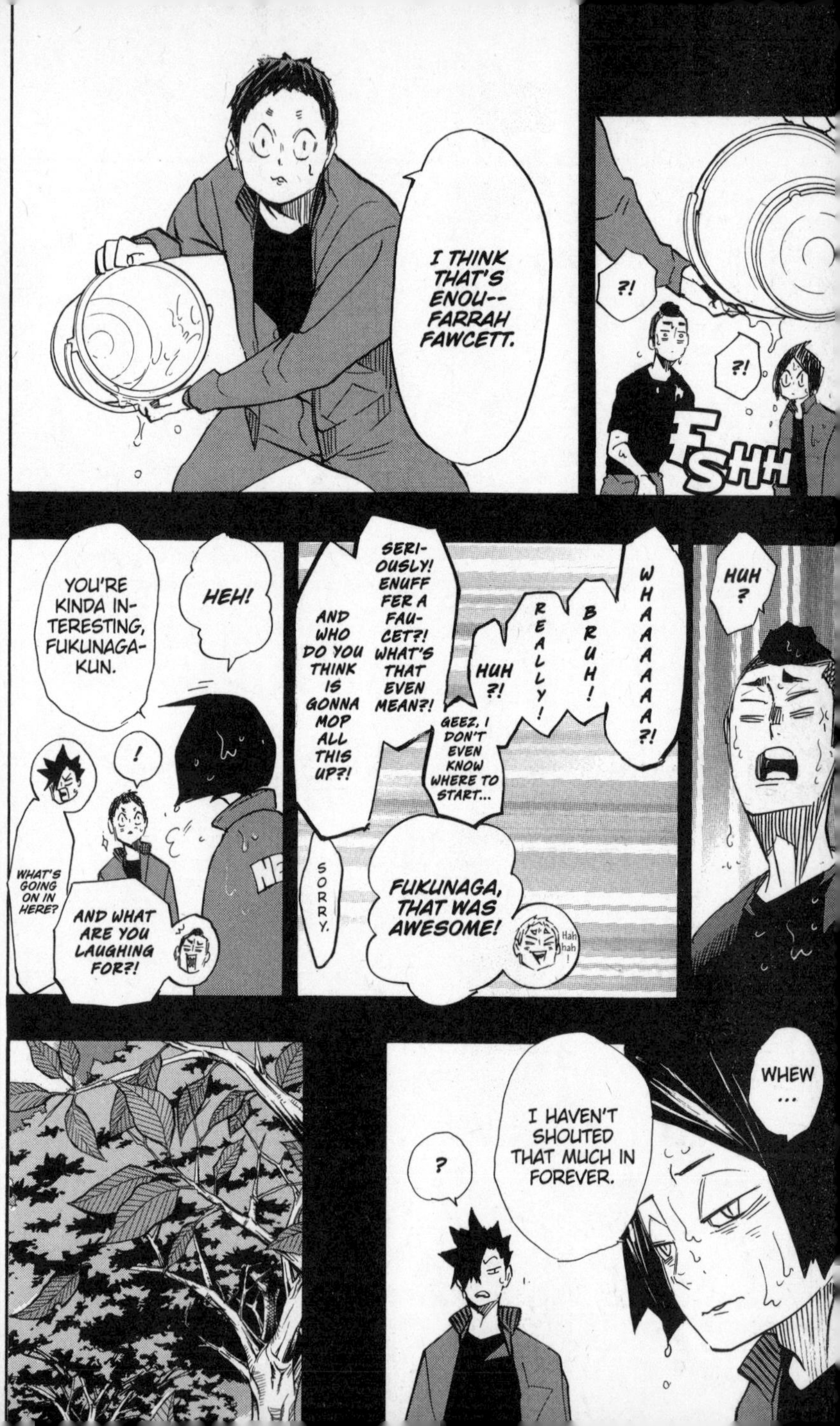
?!
?!
FSHH
I THINK THAT'S ENOU-- FARRAH FAWCETT.
HUH?
WHAAAAAAA?!
BRUH!
REALLY!
HUH?!
GEEZ, I DON'T EVEN KNOW WHERE TO START...
SERIOUSLY! ENUFF FER A FAUCET?! WHAT'S THAT EVEN MEAN?!
AND WHO DO YOU THINK IS GONNA MOP ALL THIS UP?!
FUKUNAGA, THAT WAS AWESOME!
Hah hah!
SORRY.
HEH!
YOU'RE KINDA INTERESTING, FUKUNAGA-KUN.
!
WHAT'S GOING ON IN HERE?
AND WHAT ARE YOU LAUGHING FOR?!
WHEW...
I HAVEN'T SHOUTED THAT MUCH IN FOREVER.
?

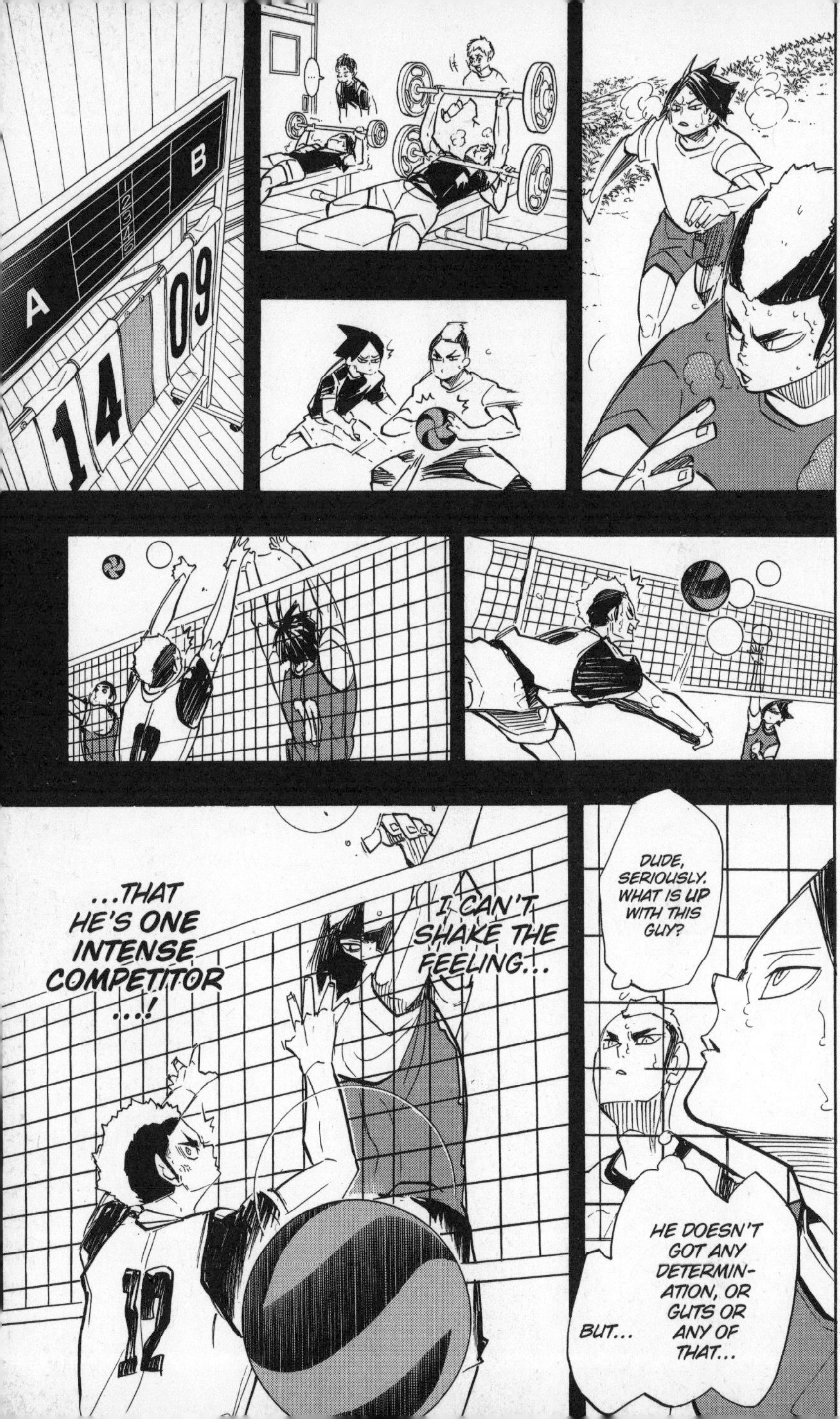
...
A
B
14
09
DUDE, SERIOUSLY. WHAT IS UP WITH THIS GUY?
HE DOESN'T GOT ANY DETERMINATION, OR GUTS OR ANY OF THAT...
BUT...
I CAN'T SHAKE THE FEELING...
...THAT HE'S ONE INTENSE COMPETITOR ...!

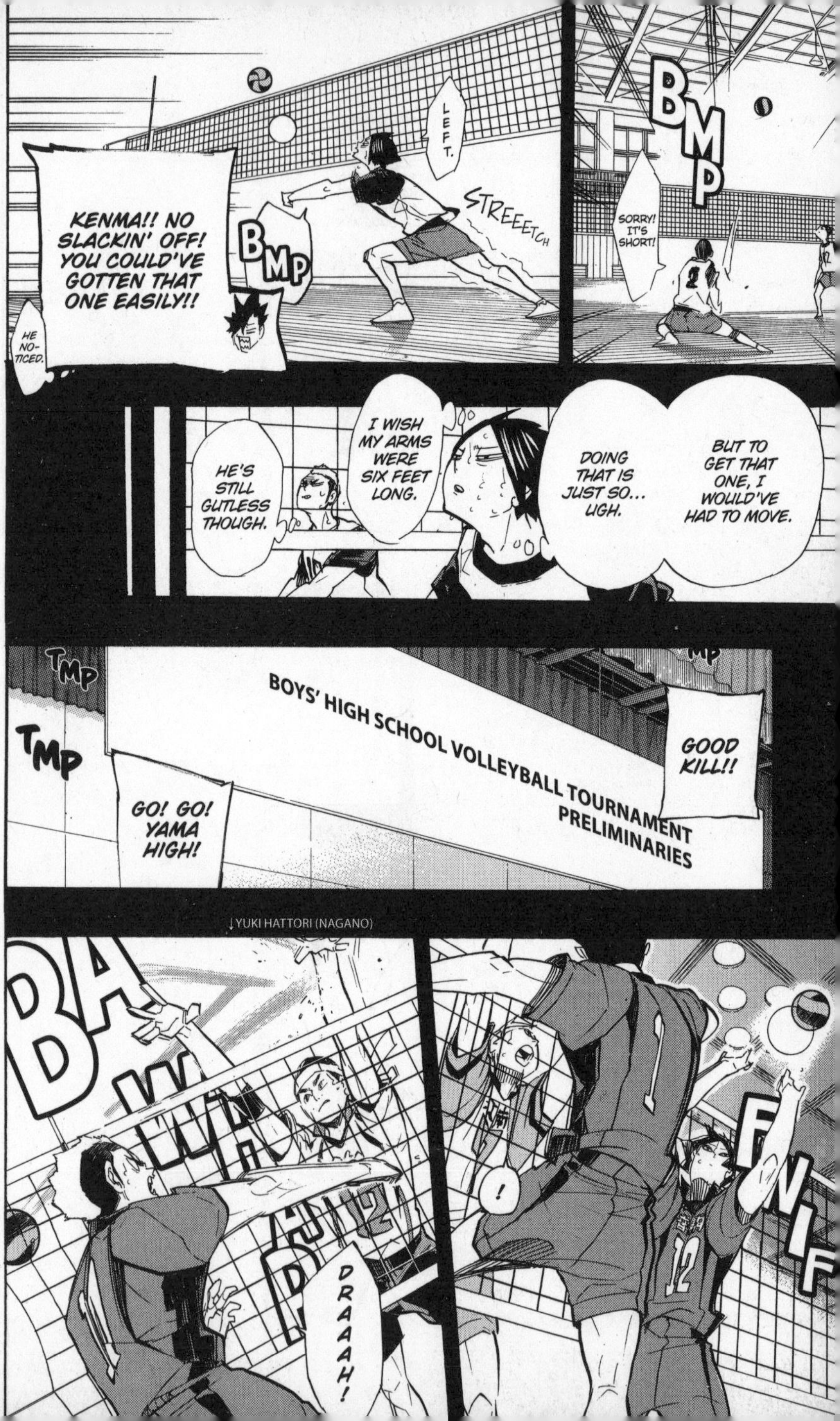
BMP
SORRY! IT'S SHORT!
LEFT.
STREEEETCH
BMP
KENMA!! NO SLACKIN' OFF! YOU COULD'VE GOTTEN THAT ONE EASILY!!
HE NOTICED.
BUT TO GET THAT ONE, I WOULD'VE HAD TO MOVE.
DOING THAT IS JUST SO... UGH.
I WISH MY ARMS WERE SIX FEET LONG.
HE'S STILL GUTLESS THOUGH.
GOOD KILL!!
BOYS' HIGH SCHOOL VOLLEYBALL TOURNAMENT PRELIMINARIES
GO! GO! YAMA HIGH!
TMP
TMP
↓YUKI HATTORI (NAGANO)
FWIF
!
DRAAAH!

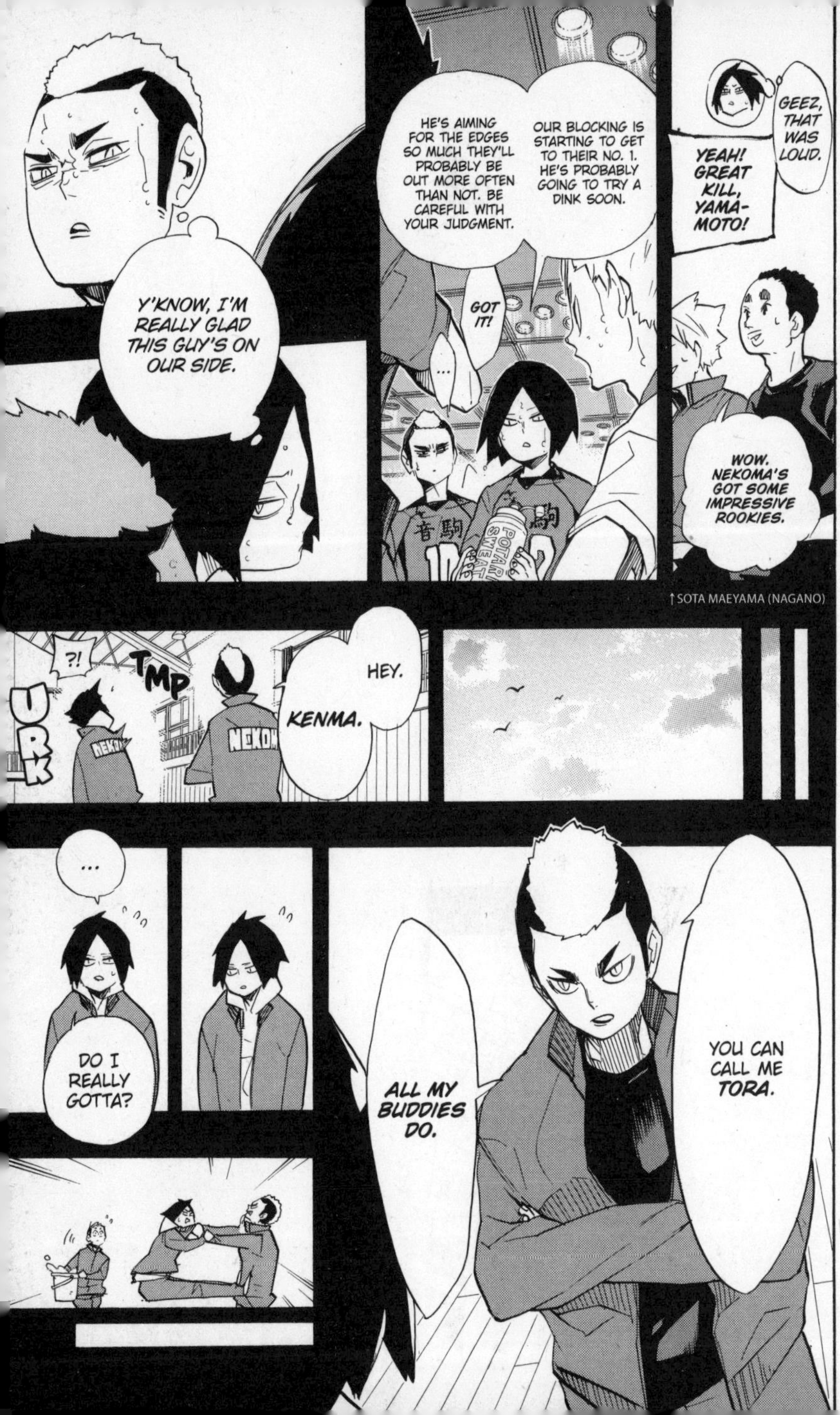
GEEZ, THAT WAS LOUD.
YEAH! GREAT KILL, YAMAMOTO!
WOW. NEKOMA'S GOT SOME IMPRESSIVE ROOKIES.
OUR BLOCKING IS STARTING TO GET TO THEIR NO. 1. HE'S PROBABLY GOING TO TRY A DINK SOON.
HE'S AIMING FOR THE EDGES SO MUCH THEY'LL PROBABLY BE OUT MORE OFTEN THAN NOT. BE CAREFUL WITH YOUR JUDGMENT.
GOT IT!
...
Y'KNOW, I'M REALLY GLAD THIS GUY'S ON OUR SIDE.
HEY.
KENMA.
TMP
?!
URK
YOU CAN CALL ME TORA.
ALL MY BUDDIES DO.
...
DO I REALLY GOTTA?

↑SOTA MAEYAMA (NAGANO)

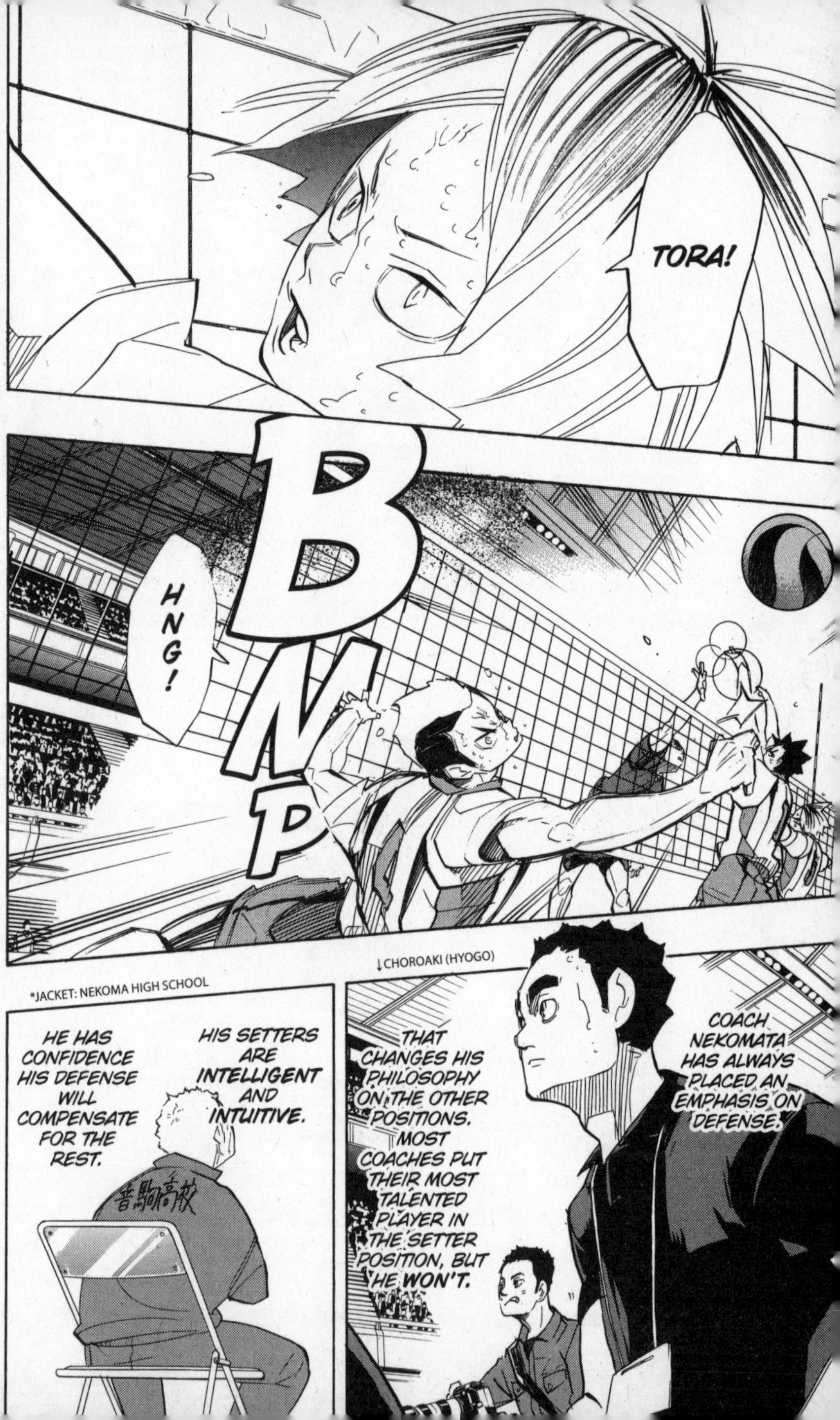
TORA!
BMP
HNG!
↓CHOROAKI (HYOGO)
COACH NEKOMATA HAS ALWAYS PLACED AN EMPHASIS ON DEFENSE.
THAT CHANGES HIS PHILOSOPHY ON THE OTHER POSITIONS. MOST COACHES PUT THEIR MOST TALENTED PLAYER IN THE SETTER POSITION, BUT HE WON'T.
*JACKET: NEKOMA HIGH SCHOOL
HIS SETTERS ARE INTELLIGENT AND INTUITIVE.
HE HAS CONFIDENCE HIS DEFENSE WILL COMPENSATE FOR THE REST.
音駒高校

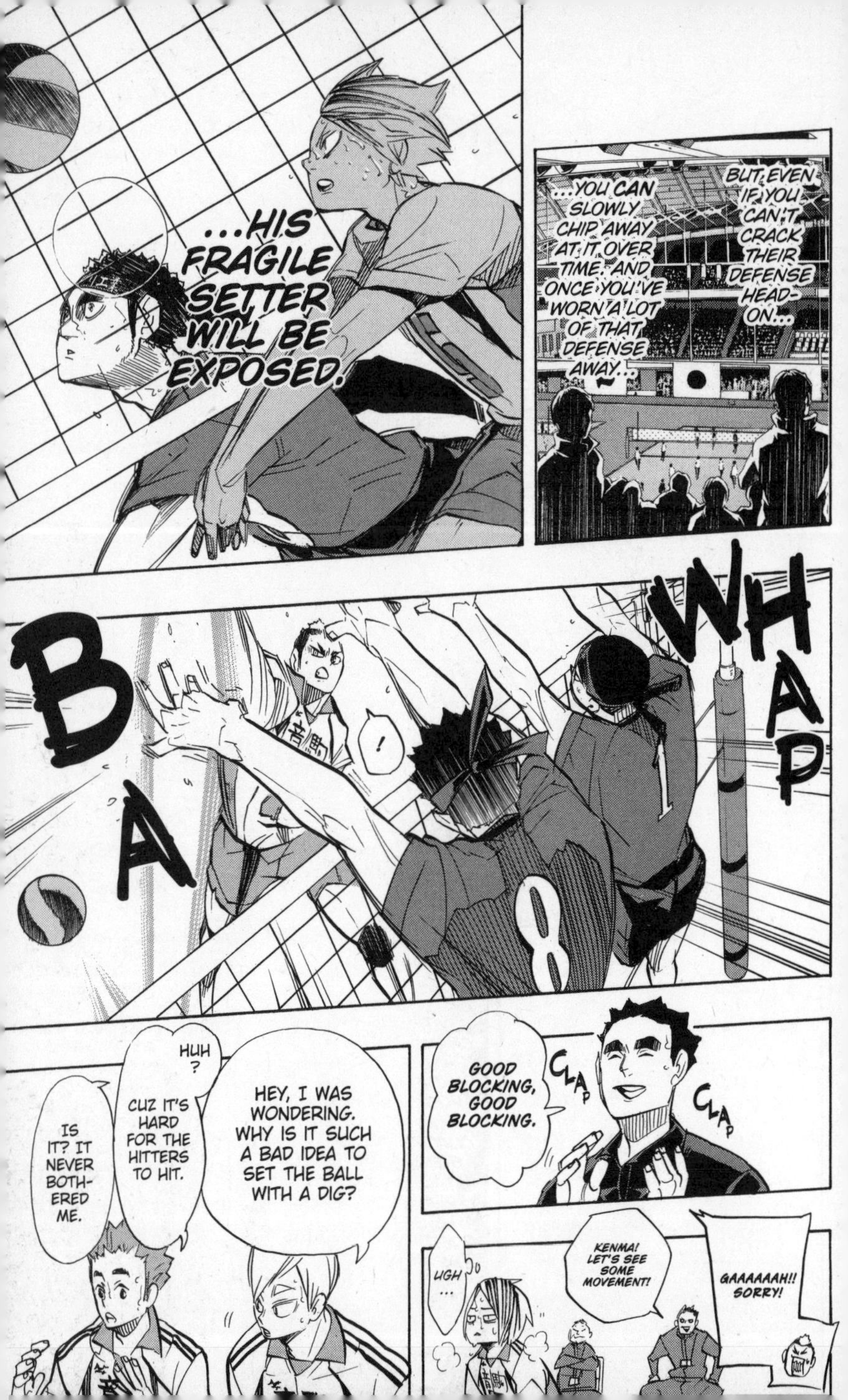

BUT EVEN IF YOU CAN'T CRACK THEIR DEFENSE HEAD-ON...
...YOU CAN SLOWLY CHIP AWAY AT IT OVER TIME. AND ONCE YOU'VE WORN A LOT OF THAT DEFENSE AWAY...
...HIS FRAGILE SETTER WILL BE EXPOSED.
WHAP
!
BA
GOOD BLOCKING, GOOD BLOCKING.
CLAP
CLAP
GAAAAAAH!! SORRY!
KENMA! LET'S SEE SOME MOVEMENT!
UGH...
HEY, I WAS WONDERING. WHY IS IT SUCH A BAD IDEA TO SET THE BALL WITH A DIG?
HUH?
CUZ IT'S HARD FOR THE HITTERS TO HIT.
IS IT? IT NEVER BOTHERED ME.

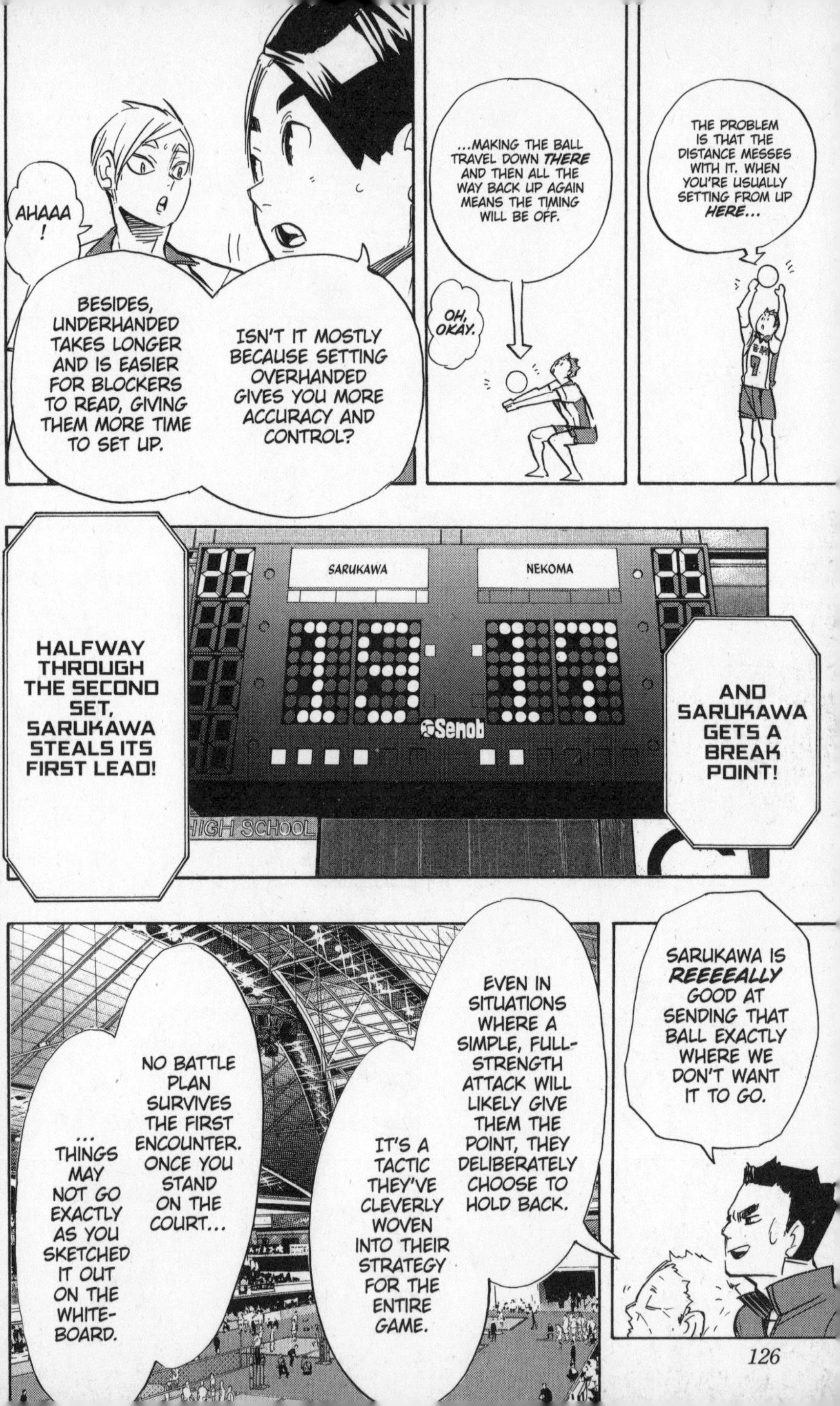
THE PROBLEM IS THAT THE DISTANCE MESSES WITH IT. WHEN YOU'RE USUALLY SETTING FROM UP *HERE*...
...MAKING THE BALL TRAVEL DOWN *THERE* AND THEN ALL THE WAY BACK UP AGAIN MEANS THE TIMING WILL BE OFF.
OH, OKAY.
ISN'T IT MOSTLY BECAUSE SETTING OVERHANDED GIVES YOU MORE ACCURACY AND CONTROL?
BESIDES, UNDERHANDED TAKES LONGER AND IS EASIER FOR BLOCKERS TO READ, GIVING THEM MORE TIME TO SET UP.
AHAAA!
AND SARUKAWA GETS A BREAK POINT!
SARUKAWA
NEKOMA
Senob
HIGH SCHOOL
HALFWAY THROUGH THE SECOND SET, SARUKAWA STEALS ITS FIRST LEAD!
SARUKAWA IS *REEEEALLY* GOOD AT SENDING THAT BALL EXACTLY WHERE WE DON'T WANT IT TO GO.
EVEN IN SITUATIONS WHERE A SIMPLE, FULL-STRENGTH ATTACK WILL LIKELY GIVE THEM THE POINT, THEY DELIBERATELY CHOOSE TO HOLD BACK.
IT'S A TACTIC THEY'VE CLEVERLY WOVEN INTO THEIR STRATEGY FOR THE ENTIRE GAME.
NO BATTLE PLAN SURVIVES THE FIRST ENCOUNTER. ONCE YOU STAND ON THE COURT...
...THINGS MAY NOT GO EXACTLY AS YOU SKETCHED IT OUT ON THE WHITEBOARD.

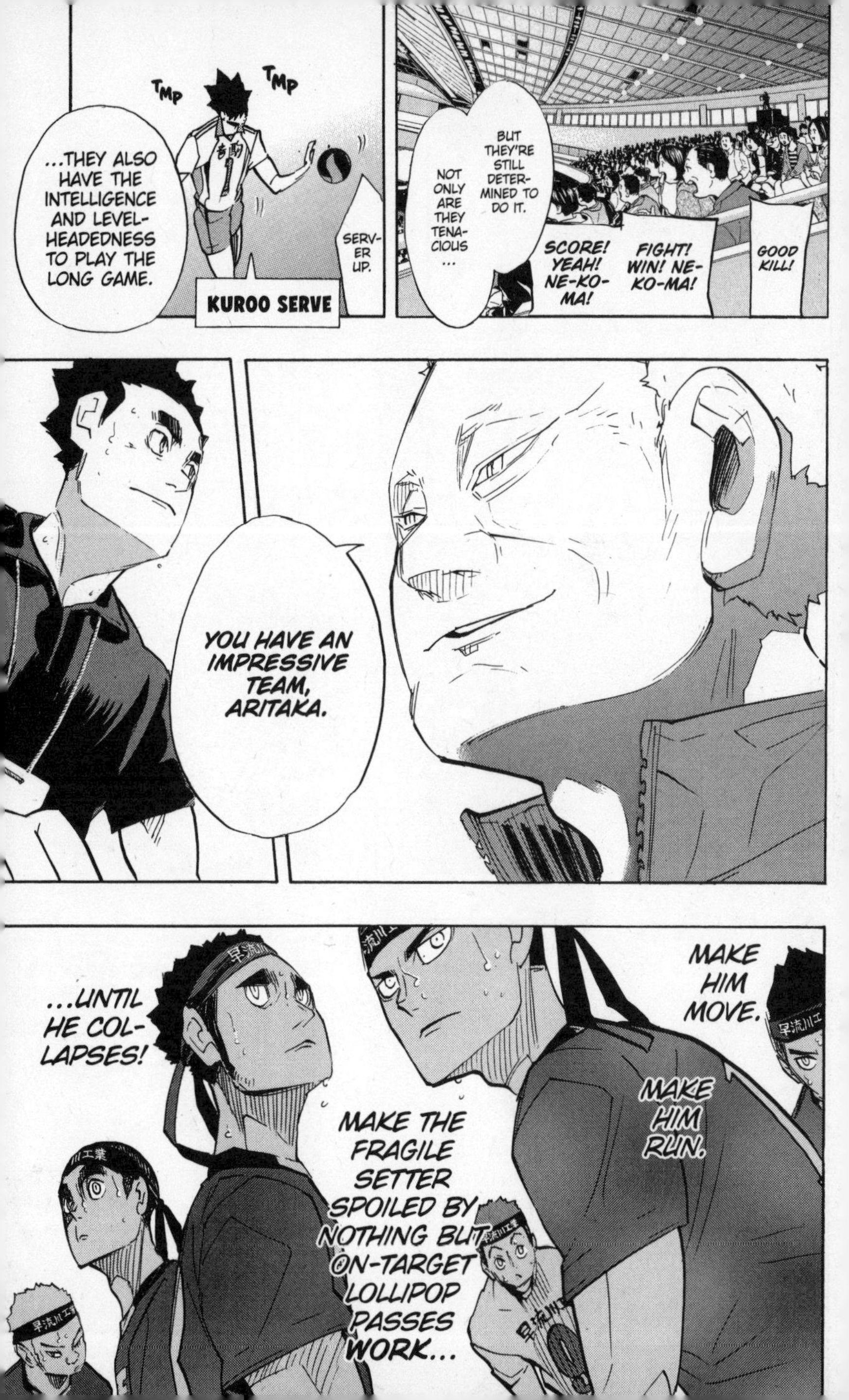
GOOD KILL!
FIGHT! WIN! NE-KO-MA!
SCORE! YEAH! NE-KO-MA!
NOT ONLY ARE THEY TENACIOUS...
BUT THEY'RE STILL DETERMINED TO DO IT.
TMP
TMP
SERVER UP.
KUROO SERVE
...THEY ALSO HAVE THE INTELLIGENCE AND LEVEL-HEADEDNESS TO PLAY THE LONG GAME.
YOU HAVE AN IMPRESSIVE TEAM, ARITAKA.
MAKE HIM MOVE.
MAKE HIM RUN.
MAKE THE FRAGILE SETTER SPOILED BY NOTHING BUT ON-TARGET LOLLIPOP PASSES WORK...
...UNTIL HE COLLAPSES!

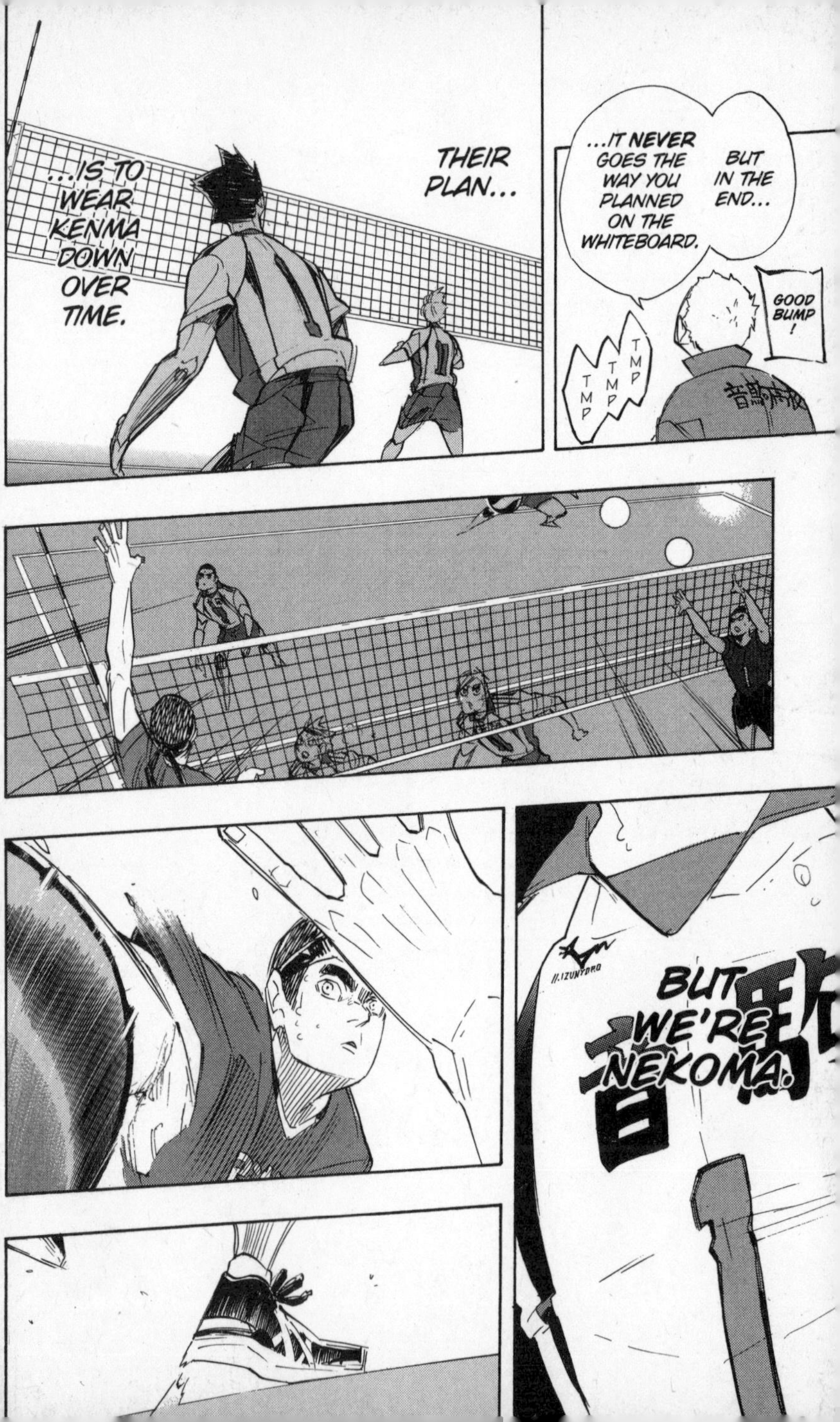
BUT IN THE END...
...IT NEVER GOES THE WAY YOU PLANNED ON THE WHITEBOARD.
TMP TMP TMP
GOOD BUMP!
THEIR PLAN...
...IS TO WEAR KENMA DOWN OVER TIME.
BUT WE'RE NEKOMA.

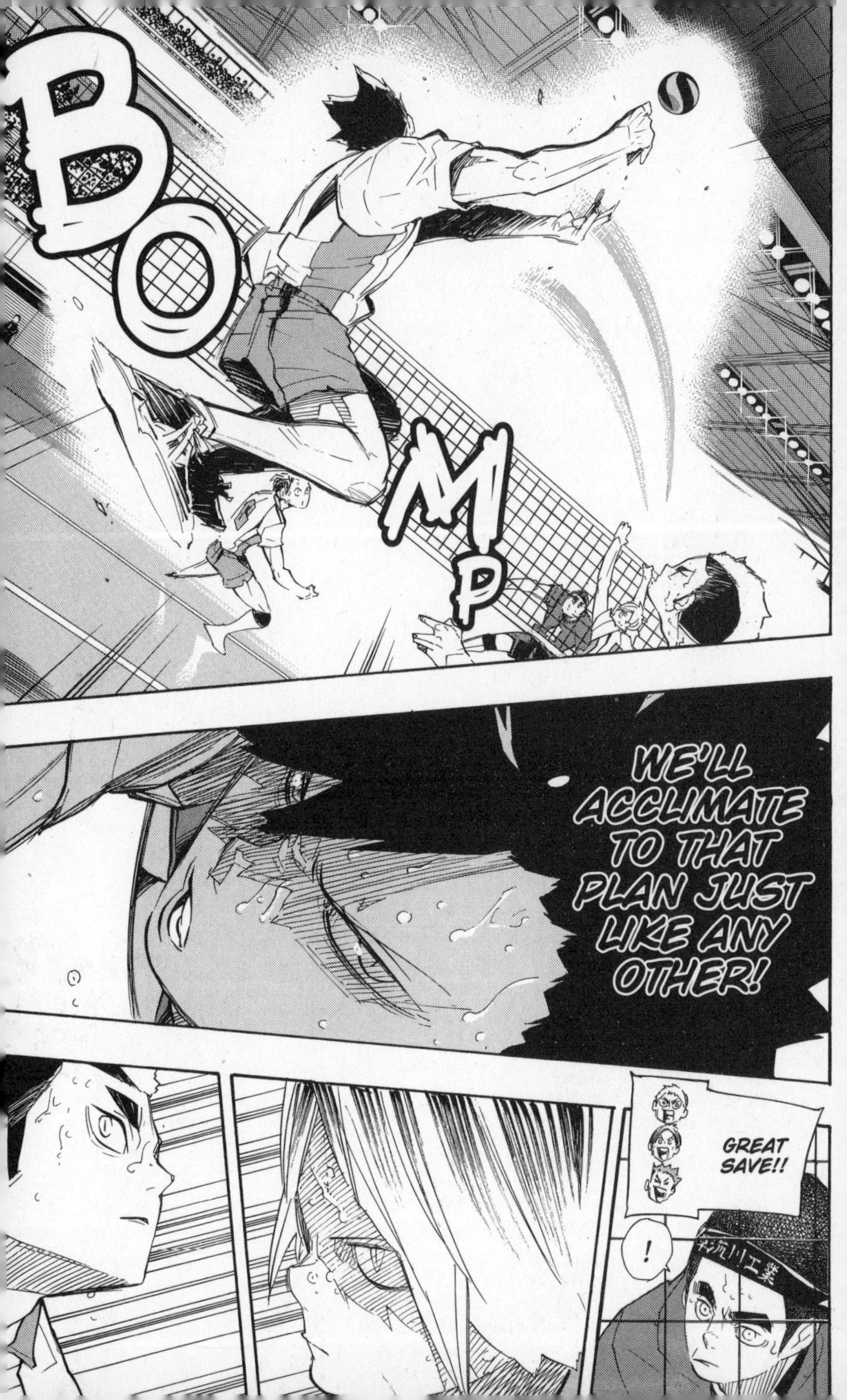
BOOMP
WE'LL ACCLIMATE TO THAT PLAN JUST LIKE ANY OTHER!
GREAT SAVE!!
!

APOLOGIES!

WE RAN A RAFFLE CONTEST WITH THE PRIZE FOR THE SELECTED WINNERS BEING AN APPEARANCE IN THE STANDS DURING CHAPTER 266. HOWEVER, WITH THE WAY THE STORY UNFOLDED, THAT HAPPENED TO BE THE ONE CHAPTER THAT DIDN'T HAVE MANY SHOTS OF THE CROWD, DESPITE BEING IN THE MIDDLE OF THE SPRING TOURNEY. I'M SORRY THE TIMING WORKED OUT SO TERRIBLY. IT WASN'T PLANNED THAT WAY, I PROMISE.

●TEAM CAPTAIN
SHIRAMINE
3RD YEAR / S
5'11"

KANAZAWA
3RD YEAR / WS
5'11"

SHIGA
3RD YEAR / MB
6'2"

WAKURA
3RD YEAR / MB
6'1"

FUKATANI
2ND YEAR / WS
5'10"

YAMASHIRO
2ND YEAR / WS
5'10"

WAJIMA
2ND YEAR / L
5'7"

MAKE THE FRAGILE SETTER SPOILED BY NOTHING BUT ON-TARGET LOLLIPOP PASSES WORK UNTIL HE COLLAPSES!!

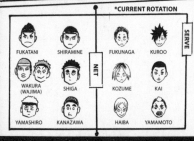

*CURRENT ROTATION

			SERVE
FUKATANI	SHIRAMINE	FUKUNAGA	KUROO
WAKURA (WAJIMA)	SHIGA	KOZUME	KAI
YAMASHIRO	KANAZAWA	HAIBA	YAMAMOTO

NET

CHAPTER 267: Trap

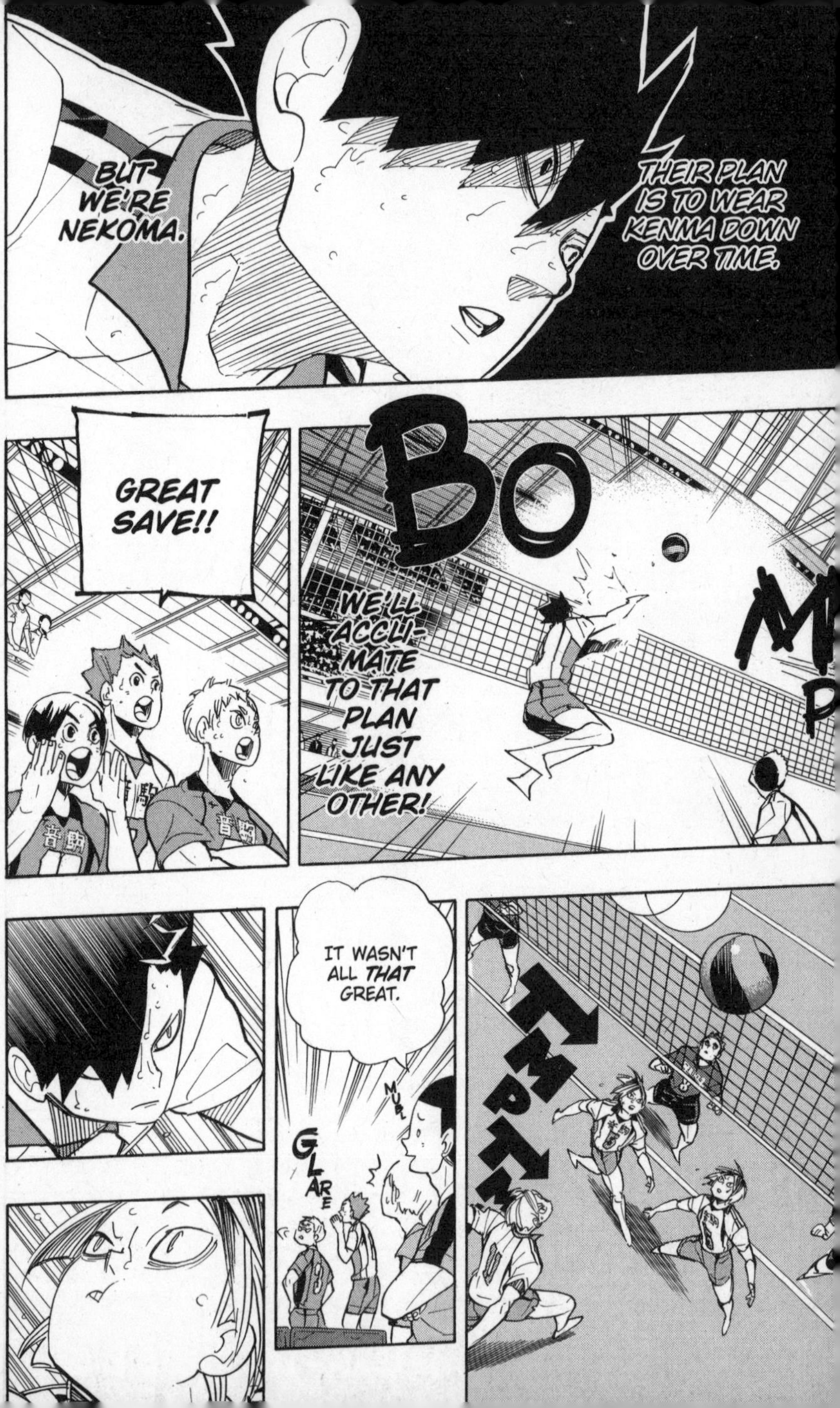
THEIR PLAN IS TO WEAR KENMA DOWN OVER TIME.
BUT WE'RE NEKOMA.
BO
WE'LL ACCLI-MATE TO THAT PLAN JUST LIKE ANY OTHER!
GREAT SAVE!!
IT WASN'T ALL *THAT* GREAT.
MUMBL
GLARE

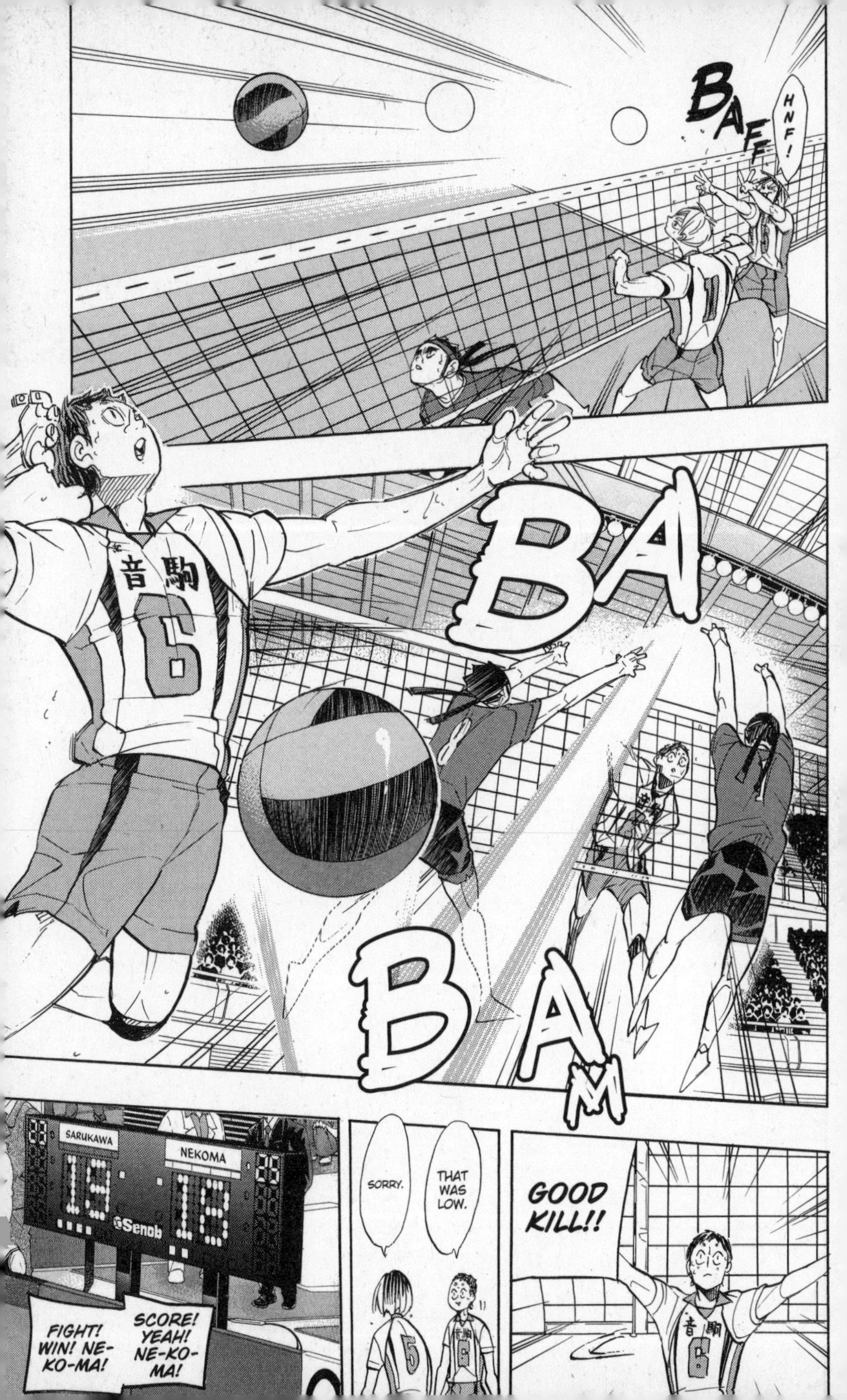

BAFF
HNF!
BA
BAM
GOOD KILL!!
THAT WAS LOW.
SORRY.
SARUKAWA
NEKOMA
Senob
SCORE! YEAH! NE-KO-MA!
FIGHT! WIN! NE-KO-MA!

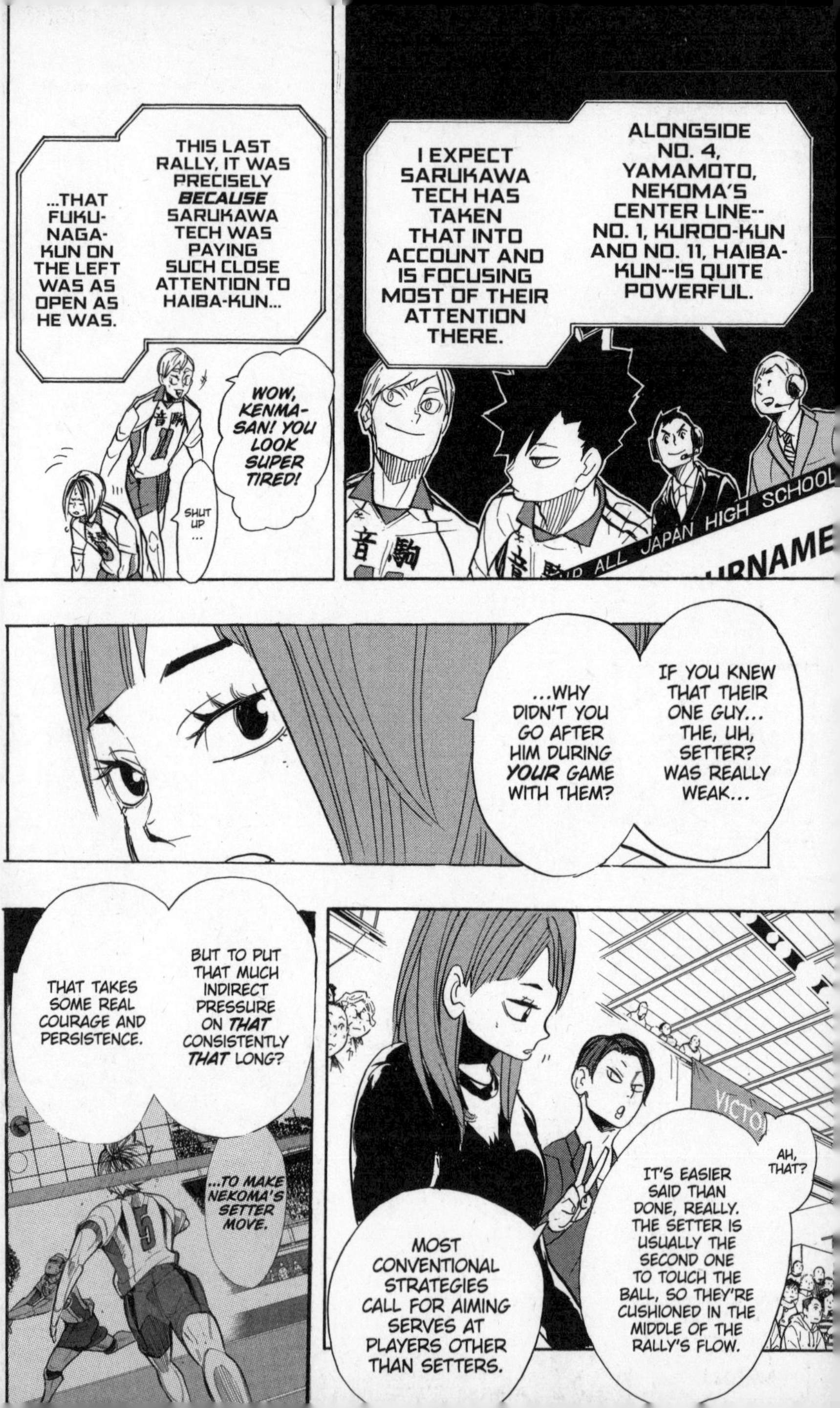
ALONGSIDE NO. 4, YAMAMOTO, NEKOMA'S CENTER LINE--NO. 1, KUROO-KUN AND NO. 11, HAIBA-KUN--IS QUITE POWERFUL.
I EXPECT SARUKAWA TECH HAS TAKEN THAT INTO ACCOUNT AND IS FOCUSING MOST OF THEIR ATTENTION THERE.
ALL JAPAN HIGH SCHOOL
THIS LAST RALLY, IT WAS PRECISELY *BECAUSE* SARUKAWA TECH WAS PAYING SUCH CLOSE ATTENTION TO HAIBA-KUN...
...THAT FUKU-NAGA-KUN ON THE LEFT WAS AS OPEN AS HE WAS.
WOW, KENMA-SAN! YOU LOOK SUPER TIRED!
SHUT UP ...
IF YOU KNEW THAT THEIR ONE GUY... THE, UH, SETTER? WAS REALLY WEAK...
...WHY DIDN'T YOU GO AFTER HIM DURING *YOUR* GAME WITH THEM?
AH, THAT?
IT'S EASIER SAID THAN DONE, REALLY. THE SETTER IS USUALLY THE SECOND ONE TO TOUCH THE BALL, SO THEY'RE CUSHIONED IN THE MIDDLE OF THE RALLY'S FLOW.
MOST CONVENTIONAL STRATEGIES CALL FOR AIMING SERVES AT PLAYERS OTHER THAN SETTERS.
BUT TO PUT THAT MUCH INDIRECT PRESSURE ON *THAT* CONSISTENTLY *THAT* LONG?
THAT TAKES SOME REAL COURAGE AND PERSISTENCE.
...TO MAKE NEKOMA'S SETTER MOVE.

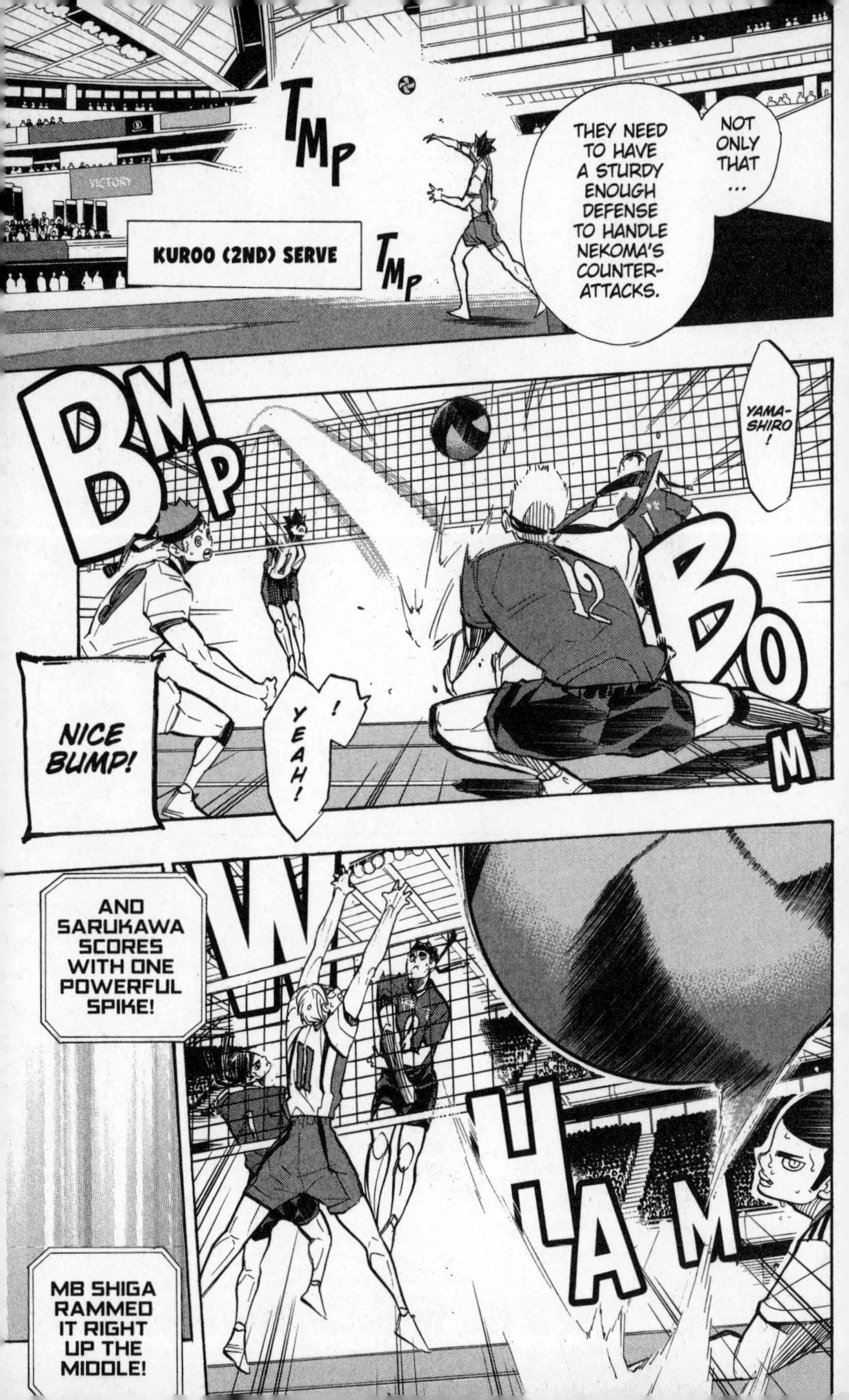
NOT ONLY THAT ...
THEY NEED TO HAVE A STURDY ENOUGH DEFENSE TO HANDLE NEKOMA'S COUNTER-ATTACKS.
TMP
TMP
KUROO (2ND) SERVE
YAMA-SHIRO!
BOOM
YEAH!!
NICE BUMP!
BMP
WHAM
AND SARUKAWA SCORES WITH ONE POWERFUL SPIKE!
MB SHIGA RAMMED IT RIGHT UP THE MIDDLE!

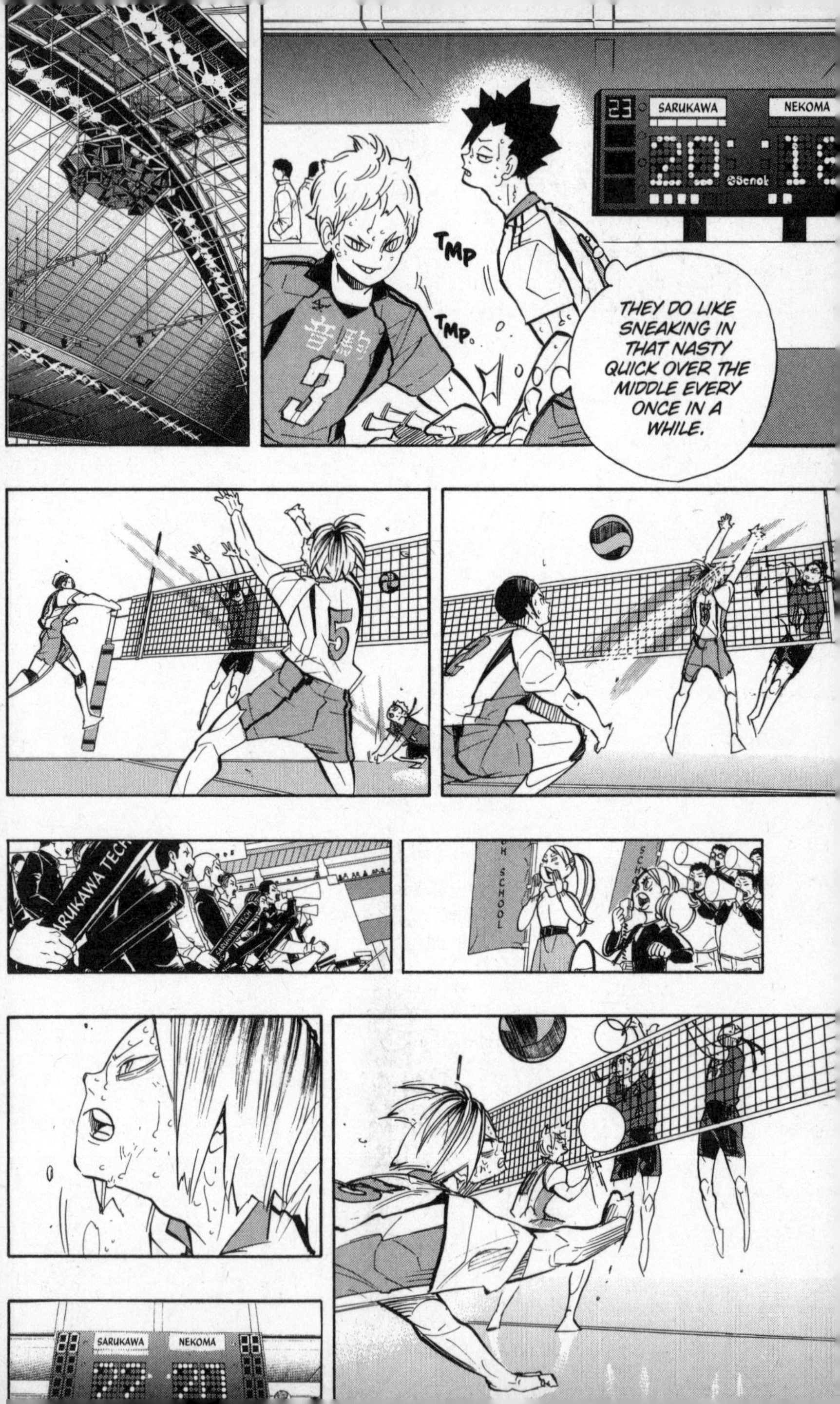
SARUKAWA
NEKOMA
TMP
TMP.
THEY DO LIKE SNEAKING IN THAT NASTY QUICK OVER THE MIDDLE EVERY ONCE IN A WHILE.
SCHOOL
SARUKAWA TECH
SARUKAWA TECH
SARUKAWA
NEKOMA

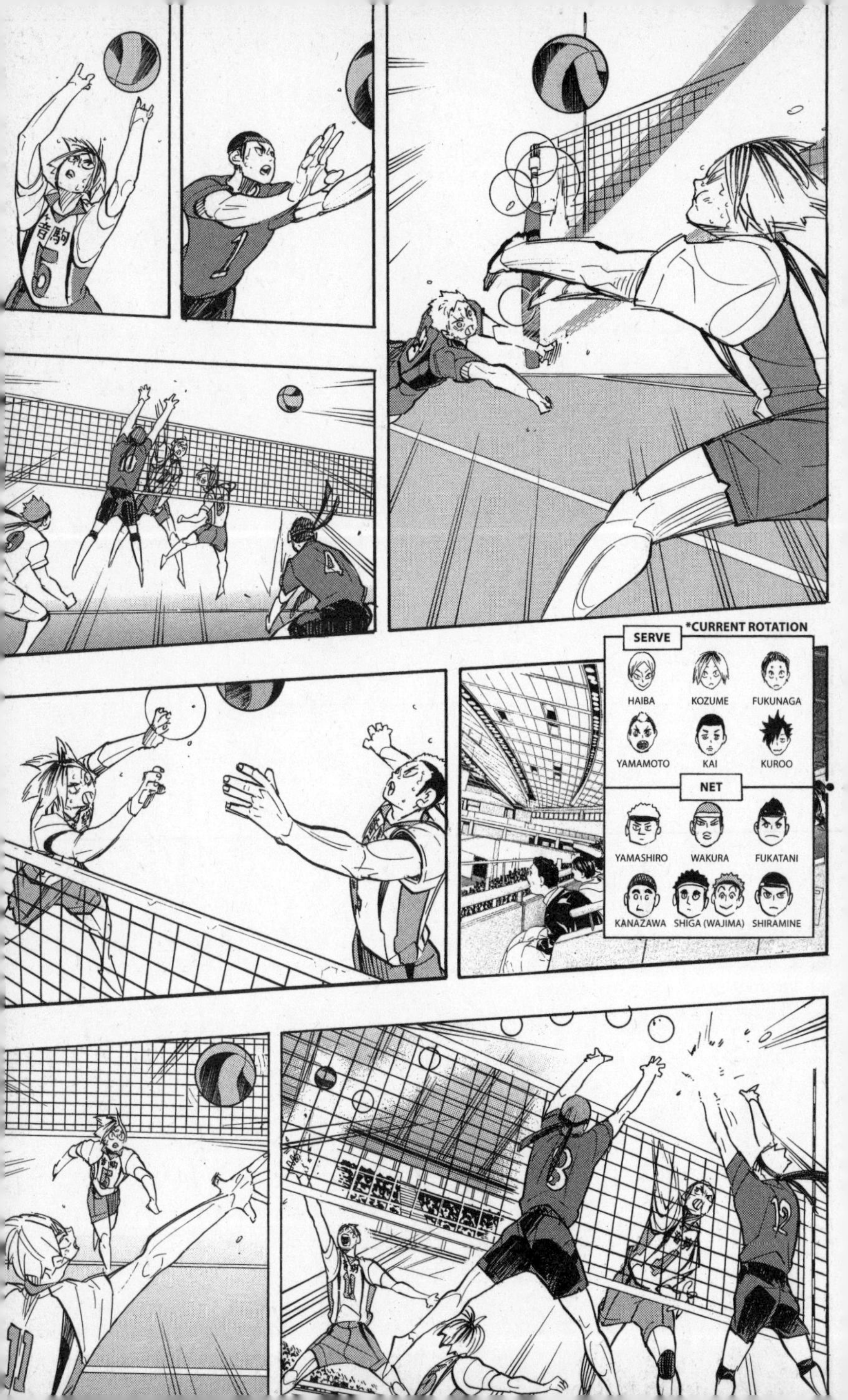
*CURRENT ROTATION
SERVE
HAIBA
KOZUME
FUKUNAGA
YAMAMOTO
KAI
KUROO
NET
YAMASHIRO
WAKURA
FUKATANI
KANAZAWA
SHIGA (WAJIMA)
SHIRAMINE

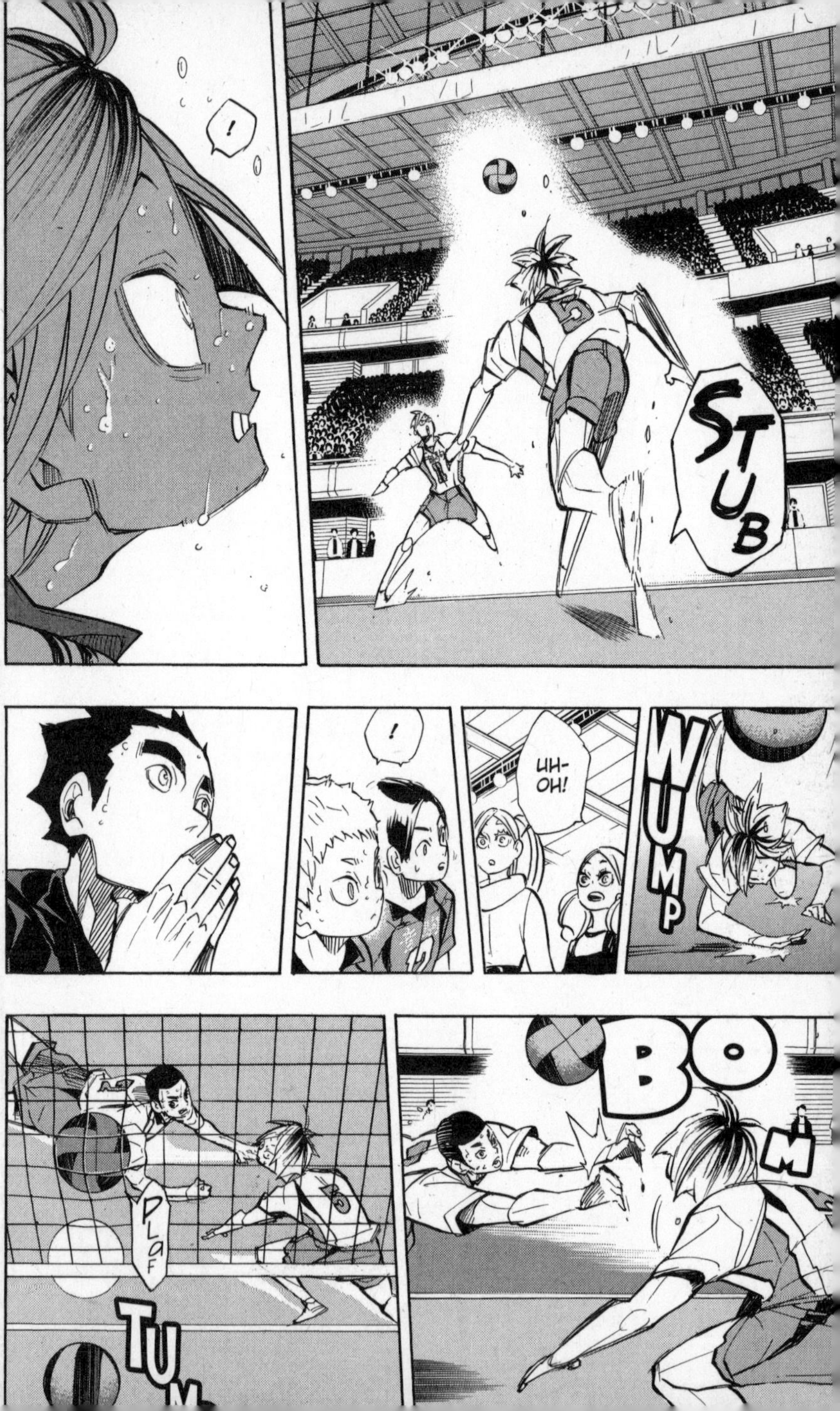
STUB
!
WUMP
UH-OH!
!
BOM
PLAF
TUM

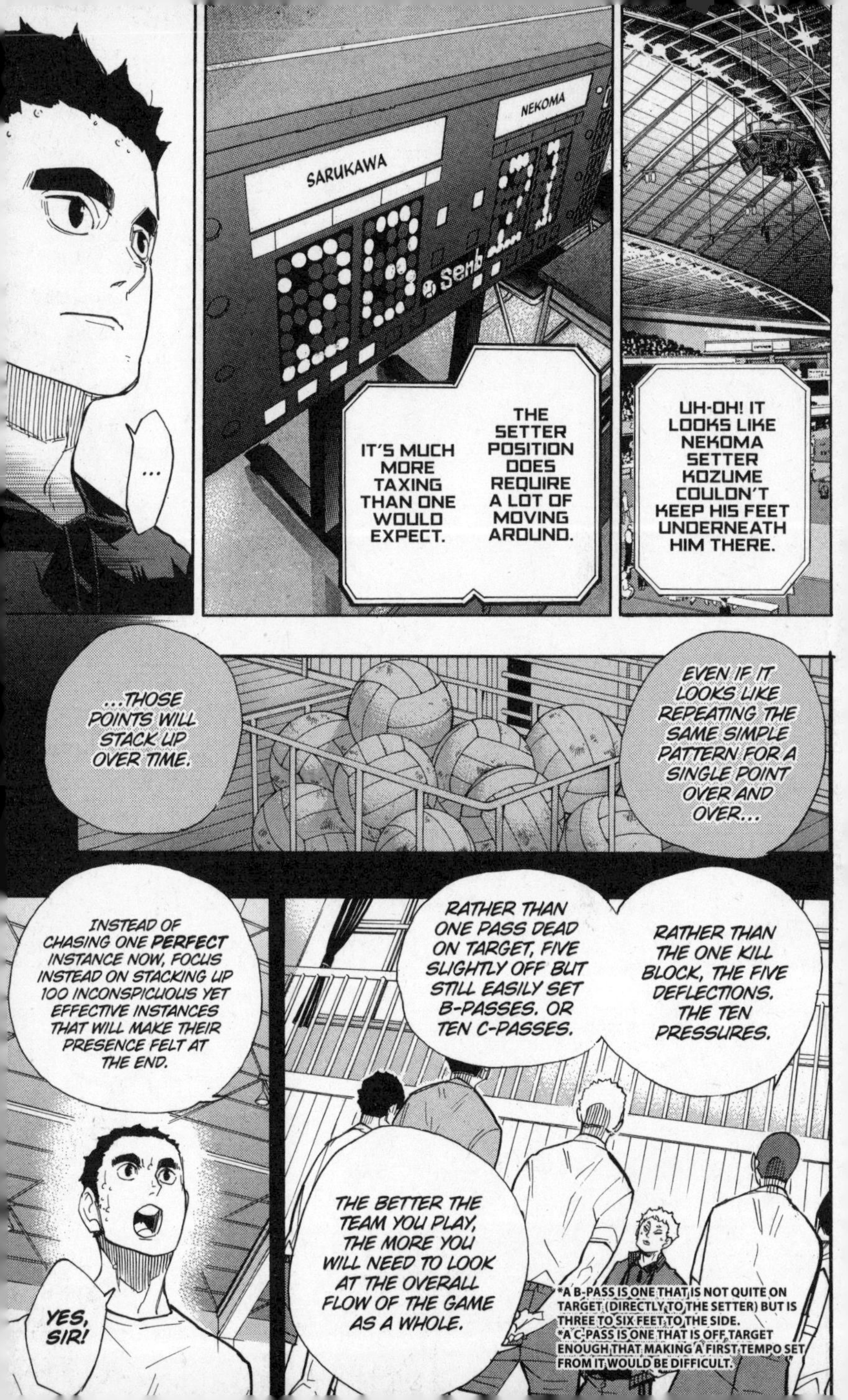
UH-OH! IT LOOKS LIKE NEKOMA SETTER KOZUME COULDN'T KEEP HIS FEET UNDERNEATH HIM THERE.
NEKOMA
SARUKAWA
THE SETTER POSITION DOES REQUIRE A LOT OF MOVING AROUND.
IT'S MUCH MORE TAXING THAN ONE WOULD EXPECT.
...
EVEN IF IT LOOKS LIKE REPEATING THE SAME SIMPLE PATTERN FOR A SINGLE POINT OVER AND OVER...
...THOSE POINTS WILL STACK UP OVER TIME.
RATHER THAN THE ONE KILL BLOCK, THE FIVE DEFLECTIONS. THE TEN PRESSURES.
RATHER THAN ONE PASS DEAD ON TARGET, FIVE SLIGHTLY OFF BUT STILL EASILY SET B-PASSES. OR TEN C-PASSES.
THE BETTER THE TEAM YOU PLAY, THE MORE YOU WILL NEED TO LOOK AT THE OVERALL FLOW OF THE GAME AS A WHOLE.
*A B-PASS IS ONE THAT IS NOT QUITE ON TARGET (DIRECTLY TO THE SETTER) BUT IS THREE TO SIX FEET TO THE SIDE.
*A C-PASS IS ONE THAT IS OFF TARGET ENOUGH THAT MAKING A FIRST TEMPO SET FROM IT WOULD BE DIFFICULT.
INSTEAD OF CHASING ONE PERFECT INSTANCE NOW, FOCUS INSTEAD ON STACKING UP 100 INCONSPICUOUS YET EFFECTIVE INSTANCES THAT WILL MAKE THEIR PRESENCE FELT AT THE END.
YES, SIR!

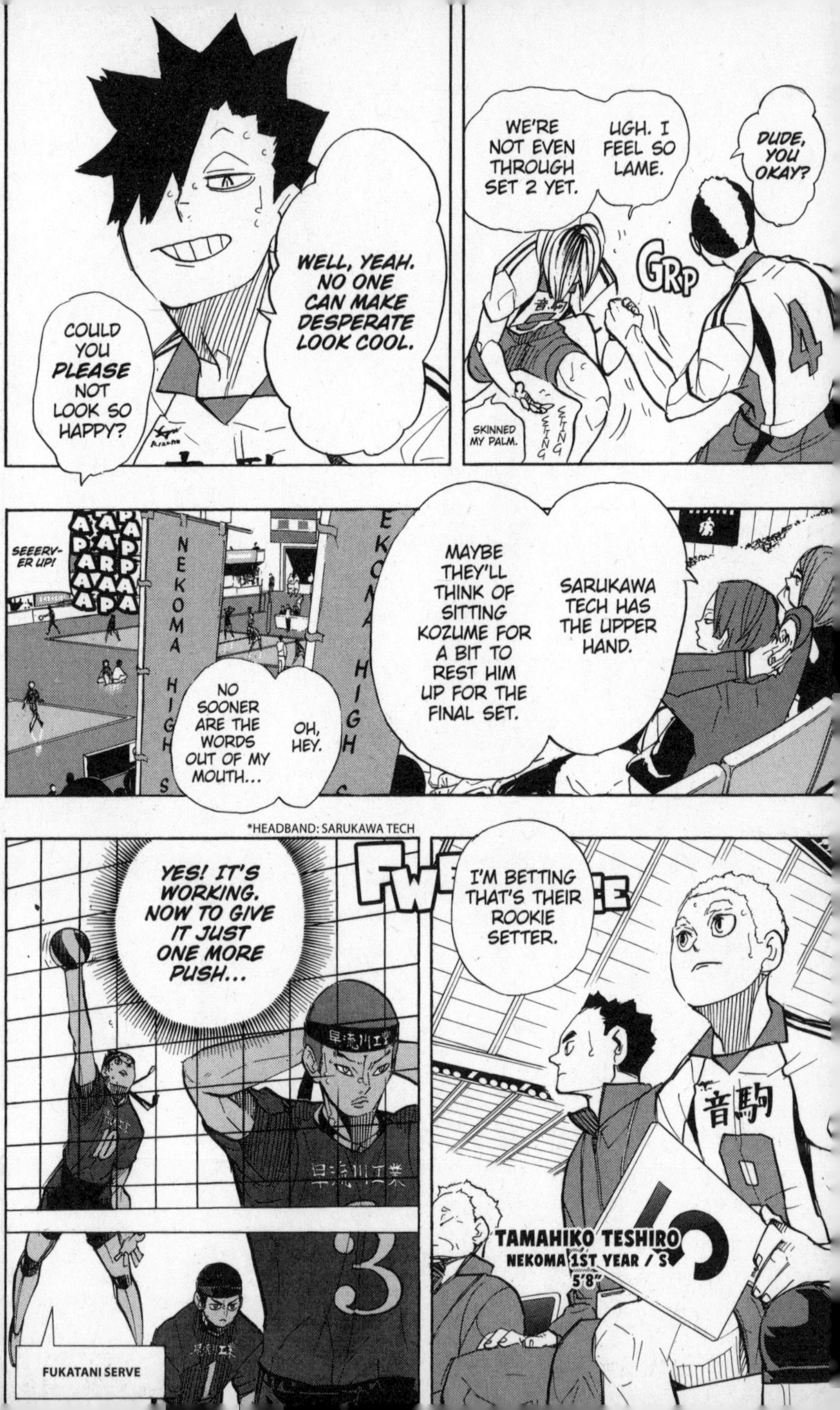
DUDE, YOU OKAY?
UGH. I FEEL SO LAME.
WE'RE NOT EVEN THROUGH SET 2 YET.
GRP
SKINNED MY PALM.
STING STING
WELL, YEAH. NO ONE CAN MAKE DESPERATE LOOK COOL.
COULD YOU PLEASE NOT LOOK SO HAPPY?
SARUKAWA TECH HAS THE UPPER HAND.
MAYBE THEY'LL THINK OF SITTING KOZUME FOR A BIT TO REST HIM UP FOR THE FINAL SET.
NEKOMA HIGH
OH, HEY.
NO SOONER ARE THE WORDS OUT OF MY MOUTH...
NEKOMA HIGH
SEEERV-ER UP!
*HEADBAND: SARUKAWA TECH
I'M BETTING THAT'S THEIR ROOKIE SETTER.
TAMAHIKO TESHIRO
NEKOMA 1ST YEAR / S
5'8"
YES! IT'S WORKING. NOW TO GIVE IT JUST ONE MORE PUSH...
FUKATANI SERVE

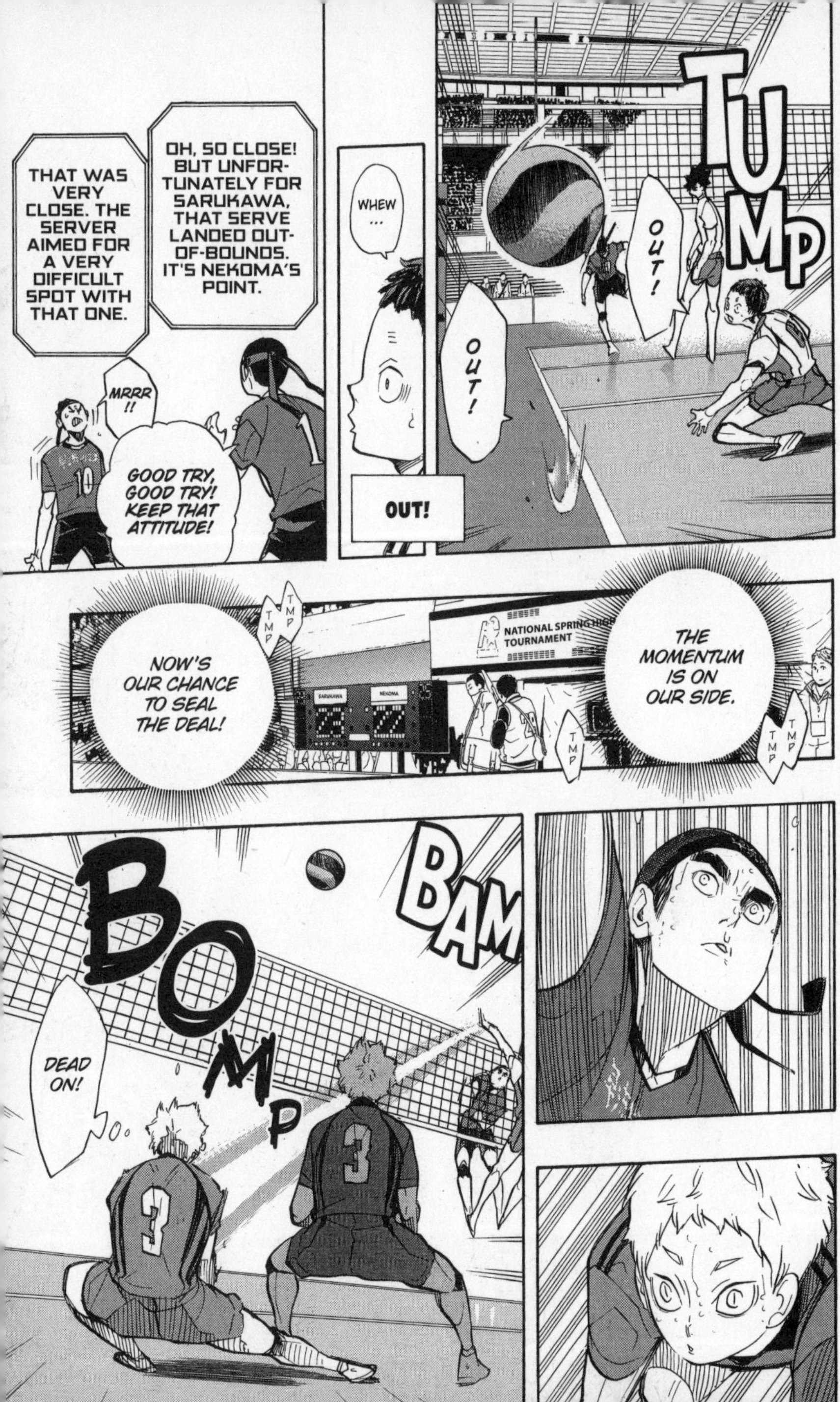
TUMP
OUT!
OUT!
WHEW ...
OUT!
OH, SO CLOSE! BUT UNFORTUNATELY FOR SARUKAWA, THAT SERVE LANDED OUT-OF-BOUNDS. IT'S NEKOMA'S POINT.
THAT WAS VERY CLOSE. THE SERVER AIMED FOR A VERY DIFFICULT SPOT WITH THAT ONE.
MRRR!!
GOOD TRY, GOOD TRY! KEEP THAT ATTITUDE!
THE MOMENTUM IS ON OUR SIDE.
TMP TMP
NATIONAL SPRING HIGH TOURNAMENT
TMP
SARUKAWA
NEKOMA
NOW'S OUR CHANCE TO SEAL THE DEAL!
TMP TMP
BAM
BOMP
DEAD ON!

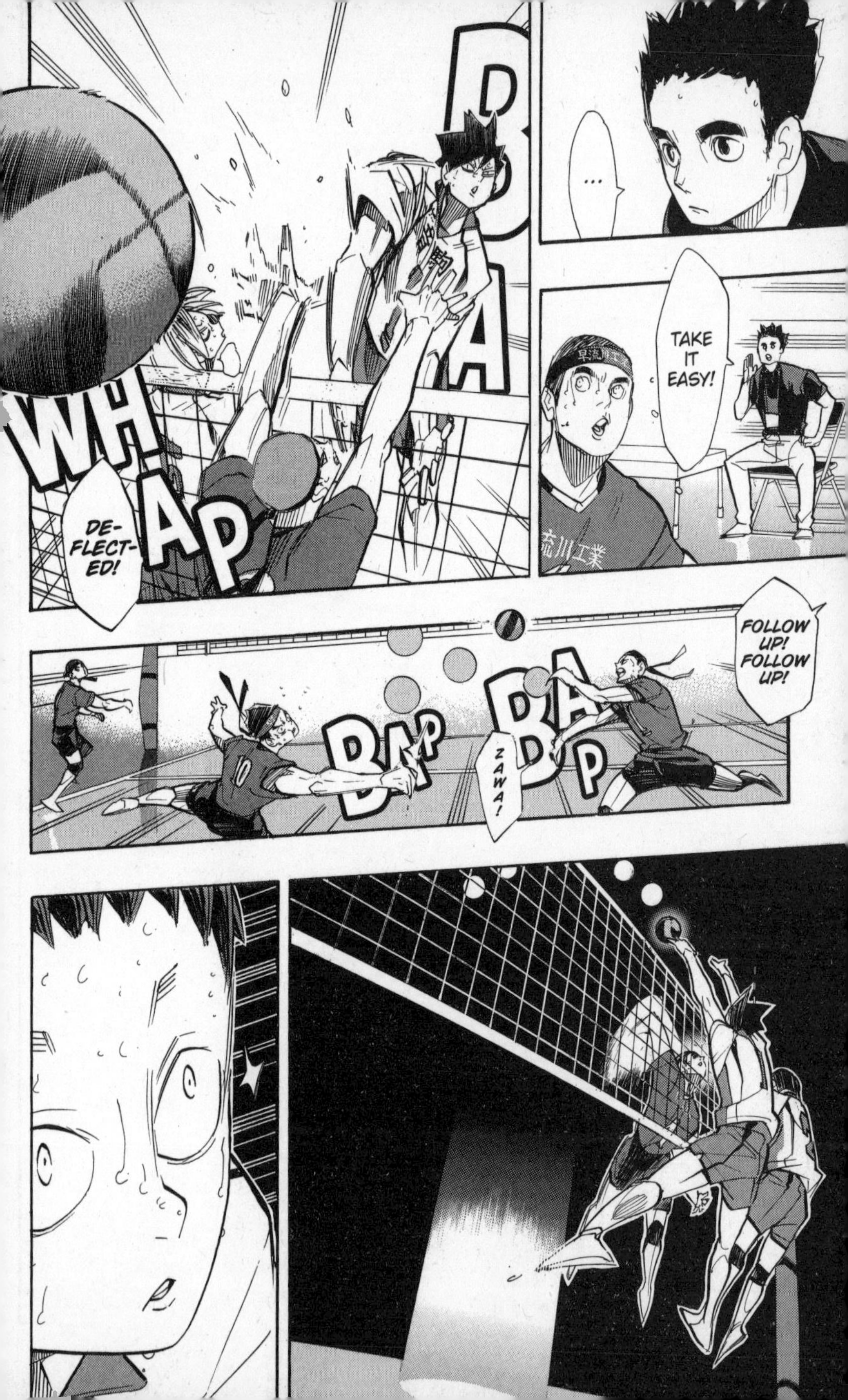
...
TAKE IT EASY!
DBA
WHAP
DE-FLECT-ED!
FOLLOW UP! FOLLOW UP!
BAP
ZAWA!
BAP

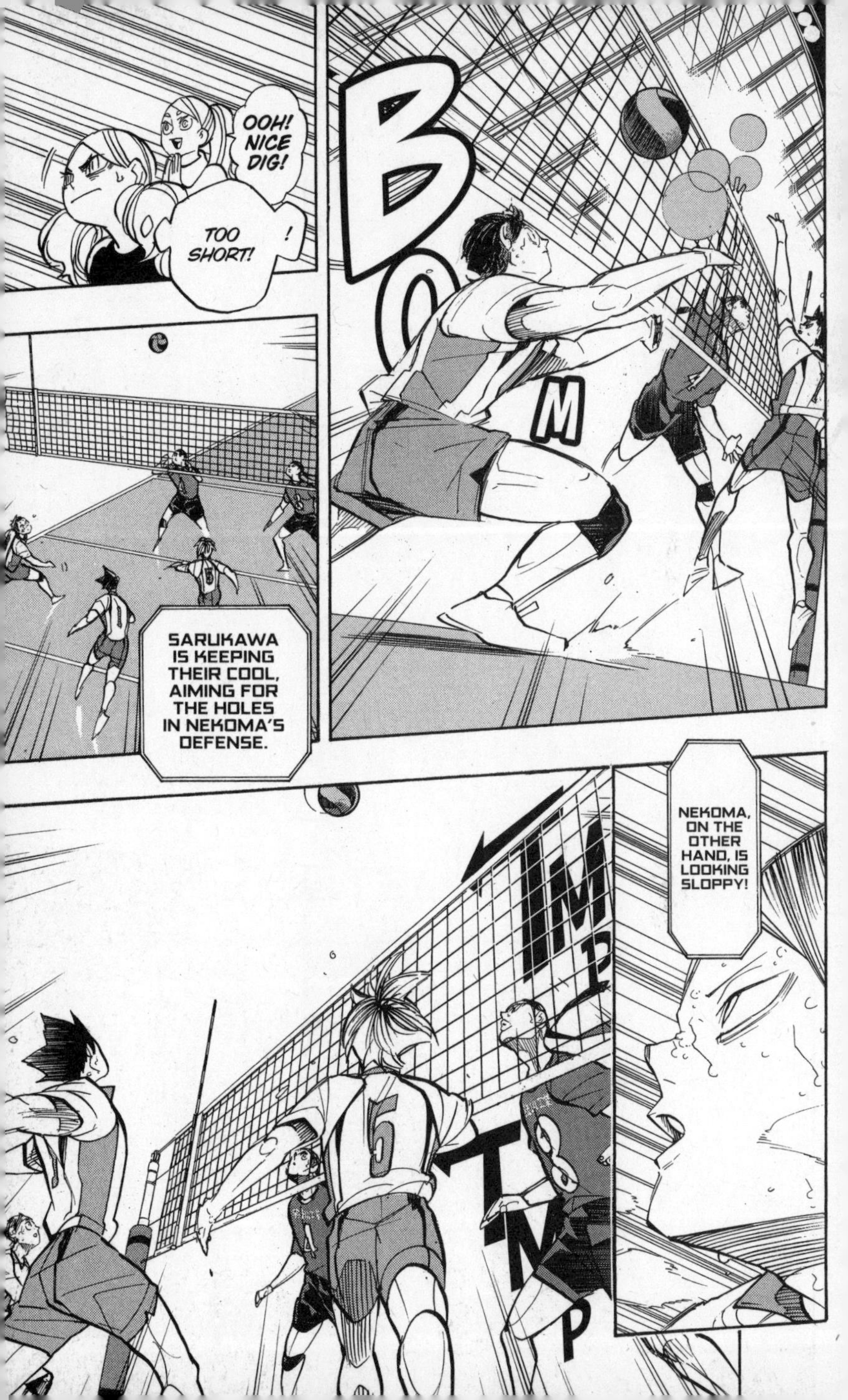
BOM
OOH! NICE DIG!
TOO SHORT!
!
SARUKAWA IS KEEPING THEIR COOL, AIMING FOR THE HOLES IN NEKOMA'S DEFENSE.
NEKOMA, ON THE OTHER HAND, IS LOOKING SLOPPY!
TMP
TMP

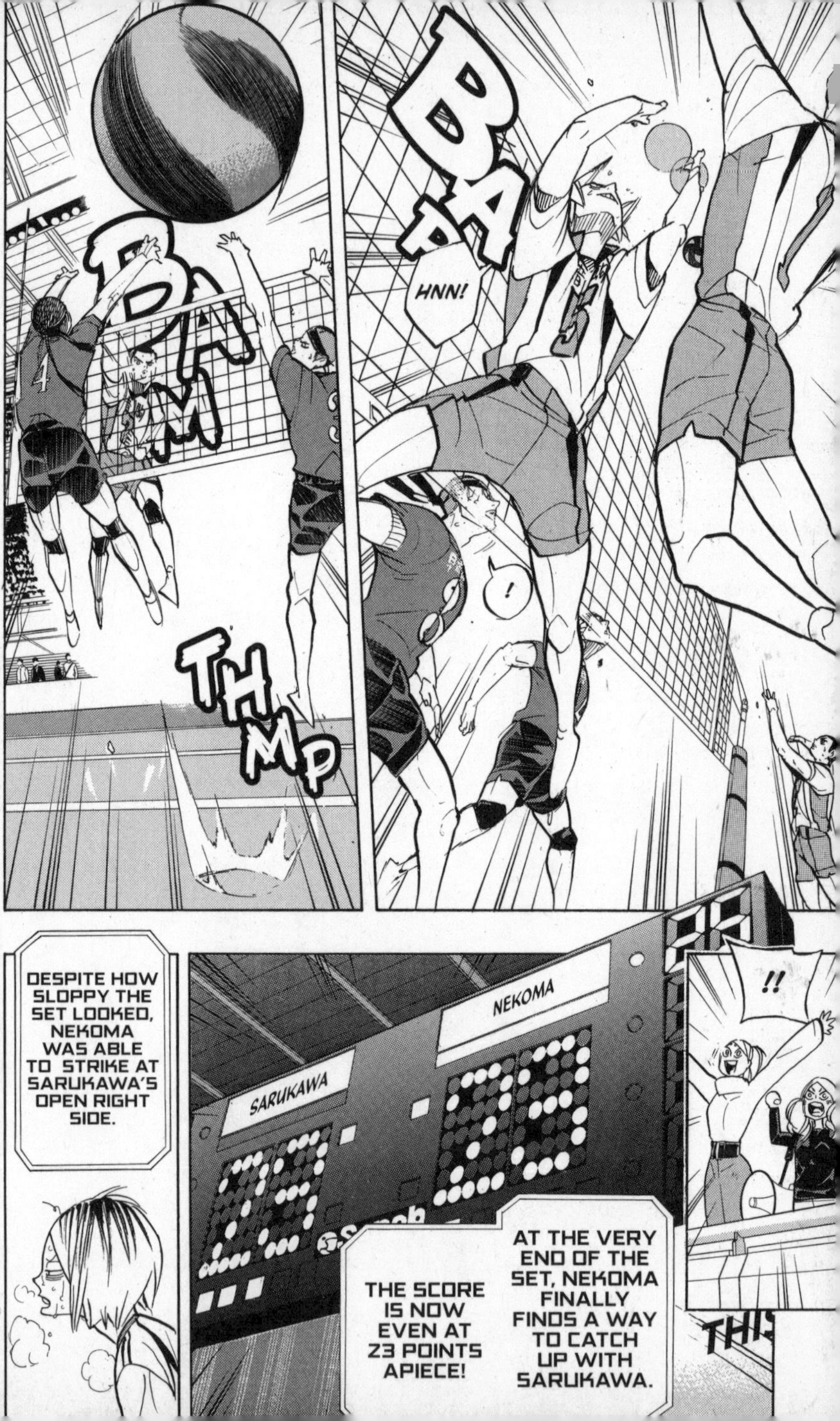
HNN!
!
BAM
THMP
!!
NEKOMA
SARUKAWA
AT THE VERY END OF THE SET, NEKOMA FINALLY FINDS A WAY TO CATCH UP WITH SARUKAWA.
THE SCORE IS NOW EVEN AT 23 POINTS APIECE!
DESPITE HOW SLOPPY THE SET LOOKED, NEKOMA WAS ABLE TO STRIKE AT SARUKAWA'S OPEN RIGHT SIDE.

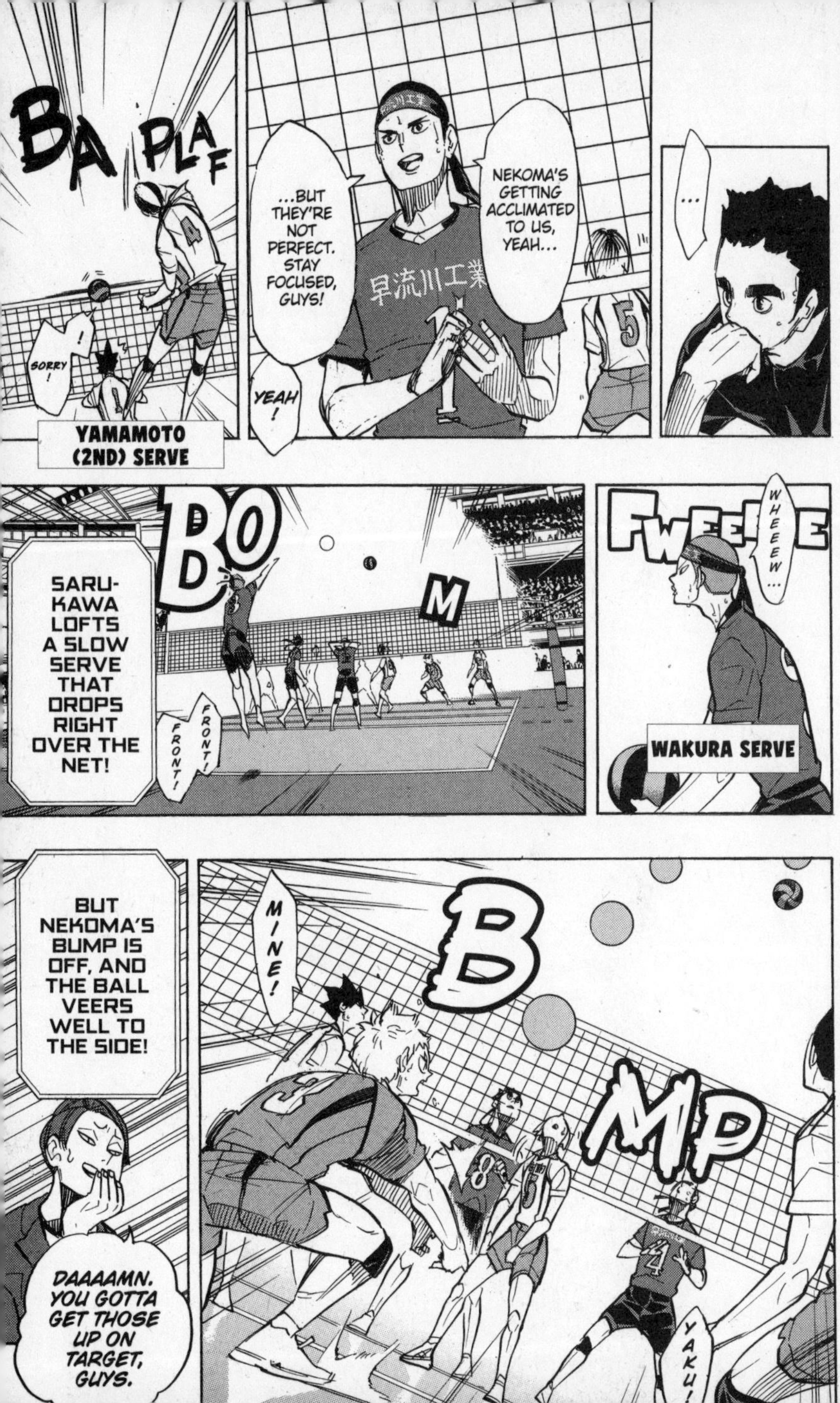
...
NEKOMA'S GETTING ACCLIMATED TO US, YEAH...
...BUT THEY'RE NOT PERFECT. STAY FOCUSED, GUYS!
YEAH!
BAPLAF
!
SORRY!
YAMAMOTO (2ND) SERVE
FWEEEE
WHEEEW...
WAKURA SERVE
BOM
SARUKAWA LOFTS A SLOW SERVE THAT DROPS RIGHT OVER THE NET!
FRONT!
FRONT!
BMP
YAKU!
MINE!
BUT NEKOMA'S BUMP IS OFF, AND THE BALL VEERS WELL TO THE SIDE!
DAAAAMN. YOU GOTTA GET THOSE UP ON TARGET, GUYS.

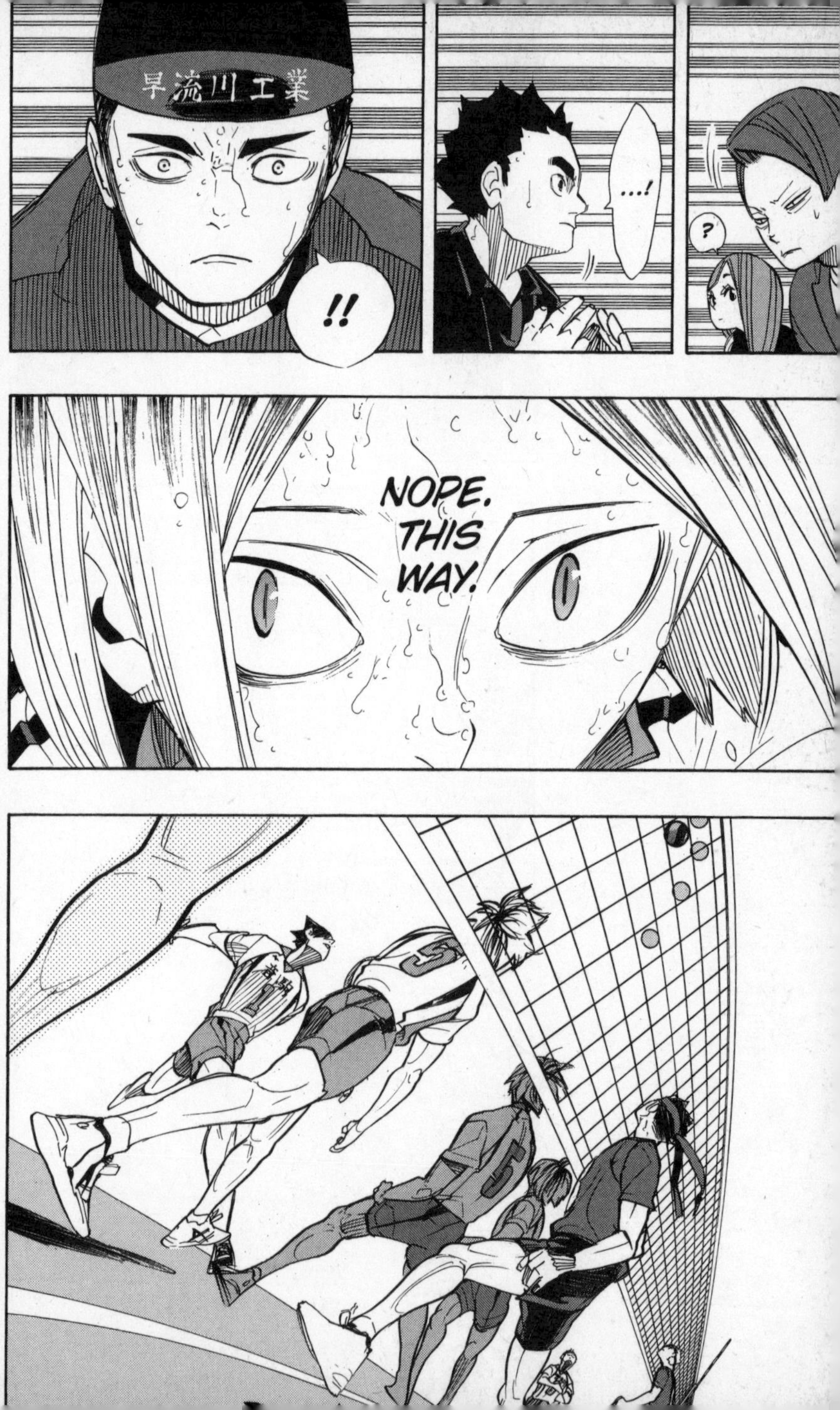
?
...!
早流川工業
!!
NOPE. THIS WAY.

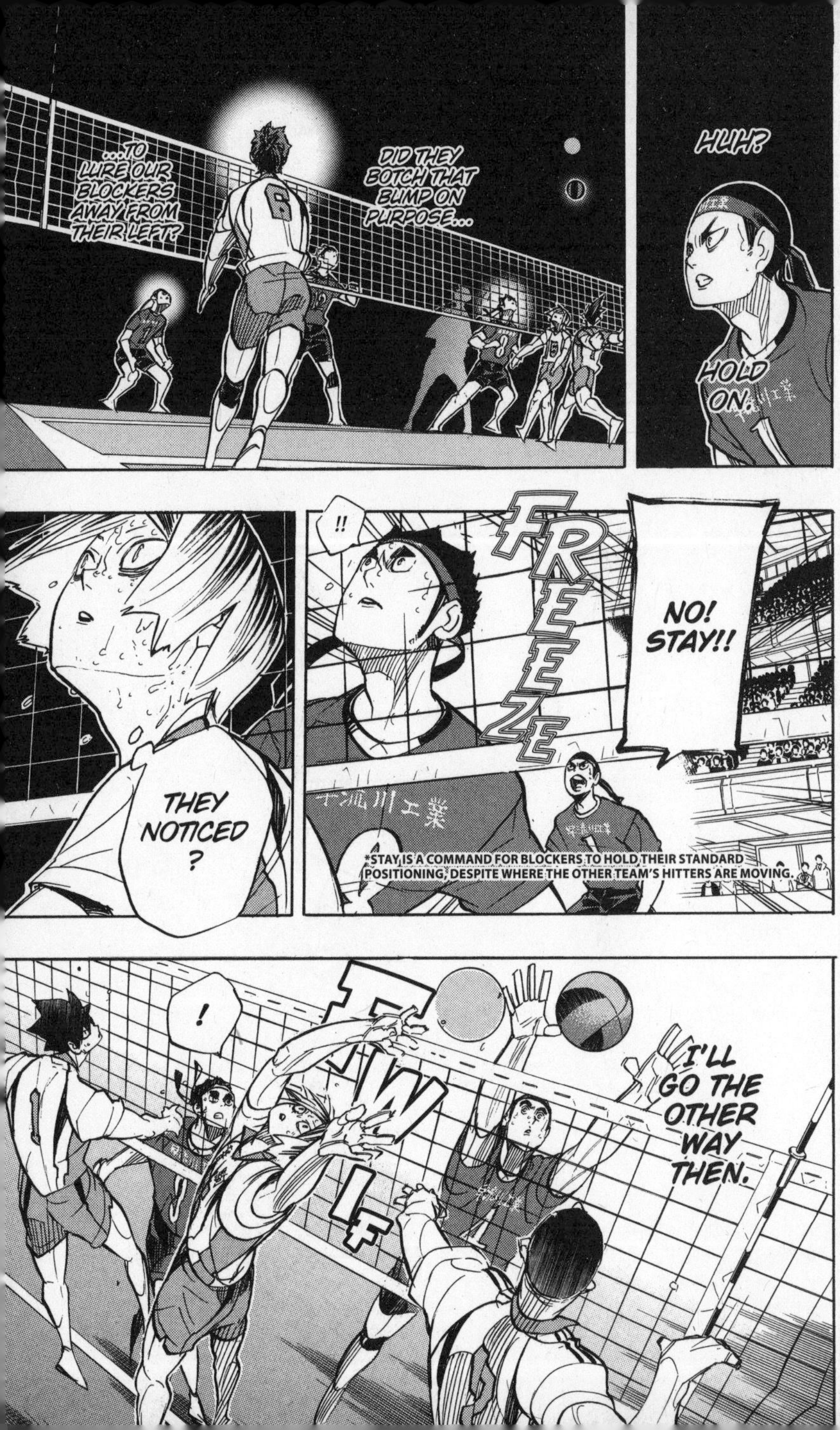
HUH?
HOLD ON.
DID THEY BOTCH THAT BUMP ON PURPOSE...
...TO LURE OUR BLOCKERS AWAY FROM THEIR LEFT?
NO! STAY!!
FREEZE
!!
*STAY IS A COMMAND FOR BLOCKERS TO HOLD THEIR STANDARD POSITIONING, DESPITE WHERE THE OTHER TEAM'S HITTERS ARE MOVING.
THEY NOTICED ?
I'LL GO THE OTHER WAY THEN.
FWIF
!

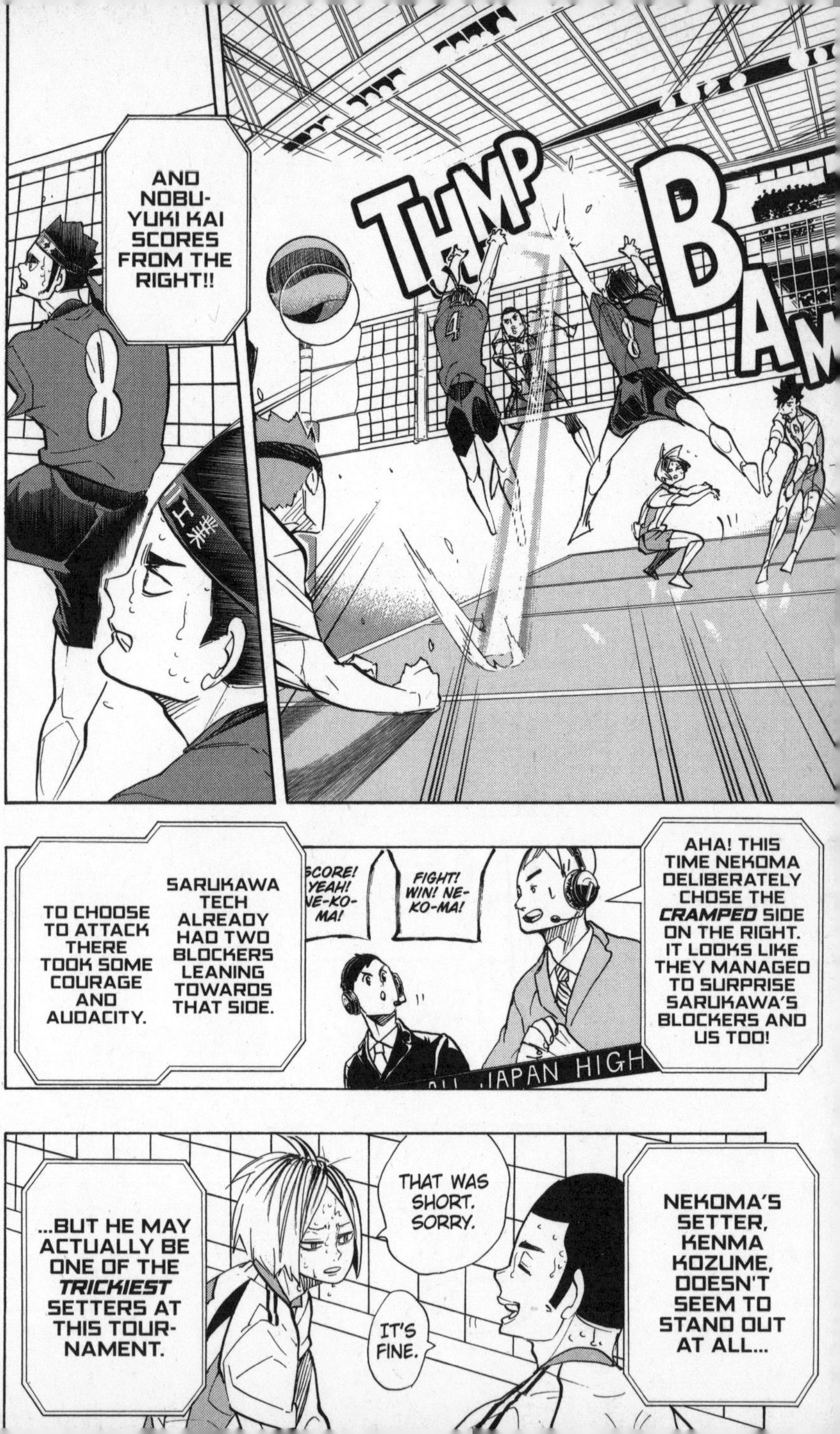
BAM
THMP
AND NOBU-YUKI KAI SCORES FROM THE RIGHT!!
AHA! THIS TIME NEKOMA DELIBERATELY CHOSE THE *CRAMPED* SIDE ON THE RIGHT. IT LOOKS LIKE THEY MANAGED TO SURPRISE SARUKAWA'S BLOCKERS AND US TOO!
FIGHT! WIN! NE-KO-MA!
SCORE! YEAH! NE-KO-MA!
SARUKAWA TECH ALREADY HAD TWO BLOCKERS LEANING TOWARDS THAT SIDE.
TO CHOOSE TO ATTACK THERE TOOK SOME COURAGE AND AUDACITY.
JAPAN HIGH
NEKOMA'S SETTER, KENMA KOZUME, DOESN'T SEEM TO STAND OUT AT ALL...
THAT WAS SHORT. SORRY.
IT'S FINE.
...BUT HE MAY ACTUALLY BE ONE OF THE *TRICKIEST* SETTERS AT THIS TOUR-NAMENT.

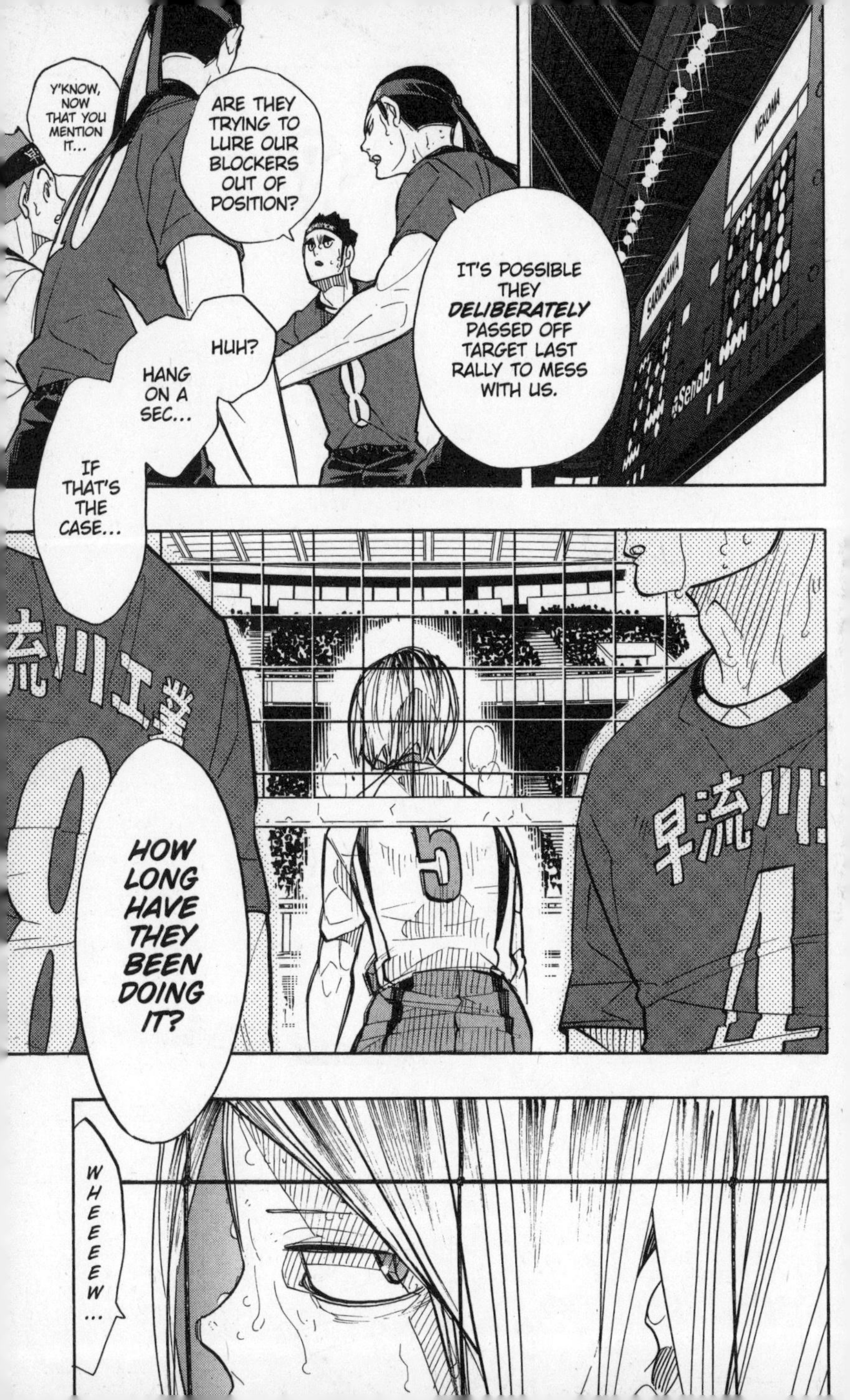

NEKOMA
SARUKAWA
IT'S POSSIBLE THEY *DELIBERATELY* PASSED OFF TARGET LAST RALLY TO MESS WITH US.
ARE THEY TRYING TO LURE OUR BLOCKERS OUT OF POSITION?
Y'KNOW, NOW THAT YOU MENTION IT...
HUH?
HANG ON A SEC...
IF THAT'S THE CASE...
HOW LONG HAVE THEY BEEN DOING IT?
WHEEEEEW...

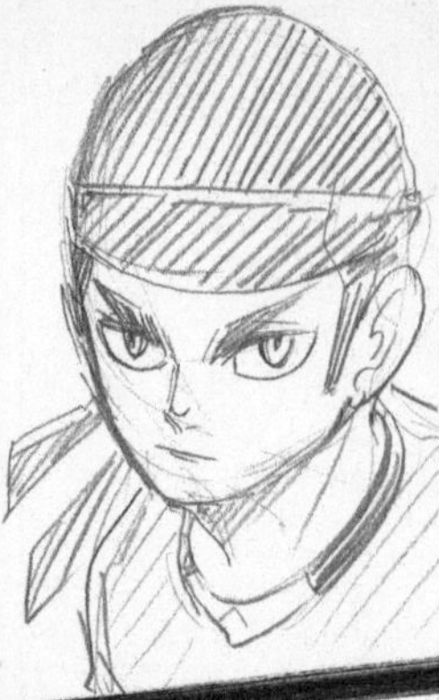

ITARU SHIRAMINE

SARUKAWA TECHNICAL HIGH SCHOOL 3RD YEAR VOLLEYBALL CLUB CAPTAIN

POSITION: SETTER

HEIGHT: 5'11"

WEIGHT: 158 LBS.
(AS OF JANUARY, 3RD YEAR OF HIGH SCHOOL)

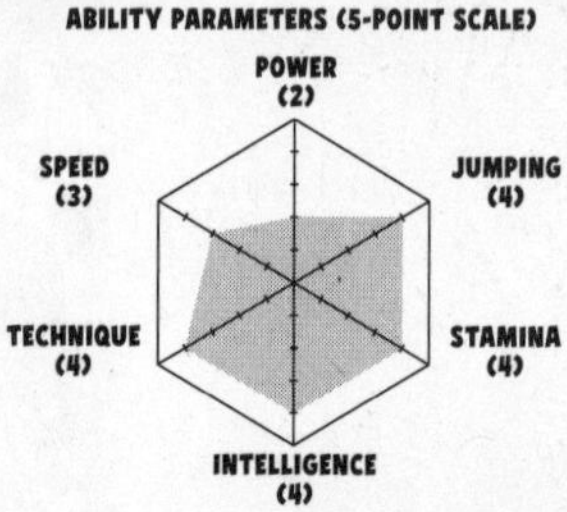
ABILITY PARAMETERS (5-POINT SCALE)
POWER (2)
JUMPING (4)
STAMINA (4)
INTELLIGENCE (4)
TECHNIQUE (4)
SPEED (3)

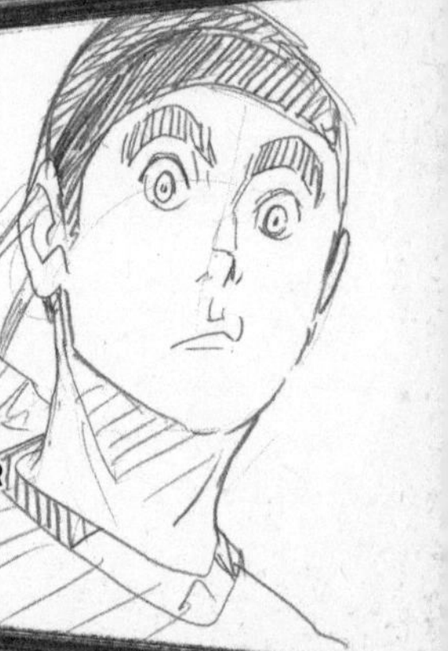

IORI KANAZAWA

SARUKAWA TECHNICAL HIGH SCHOOL 3RD YEAR

POSITION: WING SPIKER

HEIGHT: 5'11"

WEIGHT: 159 LBS.
(AS OF JANUARY, 3RD YEAR OF HIGH SCHOOL)

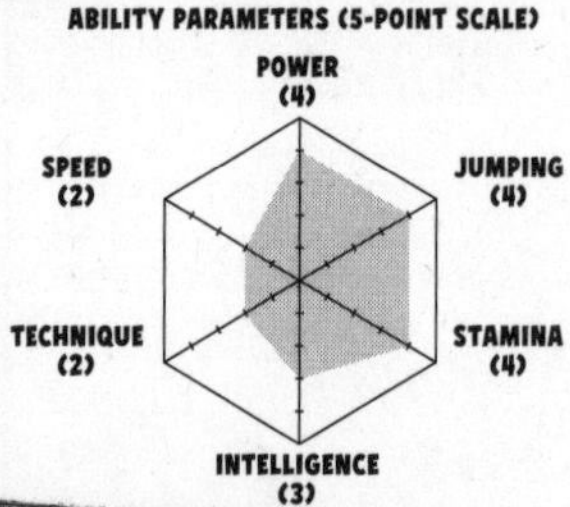
ABILITY PARAMETERS (5-POINT SCALE)
POWER (4)
JUMPING (4)
STAMINA (4)
INTELLIGENCE (3)
TECHNIQUE (2)
SPEED (2)

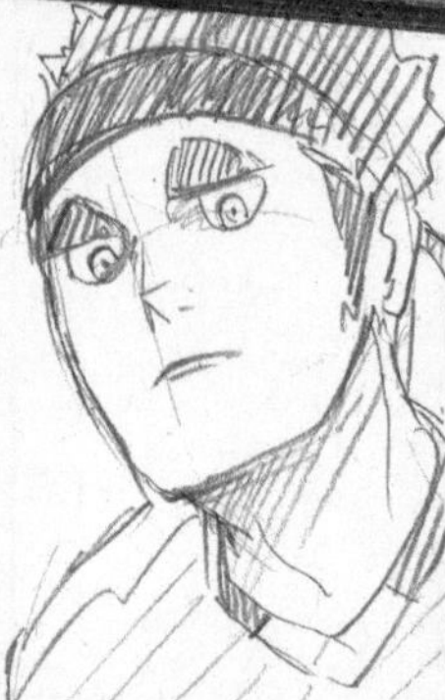

TOMONARI SHIGA

SARUKAWA TECHNICAL HIGH SCHOOL 3RD YEAR

POSITION: MIDDLE BLOCKER

HEIGHT: 6'2"

WEIGHT: 177 LBS.
(AS OF JANUARY, 3RD YEAR OF HIGH SCHOOL)

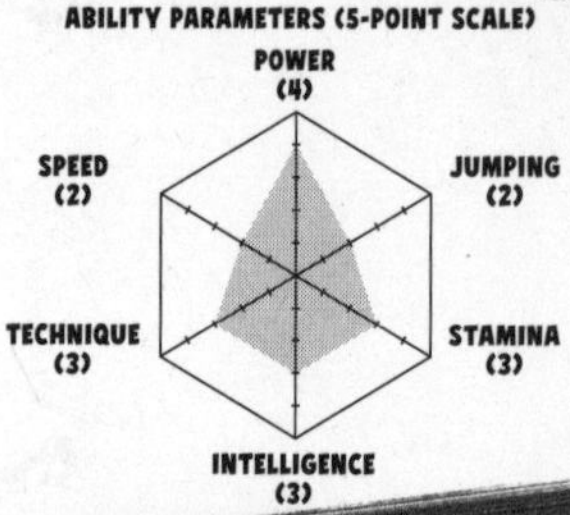
ABILITY PARAMETERS (5-POINT SCALE)
POWER (4)
JUMPING (2)
STAMINA (3)
INTELLIGENCE (3)
TECHNIQUE (3)
SPEED (2)

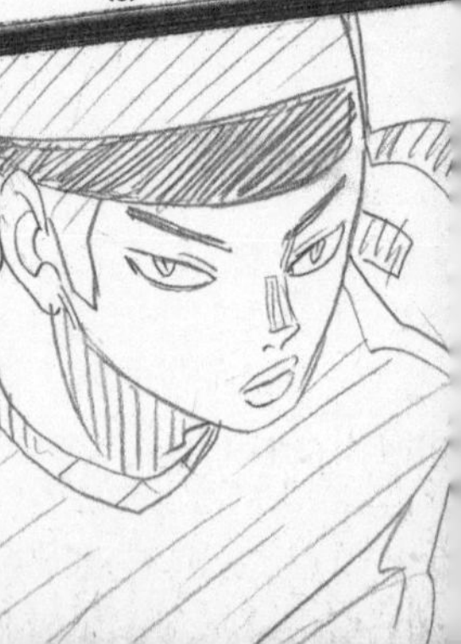

HISAHIKO WAKURA

SARUKAWA TECHNICAL HIGH SCHOOL 3RD YEAR

POSITION: MIDDLE BLOCKER

HEIGHT: 6'1"

WEIGHT: 162 LBS.
(AS OF JANUARY, 3RD YEAR OF HIGH SCHOOL)

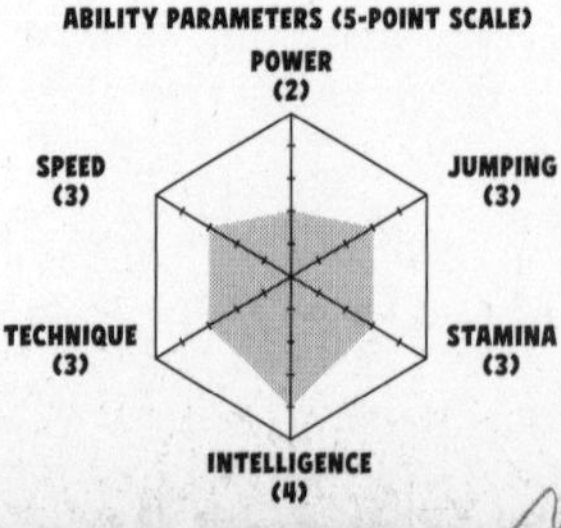
ABILITY PARAMETERS (5-POINT SCALE)
POWER (2)
JUMPING (3)
STAMINA (3)
INTELLIGENCE (4)
TECHNIQUE (3)
SPEED (3)

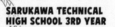

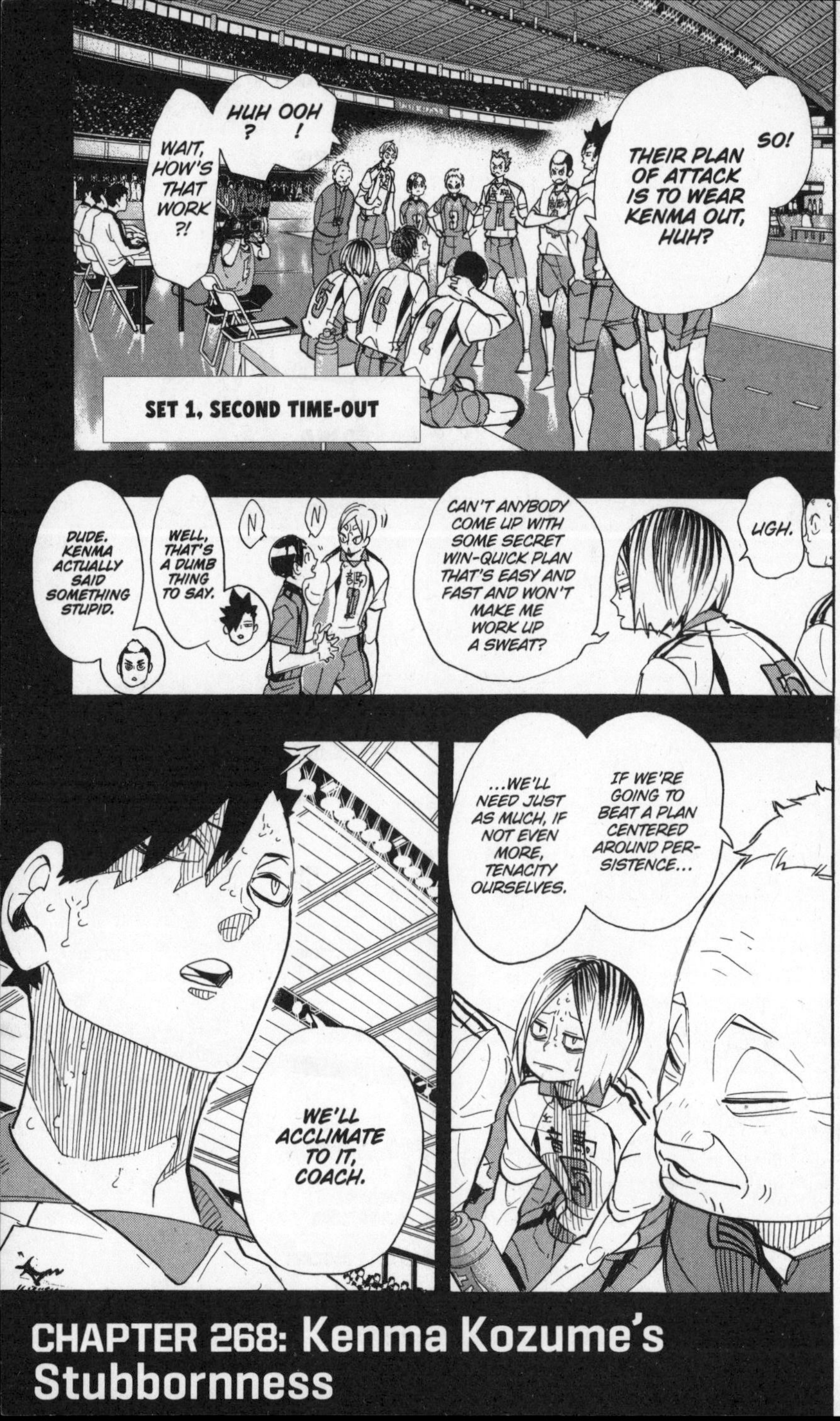
SO!
THEIR PLAN OF ATTACK IS TO WEAR KENMA OUT, HUH?
HUH? OOH!
WAIT, HOW'S THAT WORK?!
SET 1, SECOND TIME-OUT
UGH.
CAN'T ANYBODY COME UP WITH SOME SECRET WIN-QUICK PLAN THAT'S EASY AND FAST AND WON'T MAKE ME WORK UP A SWEAT?
N
N
WELL, THAT'S A DUMB THING TO SAY.
DUDE. KENMA ACTUALLY SAID SOMETHING STUPID.
IF WE'RE GOING TO BEAT A PLAN CENTERED AROUND PERSISTENCE...
...WE'LL NEED JUST AS MUCH, IF NOT EVEN MORE, TENACITY OURSELVES.
WE'LL ACCLIMATE TO IT, COACH.

CHAPTER 268: Kenma Kozume's Stubbornness

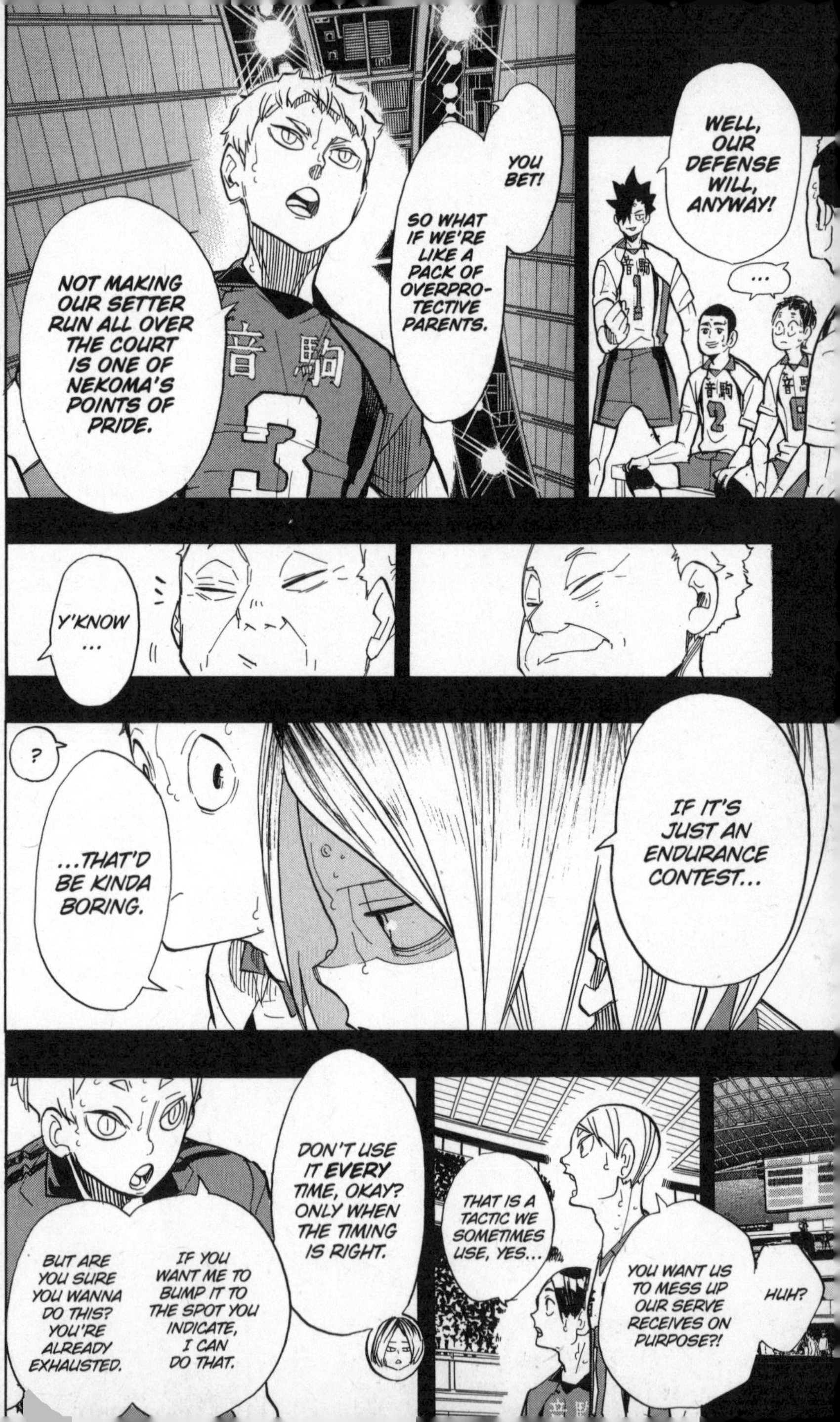
WELL, OUR DEFENSE WILL, ANYWAY!
...
YOU BET!
SO WHAT IF WE'RE LIKE A PACK OF OVERPROTECTIVE PARENTS.
NOT MAKING OUR SETTER RUN ALL OVER THE COURT IS ONE OF NEKOMA'S POINTS OF PRIDE.
Y'KNOW ...
IF IT'S JUST AN ENDURANCE CONTEST...
?
...THAT'D BE KINDA BORING.
HUH?
YOU WANT US TO MESS UP OUR SERVE RECEIVES ON PURPOSE?!
THAT IS A TACTIC WE SOMETIMES USE, YES...
DON'T USE IT **EVERY** TIME, OKAY? ONLY WHEN THE TIMING IS RIGHT.
IF YOU WANT ME TO BUMP IT TO THE SPOT YOU INDICATE, I CAN DO THAT.
BUT ARE YOU SURE YOU WANNA DO THIS? YOU'RE ALREADY EXHAUSTED.

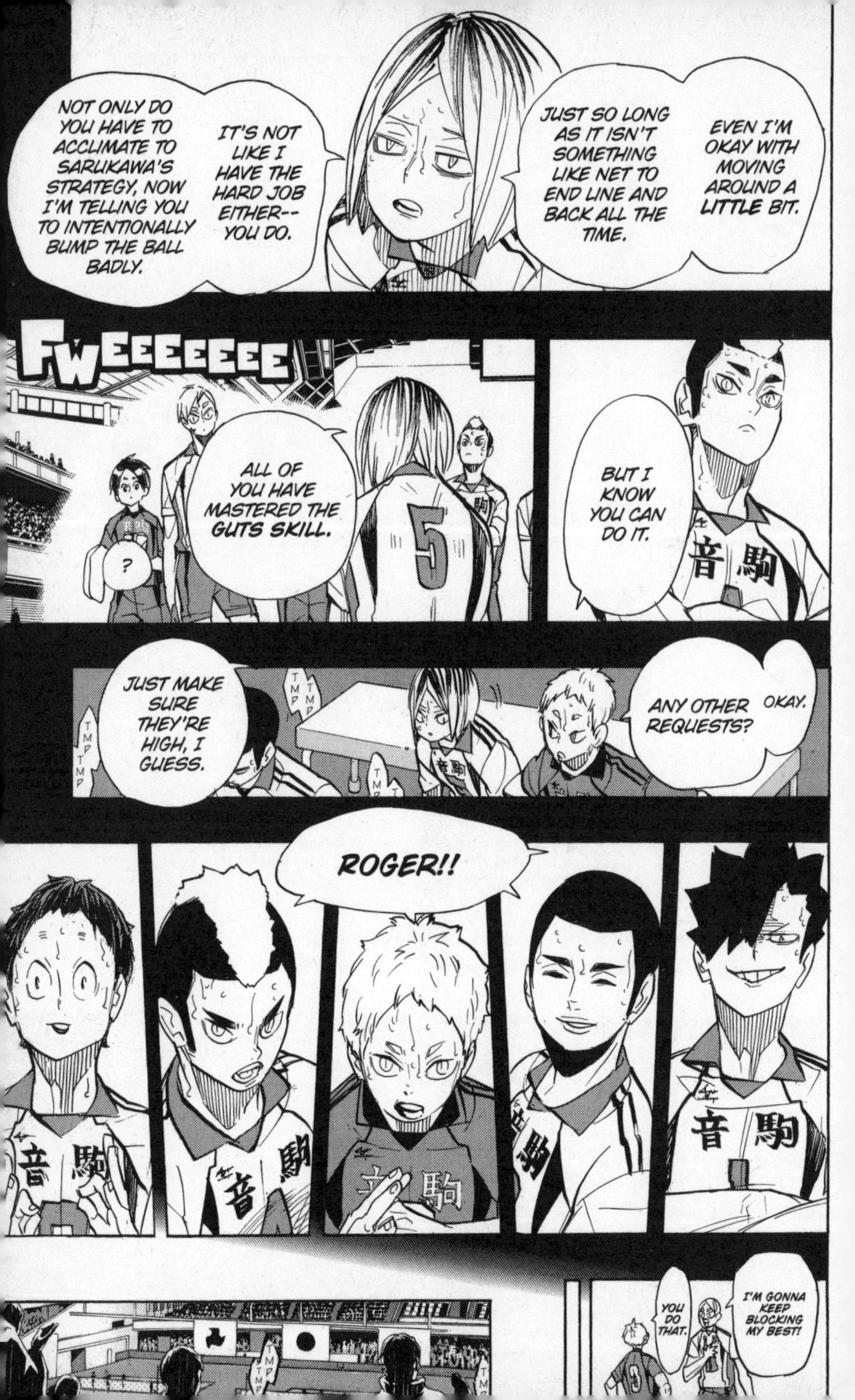
EVEN I'M OKAY WITH MOVING AROUND A LITTLE BIT.
JUST SO LONG AS IT ISN'T SOMETHING LIKE NET TO END LINE AND BACK ALL THE TIME.
IT'S NOT LIKE I HAVE THE HARD JOB EITHER--YOU DO.
NOT ONLY DO YOU HAVE TO ACCLIMATE TO SARUKAWA'S STRATEGY, NOW I'M TELLING YOU TO INTENTIONALLY BUMP THE BALL BADLY.
BUT I KNOW YOU CAN DO IT.
FWEEEEEEE
ALL OF YOU HAVE MASTERED THE GUTS SKILL.
?
OKAY.
ANY OTHER REQUESTS?
TMP TMP
JUST MAKE SURE THEY'RE HIGH, I GUESS.
TMP TMP TMP
ROGER!!
I'M GONNA KEEP BLOCKING MY BEST!
YOU DO THAT.
TMP TMP TMP

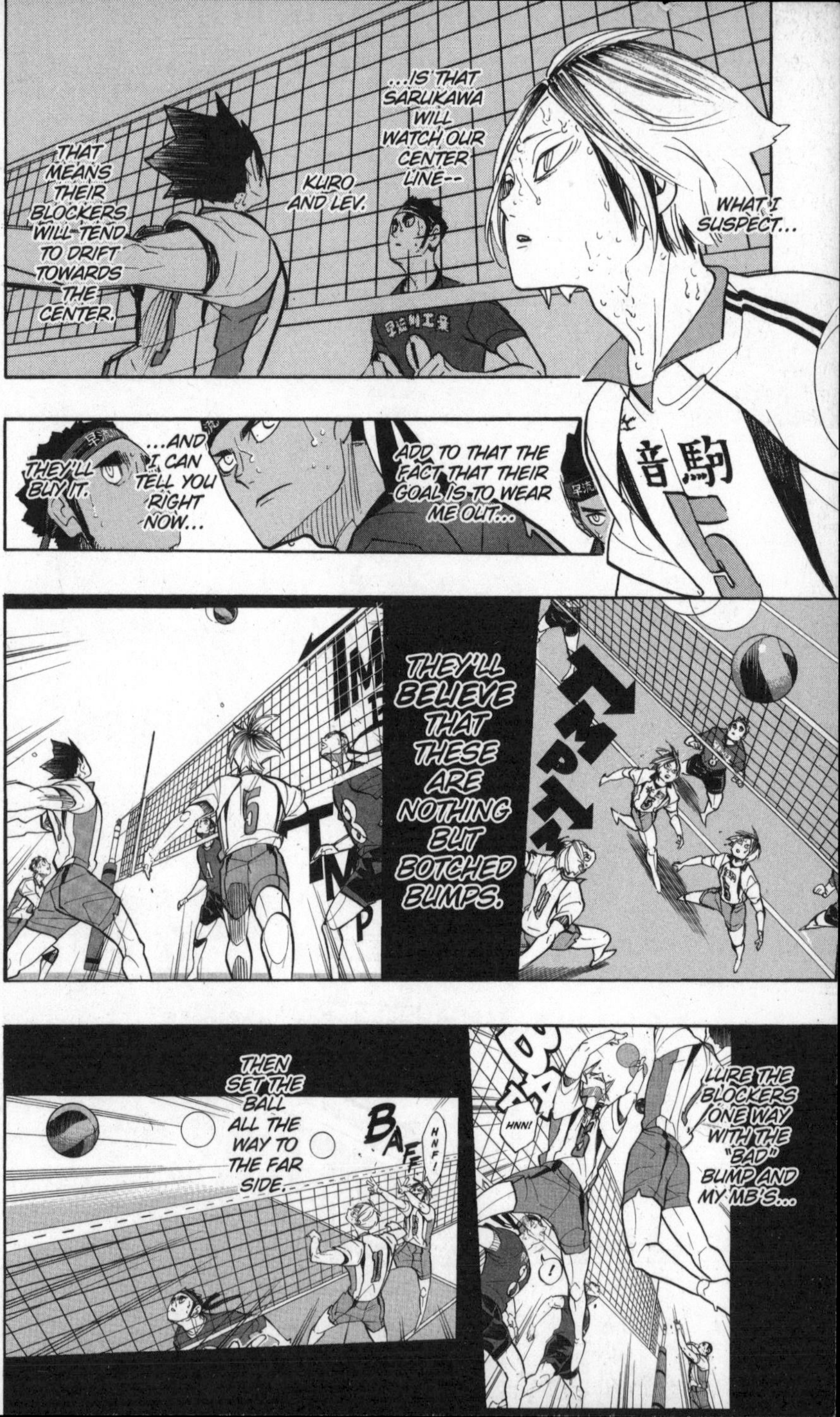
WHAT I SUSPECT...
...IS THAT SARUKAWA WILL WATCH OUR CENTER LINE--
KURO AND LEV.
THAT MEANS THEIR BLOCKERS WILL TEND TO DRIFT TOWARDS THE CENTER.
音駒
ADD TO THAT THE FACT THAT THEIR GOAL IS TO WEAR ME OUT...
...AND I CAN TELL YOU RIGHT NOW...
THEY'LL BUY IT.
THEY'LL BELIEVE THAT THESE ARE NOTHING BUT BOTCHED BUMPS.
LURE THE BLOCKERS ONE WAY WITH THE "BAD" BUMP AND MY MB'S...
HNN!
!
THEN SET THE BALL ALL THE WAY TO THE FAR SIDE.
BAFF
HNF!

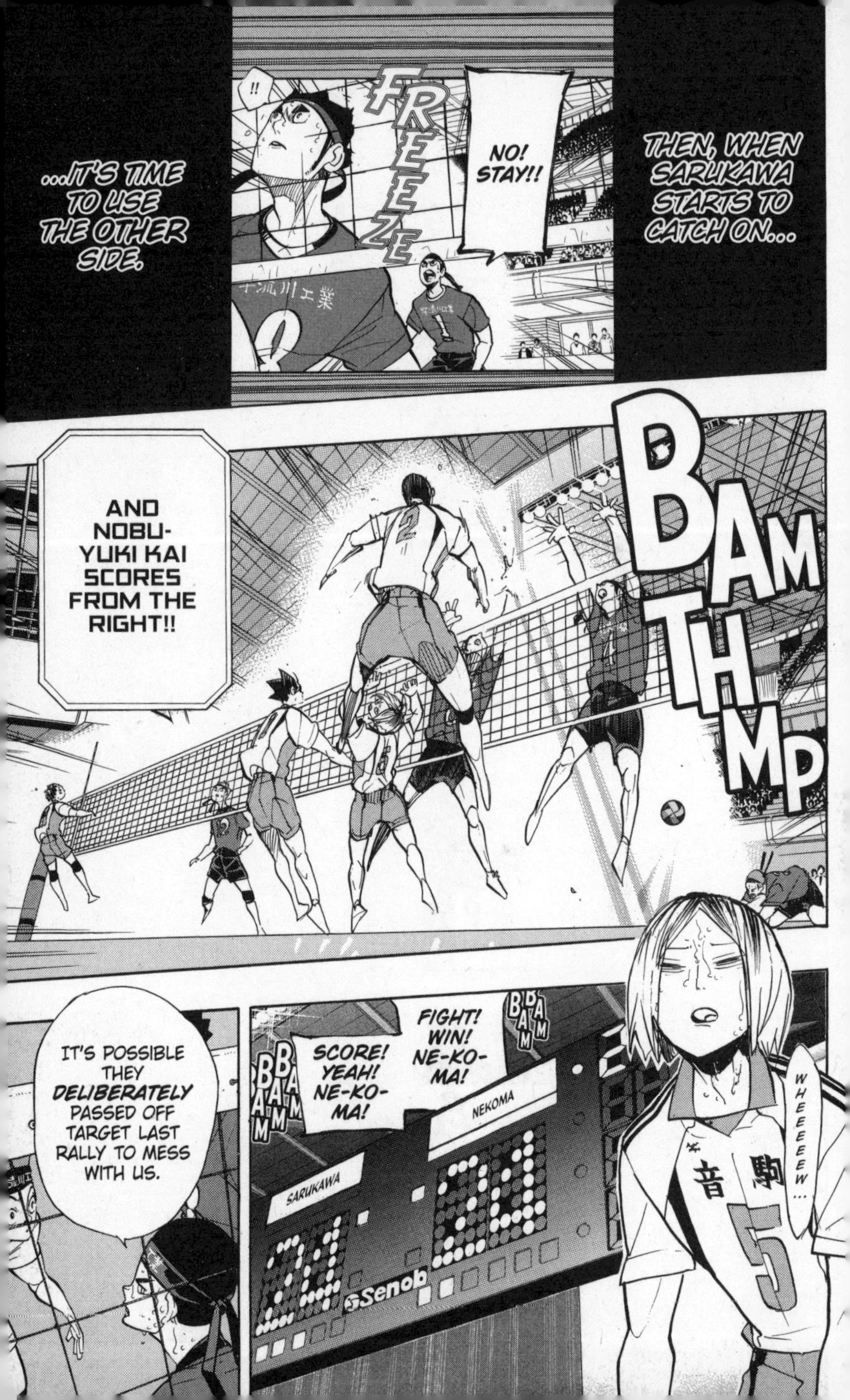
THEN, WHEN SARUKAWA STARTS TO CATCH ON...
NO! STAY!!
FREEZE
!!
...IT'S TIME TO USE THE OTHER SIDE.
BAM THUMP
AND NOBU-YUKI KAI SCORES FROM THE RIGHT!!
WHEEEEEEW...
BAM BAM
FIGHT! WIN! NE-KO-MA!
SCORE! YEAH! NE-KO-MA!
BAM BAM
NEKOMA
SARUKAWA
Senob
IT'S POSSIBLE THEY DELIBERATELY PASSED OFF TARGET LAST RALLY TO MESS WITH US.

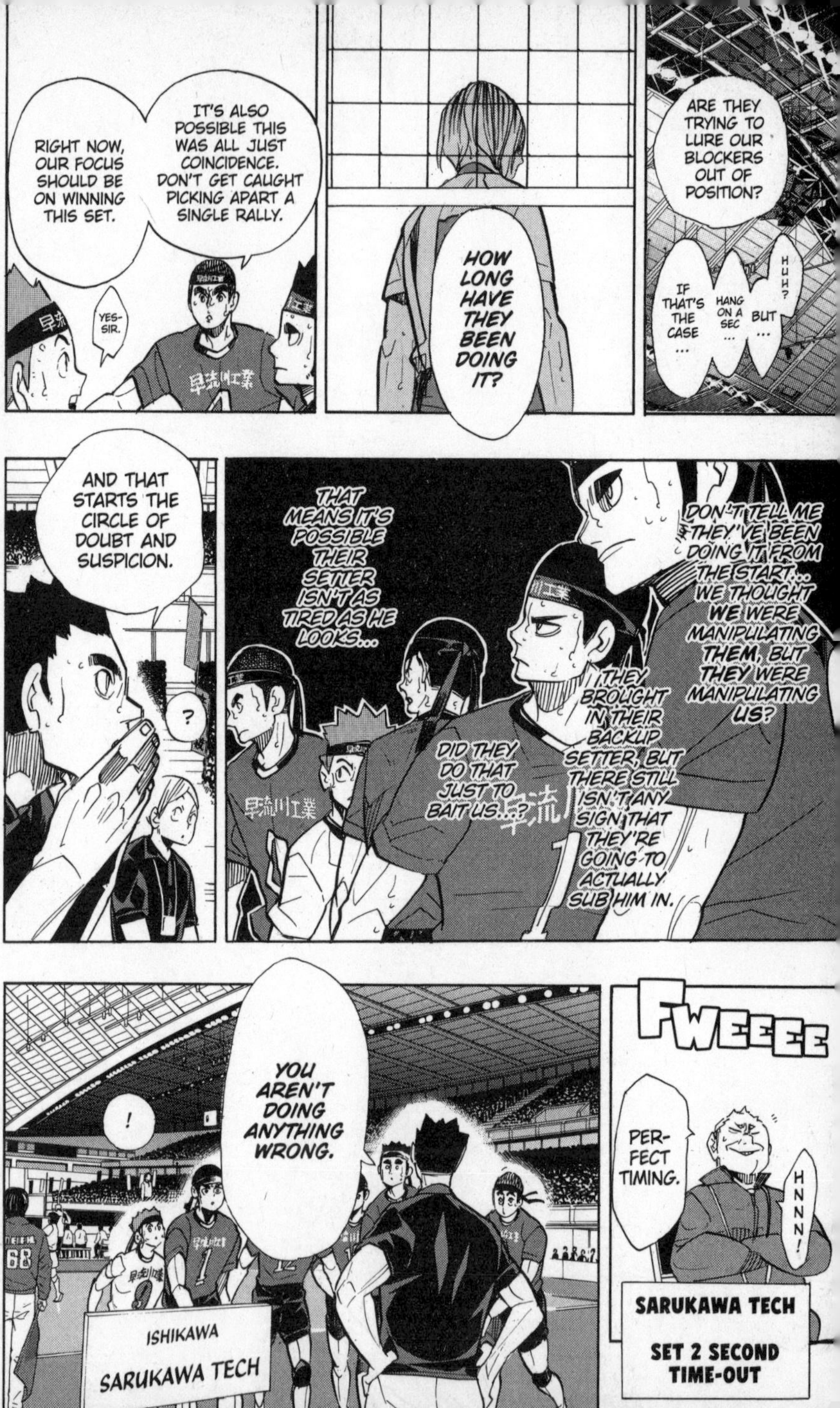
ARE THEY TRYING TO LURE OUR BLOCKERS OUT OF POSITION?
HUH?
BUT...
HANG ON A SEC...
IF THAT'S THE CASE...
HOW LONG HAVE THEY BEEN DOING IT?
IT'S ALSO POSSIBLE THIS WAS ALL JUST COINCIDENCE. DON'T GET CAUGHT PICKING APART A SINGLE RALLY.
RIGHT NOW, OUR FOCUS SHOULD BE ON WINNING THIS SET.
YES-SIR.
DON'T TELL ME THEY'VE BEEN DOING IT FROM THE START... WE THOUGHT WE WERE MANIPULATING THEM, BUT THEY WERE MANIPULATING US?
THAT MEANS IT'S POSSIBLE THEIR SETTER ISN'T AS TIRED AS HE LOOKS...
THEY BROUGHT IN THEIR BACKUP SETTER, BUT THERE STILL ISN'T ANY SIGN THAT THEY'RE GOING TO ACTUALLY SUB HIM IN.
DID THEY DO THAT JUST TO BAIT US...?
AND THAT STARTS THE CIRCLE OF DOUBT AND SUSPICION.
?
FWEEEE
PER-FECT TIMING.
HNNNN!
SARUKAWA TECH
SET 2 SECOND TIME-OUT
YOU AREN'T DOING ANYTHING WRONG.
!
ISHIKAWA
SARUKAWA TECH

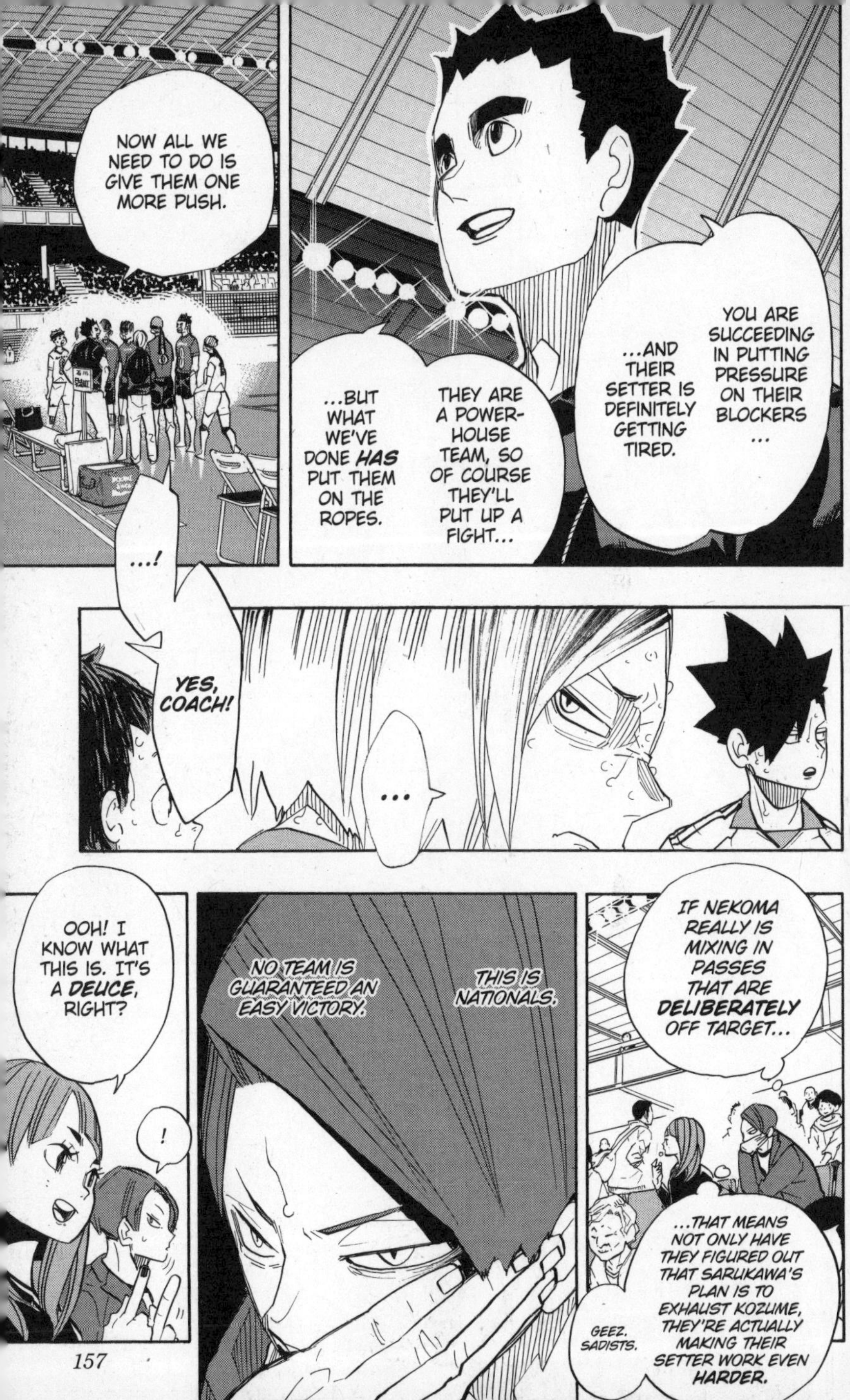
YOU ARE SUCCEEDING IN PUTTING PRESSURE ON THEIR BLOCKERS...
...AND THEIR SETTER IS DEFINITELY GETTING TIRED.
THEY ARE A POWERHOUSE TEAM, SO OF COURSE THEY'LL PUT UP A FIGHT...
...BUT WHAT WE'VE DONE **HAS** PUT THEM ON THE ROPES.
NOW ALL WE NEED TO DO IS GIVE THEM ONE MORE PUSH.
...
YES, COACH!
...!
IF NEKOMA REALLY IS MIXING IN PASSES THAT ARE **DELIBERATELY** OFF TARGET...
...THAT MEANS NOT ONLY HAVE THEY FIGURED OUT THAT SARUKAWA'S PLAN IS TO EXHAUST KOZUME, THEY'RE ACTUALLY MAKING THEIR SETTER WORK EVEN **HARDER.**
GEEZ. SADISTS.
THIS IS NATIONALS.
NO TEAM IS GUARANTEED AN EASY VICTORY.
OOH! I KNOW WHAT THIS IS. IT'S A **DEUCE**, RIGHT?
!

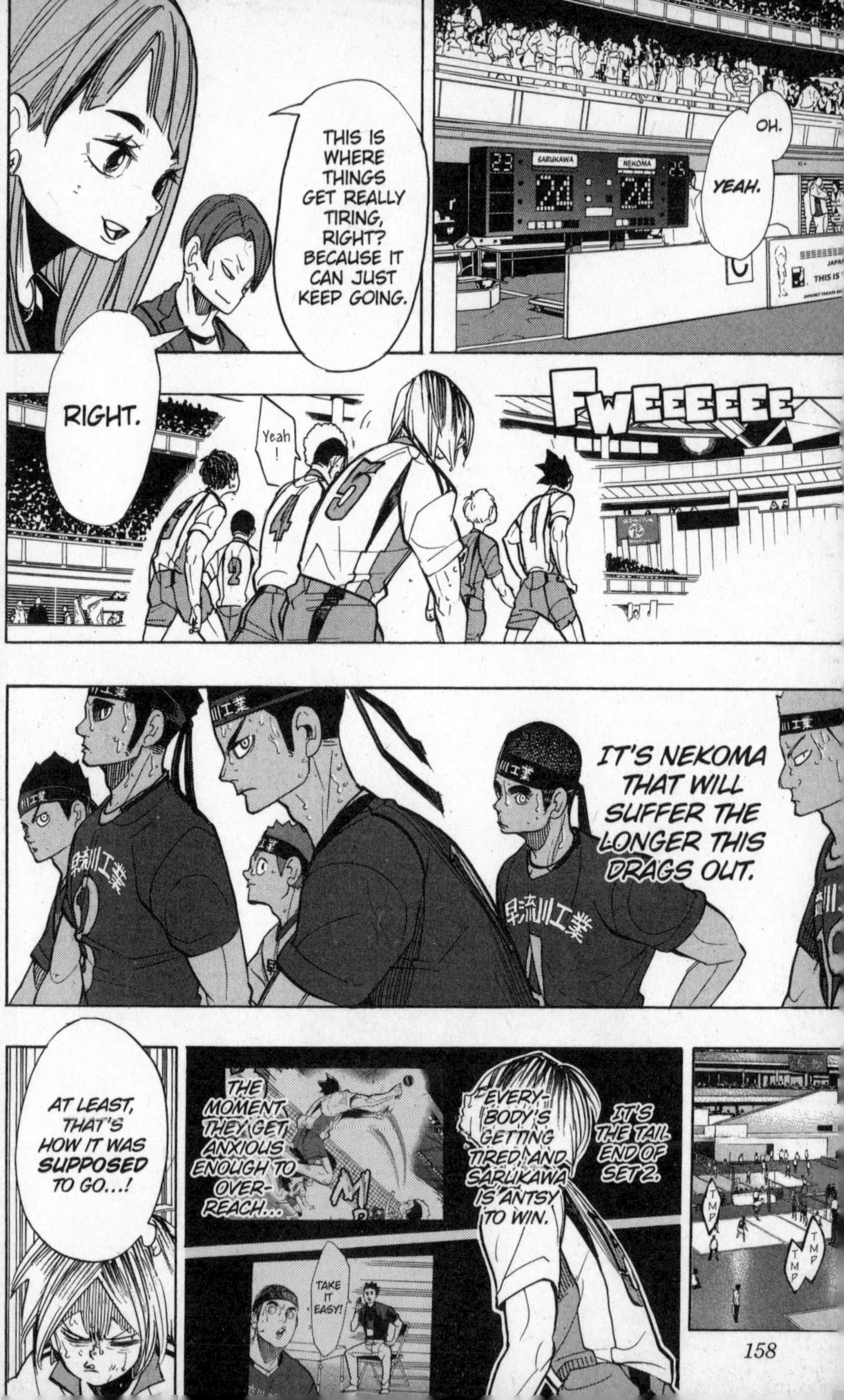
SARUKAWA
NEKOMA
24 : 24
OH.
YEAH.
THIS IS WHERE THINGS GET REALLY TIRING, RIGHT? BECAUSE IT CAN JUST KEEP GOING.
RIGHT.
FWEEEEEE
Yeah!
IT'S NEKOMA THAT WILL SUFFER THE LONGER THIS DRAGS OUT.
TMP
TMP
TMP
IT'S THE TAIL END OF SET 2.
EVERYBODY'S GETTING TIRED, AND SARUKAWA IS ANTSY TO WIN.
THE MOMENT THEY GET ANXIOUS ENOUGH TO OVER-REACH...
TAKE IT EASY!
AT LEAST, THAT'S HOW IT WAS SUPPOSED TO GO...!

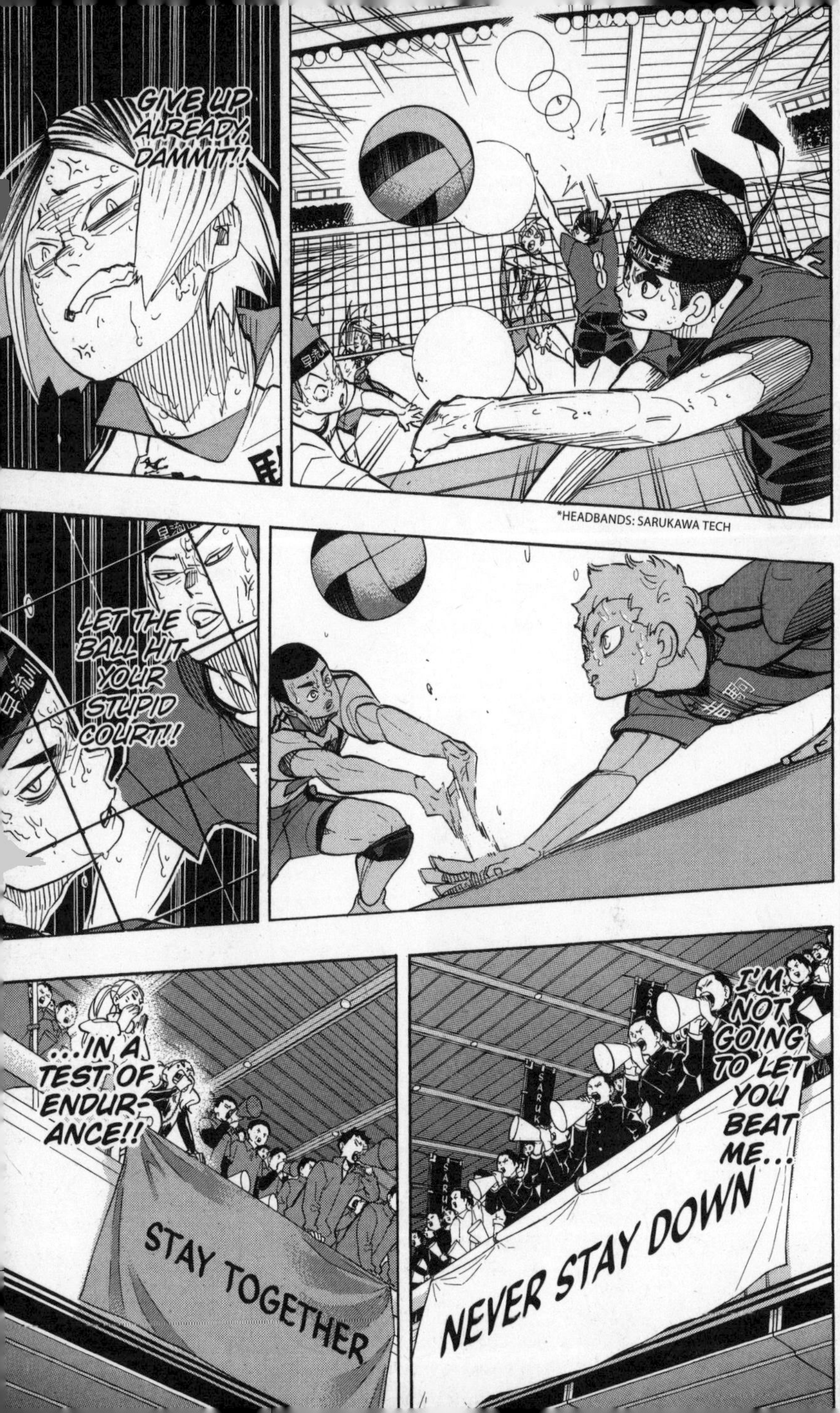
*HEADBANDS: SARUKAWA TECH
GIVE UP ALREADY, DAMMIT!!
LET THE BALL HIT YOUR STUPID COURT!!
I'M NOT GOING TO LET YOU BEAT ME...
NEVER STAY DOWN
...IN A TEST OF ENDUR-ANCE!!
STAY TOGETHER

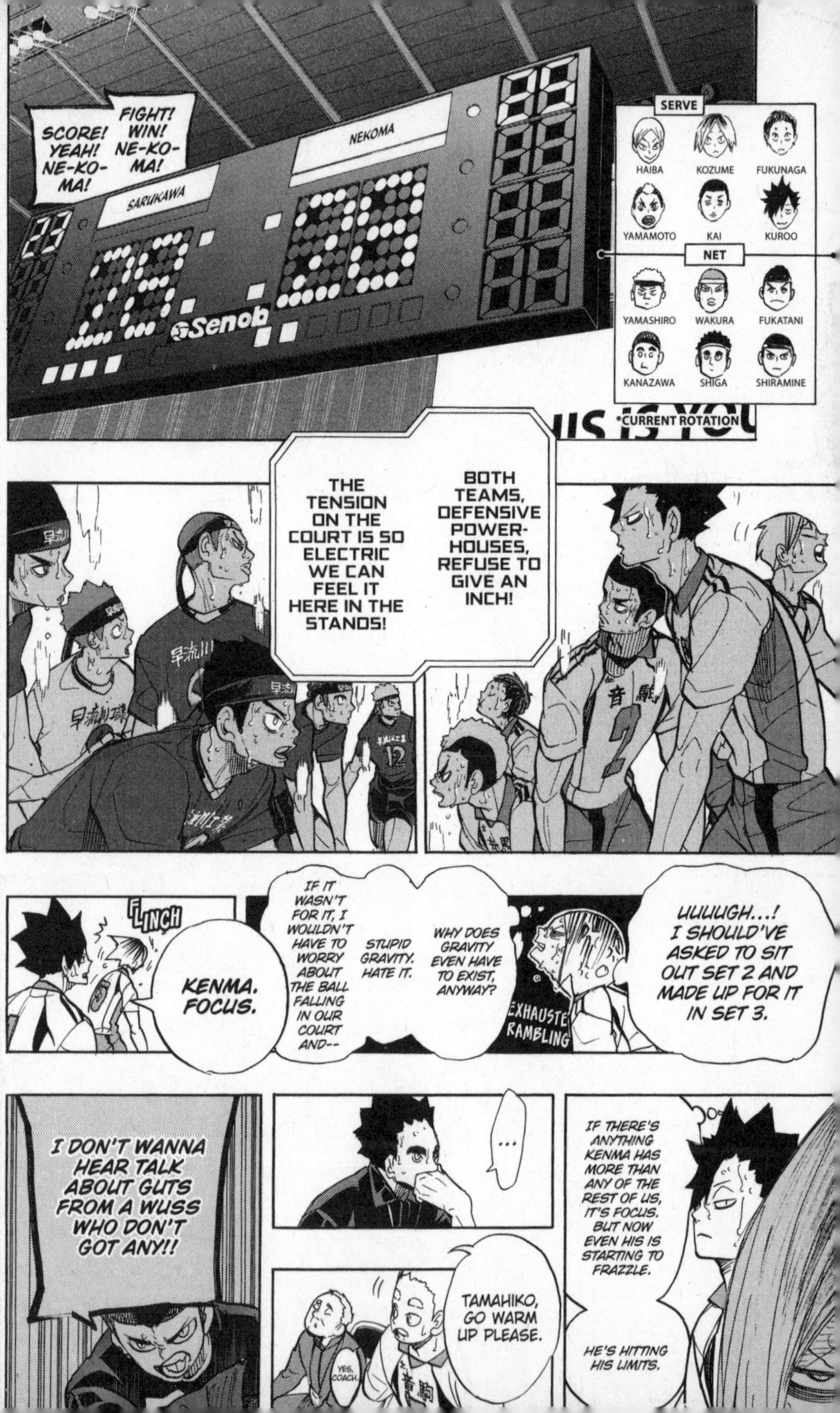

SERVE
HAIBA
KOZUME
FUKUNAGA
YAMAMOTO
KAI
KUROO
NET
YAMASHIRO
WAKURA
FUKATANI
KANAZAWA
SHIGA
SHIRAMINE
*CURRENT ROTATION
NEKOMA
SARUKAWA
Senob
FIGHT! WIN! NE-KO-MA!
SCORE! YEAH! NE-KO-MA!
BOTH TEAMS, DEFENSIVE POWERHOUSES, REFUSE TO GIVE AN INCH!
THE TENSION ON THE COURT IS SO ELECTRIC WE CAN FEEL IT HERE IN THE STANDS!
UUUUGH...! I SHOULD'VE ASKED TO SIT OUT SET 2 AND MADE UP FOR IT IN SET 3.
WHY DOES GRAVITY EVEN HAVE TO EXIST, ANYWAY?
STUPID GRAVITY. HATE IT.
IF IT WASN'T FOR IT, I WOULDN'T HAVE TO WORRY ABOUT THE BALL FALLING IN OUR COURT AND--
EXHAUSTED RAMBLING
FLINCH
KENMA. FOCUS.
IF THERE'S ANYTHING KENMA HAS MORE THAN ANY OF THE REST OF US, IT'S FOCUS. BUT NOW EVEN HIS IS STARTING TO FRAZZLE.
HE'S HITTING HIS LIMITS.
...
TAMAHIKO, GO WARM UP PLEASE.
YES, COACH.
I DON'T WANNA HEAR TALK ABOUT GUTS FROM A WUSS WHO DON'T GOT ANY!!

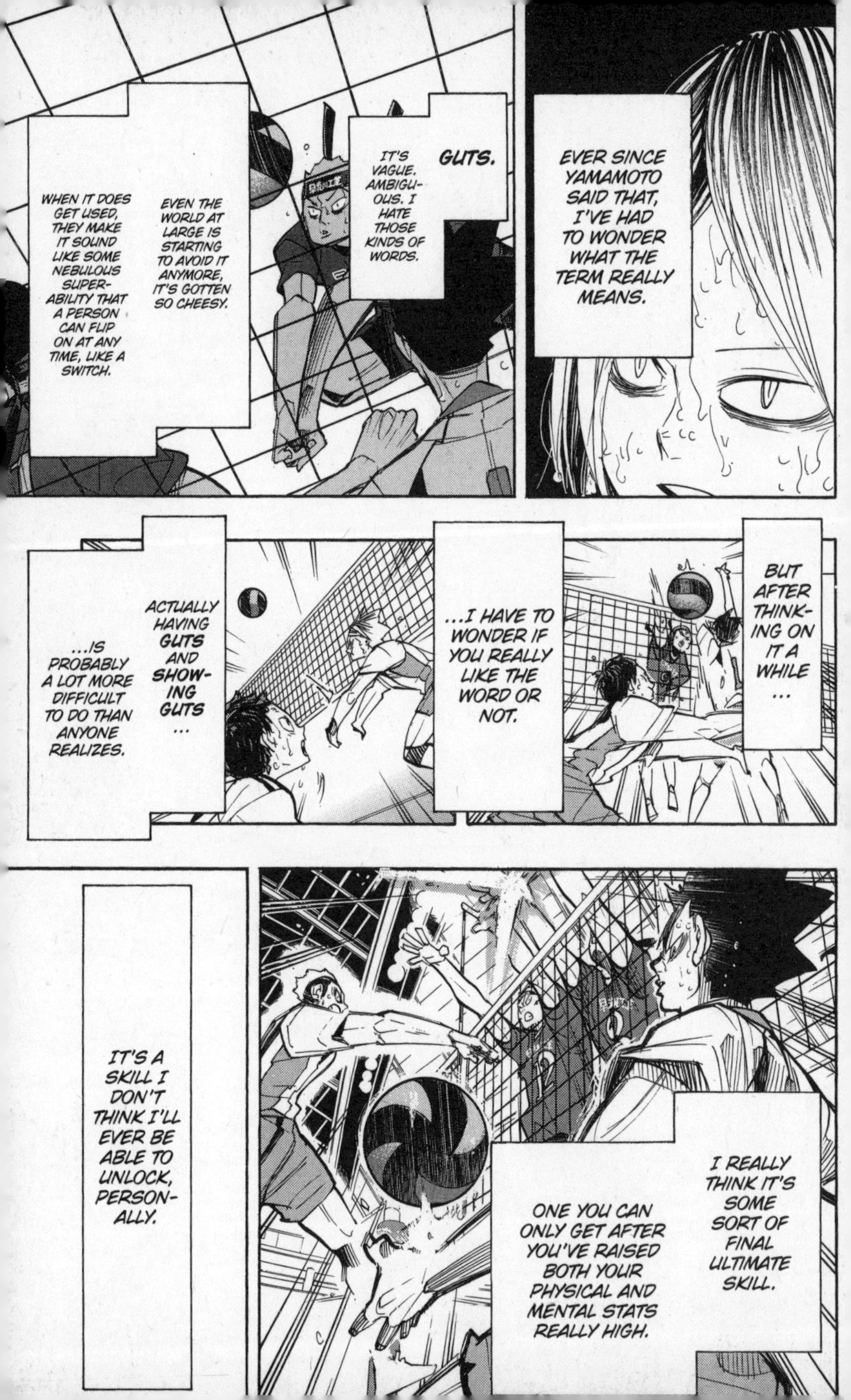
EVER SINCE YAMAMOTO SAID THAT, I'VE HAD TO WONDER WHAT THE TERM REALLY MEANS.
GUTS.
IT'S VAGUE. AMBIGUOUS. I HATE THOSE KINDS OF WORDS.
EVEN THE WORLD AT LARGE IS STARTING TO AVOID IT ANYMORE, IT'S GOTTEN SO CHEESY.
WHEN IT DOES GET USED, THEY MAKE IT SOUND LIKE SOME NEBULOUS SUPER-ABILITY THAT A PERSON CAN FLIP ON AT ANY TIME, LIKE A SWITCH.
BUT AFTER THINKING ON IT A WHILE...
...I HAVE TO WONDER IF YOU REALLY LIKE THE WORD OR NOT.
ACTUALLY HAVING GUTS AND SHOWING GUTS...
...IS PROBABLY A LOT MORE DIFFICULT TO DO THAN ANYONE REALIZES.
I REALLY THINK IT'S SOME SORT OF FINAL ULTIMATE SKILL.
ONE YOU CAN ONLY GET AFTER YOU'VE RAISED BOTH YOUR PHYSICAL AND MENTAL STATS REALLY HIGH.
IT'S A SKILL I DON'T THINK I'LL EVER BE ABLE TO UNLOCK, PERSONALLY.

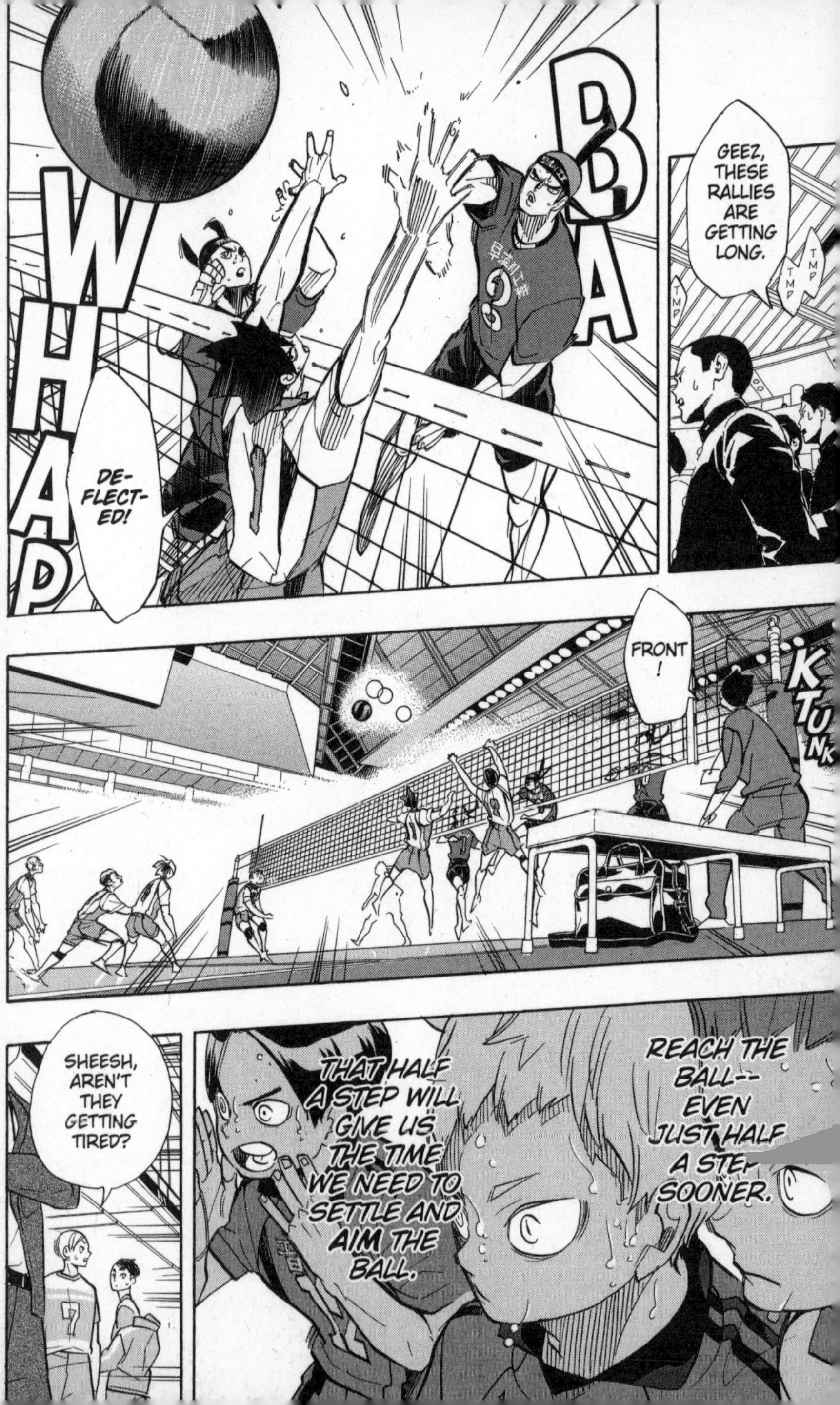
GEEZ, THESE RALLIES ARE GETTING LONG.
TMP TMP TMP TMP
BA
WHAP
DE-FLECTED!
KTUNK
FRONT!
REACH THE BALL-- EVEN JUST HALF A STEP SOONER.
THAT HALF A STEP WILL GIVE US THE TIME WE NEED TO SETTLE AND AIM THE BALL.
SHEESH, AREN'T THEY GETTING TIRED?

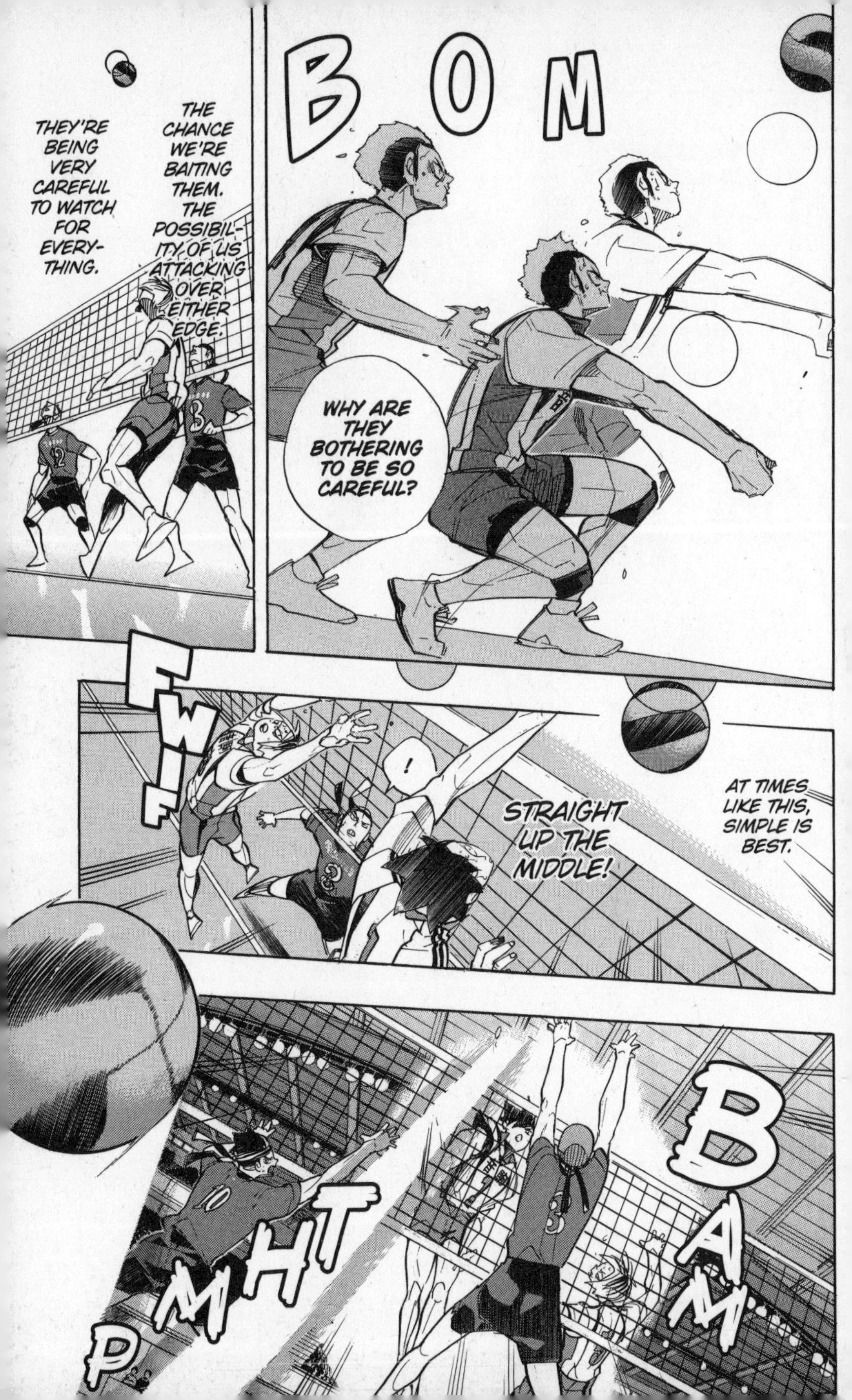
BOM
WHY ARE THEY BOTHERING TO BE SO CAREFUL?
THE CHANCE WE'RE BAITING THEM. THE POSSIBILITY OF US ATTACKING OVER EITHER EDGE.
THEY'RE BEING VERY CAREFUL TO WATCH FOR EVERYTHING.
AT TIMES LIKE THIS, SIMPLE IS BEST.
STRAIGHT UP THE MIDDLE!
!
FWIF
BAM
PMHT

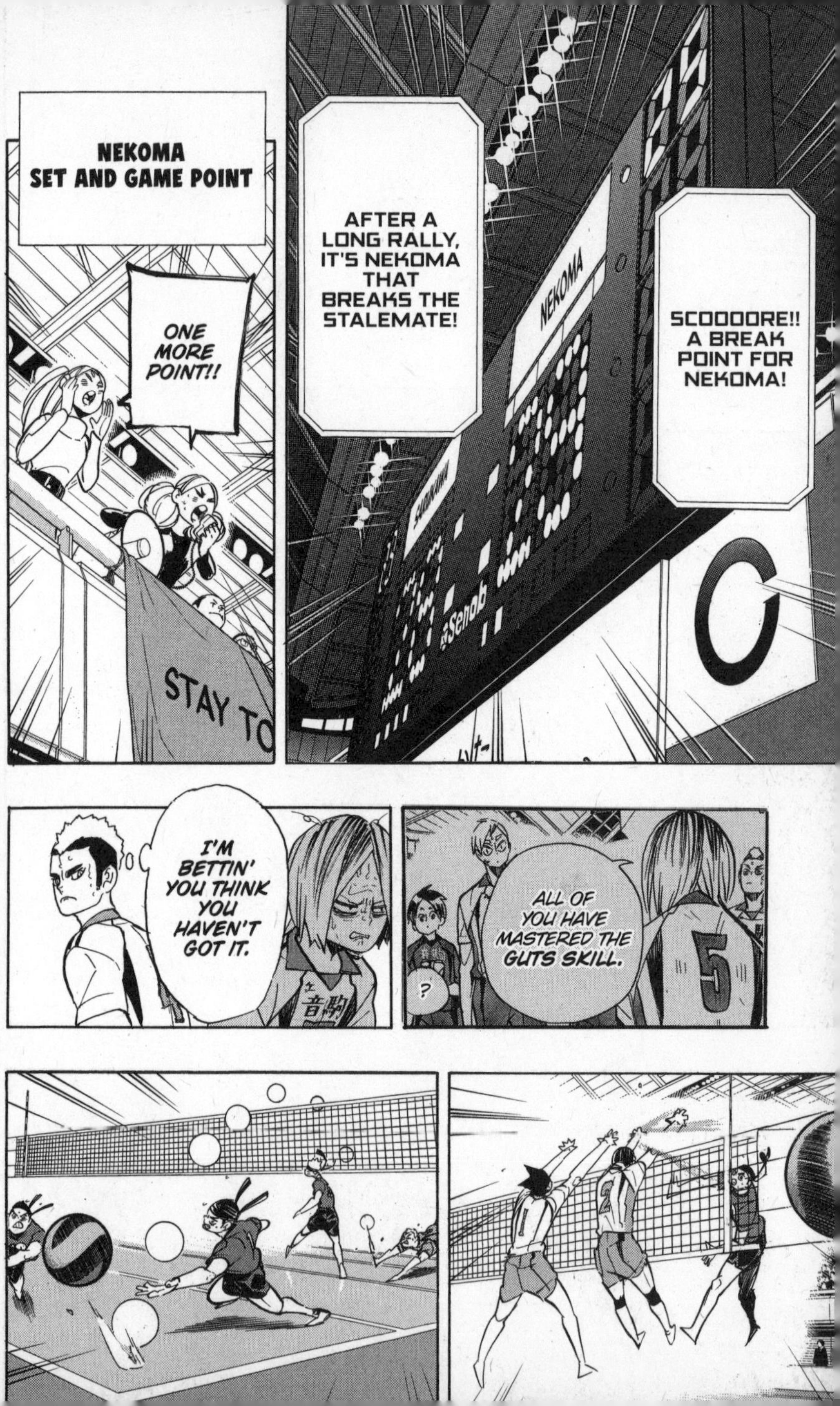
SCOOOORE!! A BREAK POINT FOR NEKOMA!
NEKOMA
AFTER A LONG RALLY, IT'S NEKOMA THAT BREAKS THE STALEMATE!
NEKOMA SET AND GAME POINT
ONE MORE POINT!!
STAY TO
ALL OF YOU HAVE MASTERED THE GUTS SKILL.
?
I'M BETTIN' YOU THINK YOU HAVEN'T GOT IT.

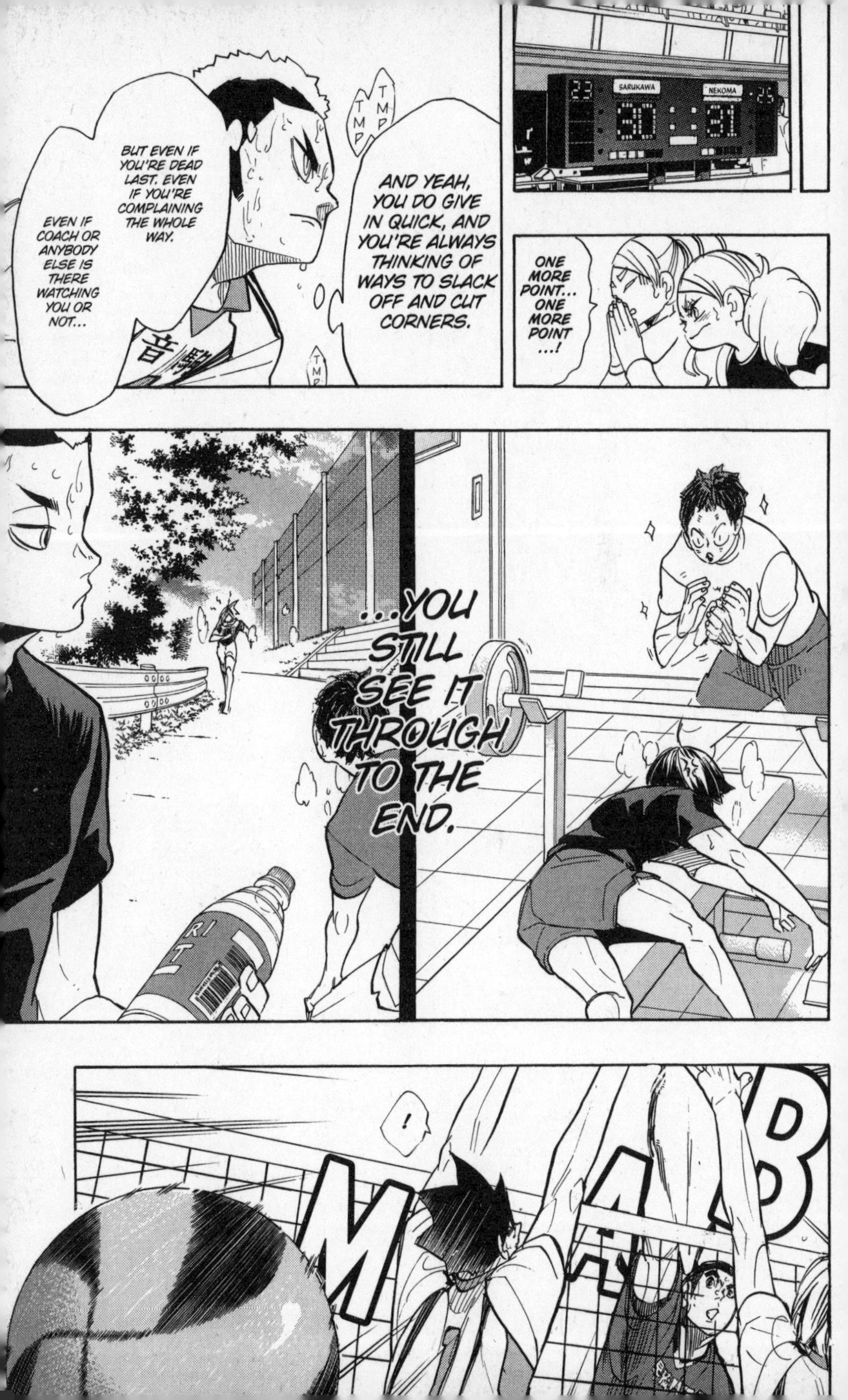

SARUKAWA
NEKOMA
30
31
ONE MORE POINT... ONE MORE POINT...!
TMP TMP
AND YEAH, YOU DO GIVE IN QUICK, AND YOU'RE ALWAYS THINKING OF WAYS TO SLACK OFF AND CUT CORNERS.
BUT EVEN IF YOU'RE DEAD LAST. EVEN IF YOU'RE COMPLAINING THE WHOLE WAY.
EVEN IF COACH OR ANYBODY ELSE IS THERE WATCHING YOU OR NOT...
TMP
...YOU STILL SEE IT THROUGH TO THE END.
!
BAM

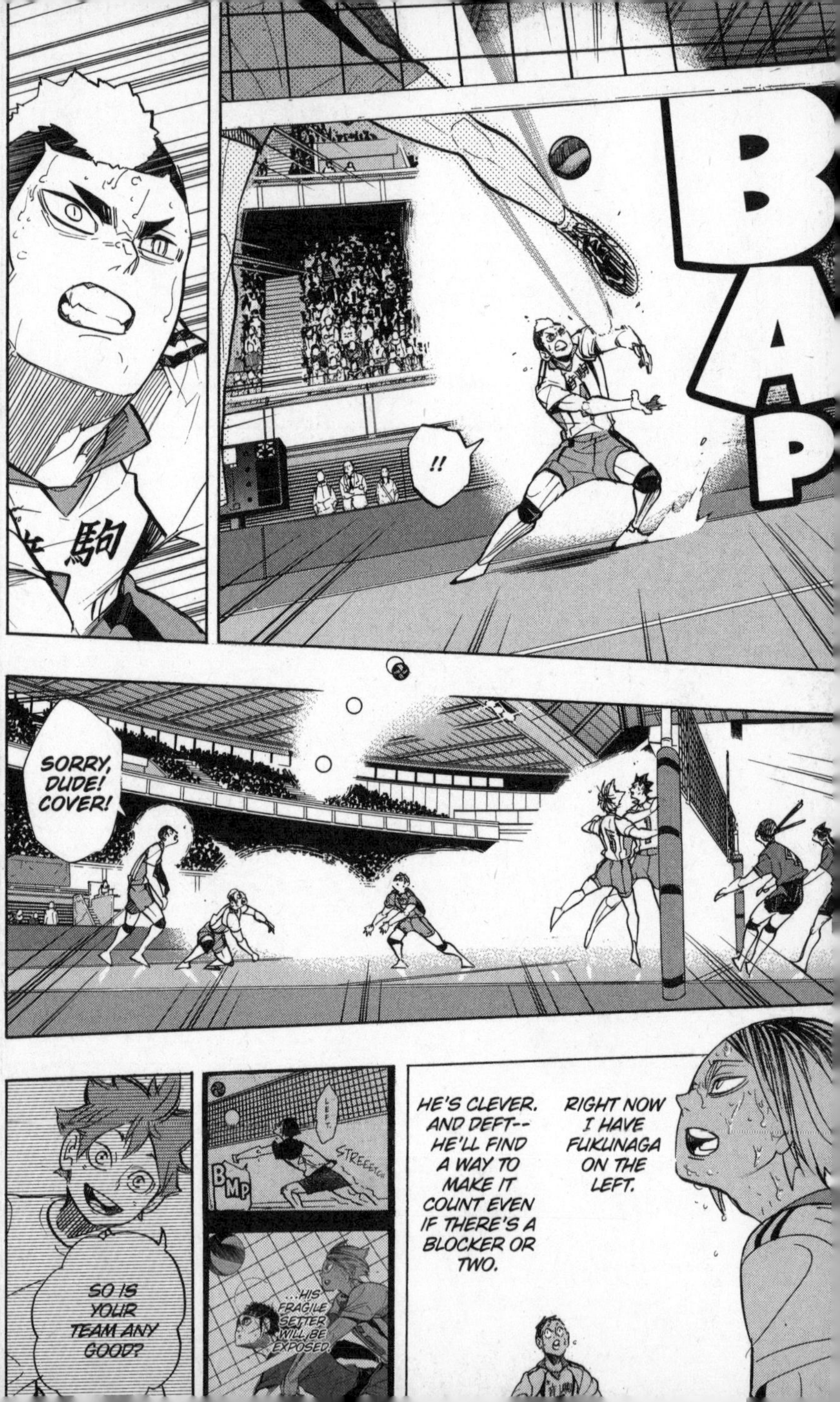
BAP
!!
SORRY, DUDE! COVER!
RIGHT NOW I HAVE FUKUNAGA ON THE LEFT.
HE'S CLEVER. AND DEFT-- HE'LL FIND A WAY TO MAKE IT COUNT EVEN IF THERE'S A BLOCKER OR TWO.
BMP
...HIS FRAGILE SETTER WILL BE EXPOSED.
SO IS YOUR TEAM ANY GOOD?

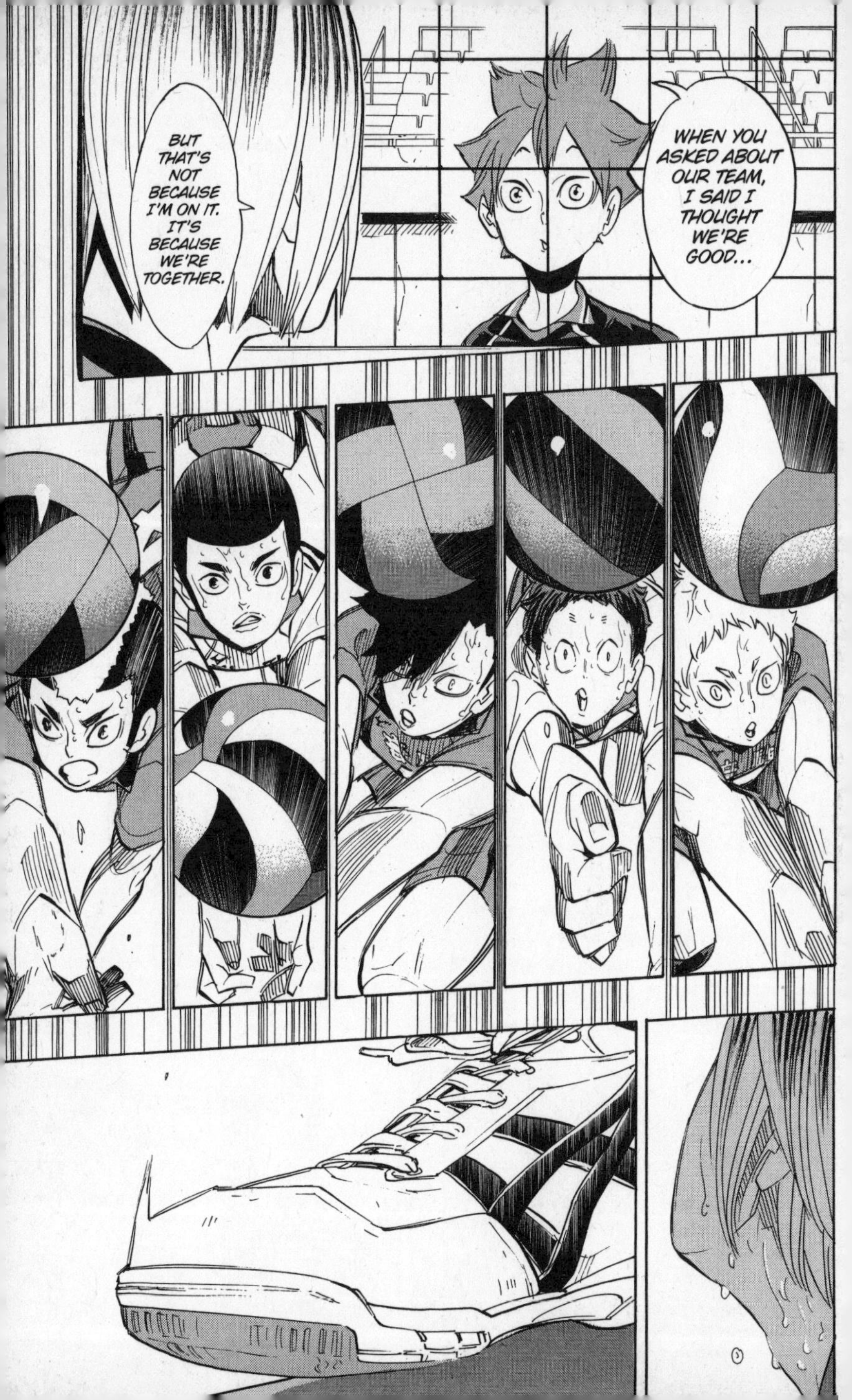
WHEN YOU ASKED ABOUT OUR TEAM, I SAID I THOUGHT WE'RE GOOD...
BUT THAT'S NOT BECAUSE I'M ON IT. IT'S BECAUSE WE'RE TOGETHER.

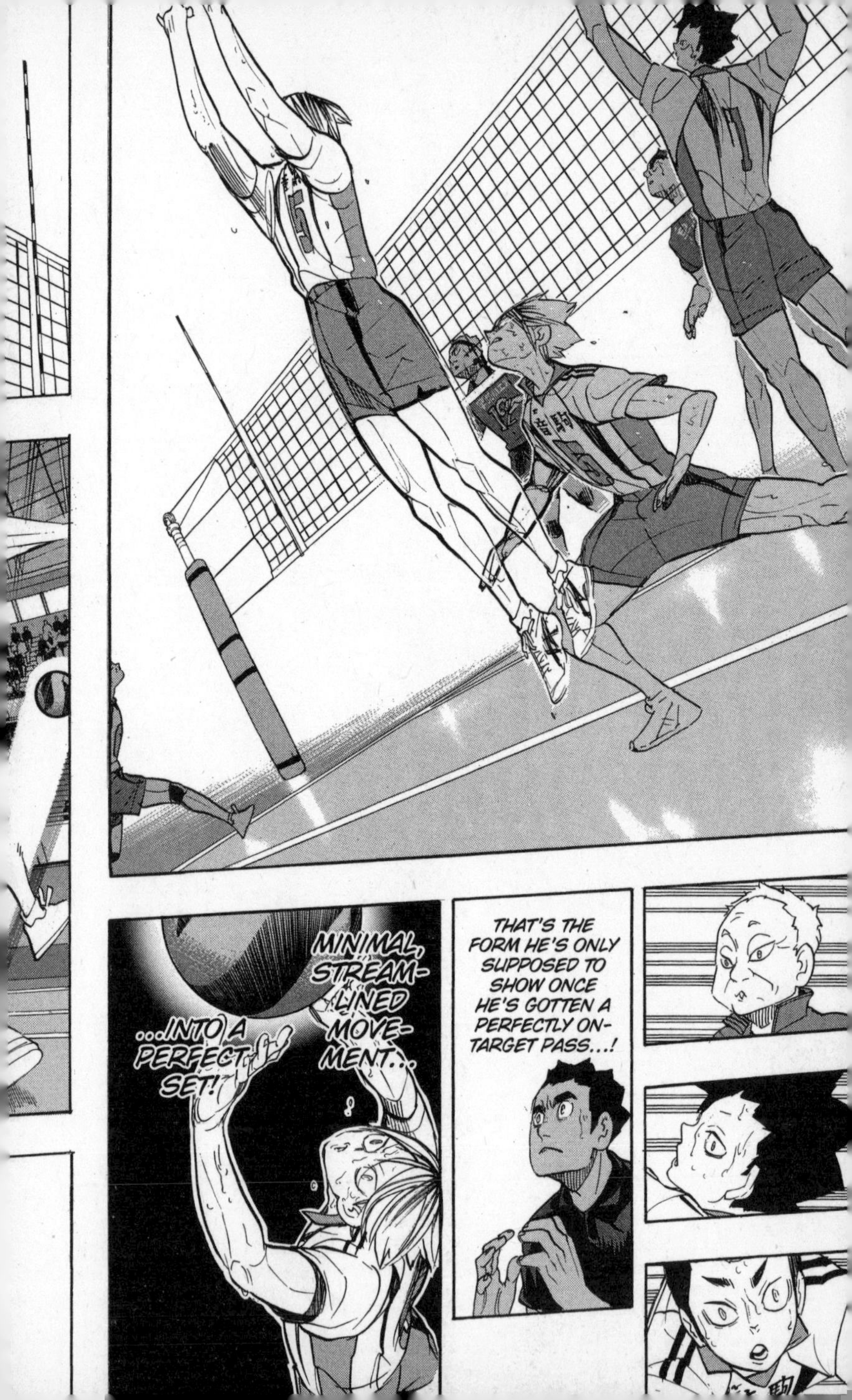
THAT'S THE FORM HE'S ONLY SUPPOSED TO SHOW ONCE HE'S GOTTEN A PERFECTLY ON-TARGET PASS...!
MINIMAL, STREAM-LINED MOVE-MENT...
...INTO A PERFECT SET!

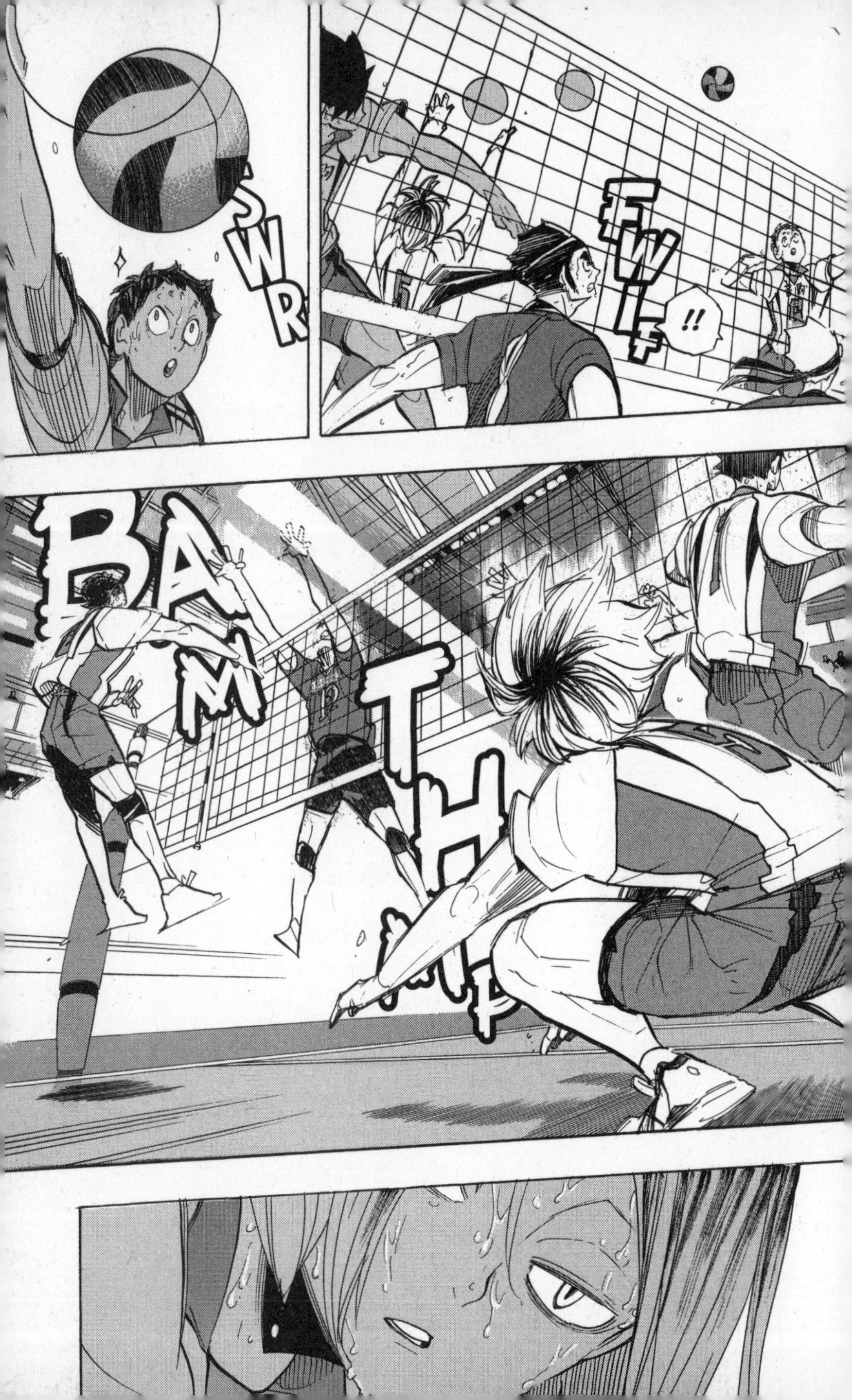
FWIT
!!
SWR
BAM
TH

KENRO FUKATANI

SARUKAWA TECHNICAL HIGH SCHOOL 2ND YEAR

POSITION: WING SPIKER

HEIGHT: 5'10"

WEIGHT: 150 LBS.
(AS OF JANUARY, 2ND YEAR OF HIGH SCHOOL)

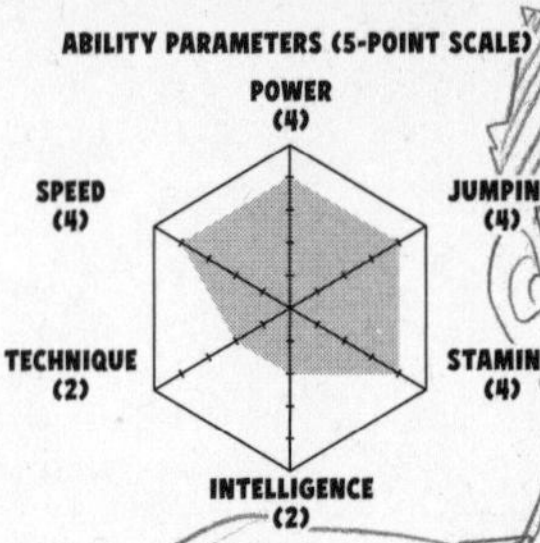
ABILITY PARAMETERS (5-POINT SCALE)
POWER (4)
JUMPING (4)
STAMINA (4)
INTELLIGENCE (2)
TECHNIQUE (2)
SPEED (4)

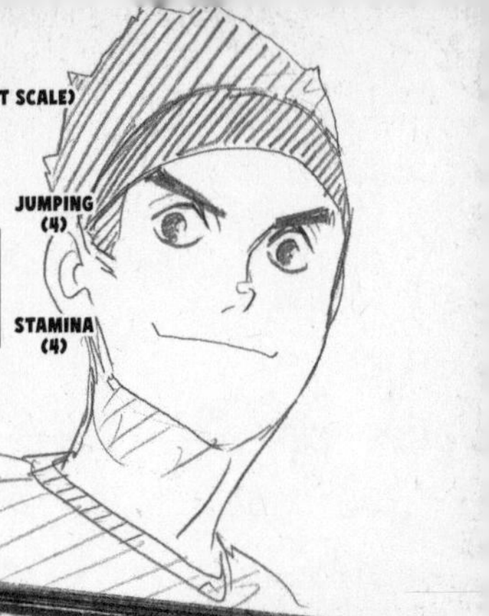

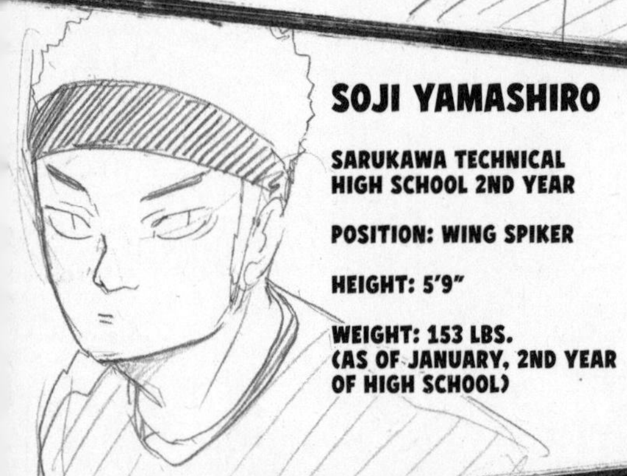

SOJI YAMASHIRO

SARUKAWA TECHNICAL HIGH SCHOOL 2ND YEAR

POSITION: WING SPIKER

HEIGHT: 5'9"

WEIGHT: 153 LBS.
(AS OF JANUARY, 2ND YEAR OF HIGH SCHOOL)

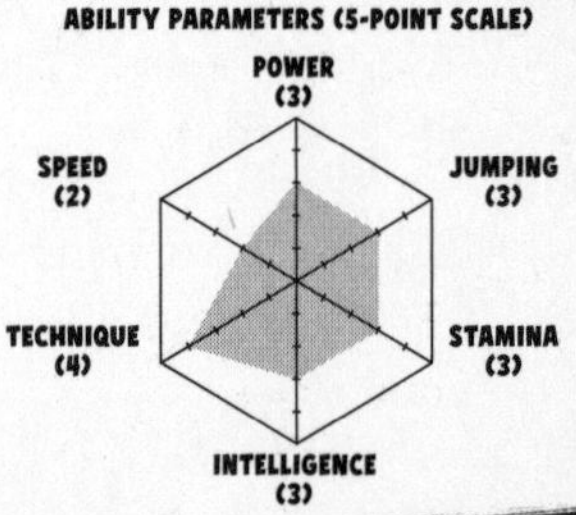
ABILITY PARAMETERS (5-POINT SCALE)
POWER (3)
JUMPING (3)
STAMINA (3)
INTELLIGENCE (3)
TECHNIQUE (4)
SPEED (2)

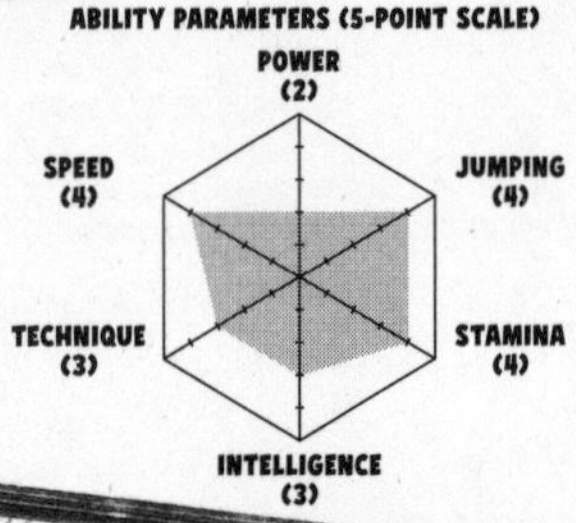
ABILITY PARAMETERS (5-POINT SCALE)
POWER (2)
JUMPING (4)
STAMINA (4)
INTELLIGENCE (3)
TECHNIQUE (3)
SPEED (4)

TOMOKAZU WAJIMA

SARUKAWA TECHNICAL HIGH SCHOOL 2ND YEAR

POSITION: LIBERO

HEIGHT: 5'7"

WEIGHT: 136 LBS.
(AS OF JANUARY, 2ND YEAR OF HIGH SCHOOL)

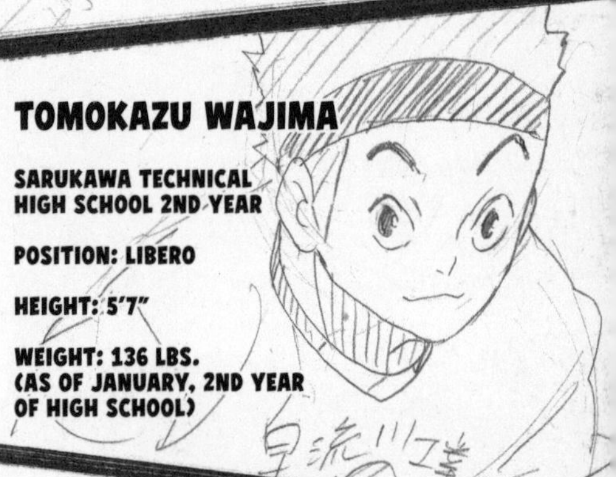

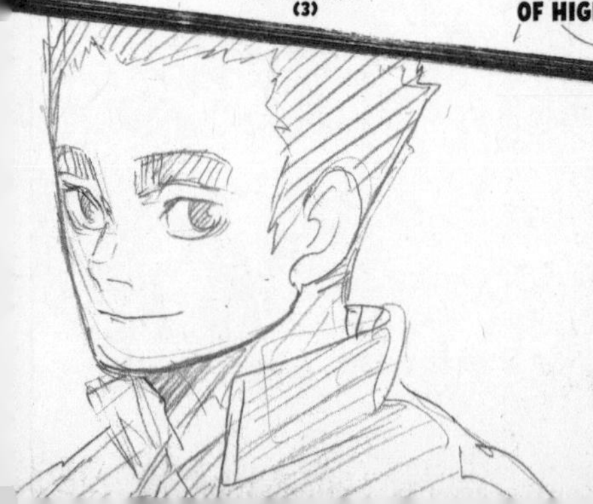

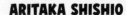

ARITAKA SHISHIO

SARUKAWA TECHNICAL HIGH SCHOOL HEAD COACH

AGE: 39

CURRENT WORRY: IS IT TIME TO GIVE UP HIS FLIP PHONE FOR A SMART PHONE?

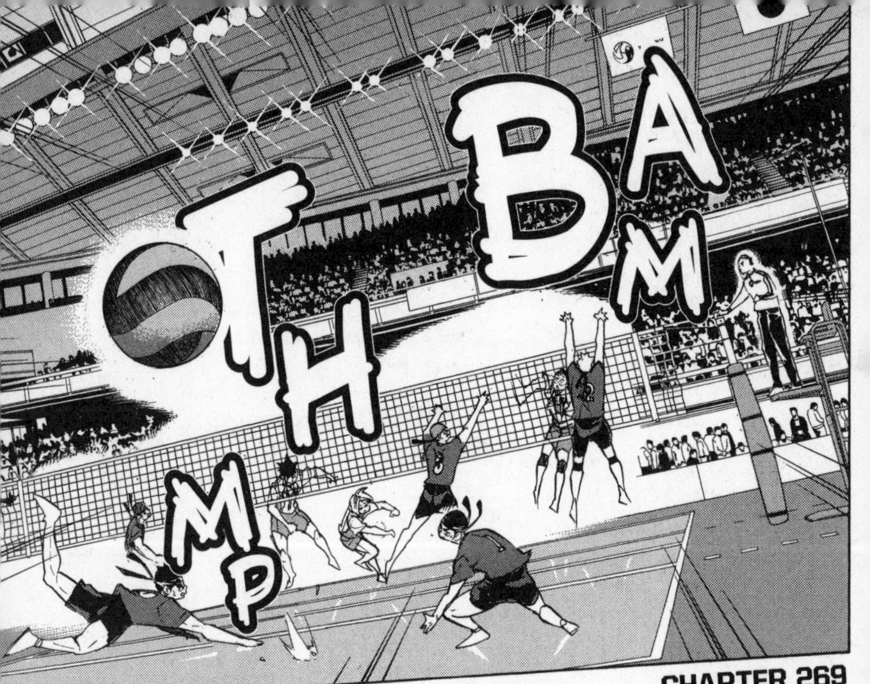
THOMP
BAM

CHAPTER 269

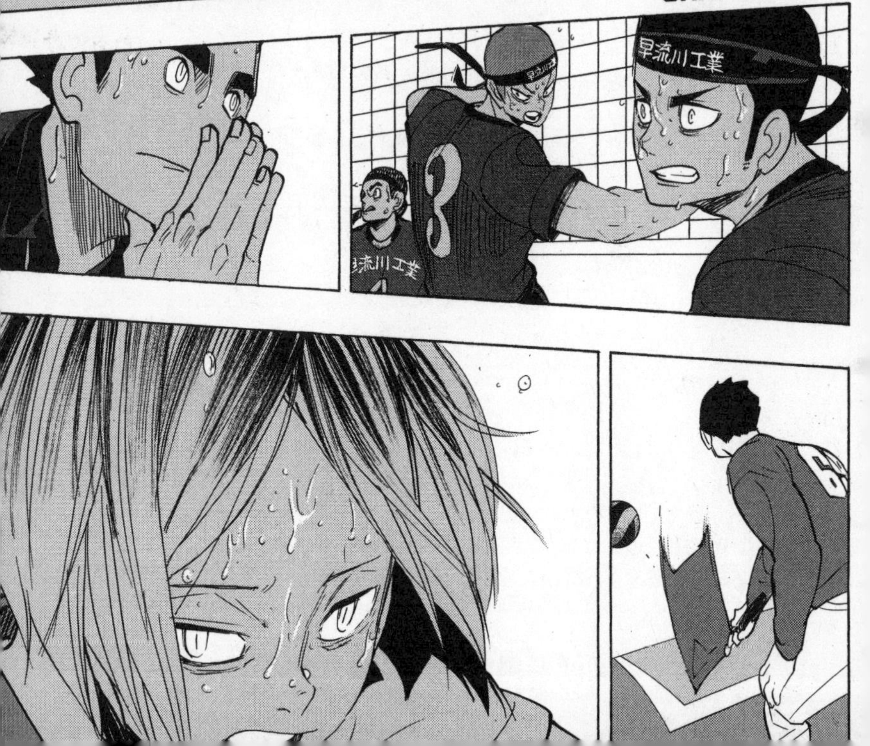
早流川工業

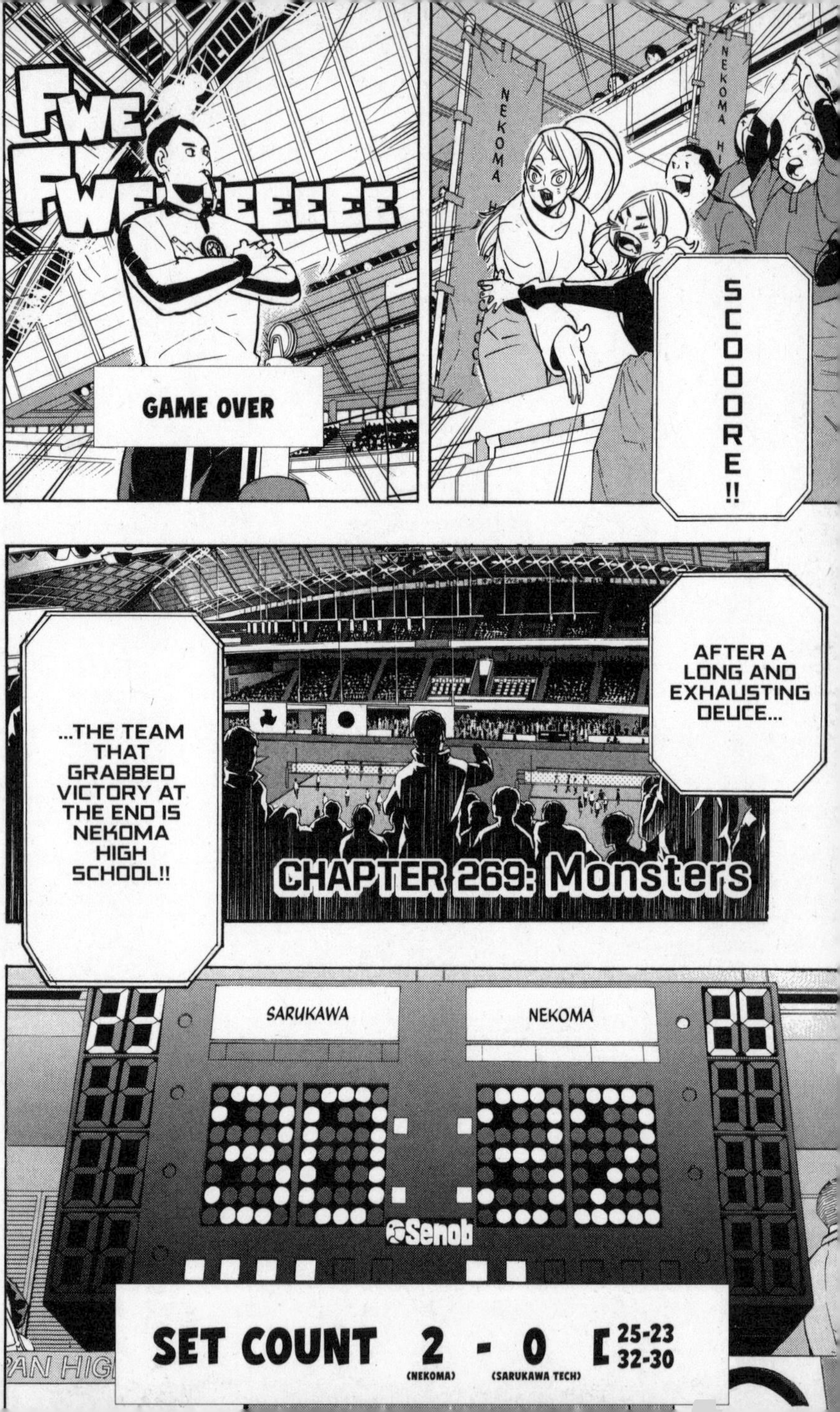
SCOOORE!!
FWE FWEEEEEE
GAME OVER
AFTER A LONG AND EXHAUSTING DEUCE...
...THE TEAM THAT GRABBED VICTORY AT THE END IS NEKOMA HIGH SCHOOL!!
CHAPTER 269: Monsters
SARUKAWA
NEKOMA
Senob
SET COUNT 2 - 0 [25-23 32-30
(NEKOMA)
(SARUKAWA TECH)

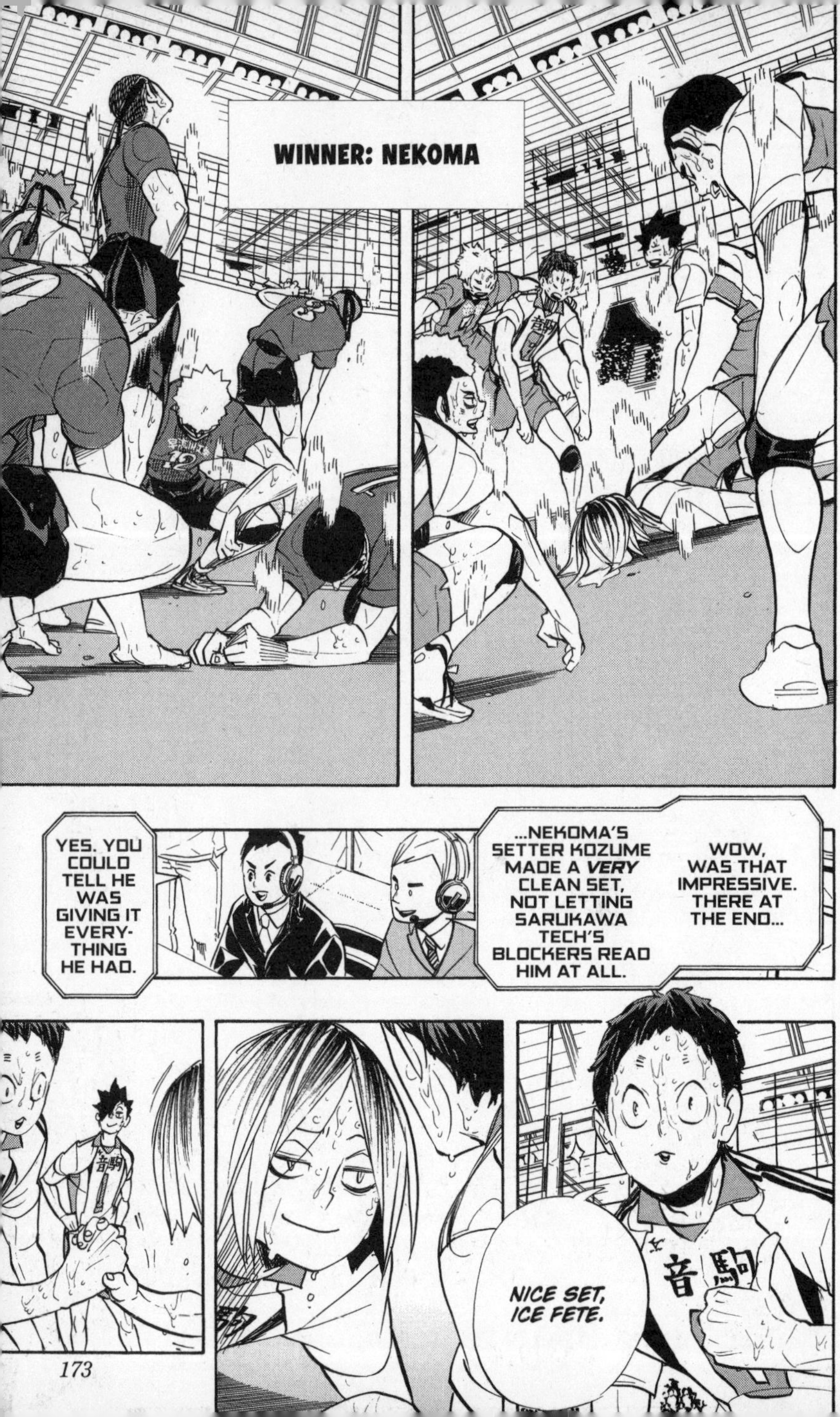
WINNER: NEKOMA
WOW, WAS THAT IMPRESSIVE. THERE AT THE END...
...NEKOMA'S SETTER KOZUME MADE A *VERY* CLEAN SET, NOT LETTING SARUKAWA TECH'S BLOCKERS READ HIM AT ALL.
YES. YOU COULD TELL HE WAS GIVING IT EVERY-THING HE HAD.
NICE SET, ICE FETE.

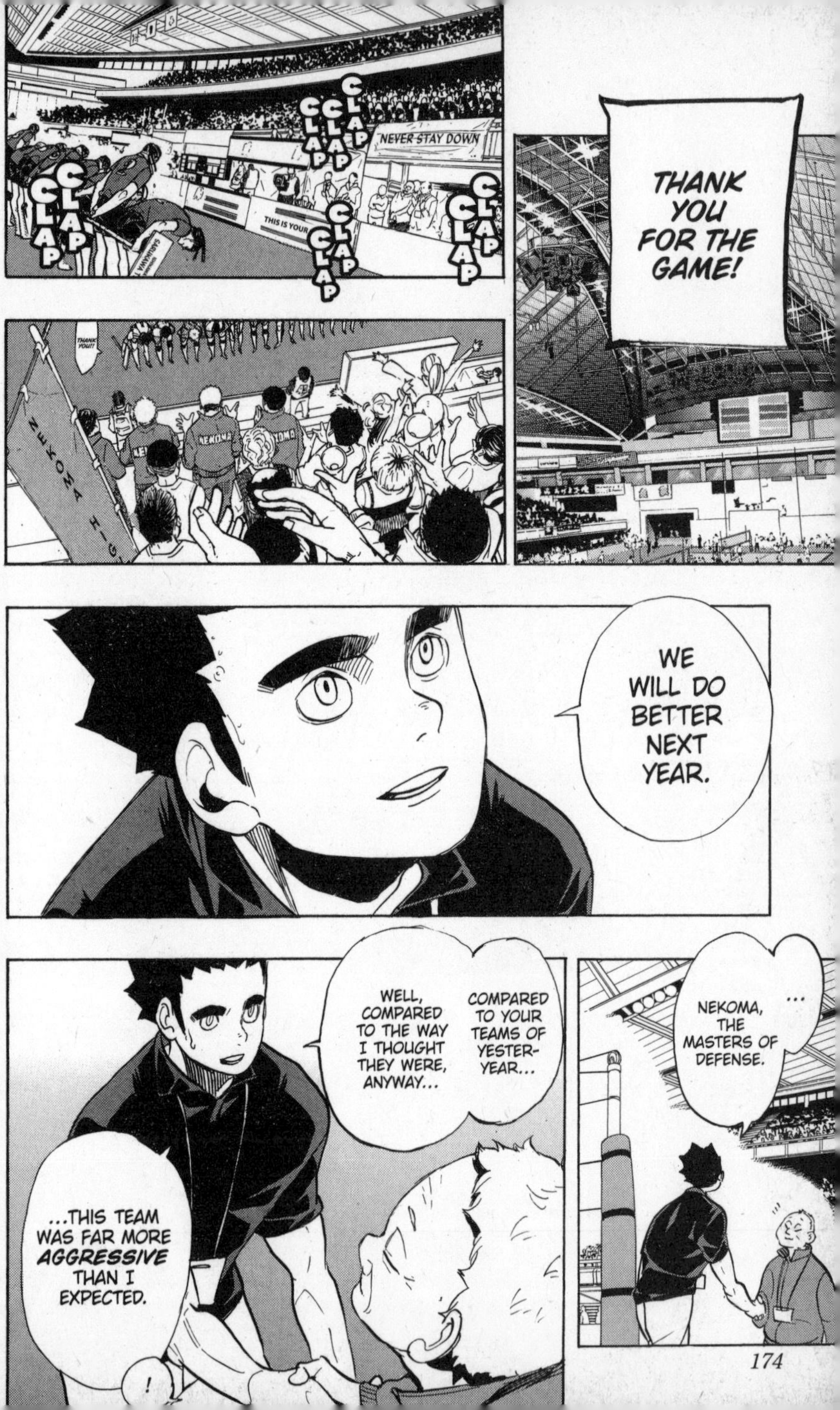
THANK YOU FOR THE GAME!
CLAP CLAP CLAP
NEVER STAY DOWN
CLAP CLAP
THIS IS YOUR
CLAP CLAP
CLAP CLAP
THANK YOU!!
NEKOMA
WE WILL DO BETTER NEXT YEAR.
...
NEKOMA, THE MASTERS OF DEFENSE.
COMPARED TO YOUR TEAMS OF YESTER-YEAR...
WELL, COMPARED TO THE WAY I THOUGHT THEY WERE, ANYWAY...
...THIS TEAM WAS FAR MORE *AGGRESSIVE* THAN I EXPECTED.
!

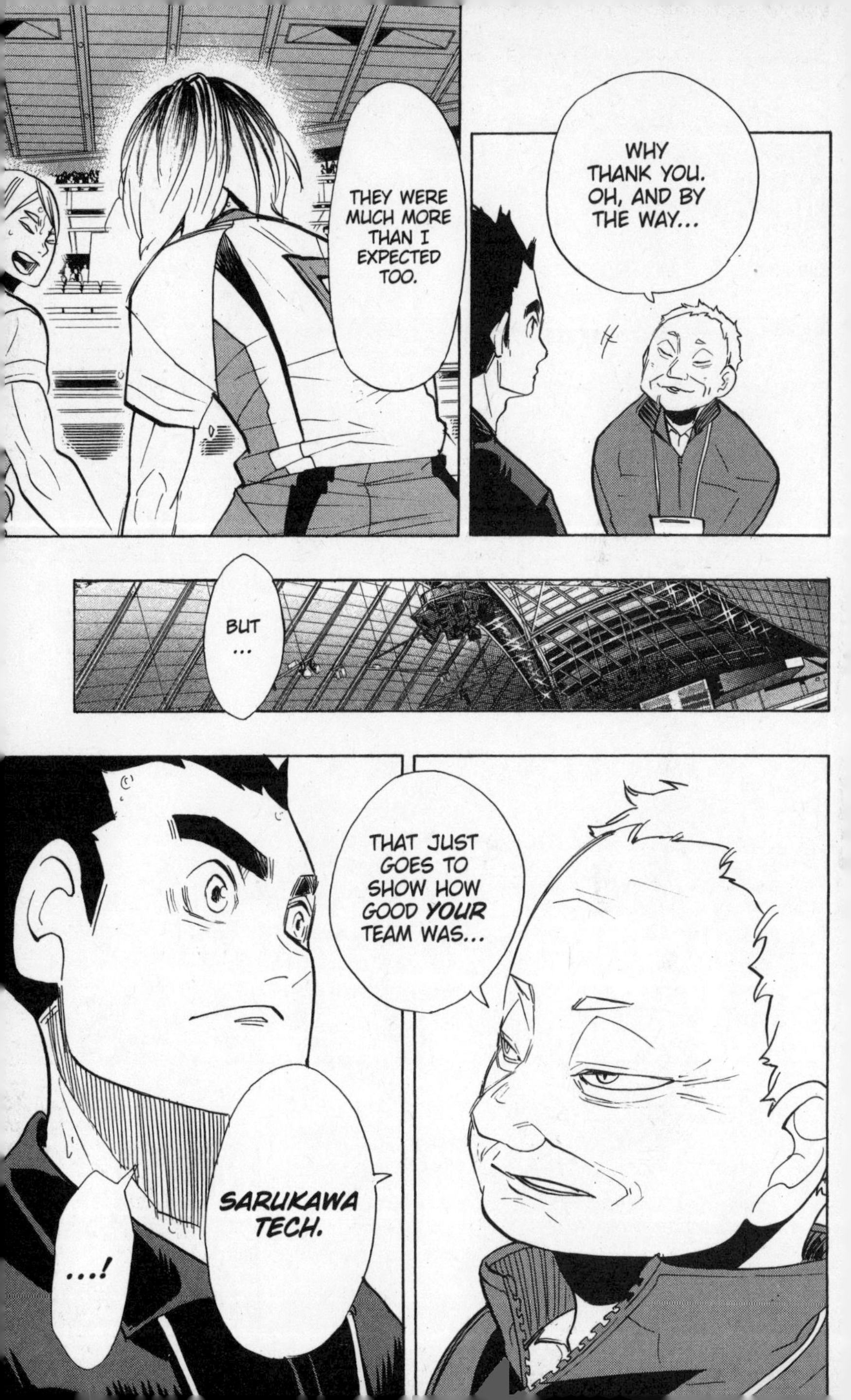
WHY THANK YOU. OH, AND BY THE WAY...
THEY WERE MUCH MORE THAN I EXPECTED TOO.
BUT ...
THAT JUST GOES TO SHOW HOW GOOD YOUR TEAM WAS...
SARUKAWA TECH.
...!

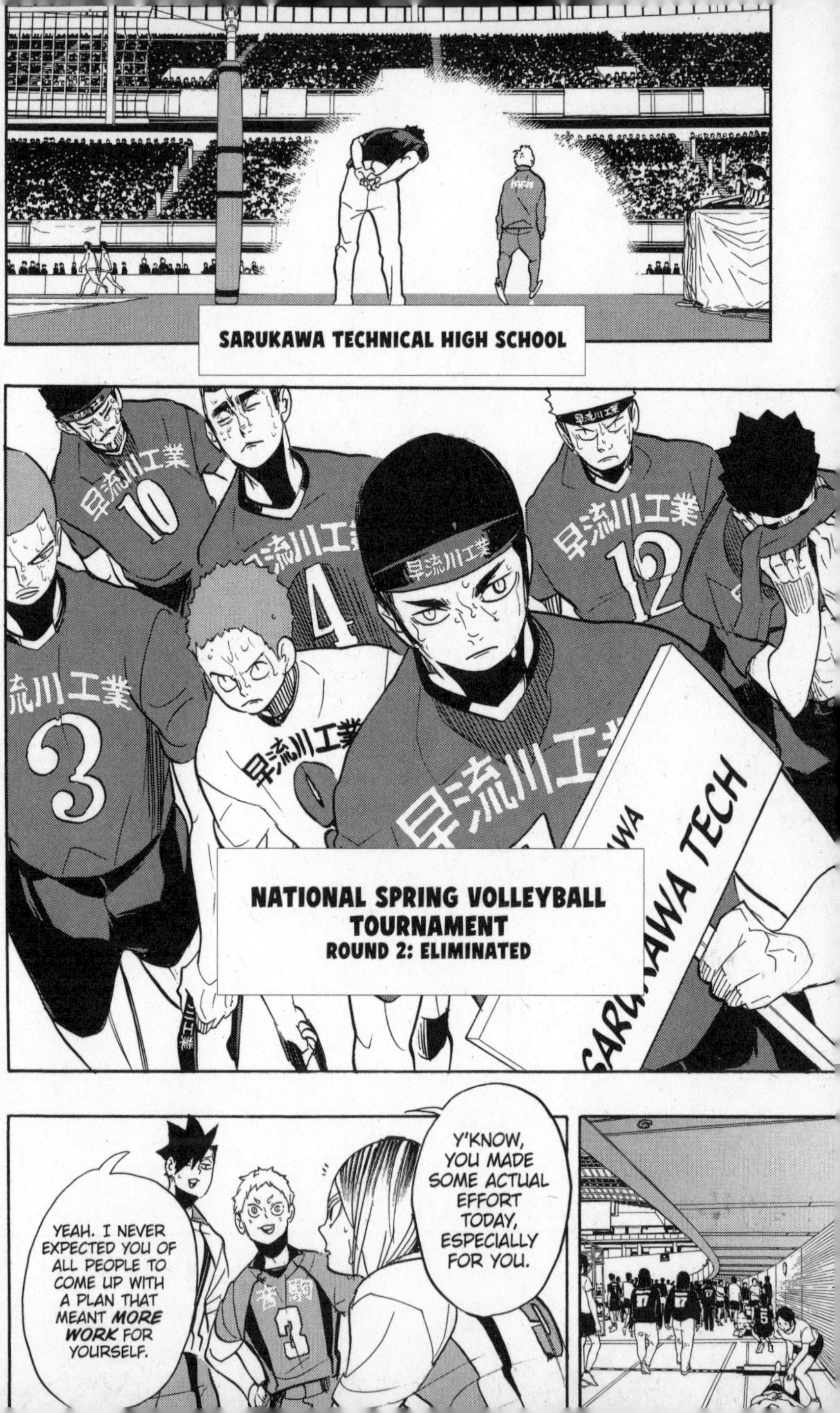
SARUKAWA TECHNICAL HIGH SCHOOL
SARUKAWA TECH
NATIONAL SPRING VOLLEYBALL TOURNAMENT
ROUND 2: ELIMINATED
Y'KNOW, YOU MADE SOME ACTUAL EFFORT TODAY, ESPECIALLY FOR YOU.
YEAH. I NEVER EXPECTED YOU OF ALL PEOPLE TO COME UP WITH A PLAN THAT MEANT MORE WORK FOR YOURSELF.

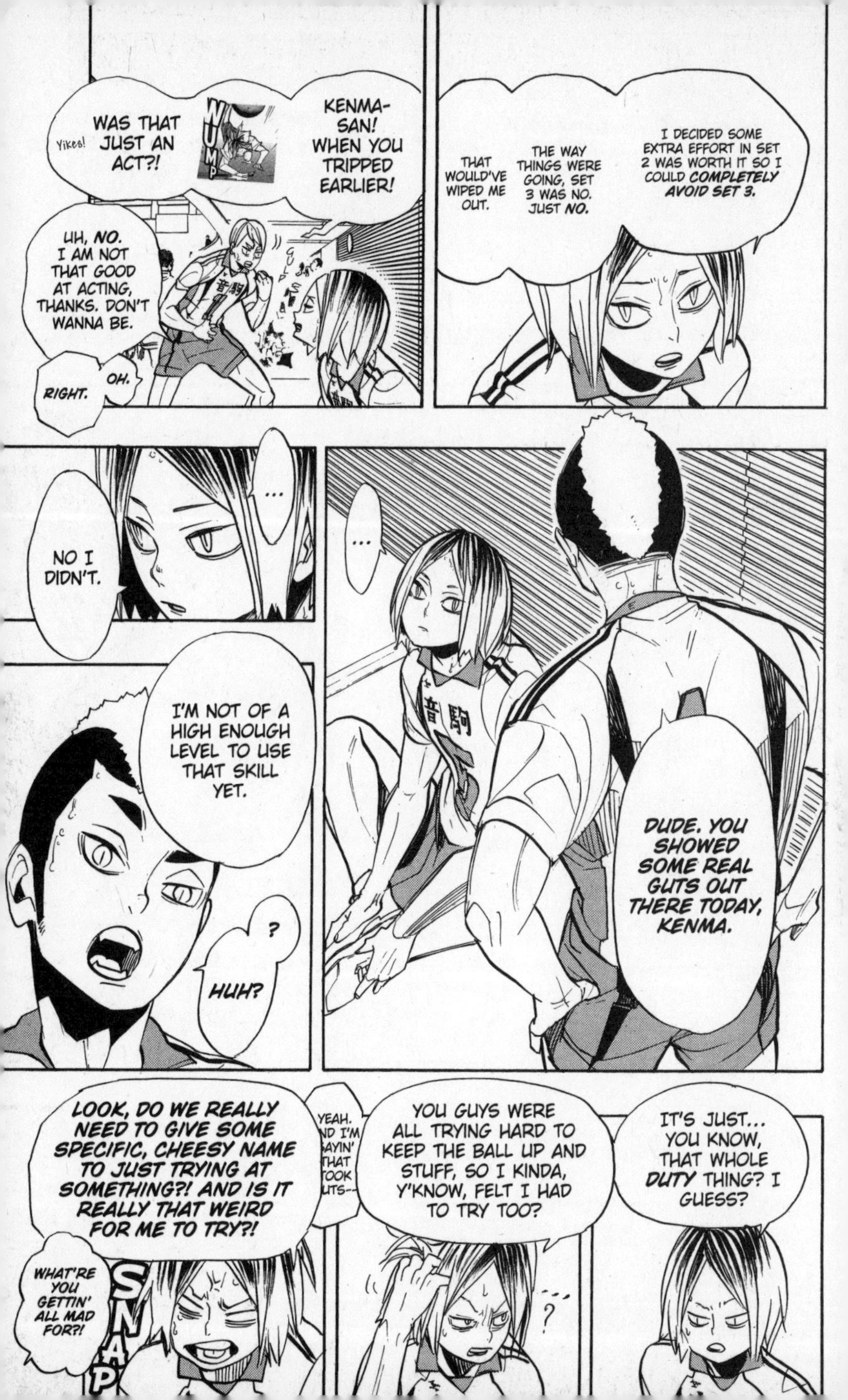
I DECIDED SOME EXTRA EFFORT IN SET 2 WAS WORTH IT SO I COULD COMPLETELY AVOID SET 3.
THE WAY THINGS WERE GOING, SET 3 WAS NO. JUST NO.
THAT WOULD'VE WIPED ME OUT.
KENMA-SAN! WHEN YOU TRIPPED EARLIER!
WUMP
WAS THAT JUST AN ACT?!
Yikes!
UH, NO. I AM NOT THAT GOOD AT ACTING, THANKS. DON'T WANNA BE.
OH.
RIGHT.
...
DUDE. YOU SHOWED SOME REAL GUTS OUT THERE TODAY, KENMA.
...
NO I DIDN'T.
I'M NOT OF A HIGH ENOUGH LEVEL TO USE THAT SKILL YET.
?
HUH?
IT'S JUST... YOU KNOW, THAT WHOLE DUTY THING? I GUESS?
YOU GUYS WERE ALL TRYING HARD TO KEEP THE BALL UP AND STUFF, SO I KINDA, Y'KNOW, FELT I HAD TO TRY TOO?
...?
YEAH. ND I'M AYIN' THAT TOOK UTS--
LOOK, DO WE REALLY NEED TO GIVE SOME SPECIFIC, CHEESY NAME TO JUST TRYING AT SOMETHING?! AND IS IT REALLY THAT WEIRD FOR ME TO TRY?!
SNAP
WHAT'RE YOU GETTIN' ALL MAD FOR?!

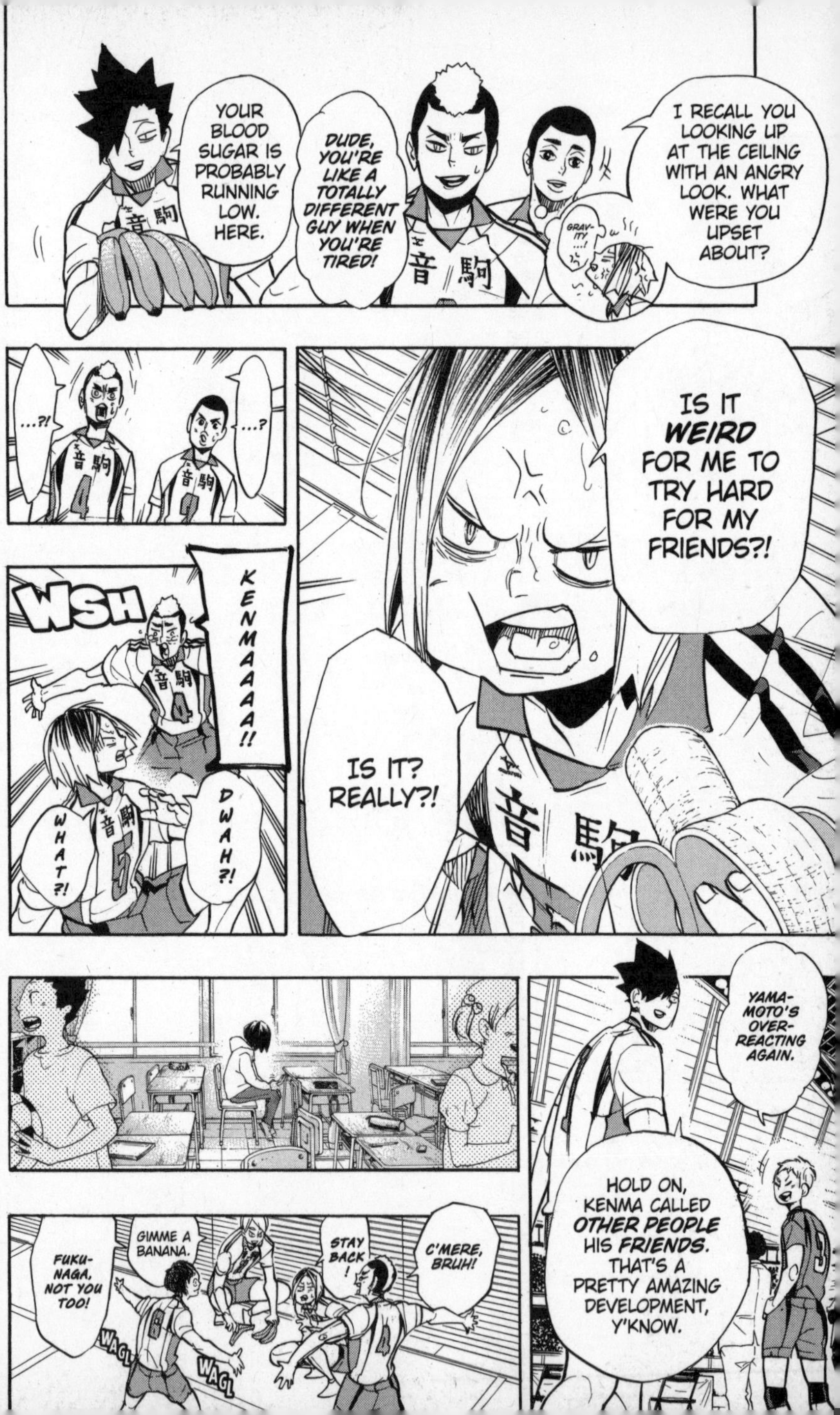
I RECALL YOU LOOKING UP AT THE CEILING WITH AN ANGRY LOOK. WHAT WERE YOU UPSET ABOUT?
GRAV-ITY ...!
DUDE, YOU'RE LIKE A TOTALLY DIFFERENT GUY WHEN YOU'RE TIRED!
YOUR BLOOD SUGAR IS PROBABLY RUNNING LOW. HERE.
IS IT *WEIRD* FOR ME TO TRY HARD FOR MY FRIENDS?!
IS IT? REALLY?!
...?
...?!
KENMAAAAA!!
WSH
DWAH?!
WHAT?!
YAMA-MOTO'S OVER-REACTING AGAIN.
HOLD ON, KENMA CALLED *OTHER PEOPLE* HIS *FRIENDS*. THAT'S A PRETTY AMAZING DEVELOPMENT, Y'KNOW.
C'MERE, BRUH!
STAY BACK!
GIMME A BANANA.
FUKU-NAGA, NOT YOU TOO!
WAGL
WAGL

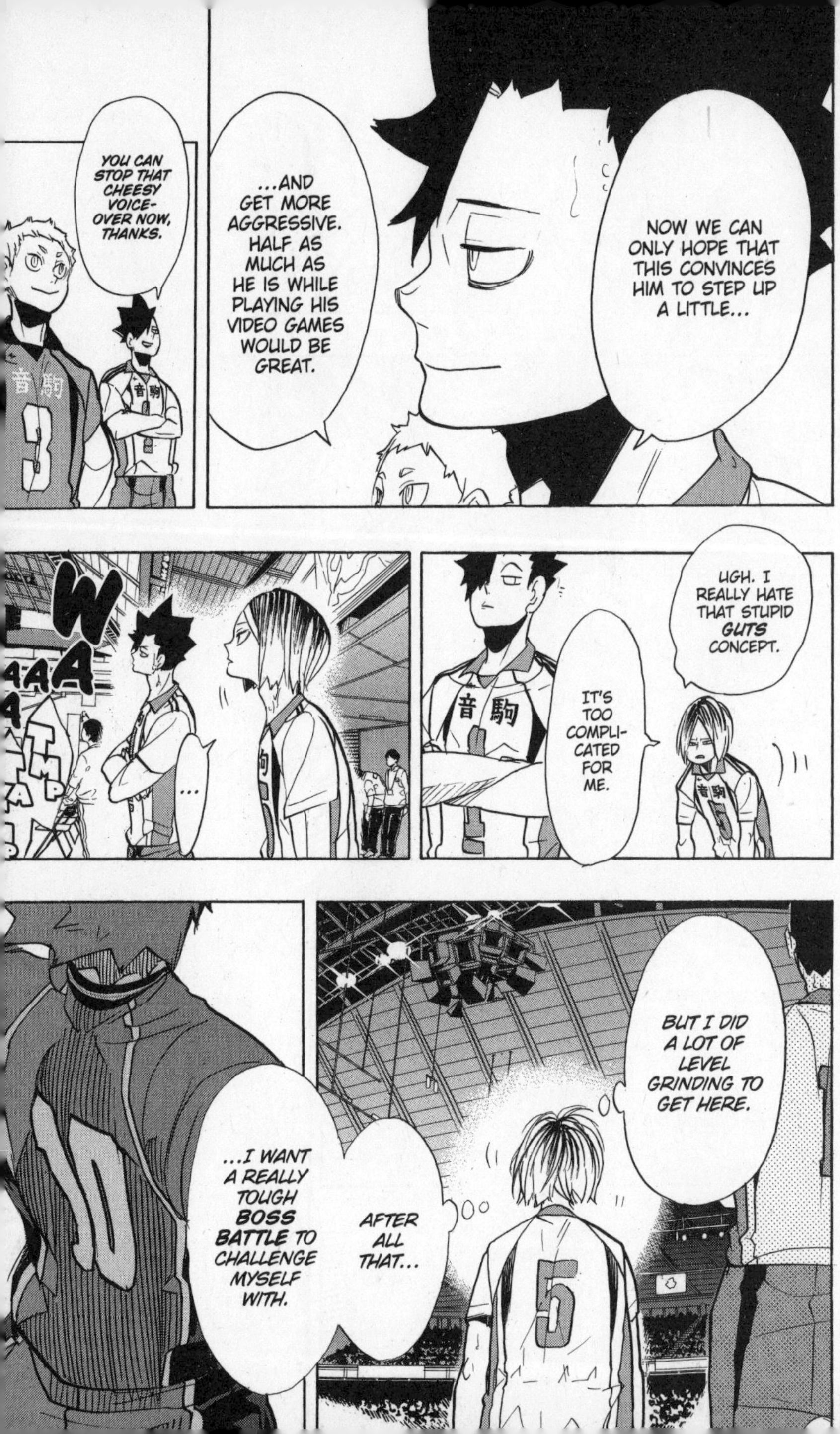
NOW WE CAN ONLY HOPE THAT THIS CONVINCES HIM TO STEP UP A LITTLE...
...AND GET MORE AGGRESSIVE. HALF AS MUCH AS HE IS WHILE PLAYING HIS VIDEO GAMES WOULD BE GREAT.
YOU CAN STOP THAT CHEESY VOICE-OVER NOW, THANKS.
UGH. I REALLY HATE THAT STUPID GUTS CONCEPT.
IT'S TOO COMPLICATED FOR ME.
WAAAA
...
BUT I DID A LOT OF LEVEL GRINDING TO GET HERE.
AFTER ALL THAT...
...I WANT A REALLY TOUGH BOSS BATTLE TO CHALLENGE MYSELF WITH.

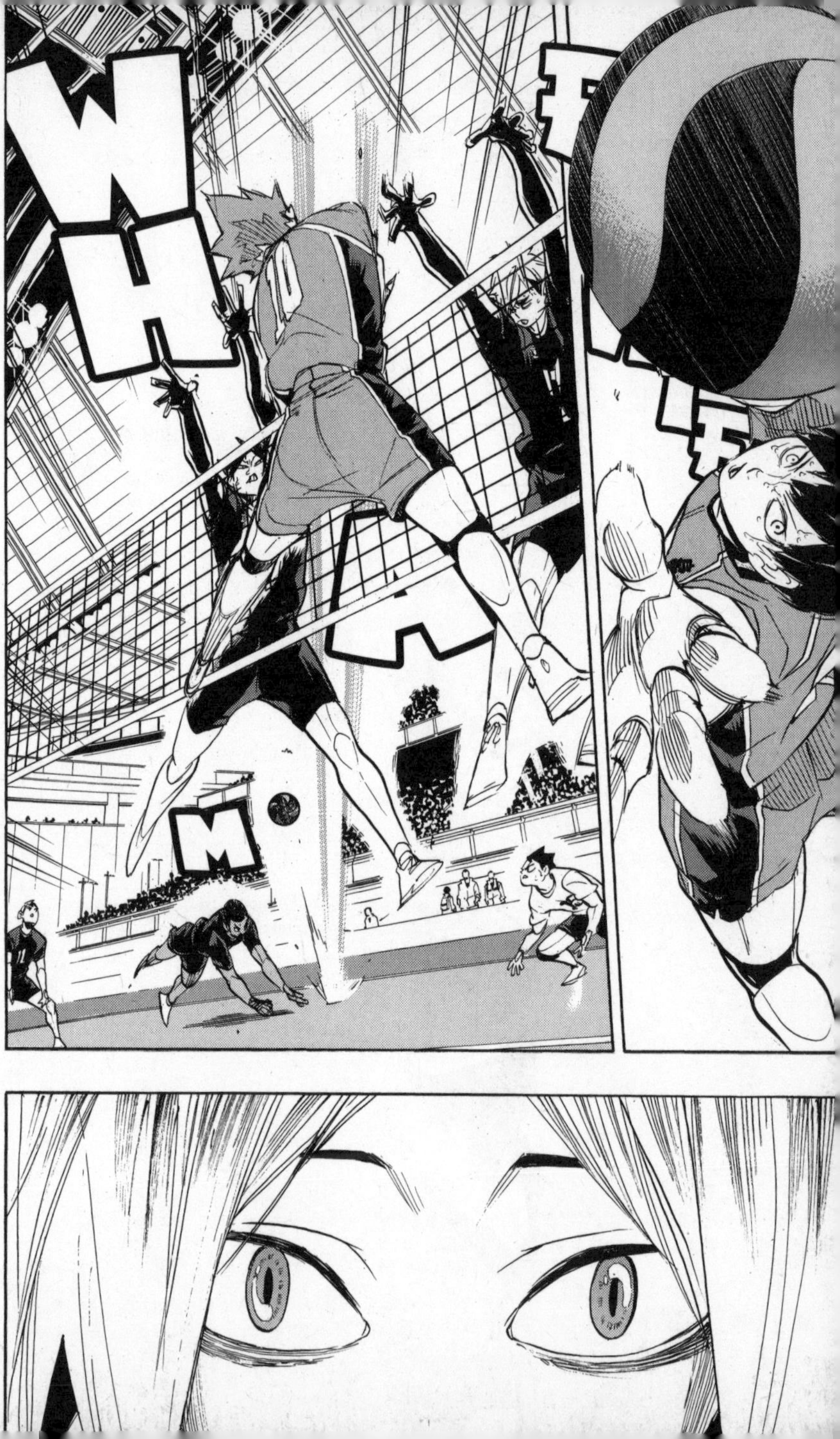
WHAM

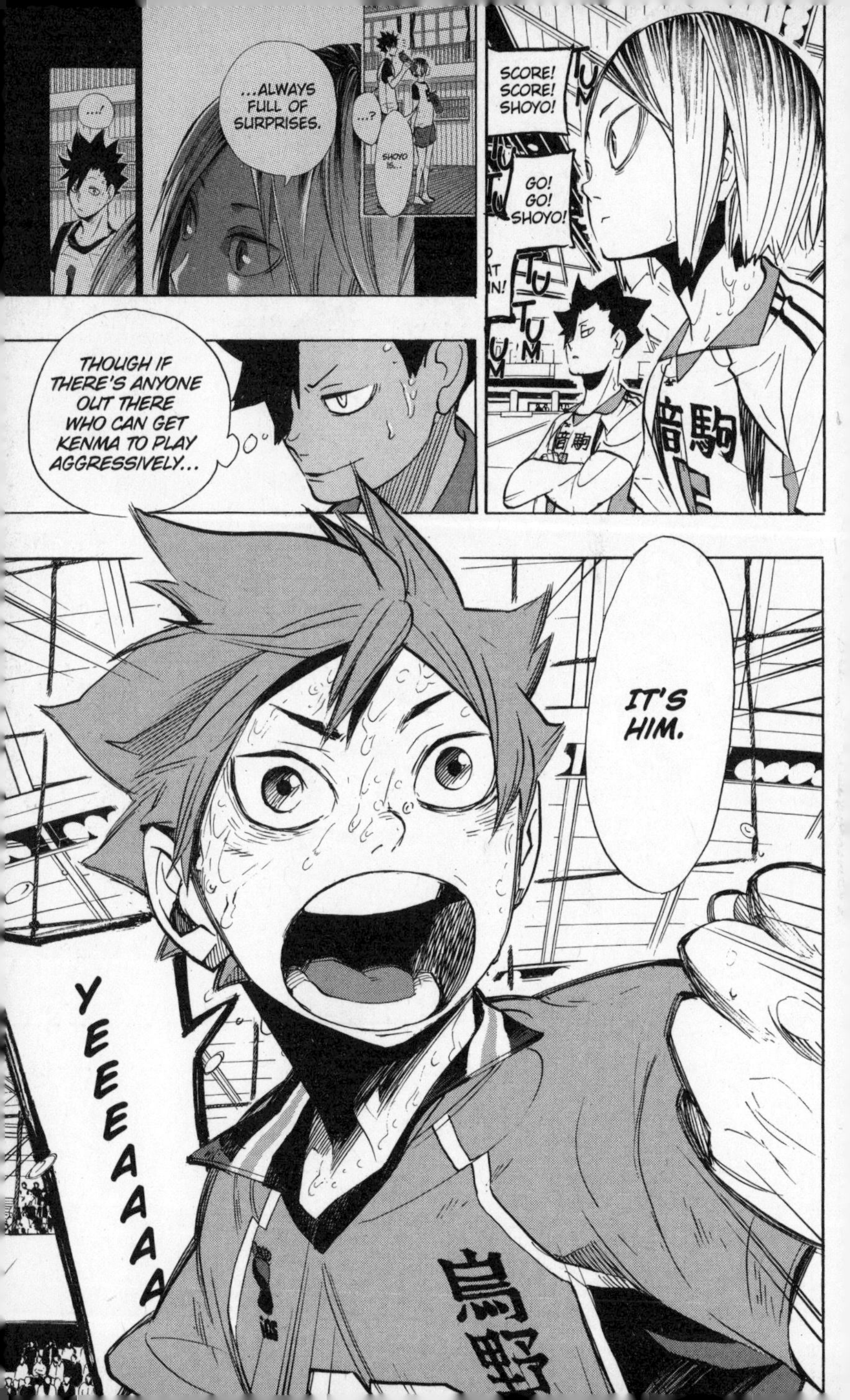
SCORE! SCORE! SHOYO!
TUTUM
GO! GO! SHOYO!
TUTUM
TUTUM
SHOYO IS...
...?
...ALWAYS FULL OF SURPRISES.
...!
THOUGH IF THERE'S ANYONE OUT THERE WHO CAN GET KENMA TO PLAY AGGRESSIVELY...
IT'S HIM.
YEEEAAAA

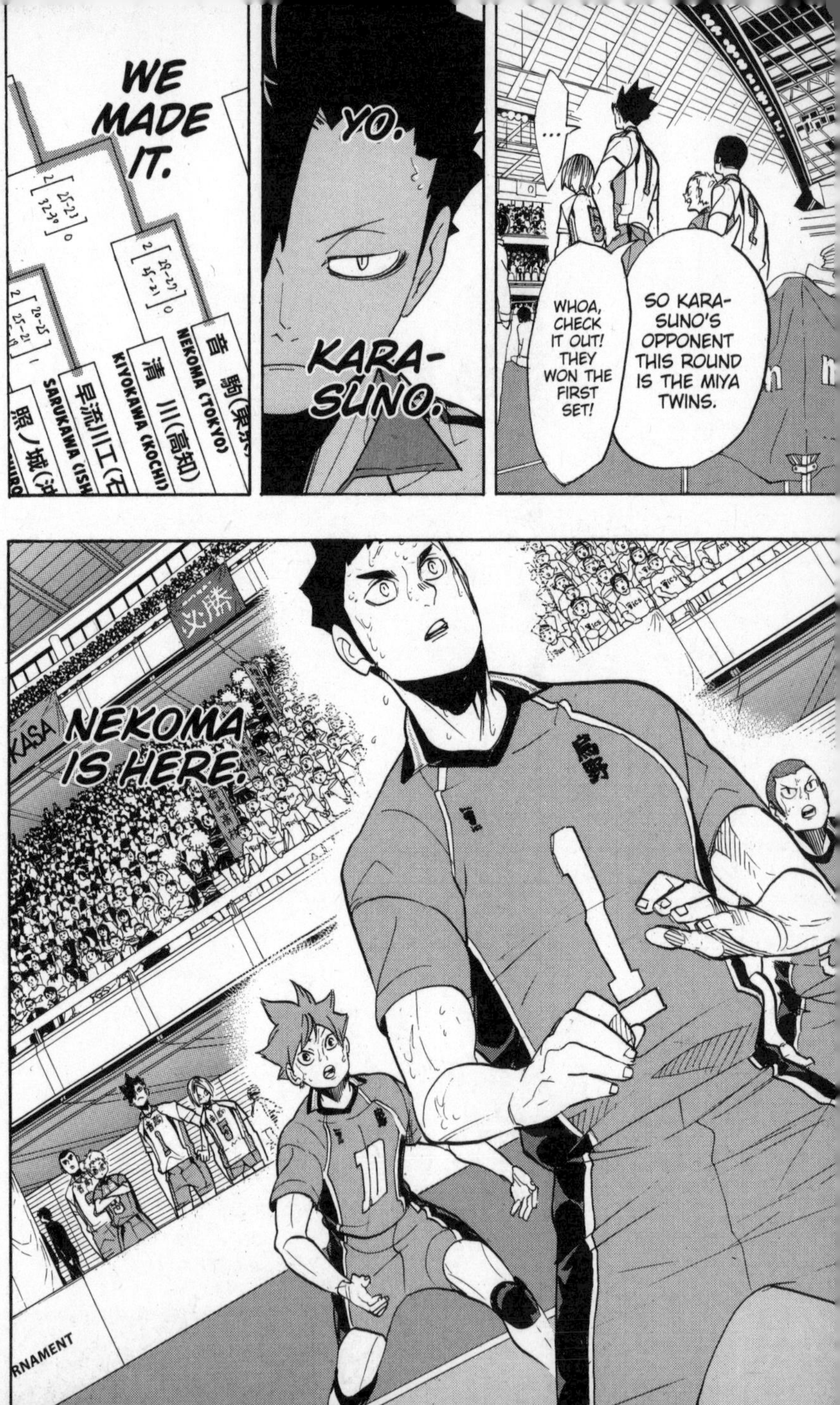

...
SO KARA-SUNO'S OPPONENT THIS ROUND IS THE MIYA TWINS.
WHOA, CHECK IT OUT! THEY WON THE FIRST SET!
YO.
KARA-SUNO.
WE MADE IT.
NEKOMA (TOKYO)
清 川(高知)
KIYOKAWA (KOCHI)
NEKOMA IS HERE.

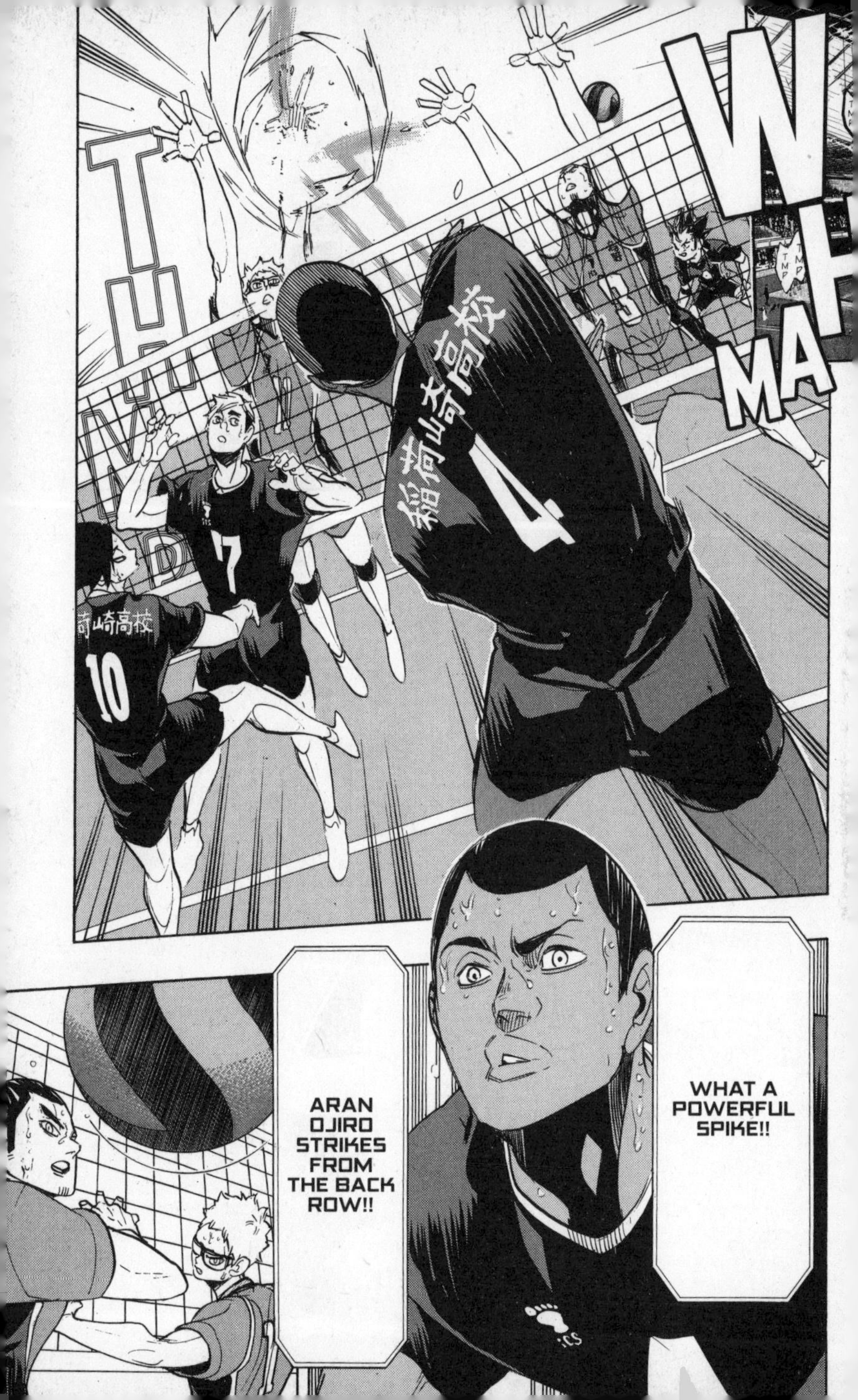
稲荷崎高校
WHAT A POWERFUL SPIKE!!
ARAN OJIRO STRIKES FROM THE BACK ROW!!

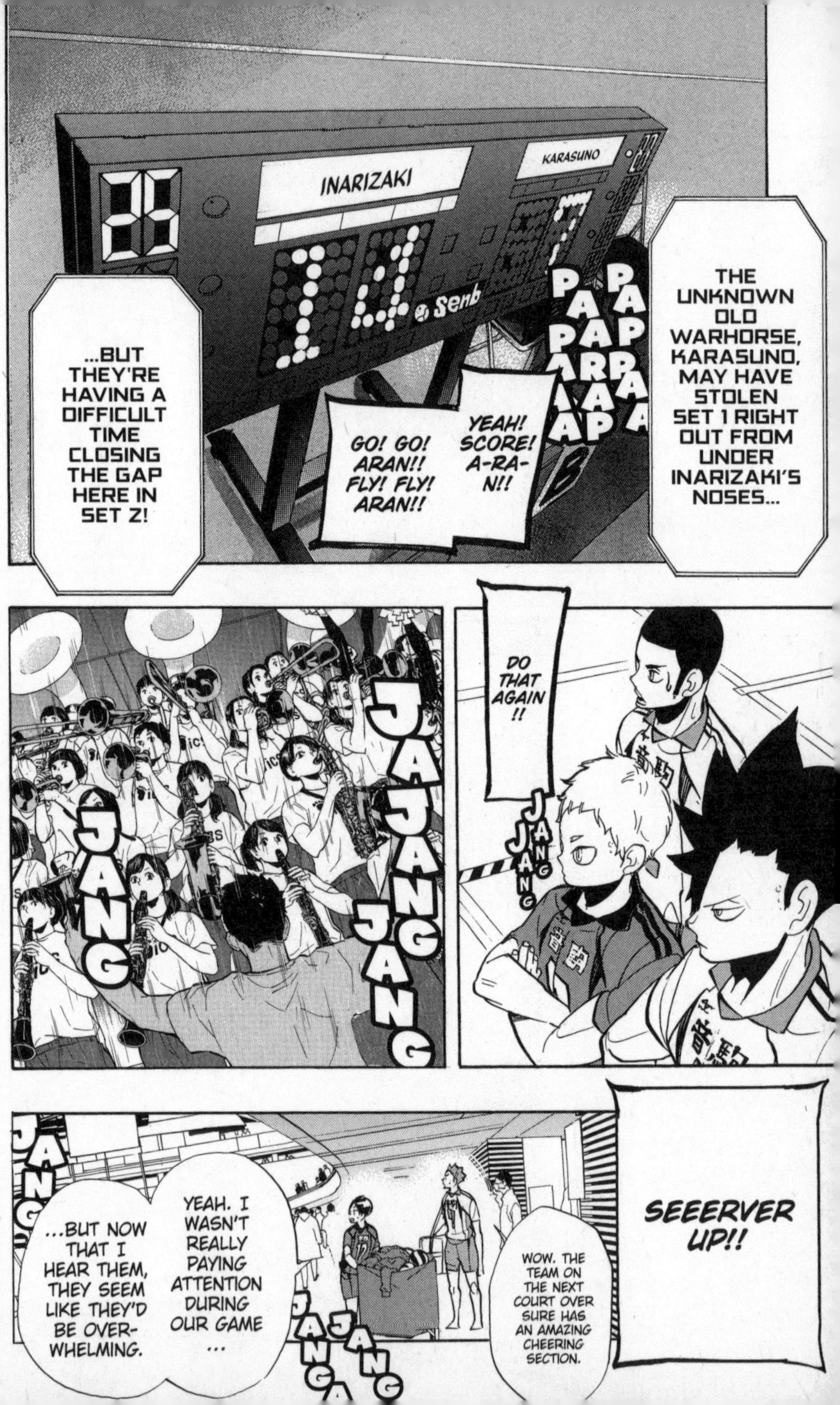
INARIZAKI
KARASUNO
THE UNKNOWN OLD WARHORSE, KARASUNO, MAY HAVE STOLEN SET 1 RIGHT OUT FROM UNDER INARIZAKI'S NOSES...
PAPARAPA
YEAH! SCORE! A-RA-N!!
GO! GO! ARAN!! FLY! FLY! ARAN!!
...BUT THEY'RE HAVING A DIFFICULT TIME CLOSING THE GAP HERE IN SET 2!
DO THAT AGAIN!!
JAJANG JANG
JAJANG JANG
JANG
SEEERVER UP!!
WOW. THE TEAM ON THE NEXT COURT OVER SURE HAS AN AMAZING CHEERING SECTION.
YEAH. I WASN'T REALLY PAYING ATTENTION DURING OUR GAME...
...BUT NOW THAT I HEAR THEM, THEY SEEM LIKE THEY'D BE OVER-WHELMING.
JAJANG JANG

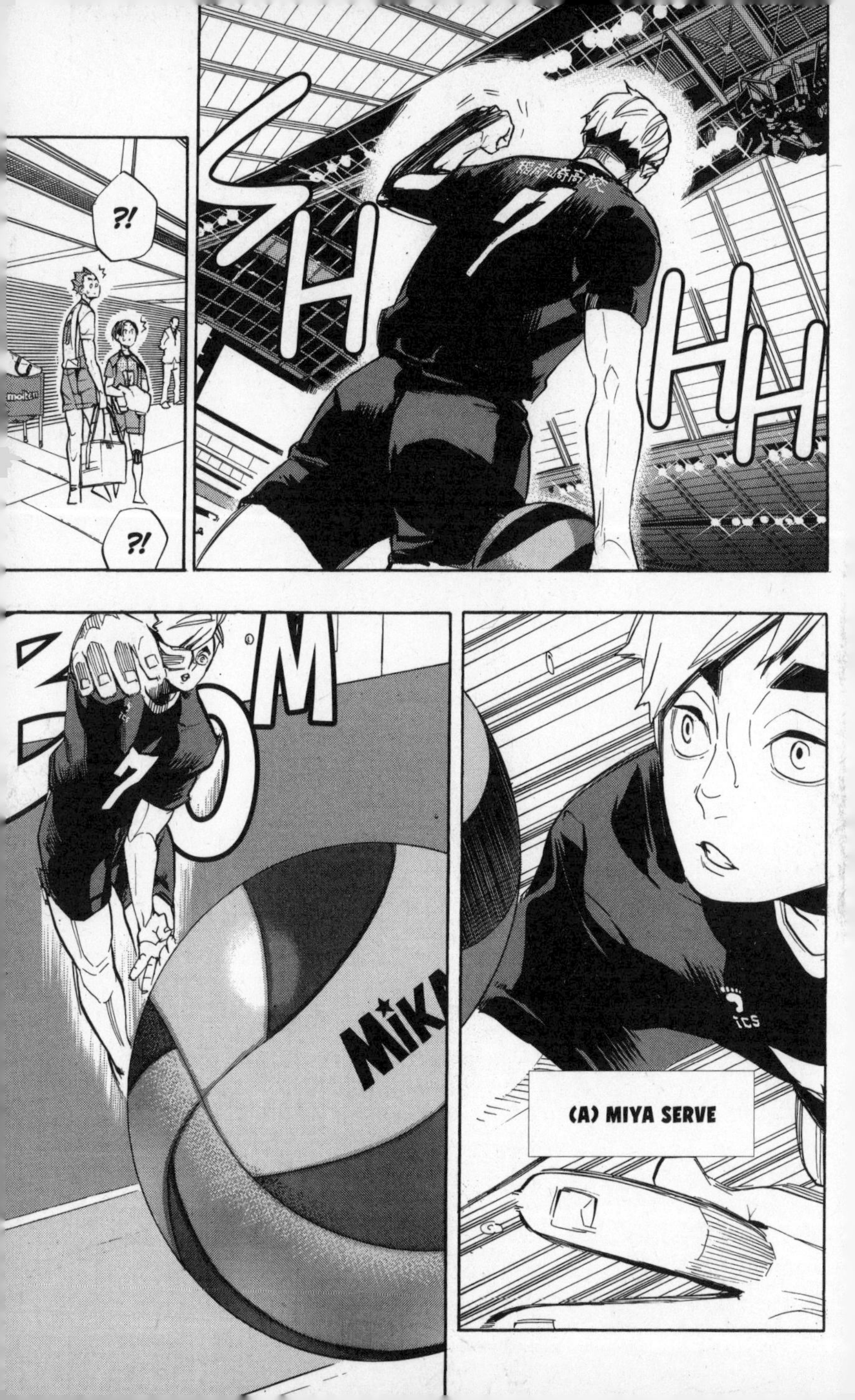
SHHHH
稲荷崎高校
?!
?!
(A) MIYA SERVE
M
MIKA

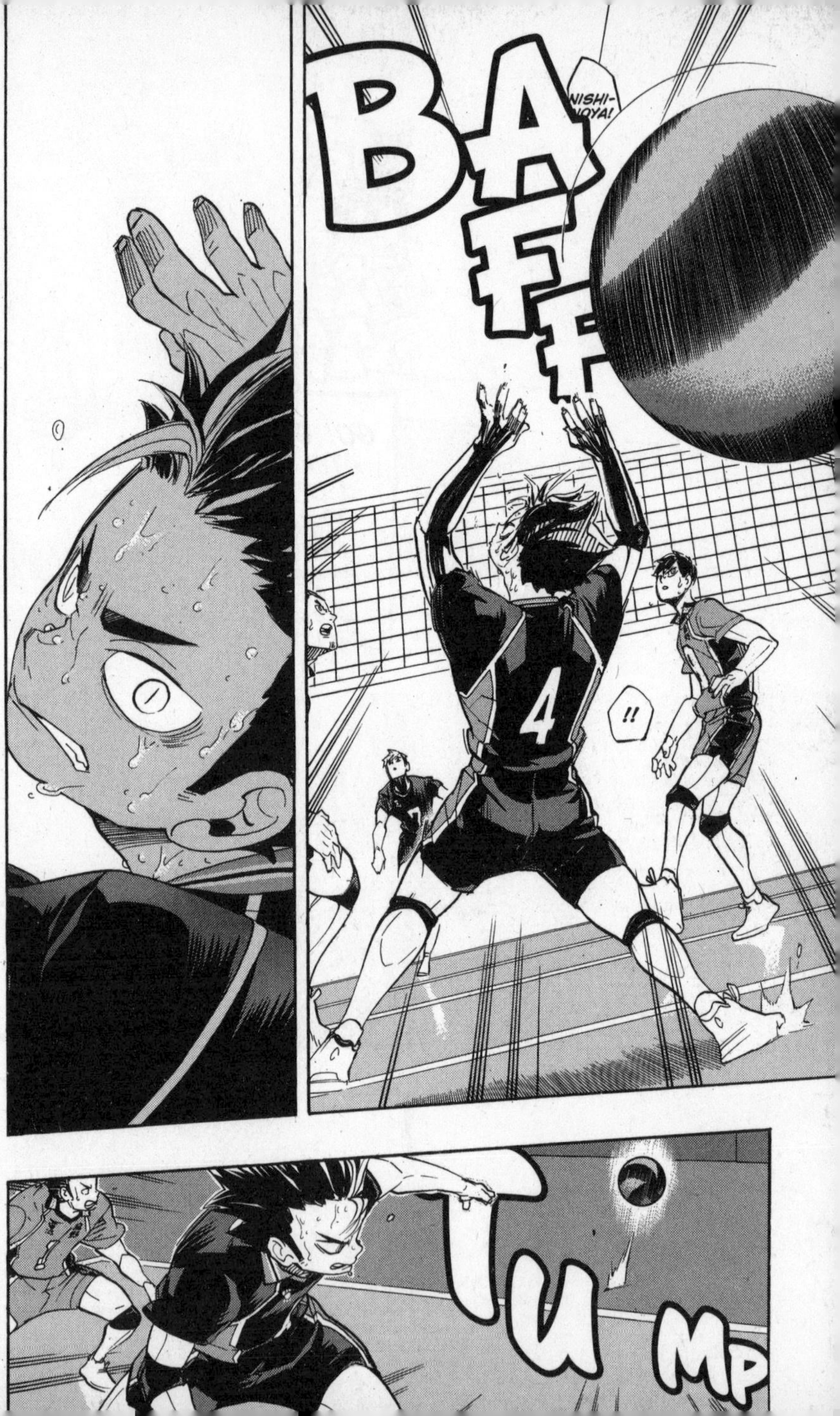
BAFF
NISHI-NOYA!
!!
TUMP

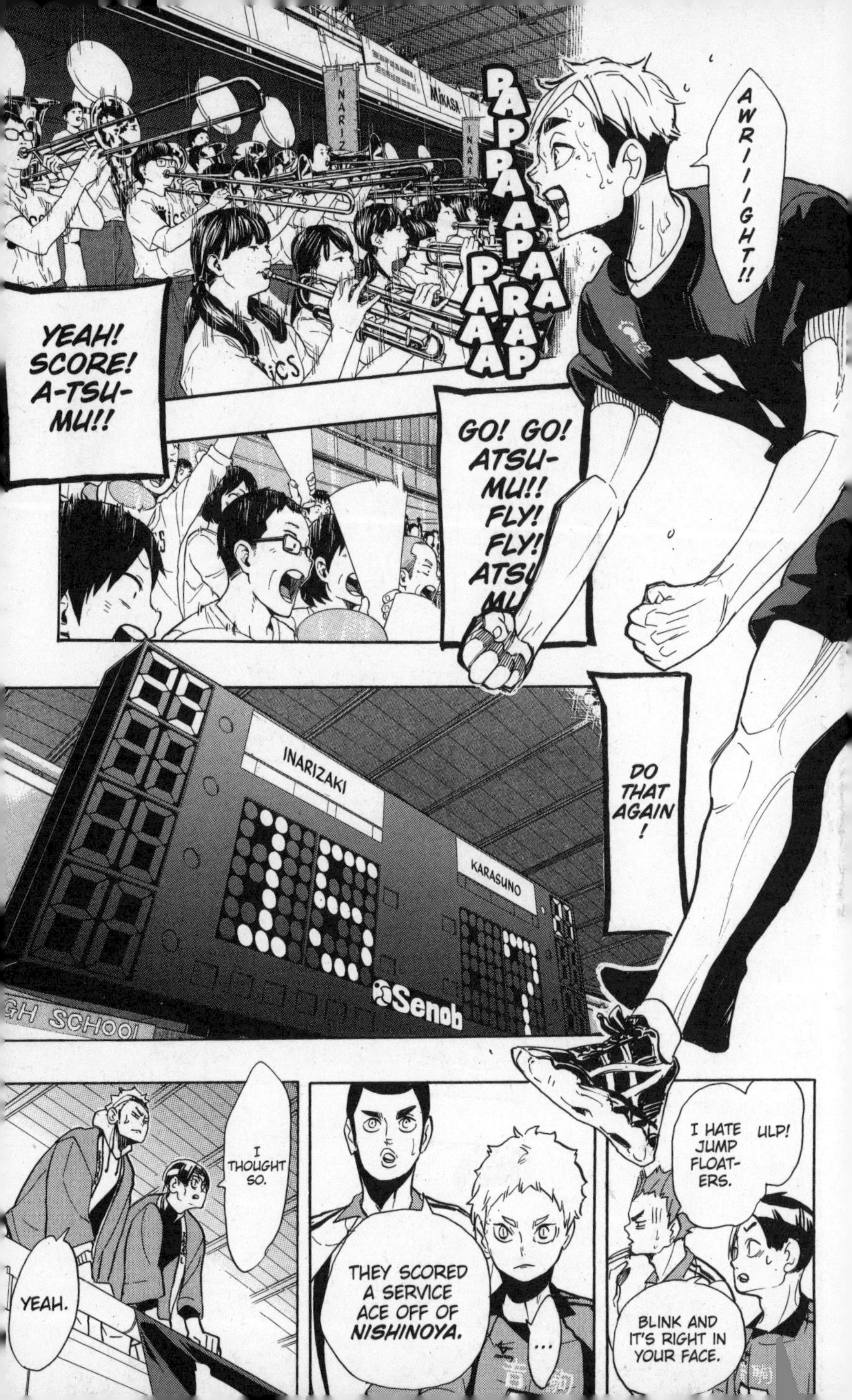
AWRIIIGHT!!
PAPPAAPAA
RAAP
PAAA
YEAH! SCORE! A-TSU-MU!!
GO! GO! ATSU-MU!! FLY! FLY! ATSU MU
DO THAT AGAIN!
INARIZAKI
KARASUNO
Senob
GH SCHOOL
I HATE JUMP FLOATERS.
ULP!
BLINK AND IT'S RIGHT IN YOUR FACE.
THEY SCORED A SERVICE ACE OFF OF NISHINOYA.
...
I THOUGHT SO.
YEAH.

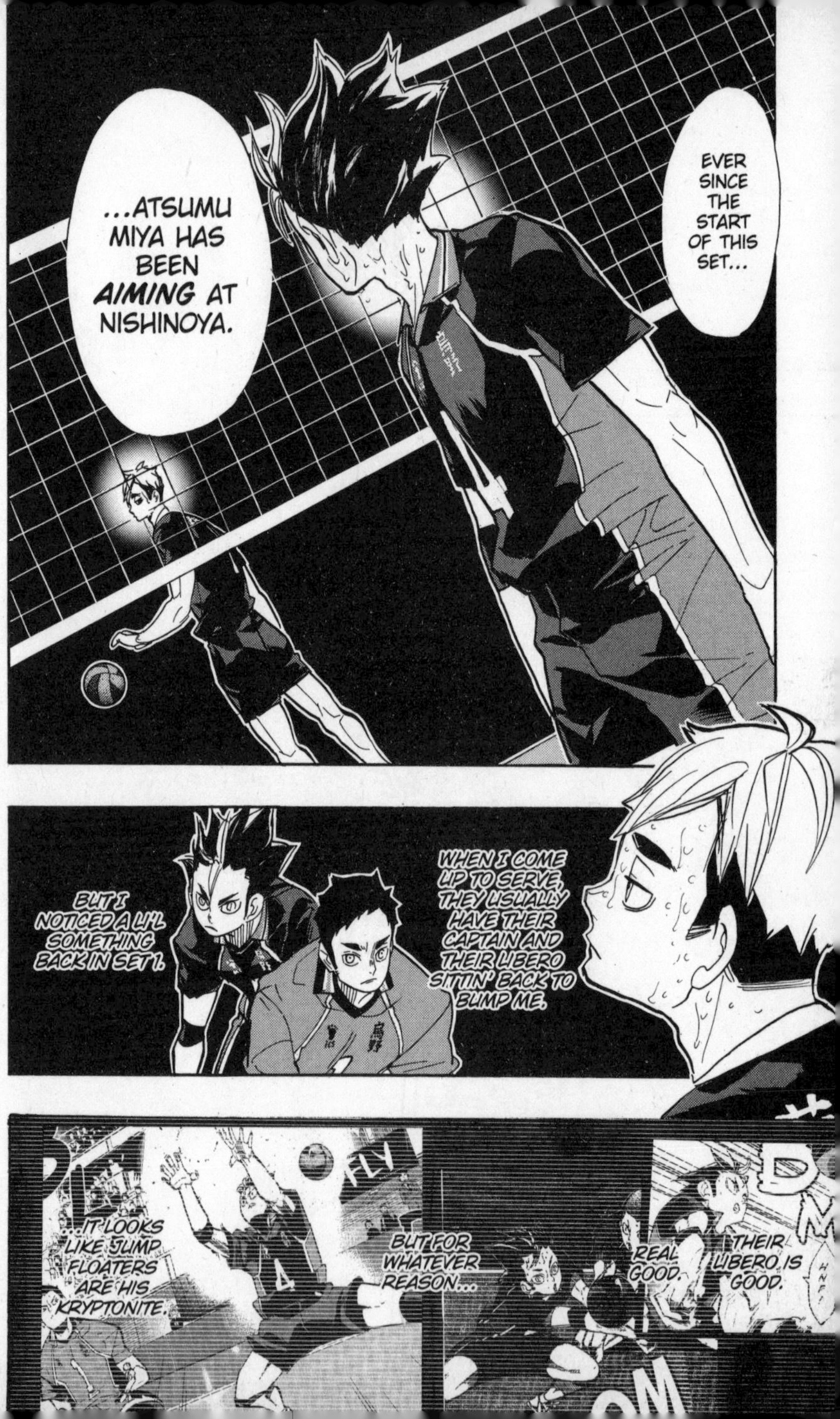

EVER SINCE THE START OF THIS SET...
...ATSUMU MIYA HAS BEEN AIMING AT NISHINOYA.
WHEN I COME UP TO SERVE, THEY USUALLY HAVE THEIR CAPTAIN AND THEIR LIBERO SITTIN' BACK TO BUMP ME.
BUT I NOTICED A LI'L SOMETHING BACK IN SET 1.
THEIR LIBERO IS GOOD.
HNF!
REAL GOOD.
BUT FOR WHATEVER REASON...
FLY
...IT LOOKS LIKE JUMP FLOATERS ARE HIS KRYPTONITE.

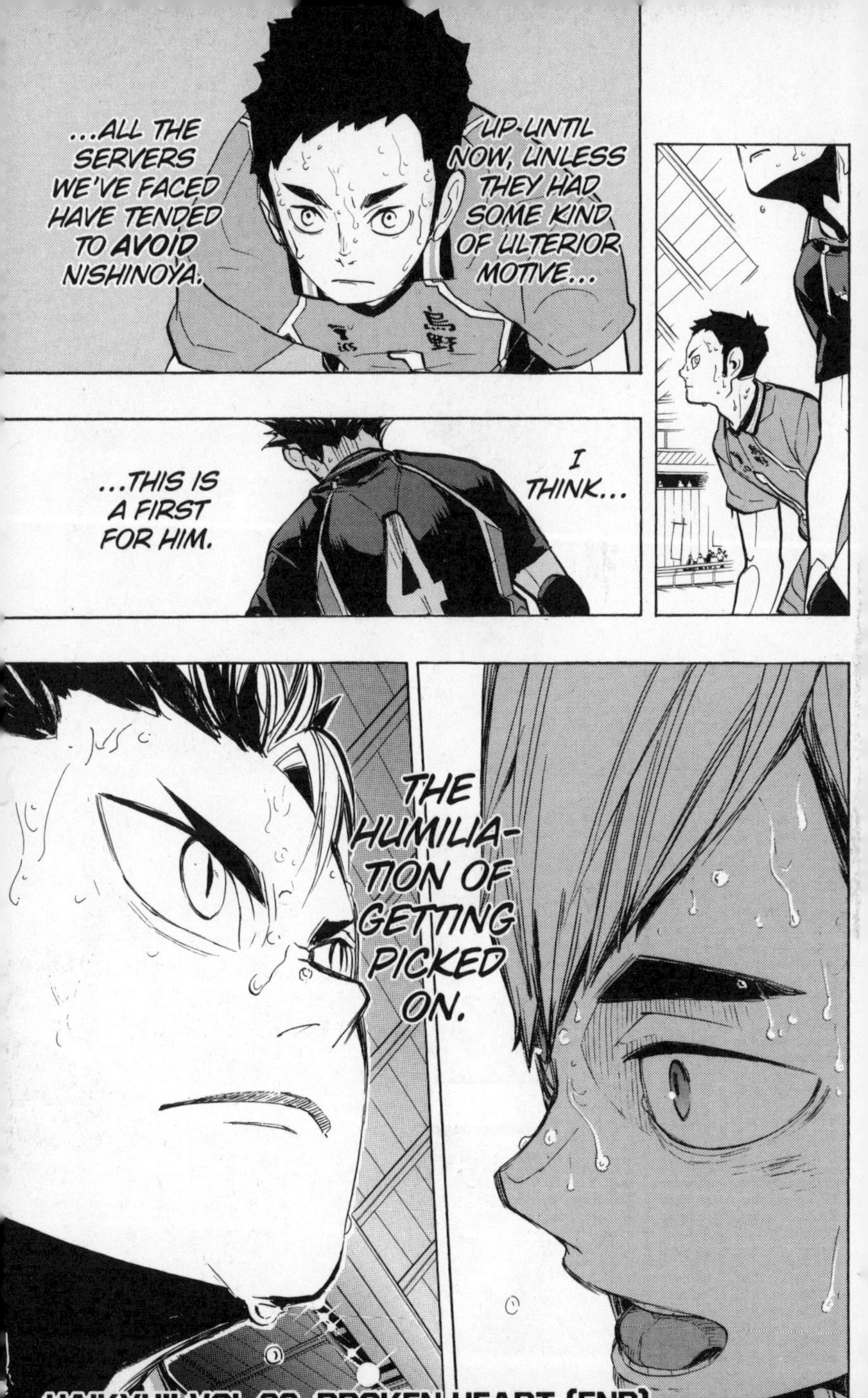
UP-UNTIL NOW, UNLESS THEY HAD SOME KIND OF ULTERIOR MOTIVE...
...ALL THE SERVERS WE'VE FACED HAVE TENDED TO AVOID NISHINOYA.
I THINK...
...THIS IS A FIRST FOR HIM.
THE HUMILIA-TION OF GETTING PICKED ON.

HAIKYU!! VOL 30: BROKEN HEART (END)

IRE

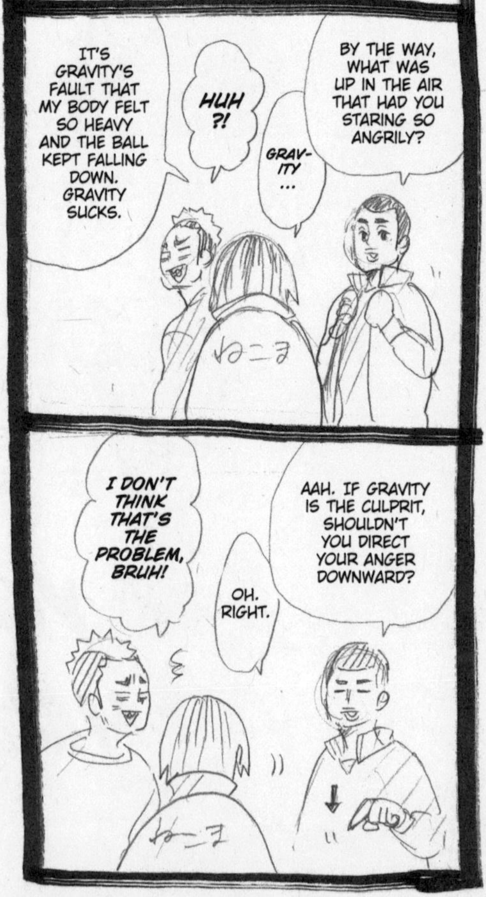
BY THE WAY, WHAT WAS UP IN THE AIR THAT HAD YOU STARING SO ANGRILY?
GRAVITY...
HUH?!
IT'S GRAVITY'S FAULT THAT MY BODY FELT SO HEAVY AND THE BALL KEPT FALLING DOWN. GRAVITY SUCKS.
AAH. IF GRAVITY IS THE CULPRIT, SHOULDN'T YOU DIRECT YOUR ANGER DOWNWARD?
OH. RIGHT.
I DON'T THINK THAT'S THE PROBLEM, BRUH!

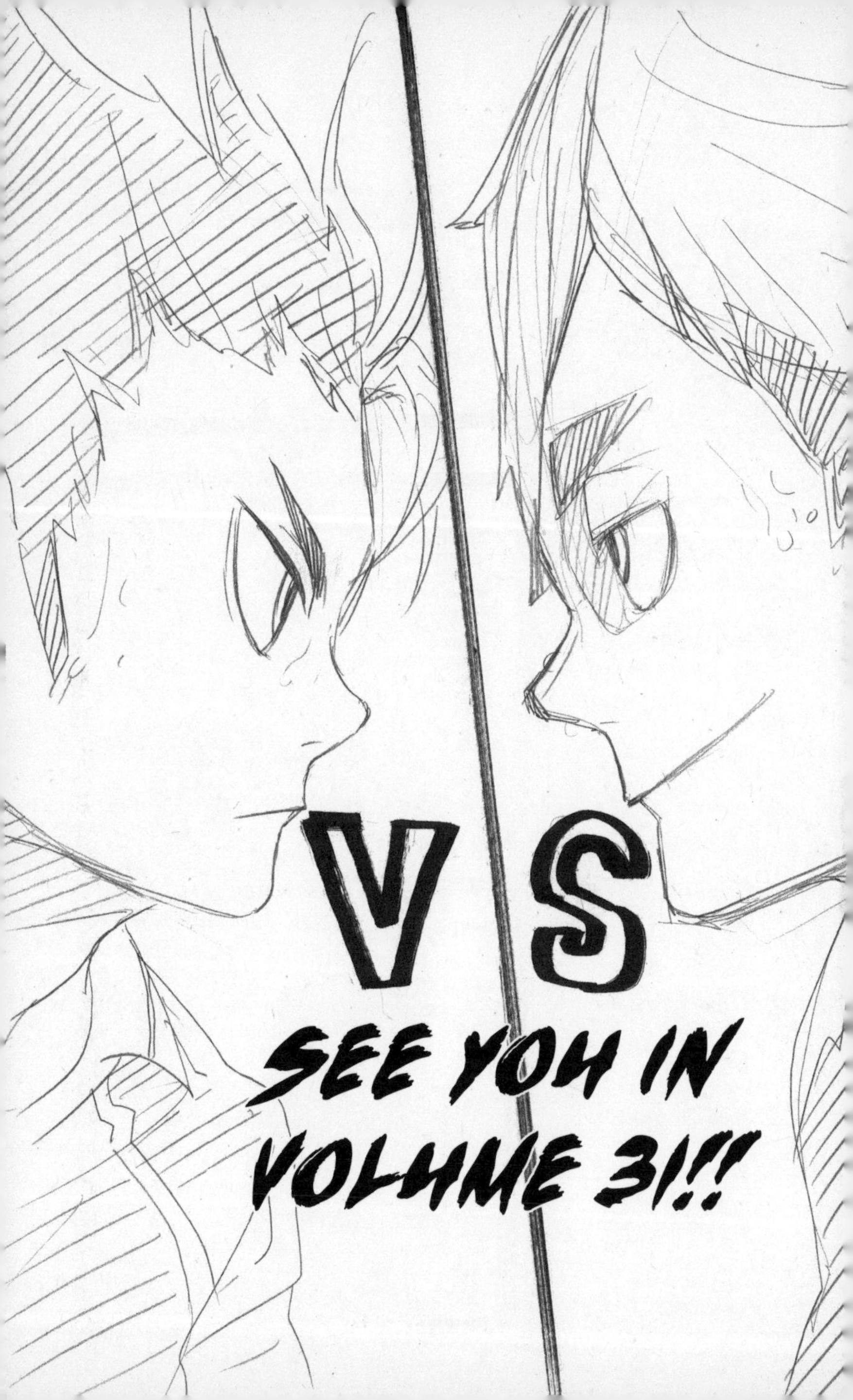
VS
SEE YOU IN VOLUME 31!!

EDITOR'S NOTES

The English edition of Haikyu!! maintains the honorifics used in the original Japanese version. For those of you who are new to these terms, here's a brief explanation to help with your reading experience!

When saying someone's name in Japanese, a suffix is often attached to indicate how familiar the speaker is with the person. Some are more polite and respectful, while others are endearing.

1. **-kun** is often used for young men or boys, usually someone you are familiar with.

2. **-chan** is used for young children and can be used as a term of endearment.

3. **-san** is used for someone you respect or are not close to, or to be polite.

4. **Senpai** is used for someone who is older than you or in a higher position or grade in school.

5. **Kohai** is used for someone who is younger than you or in a lower position or grade in school.

6. **Sensei** means teacher.

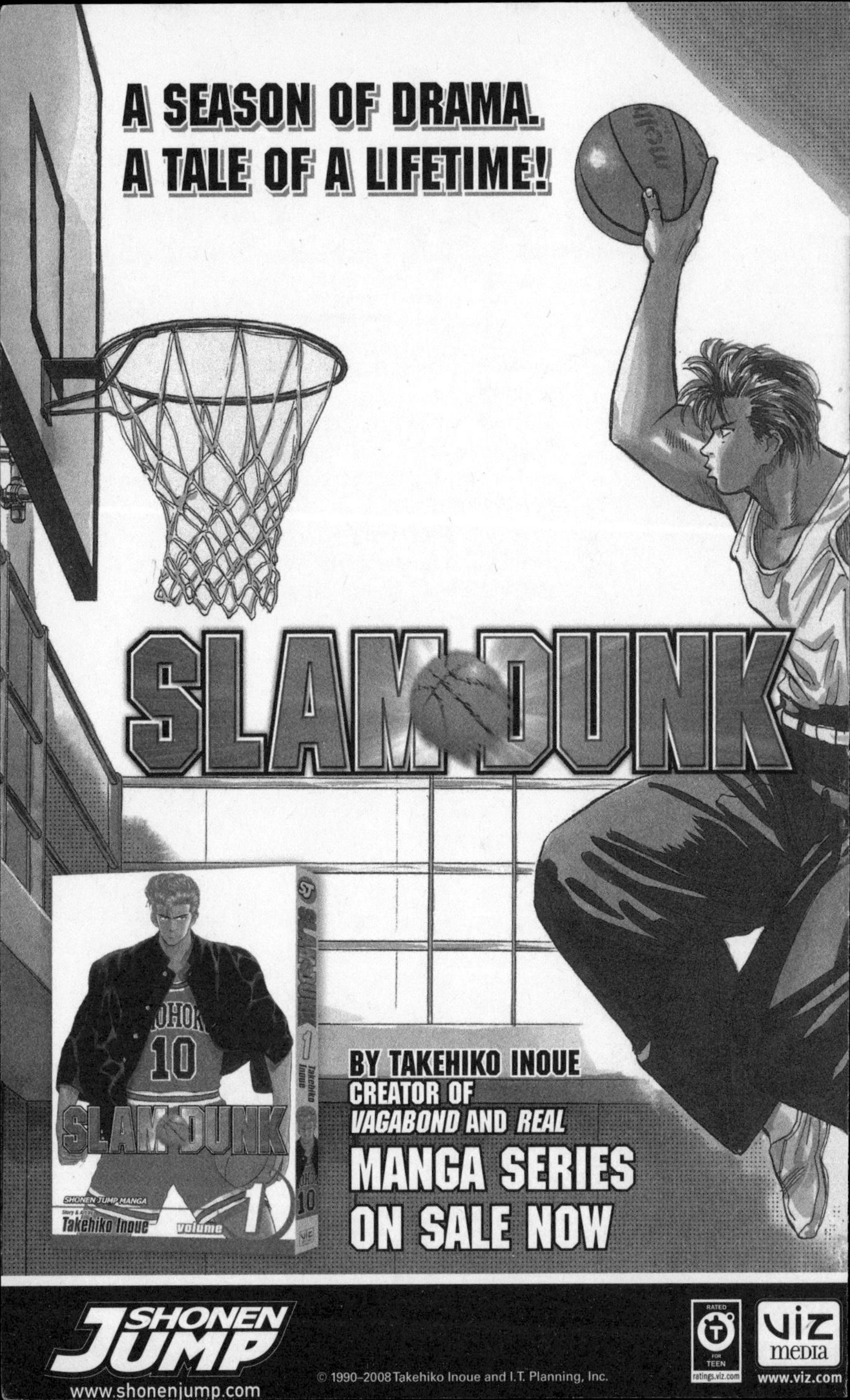
A SEASON OF DRAMA.
A TALE OF A LIFETIME!
SLAM DUNK
SHOHOKU
10
SLAM DUNK
SHONEN JUMP MANGA
Takehiko Inoue
volume 1
BY TAKEHIKO INOUE
CREATOR OF
VAGABOND AND REAL
MANGA SERIES
ON SALE NOW
SHONEN JUMP
www.shonenjump.com
© 1990–2008 Takehiko Inoue and I.T. Planning, Inc.
RATED T FOR TEEN
ratings.viz.com
VIZ media
www.viz.com

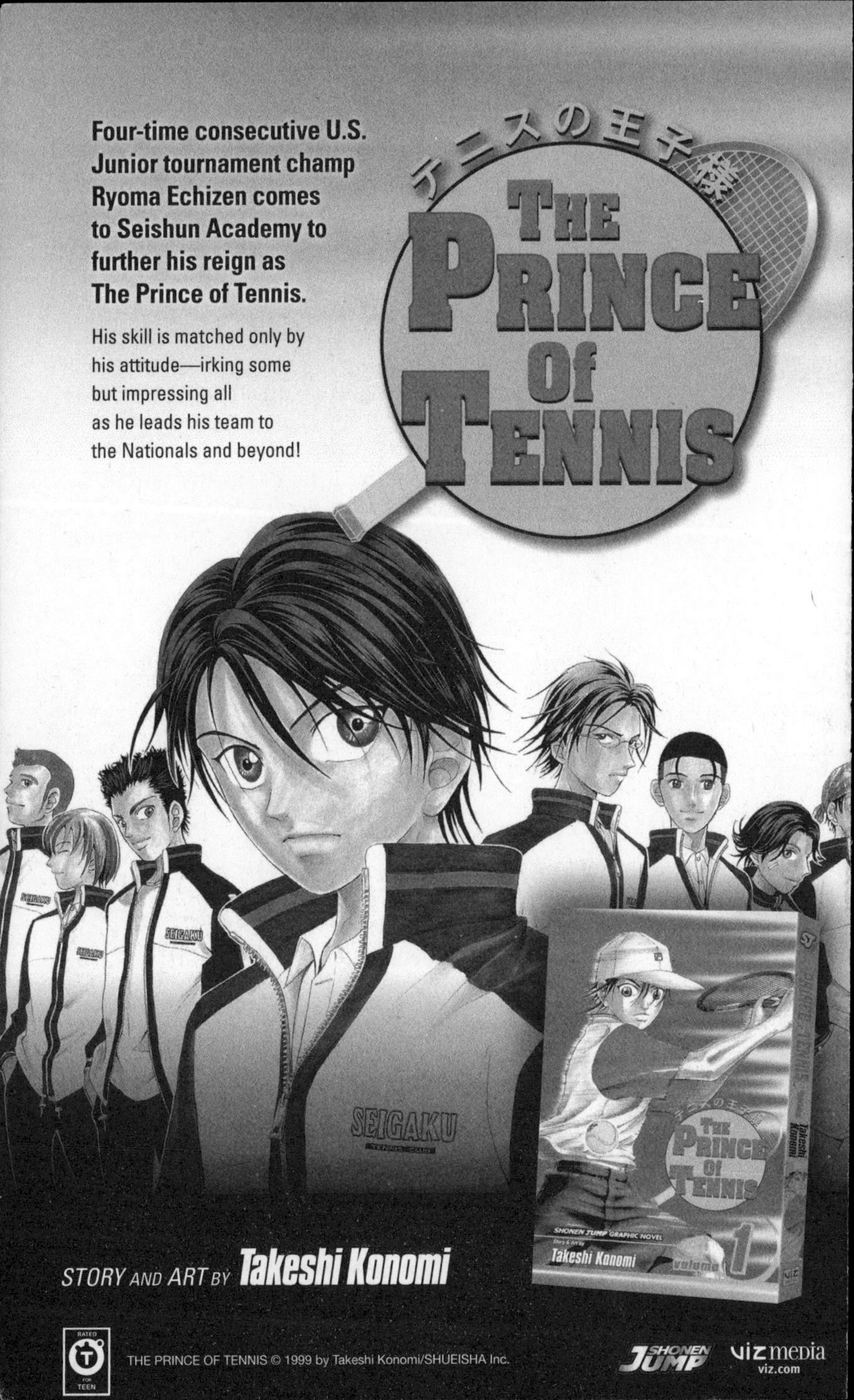
テニスの王子様
THE PRINCE OF TENNIS
Four-time consecutive U.S. Junior tournament champ Ryoma Echizen comes to Seishun Academy to further his reign as The Prince of Tennis.
His skill is matched only by his attitude—irking some but impressing all as he leads his team to the Nationals and beyond!
SEIGAKU
STORY AND ART BY Takeshi Konomi
THE PRINCE OF TENNIS
SHONEN JUMP GRAPHIC NOVEL
Takeshi Konomi
volume 1
RATED T FOR TEEN
THE PRINCE OF TENNIS © 1999 by Takeshi Konomi/SHUEISHA Inc.
SHONEN JUMP
viz media
viz.com

IN A SAVAGE WORLD RULED BY THE PURSUIT OF THE MOST DELICIOUS FOODS, IT'S EITHER EAT OR BE EATEN!

"The most bizarrely entertaining manga out there on comic shelves. *Toriko* is a great series. If you're looking for an weirdly fun book or a fighting manga with a bizarre take, this is the story for you to read."

—ComicAttack.com

TORIKO

Story and Art by Mitsutoshi Shimabukuro

In an era where the world's gone crazy for increasingly bizarre gourmet foods, only Gourmet Hunter Toriko can hunt down the ferocious ingredients that supply the world's best restaurants. Join Toriko as he tracks and defeats the tastiest and most dangerous animals with his bare hands.

www.shonenjump.com   www.viz.com

ON SALE NOW
YU-GI-OH! ARC-V

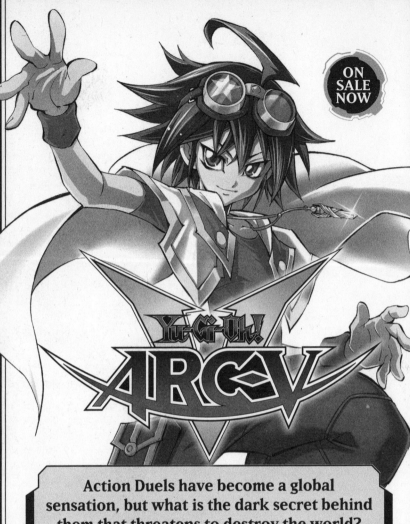

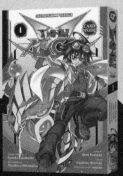

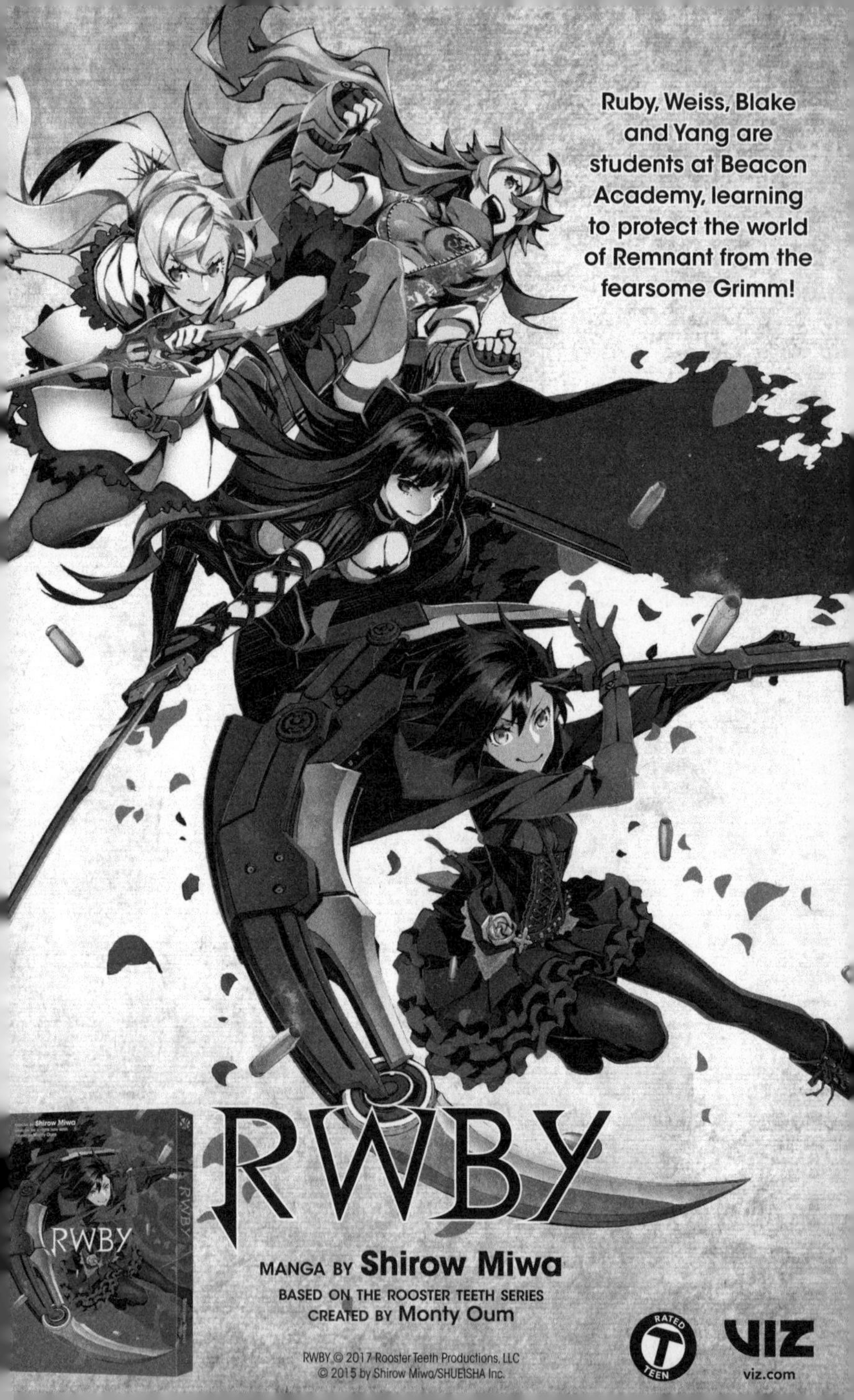
Ruby, Weiss, Blake and Yang are students at Beacon Academy, learning to protect the world of Remnant from the fearsome Grimm!
RWBY
MANGA BY Shirow Miwa
BASED ON THE ROOSTER TEETH SERIES
CREATED BY Monty Oum
RATED T TEEN
VIZ
viz.com
RWBY © 2017 Rooster Teeth Productions, LLC
© 2015 by Shirow Miwa/SHUEISHA Inc.